Anders Zorn
Paintings and Drawings

By Jessica Findley

Second Edition

*****   I0477287

Anders Zorn: Paintings and Drawings
*****

Foreword

Anders Leonard Zorn (1860 –1920) was Sweden's artist who obtained international success as a painter, sculptor and printmaker in etching. Zorn was born in Yvraden, a hamlet in the village of Utmeland in the parish of Mora, Dalarna, and was raised on his grandparents' farm in Yvraden. He studied until the age of twelve in the school at Mora Strand before progressing in the autumn of 1872 to a secondary grammar school in Enköping.

From 1875–1880 Zorn studied at Royal Swedish Academy of Arts in Stockholm, Sweden. He traveled extensively to London, Paris, the Balkans, Spain, Italy and the United States, becoming an international success as one of the most acclaimed painters of his era. While his early works were often brilliant, luminous watercolors, by 1887 he had switched firmly to oils.

In 1886, Anders Zorn and his wife Emma had bought land close to Mora church and here they moved a cottage from his maternal grandfather's farm. When Anders and Emma Zorn decided to return to Sweden after several years abroad, they began to enlarge the cottage. Zorngården was completed in 1910.

In 1893, the Columbian World Fair was arranged in Chicago. Zorn was chosen as the superintendent of the Swedish art exhibition and travelled to the States. He stayed for almost a year. This trip to the USA, the first of seven, was very important for him. Zorn enjoyed the American lifestyle and felt at home there. This first trip to the States was also of great importance for his art. Subsequent visits to the USA were in 1896-1897, and 1898-1899, 1900-1901, 1903-1904, 1907, and 1911. He generally travelled during the fall, winter and spring. The 1907 trip was primarily for pleasure, but the others included a large number of paintings, mostly portraits. Naturally, the high points were the commissions to portray American presidents. One of the benefits of the presidential portraits was the number of commissions that Zorn received in the USA.

Beginning in 1910, Zorn focused on developing his control of the technique and motif. He accomplished this with such certainty that the process of painting can assume the dominant role, sometimes to the detriment of the work's emotional expression.

Zorn's health deteriorated markedly during his last years. He died on August 22, 1920. The funeral was conducted by Archbishop Nathan Söderblom and attended among others by representatives of the Swedish royal family and many cultural personalities. He is buried in Mora Cemetery.

Etchings

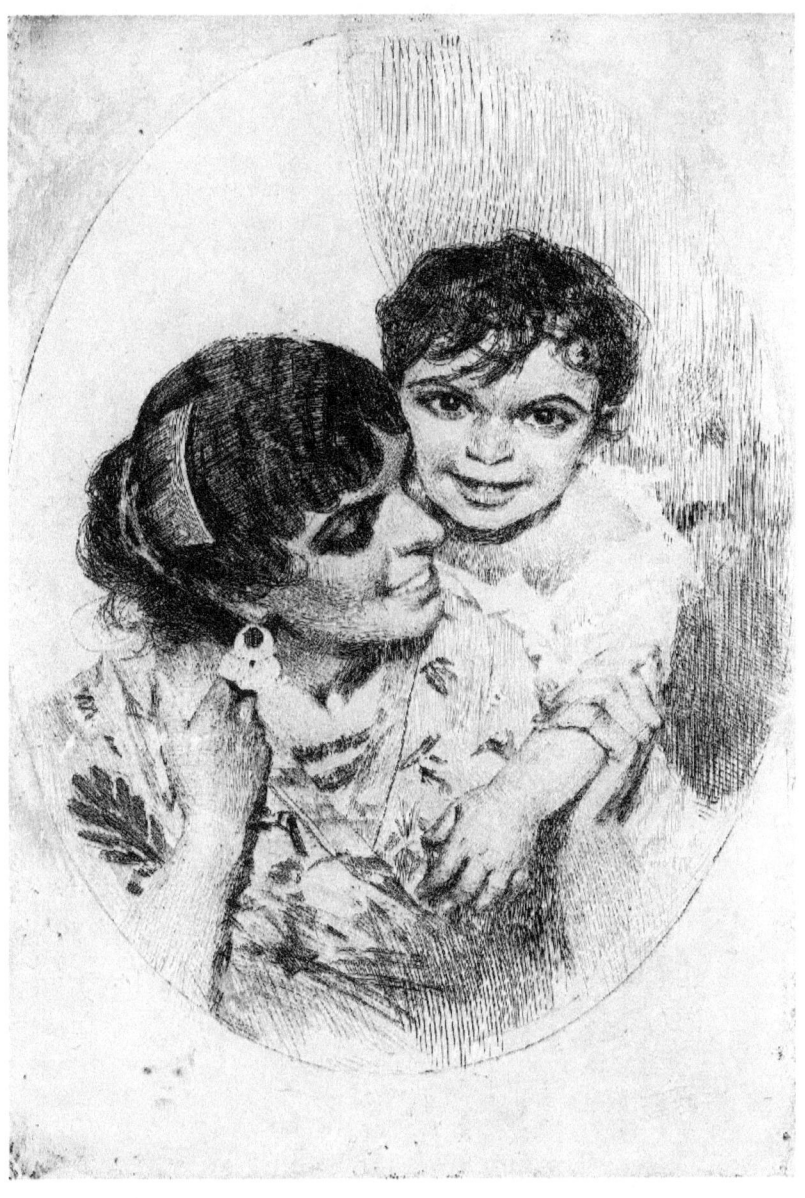

Motherly Happiness III, 1883, etching

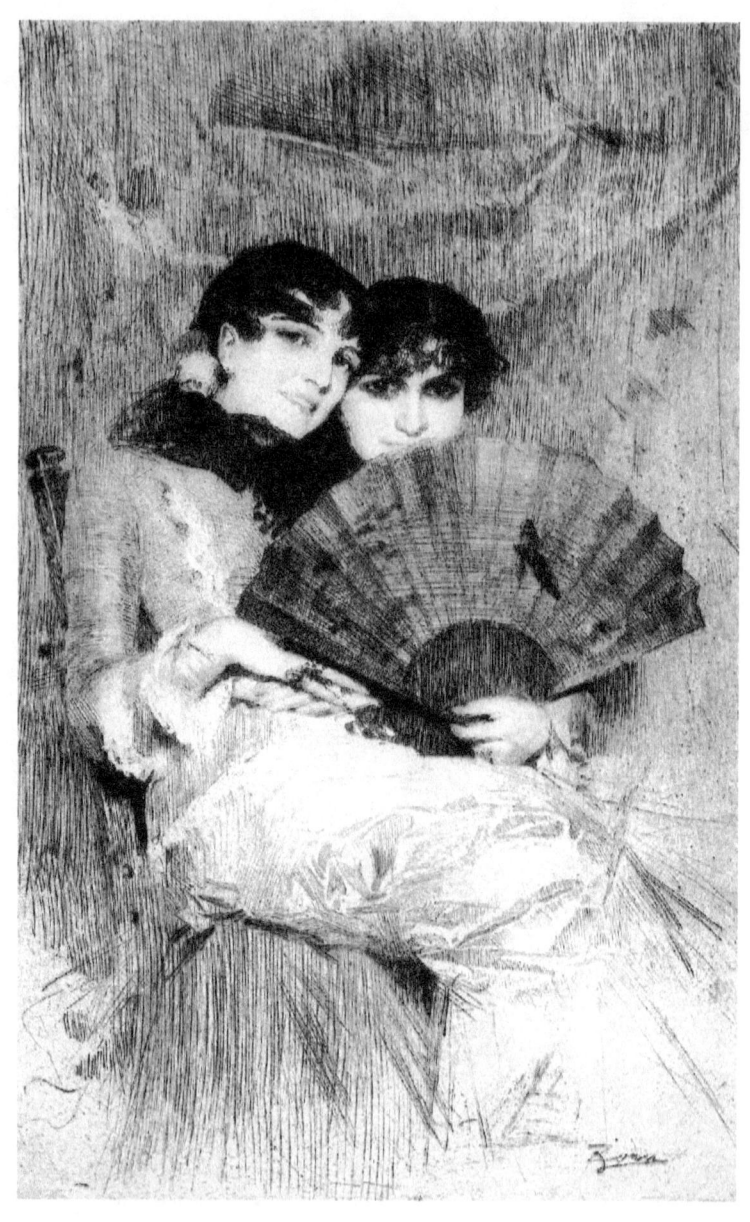

The Cousins, 1883, etching

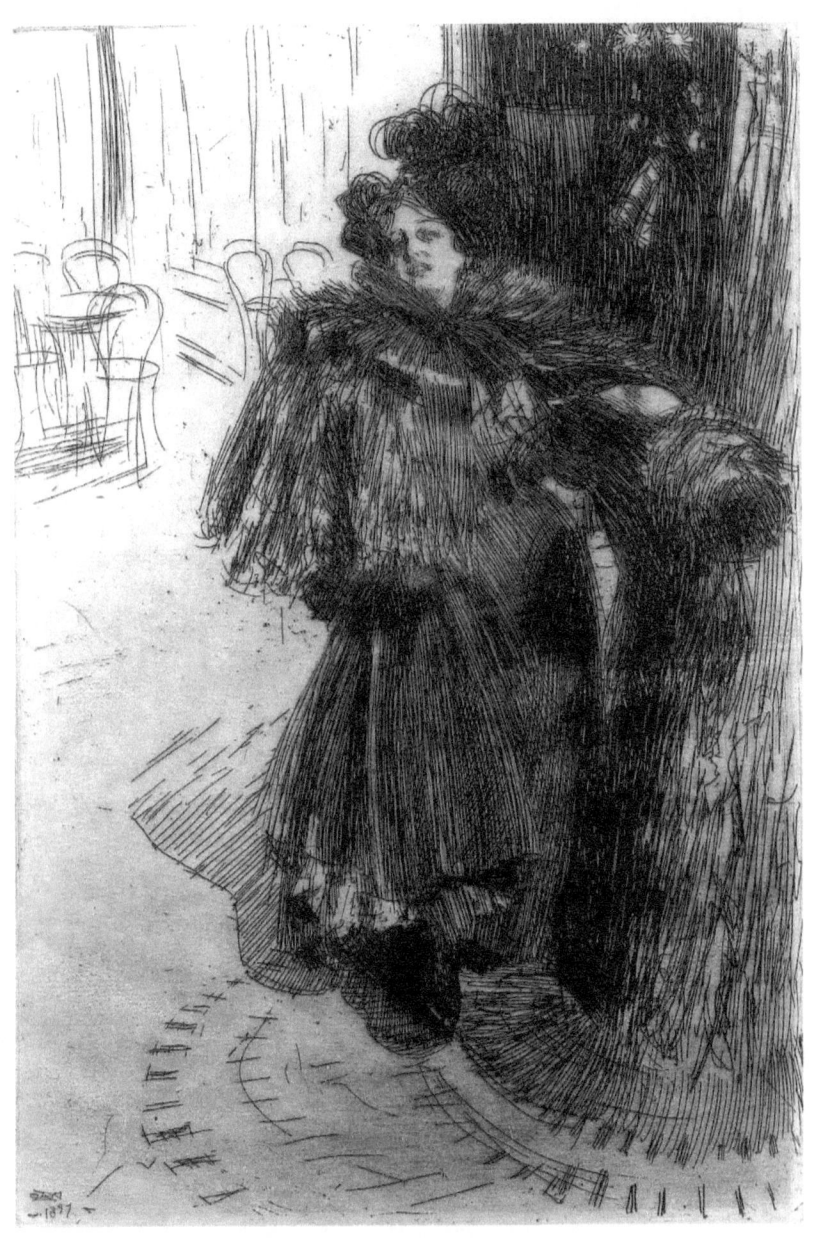

Night Effect III, 1897, etching

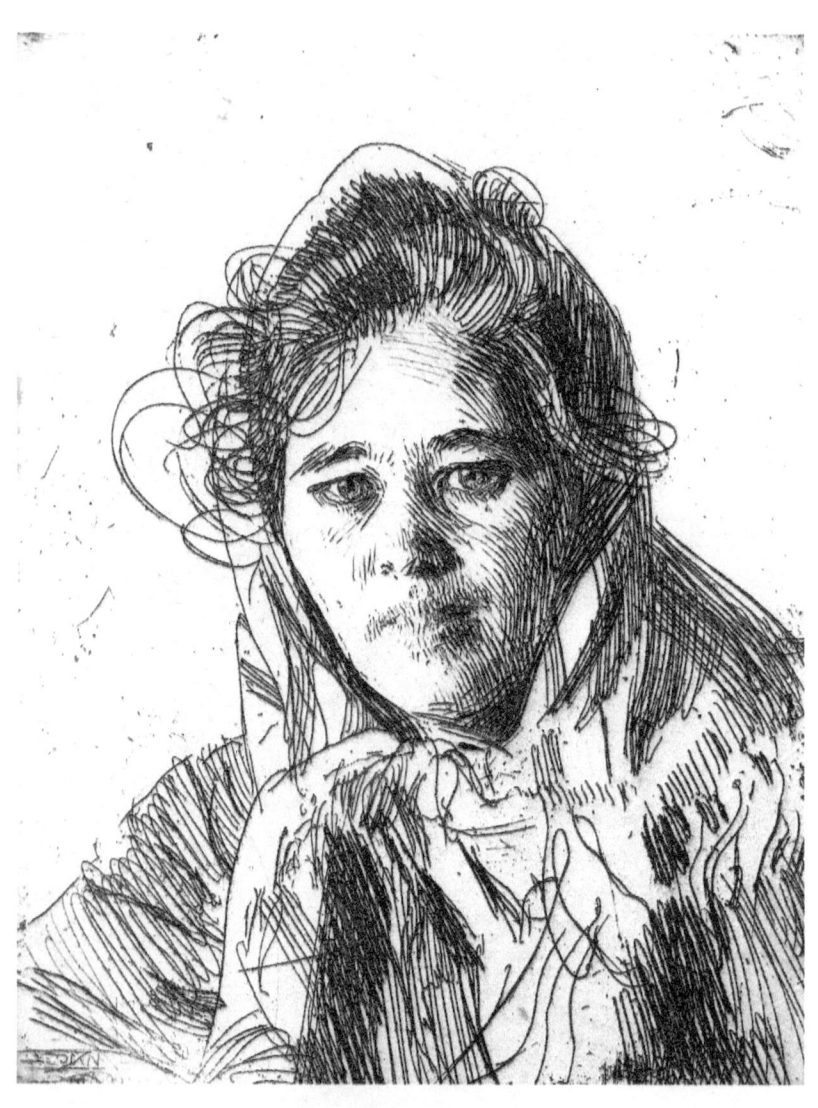

Krakbergs Anna, 1903, etching

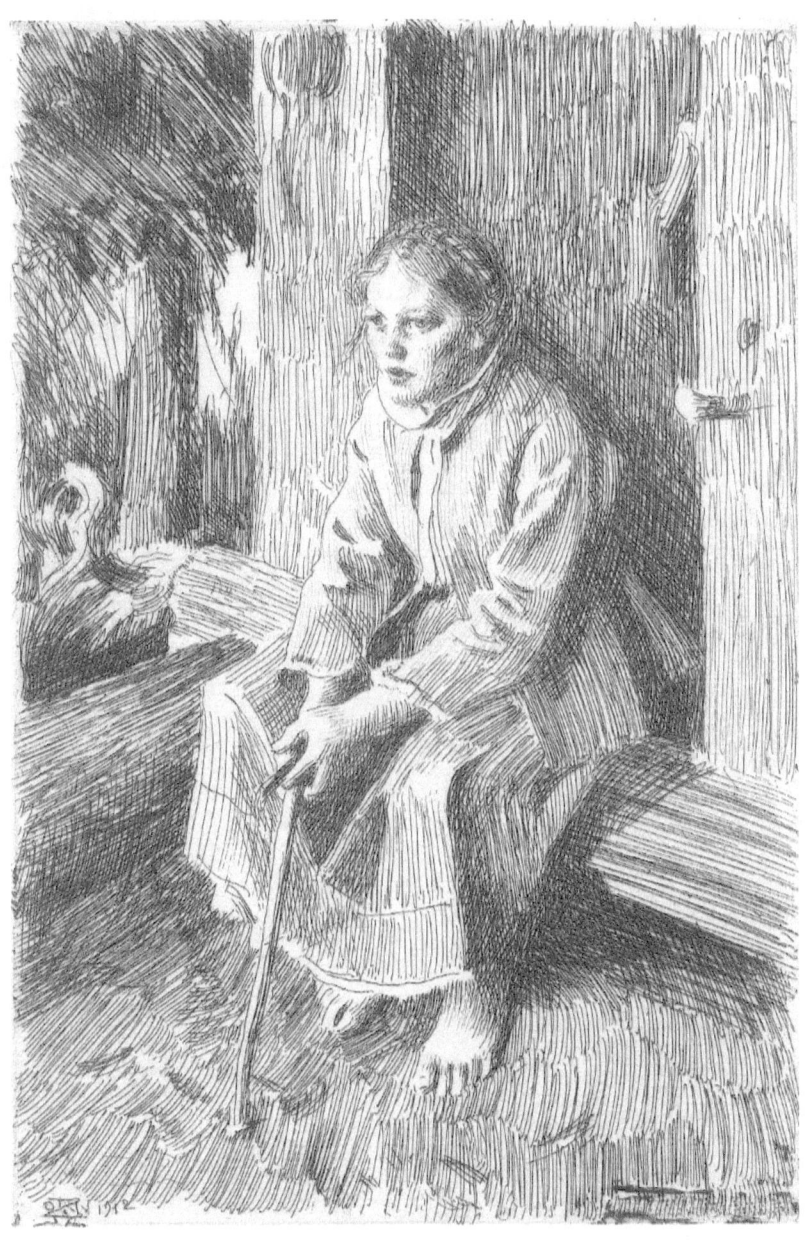

The Herding Maiden's Sunday, 1912, etching

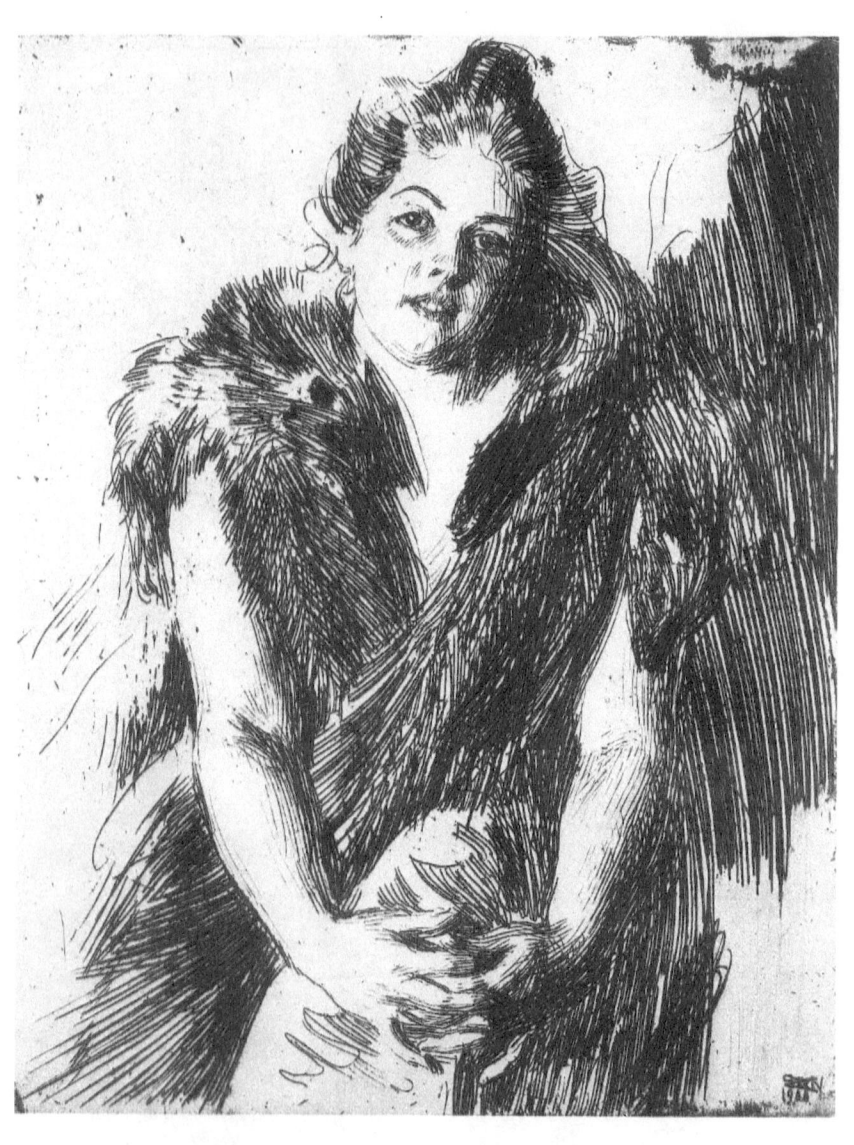

Maja von Heijne, 1911, etching

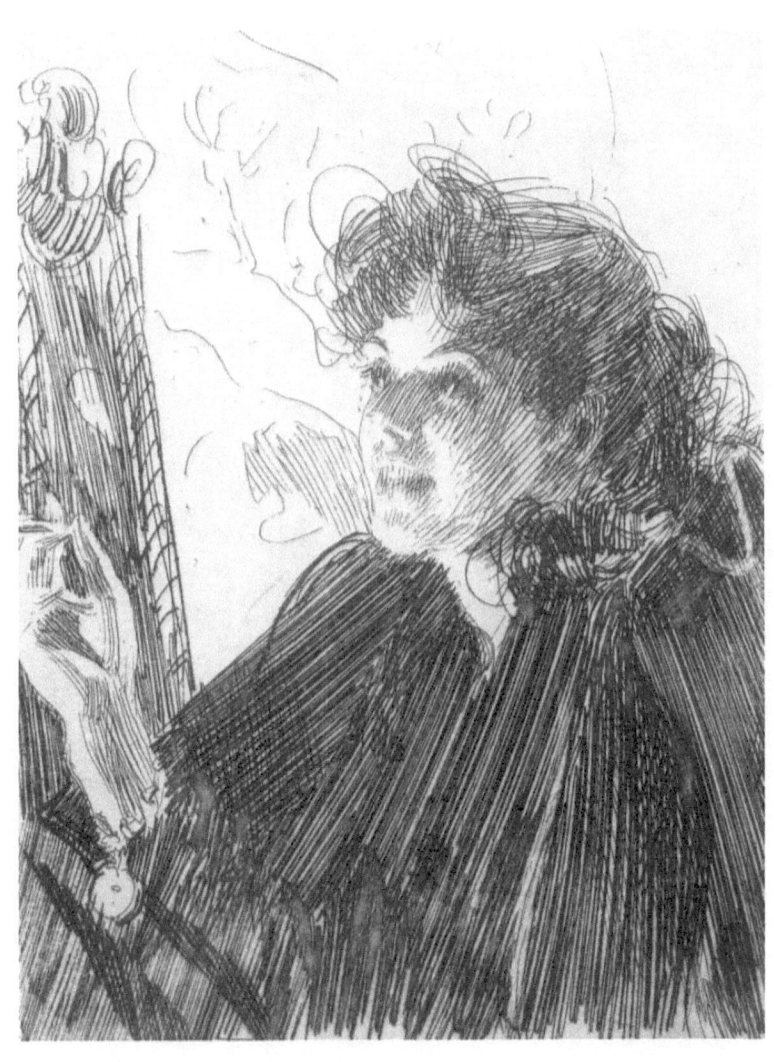

Cigarette Smoker II, 1891, etching

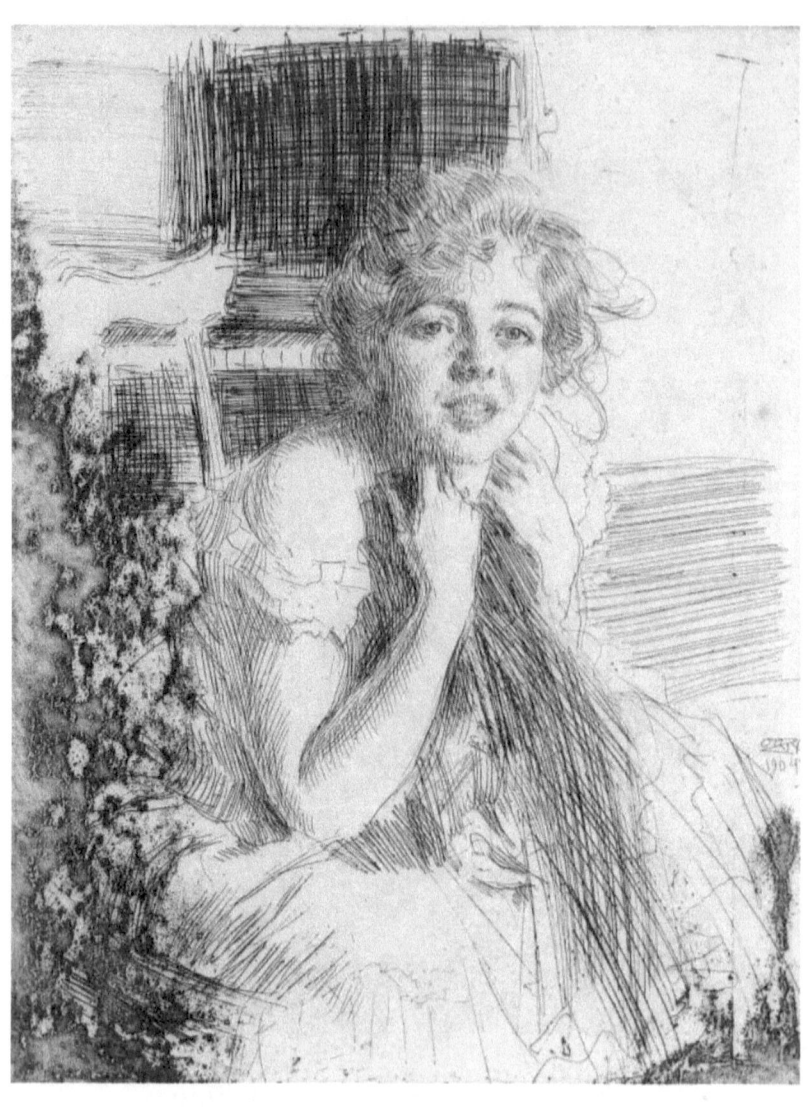

Emma Rasmussen, 1904, etching

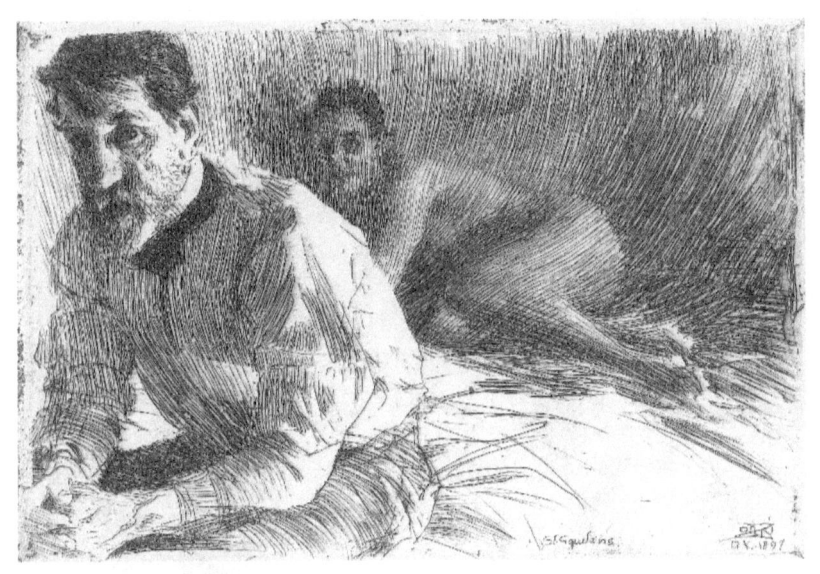

August Saint-Gaudens II, 1897, etching

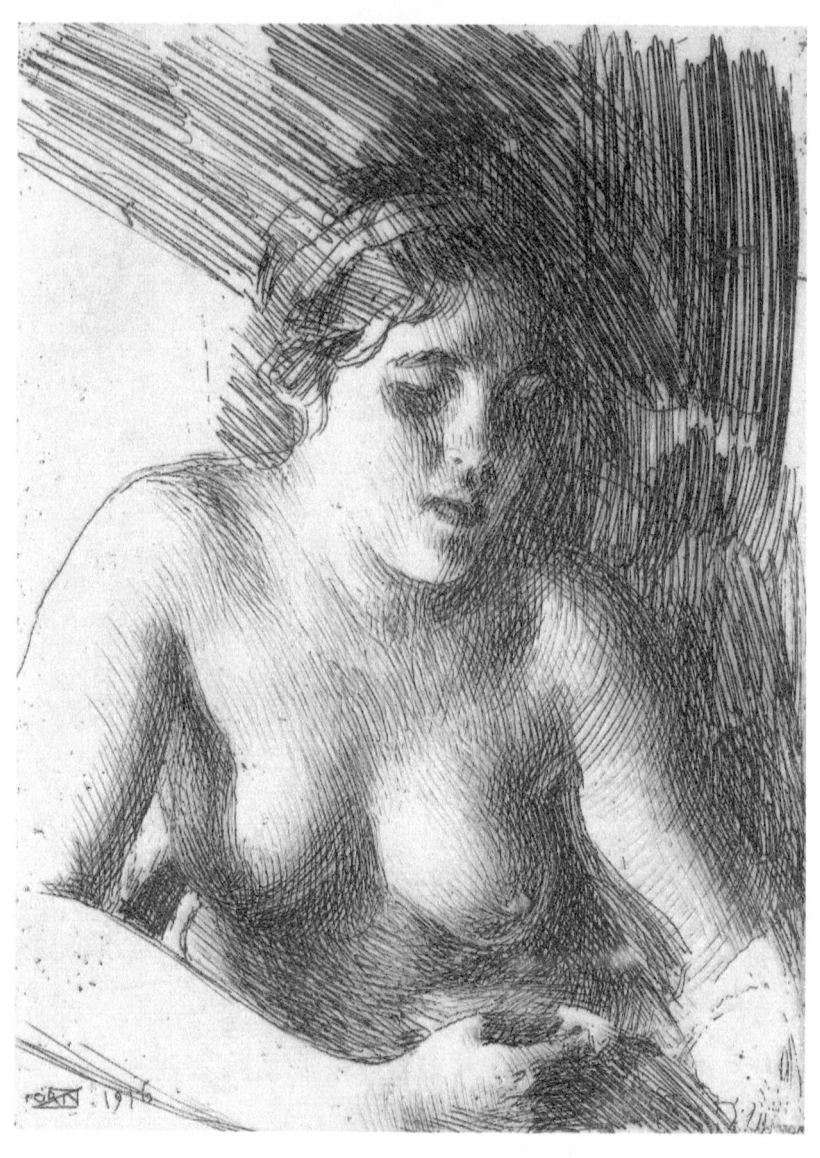

Bust, 1915, etching

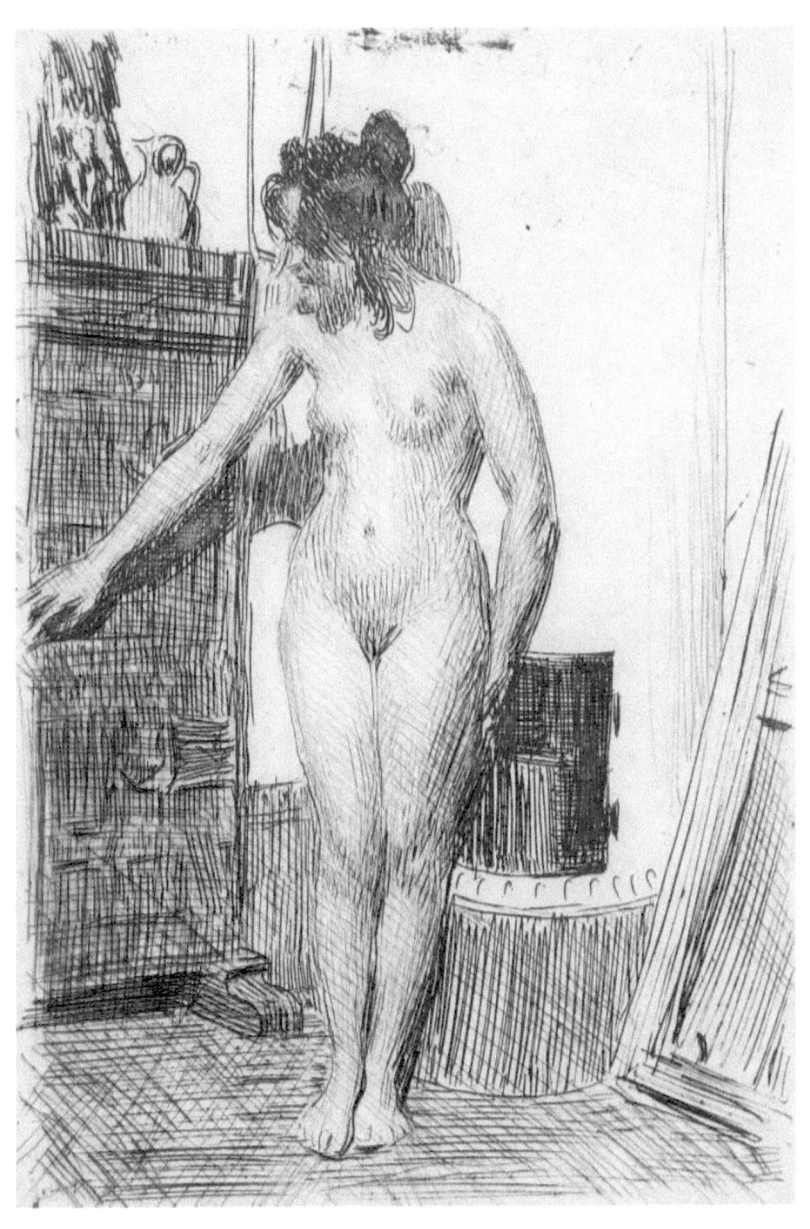

At the Tile Stove, 1903, etching

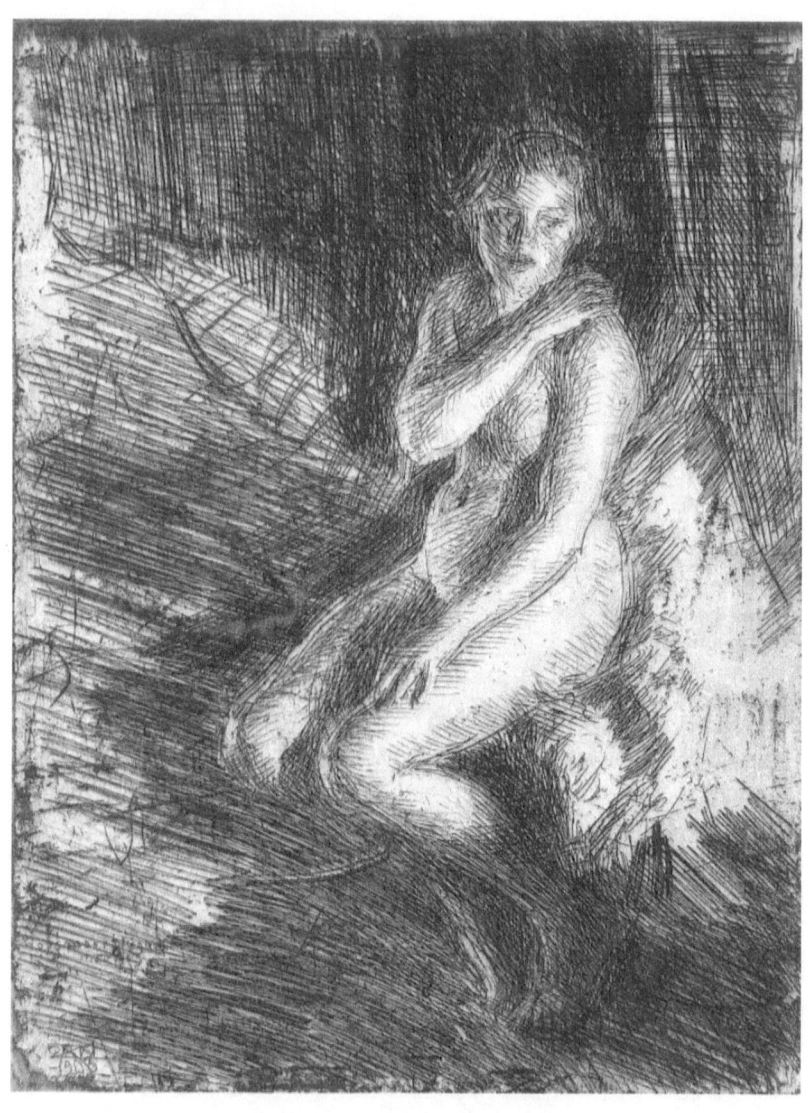

Berit, 1905, etching

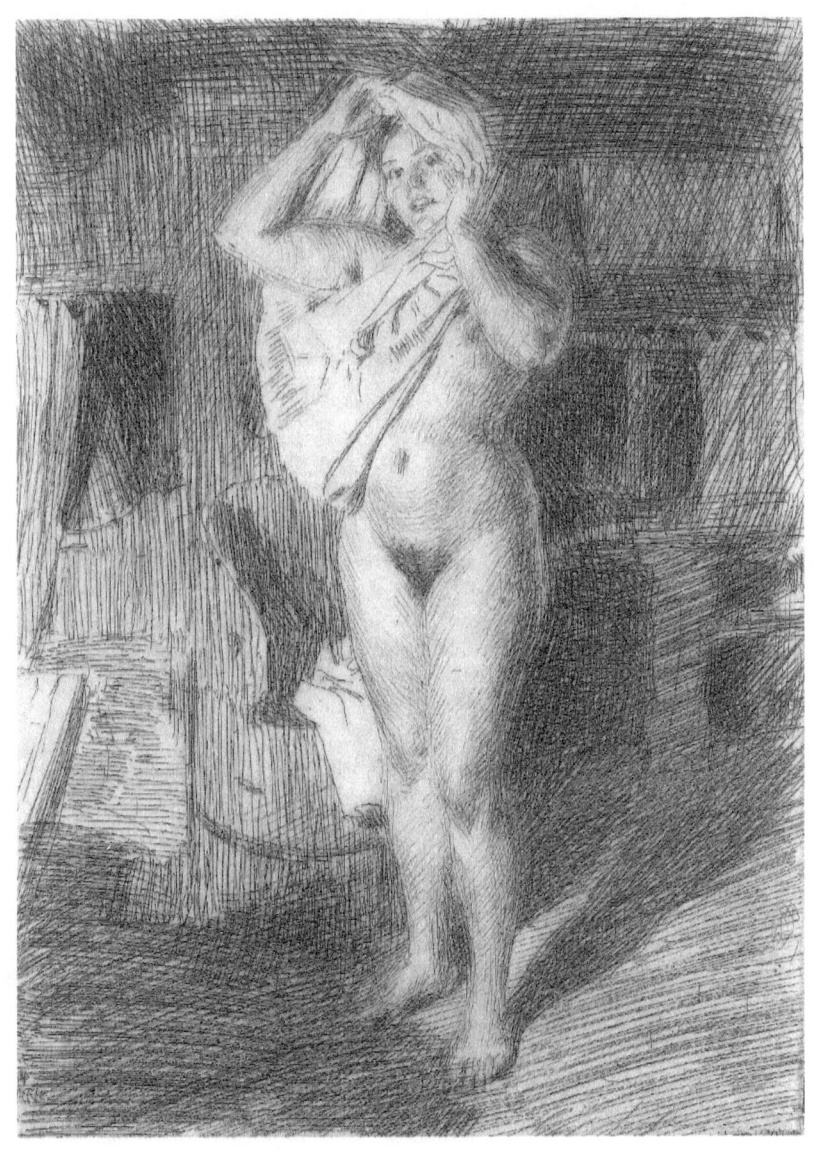

Berserk, 1914, etching

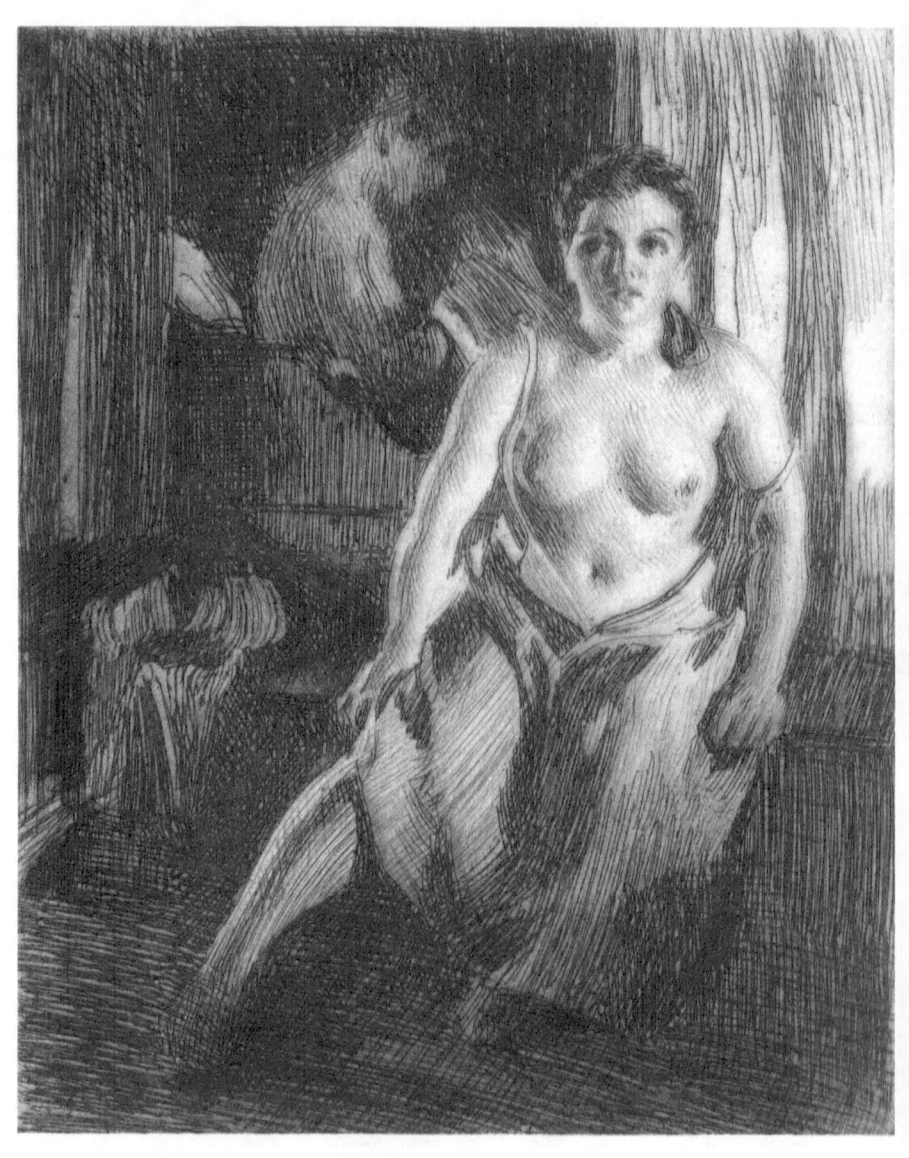

By the Bed Stool, 1914, etching

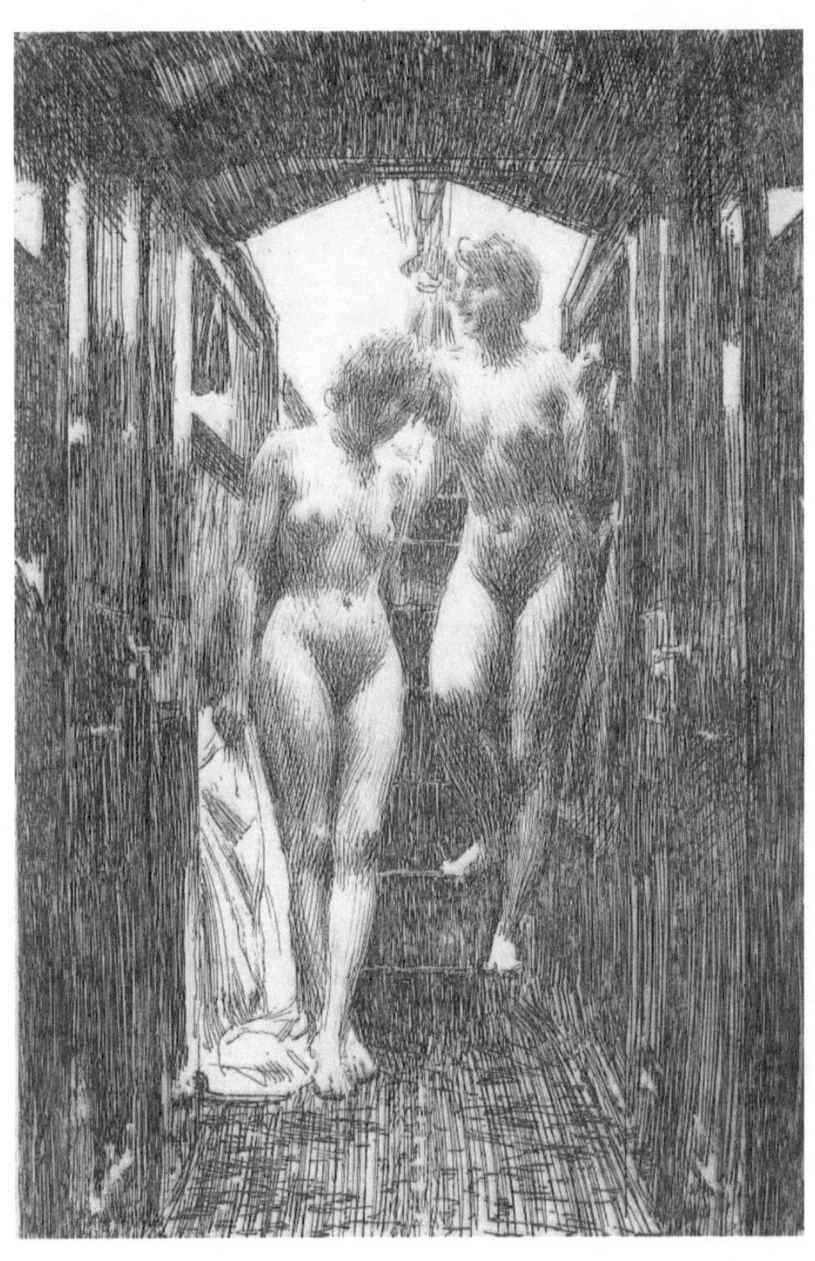

Cabin, 1917, etching

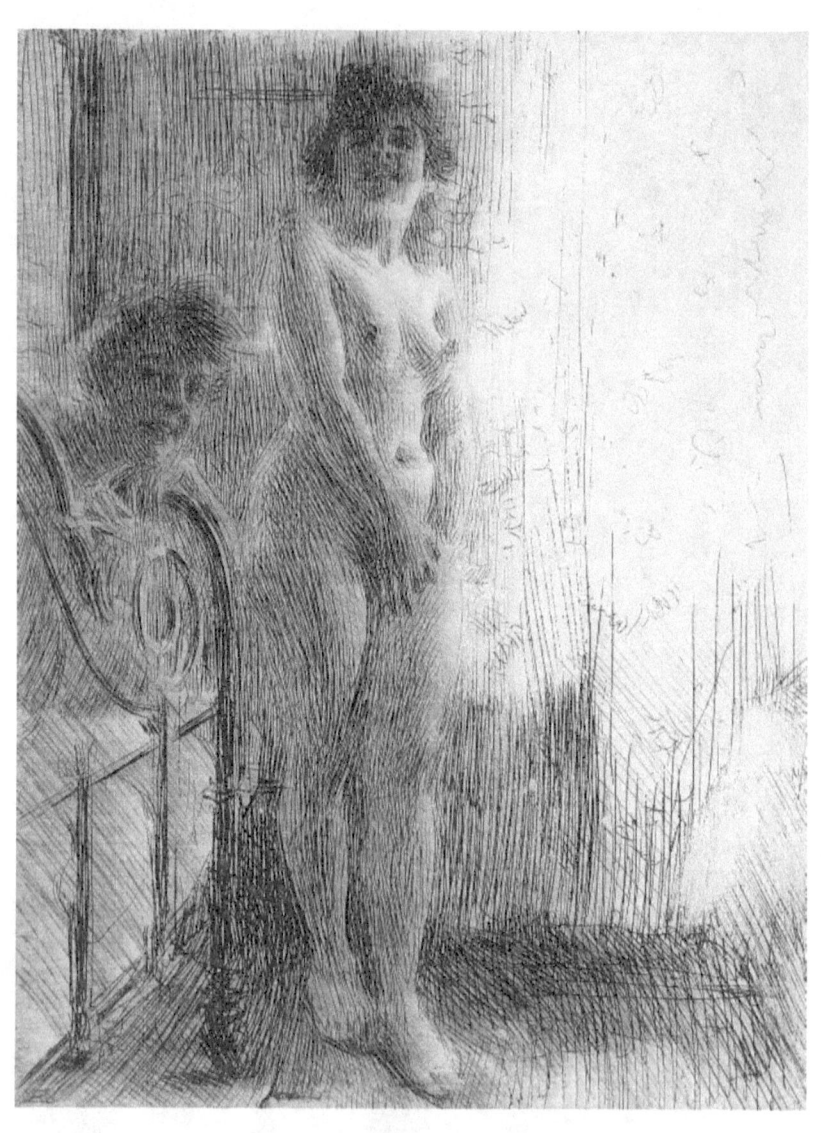

Dim Corner, 1903, etching

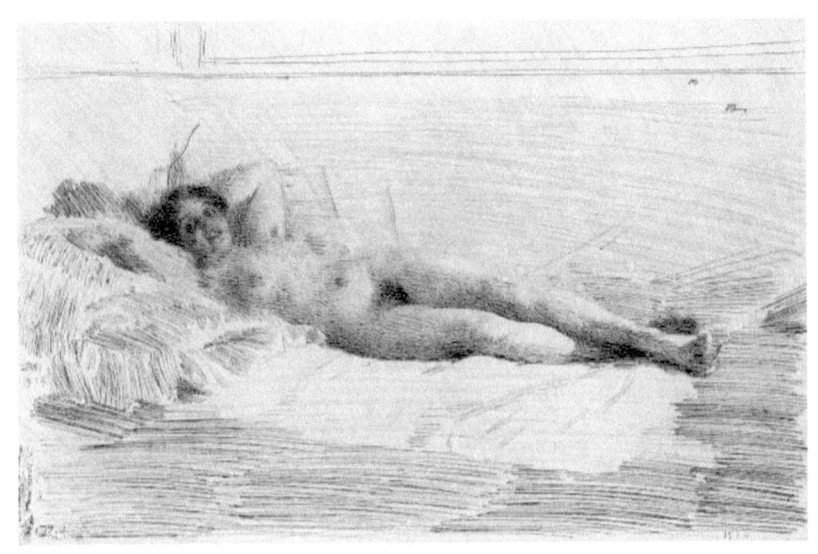

Elin, 1914, etching

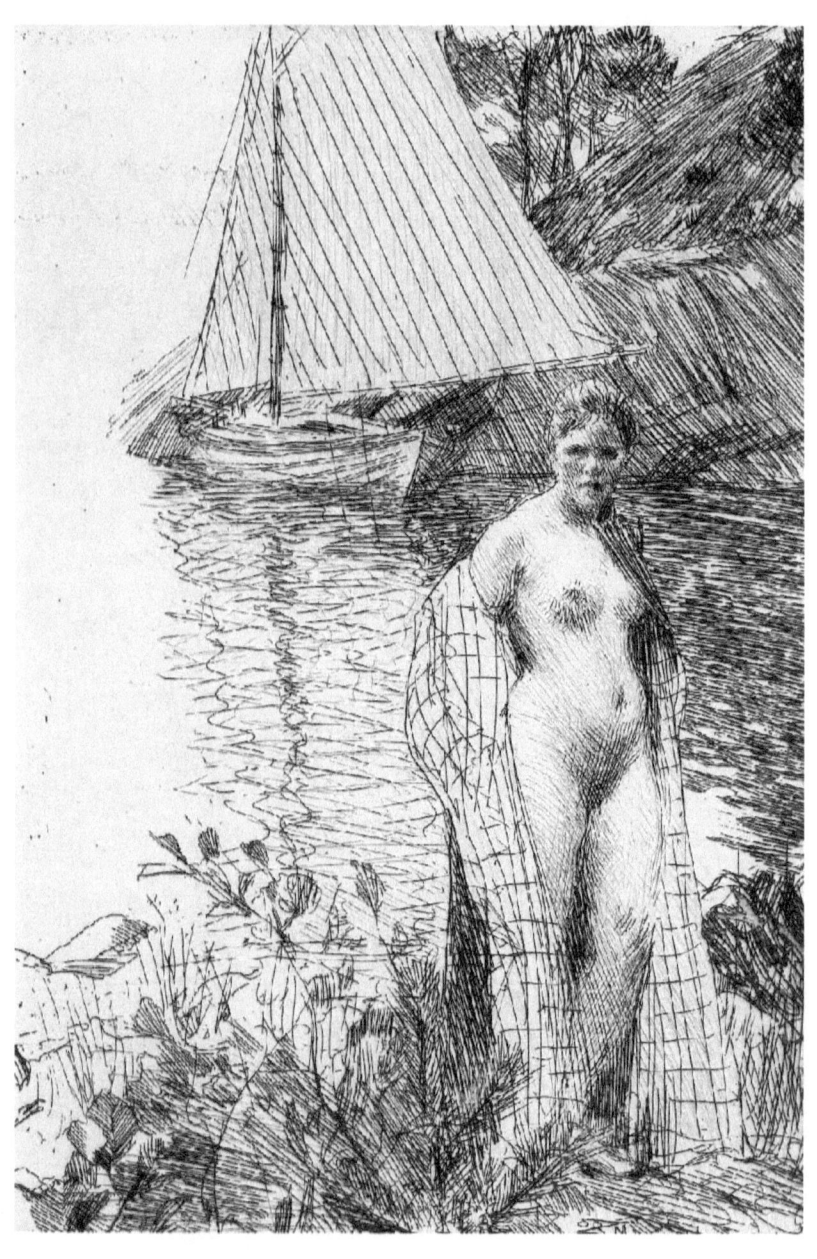

My Model and My Boat, 1894, etching

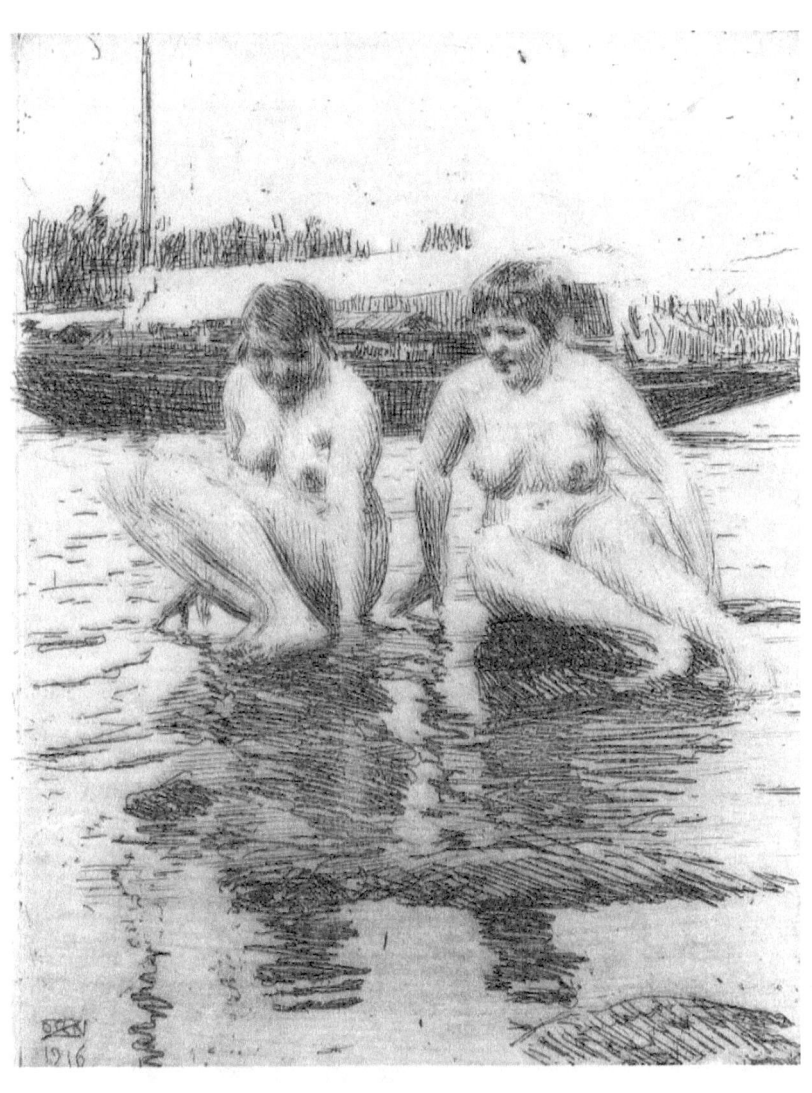

My Models, 1916, etching

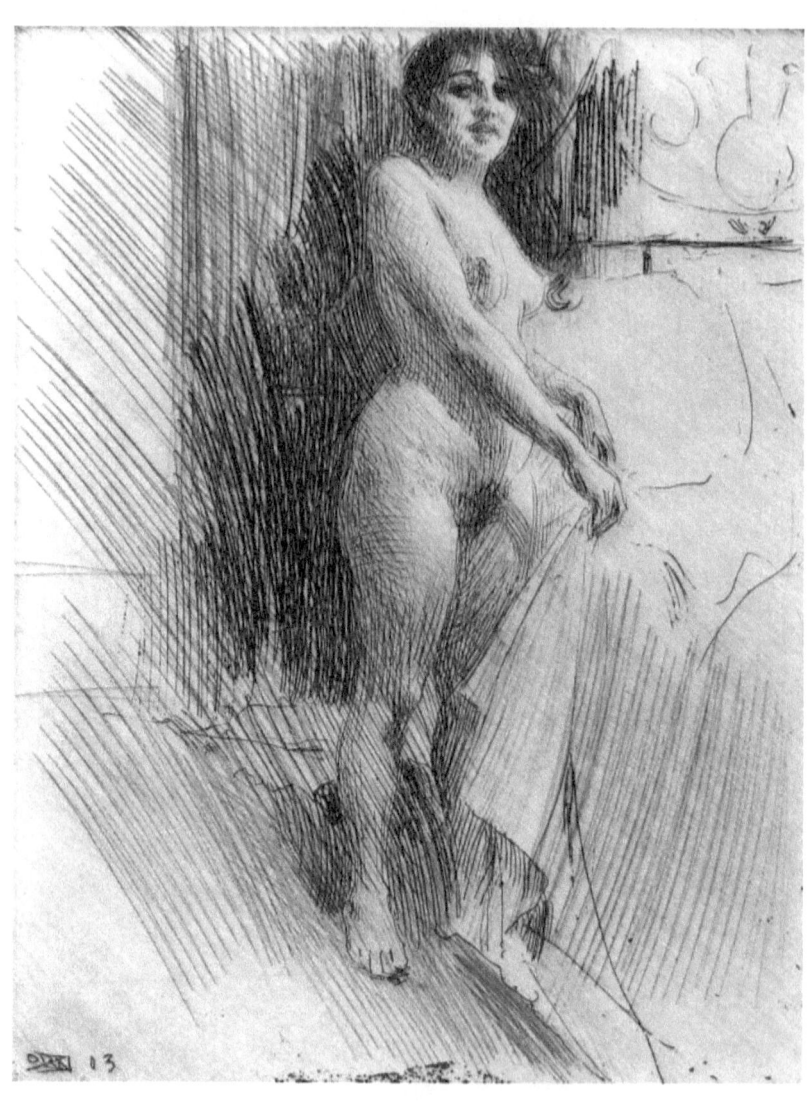

Nanette, 1903, etching

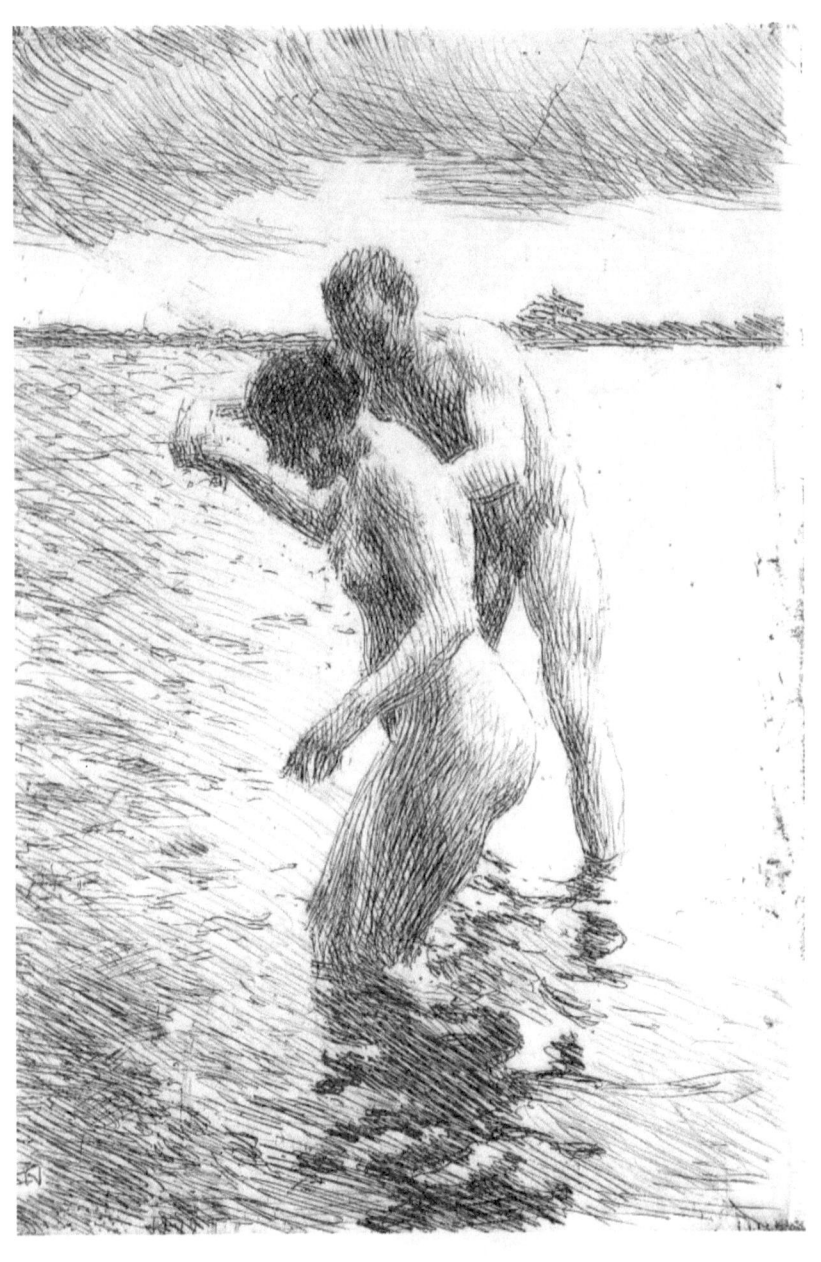

Pilot, 1919, etching

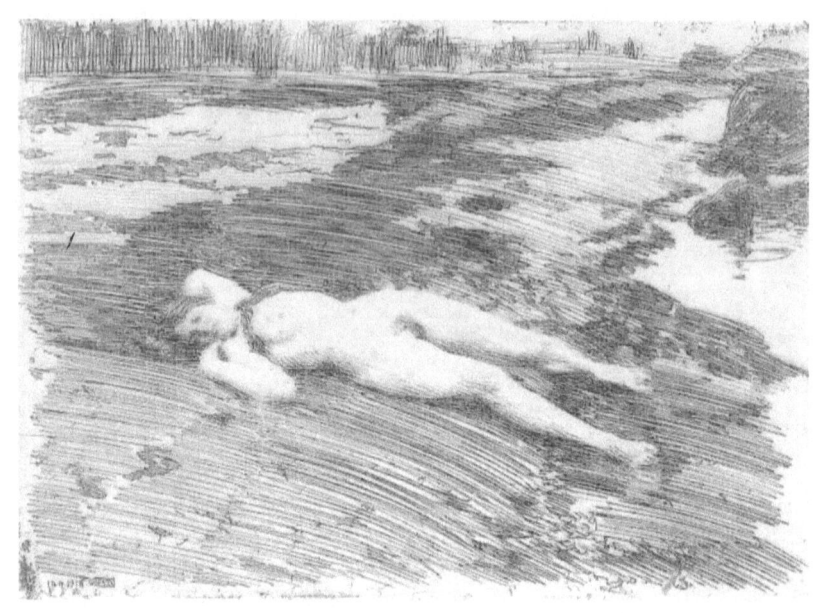

On the Sands, 1916, etching

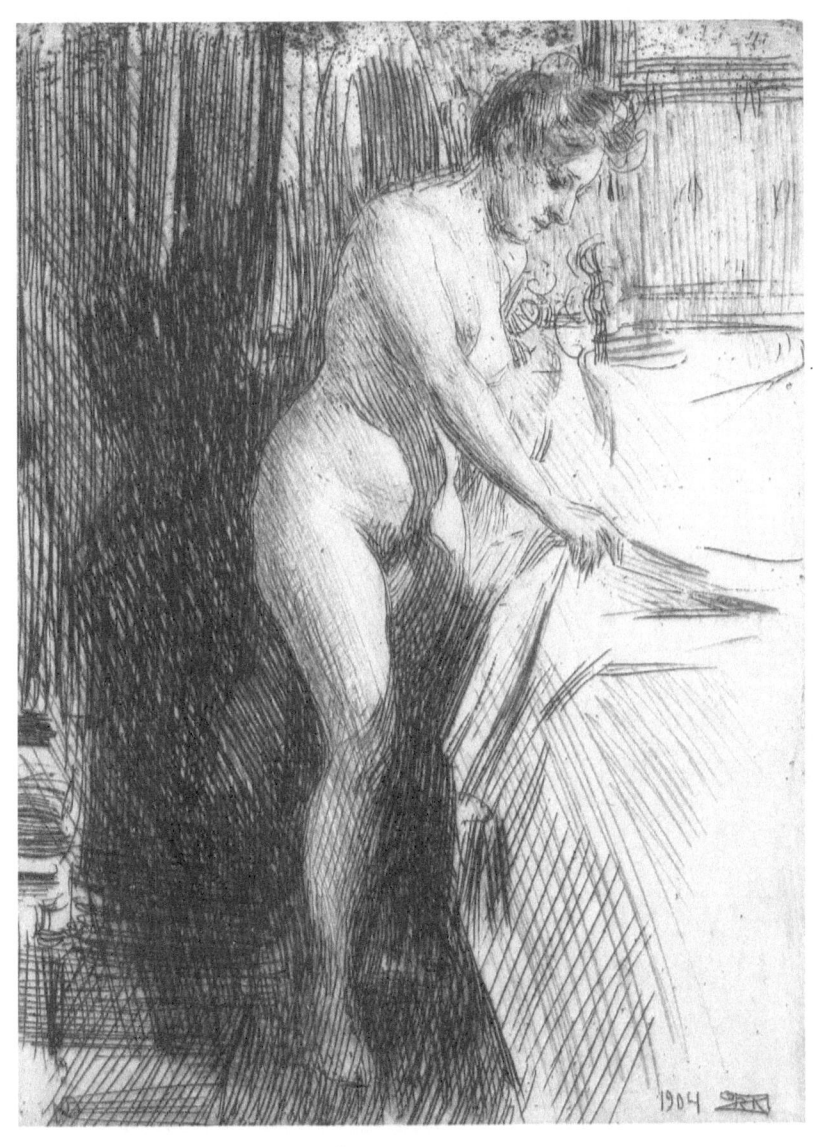

Olandine, 1904, etching

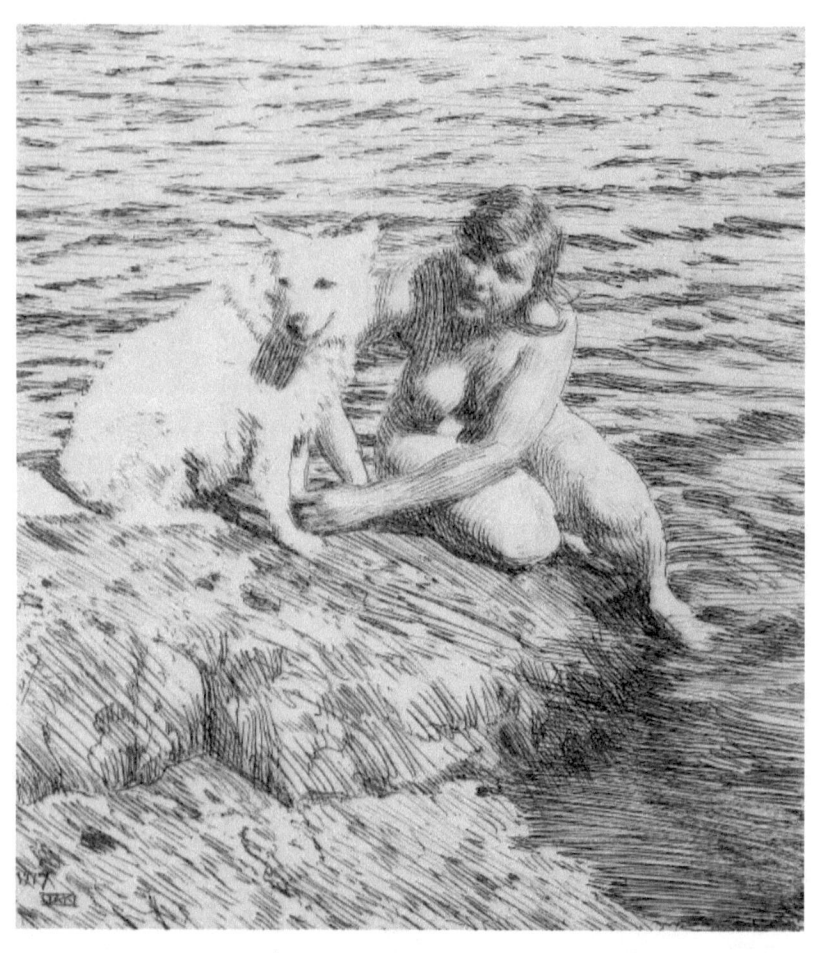

Sappo, 1917, etching

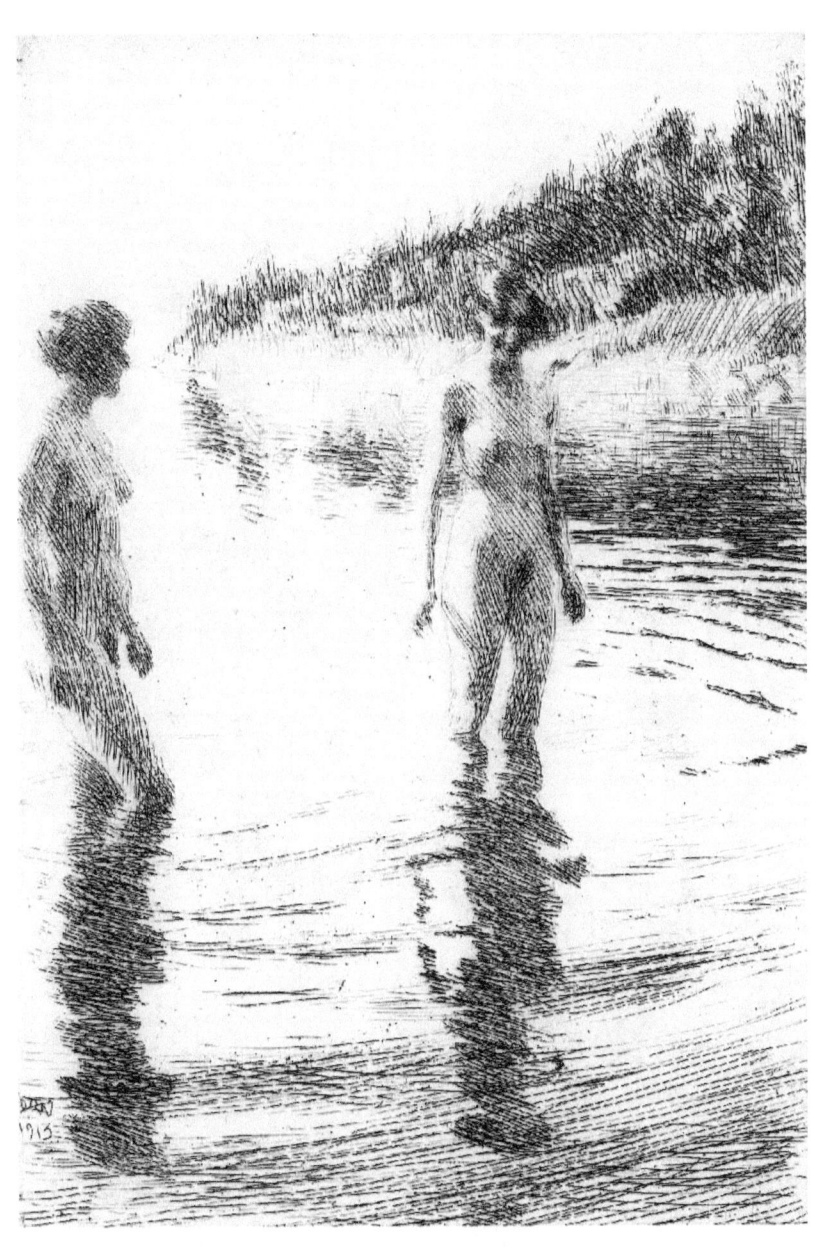

Shallow, 1913, etching

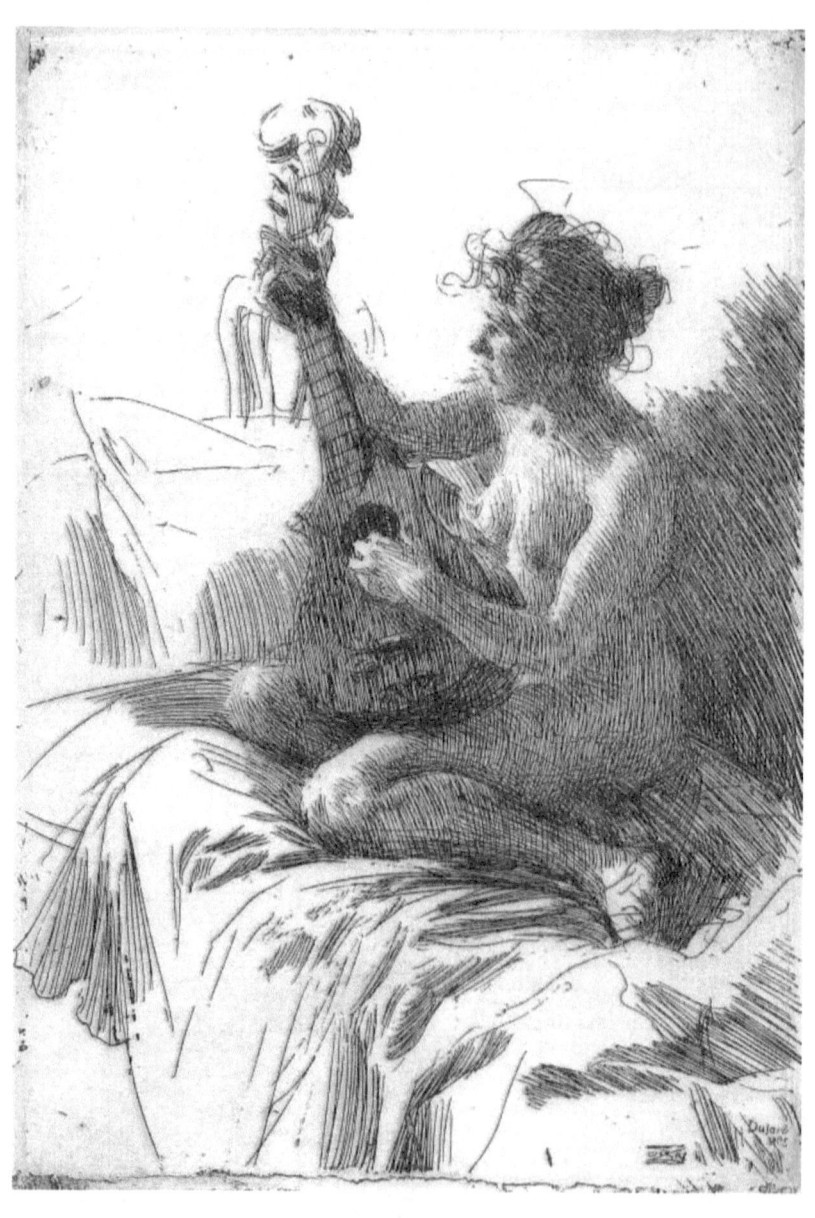

Souvenir - The Guitar, 1895, etching

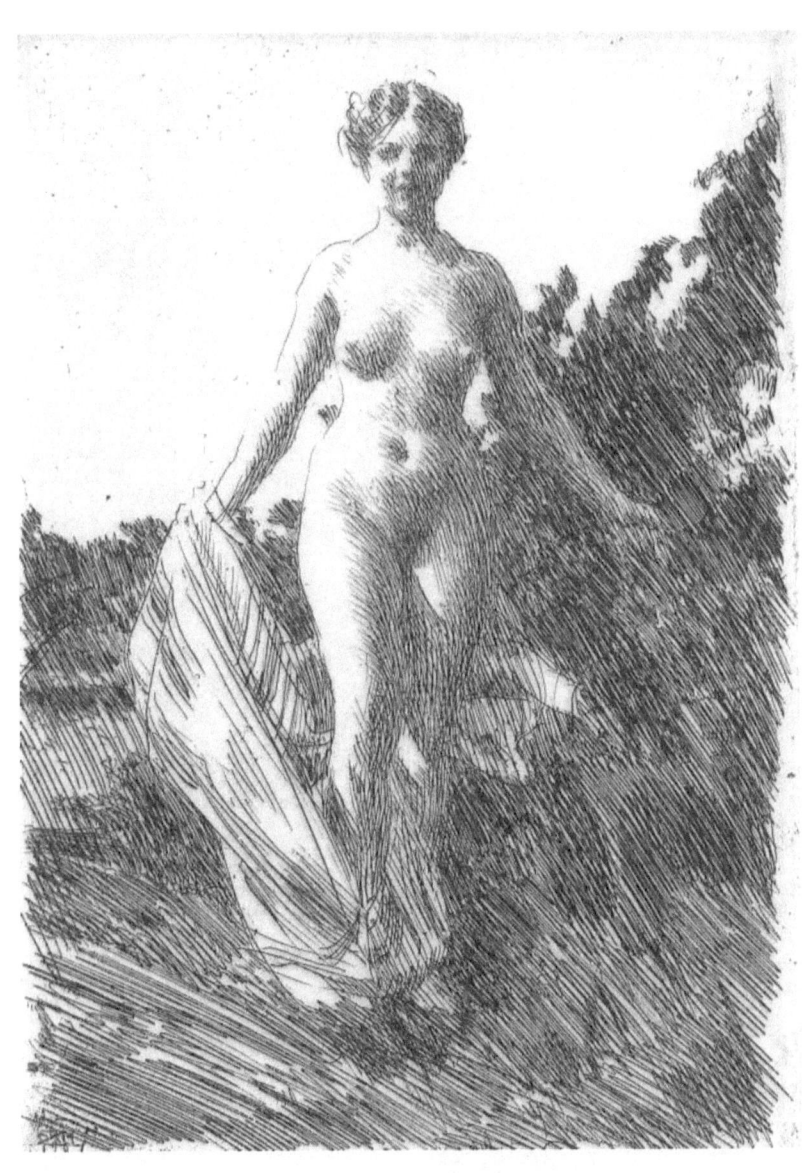

Summer, 1907, etching

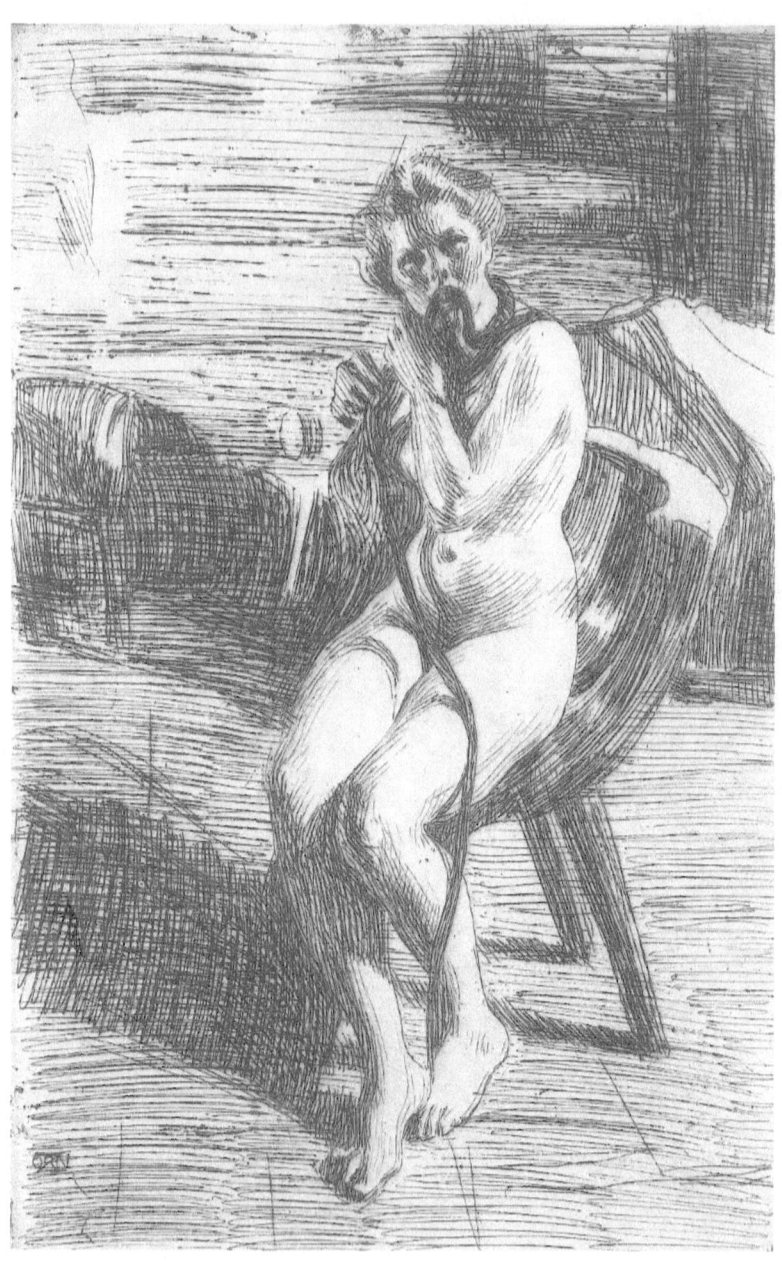

The Braid, 1912, etching

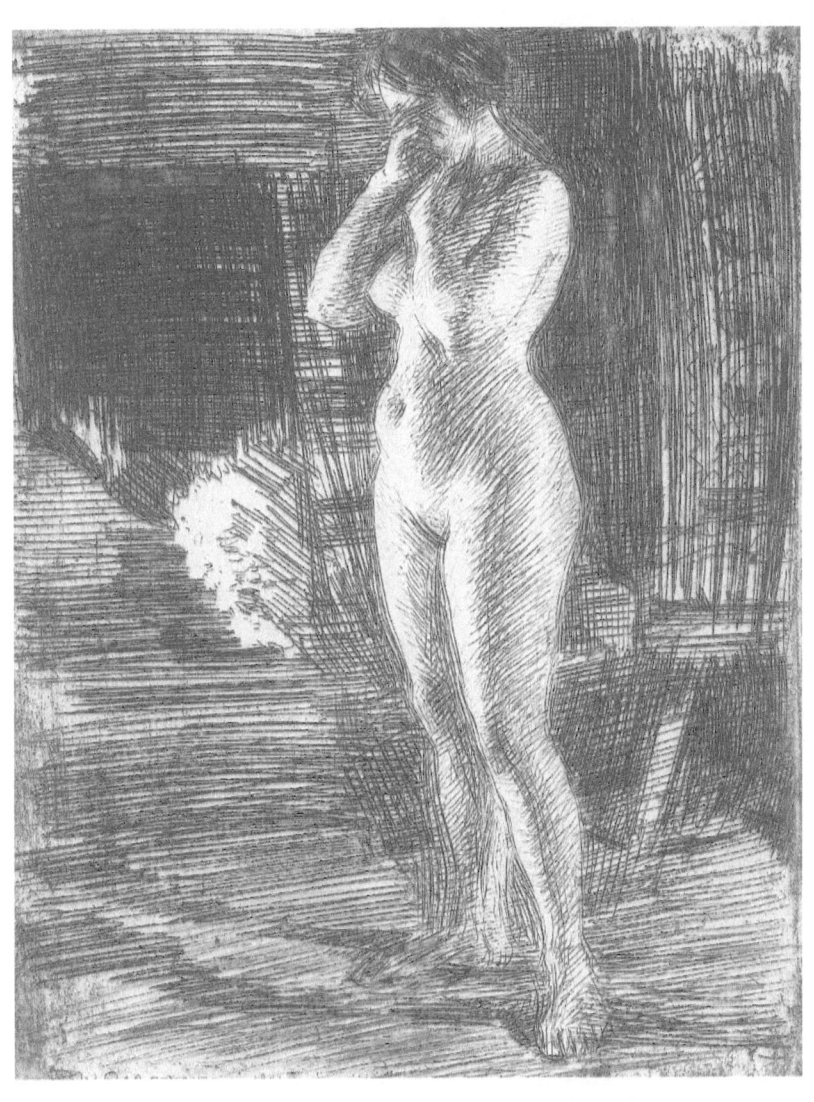

The First Séance, 1906, etching

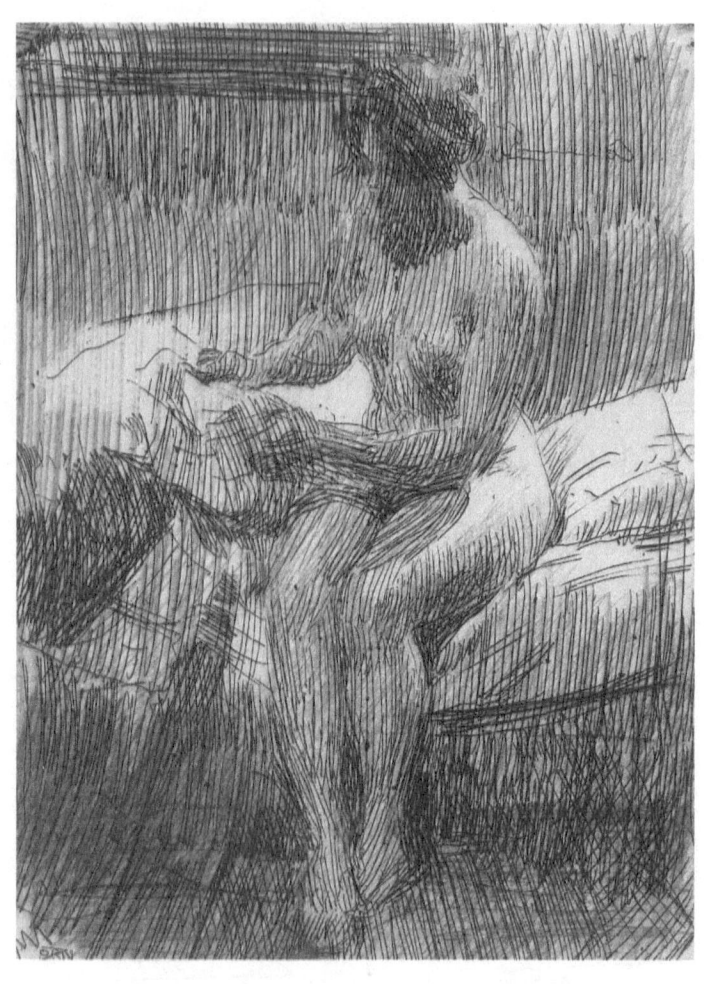

The Model Reading Letters, 1910, etching

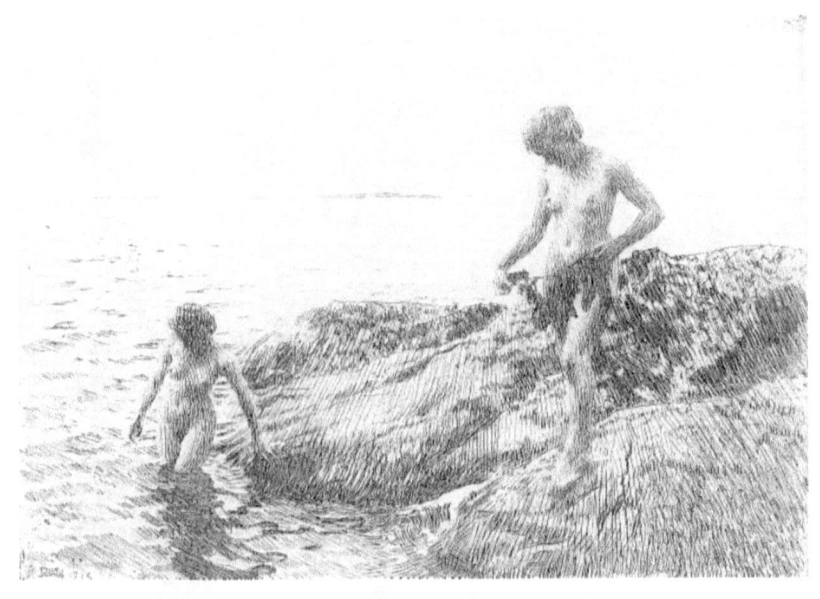

The Outer Skerries, 1913, etching

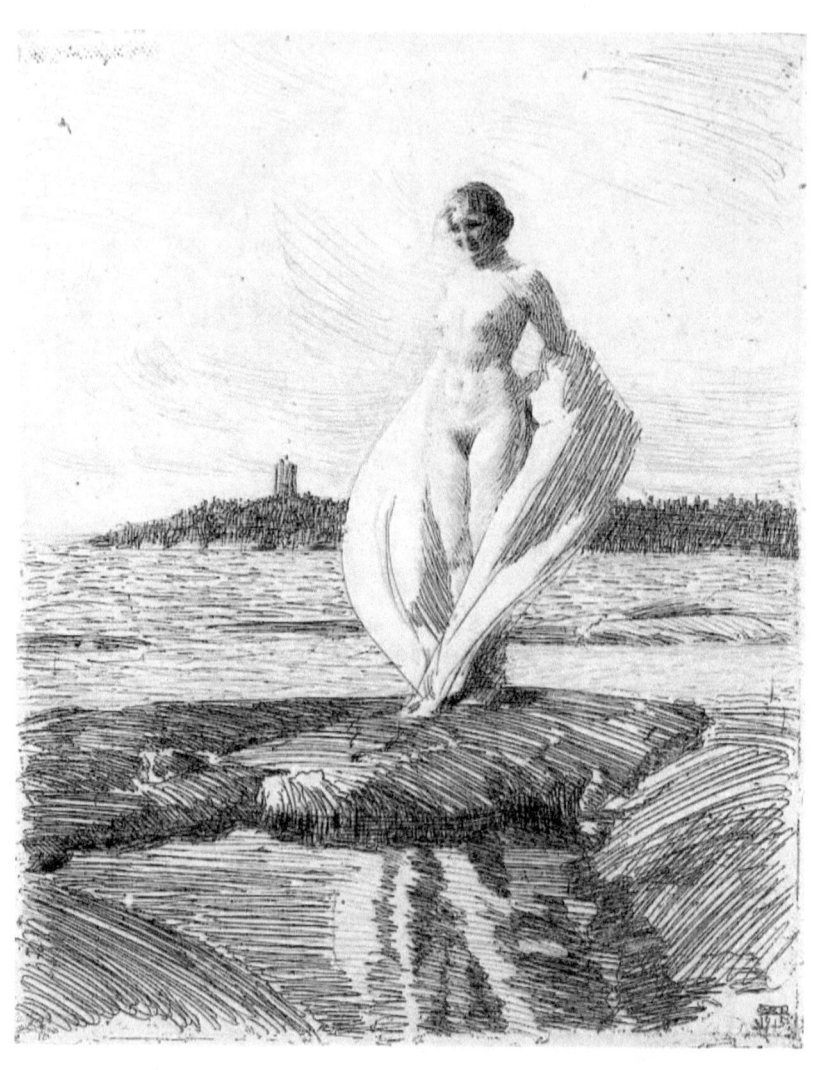

The Swan, 1915, etching

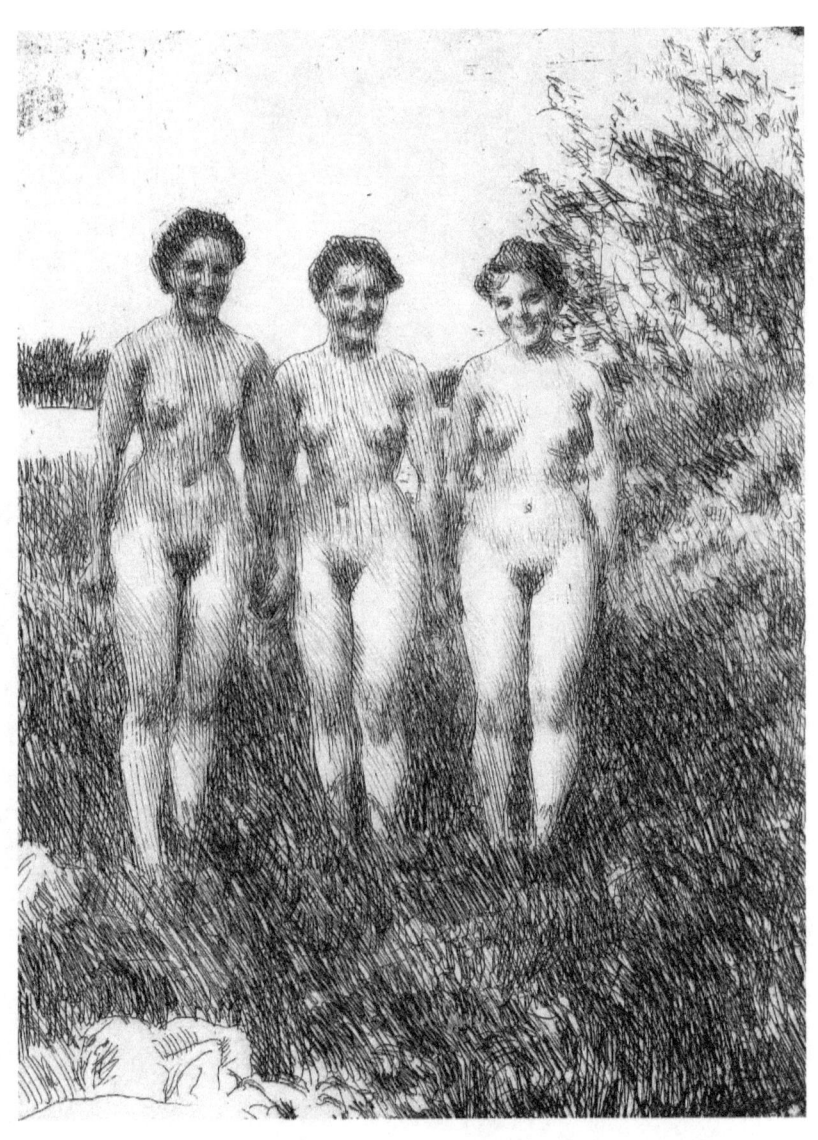

Three Sisters, 1913, etching

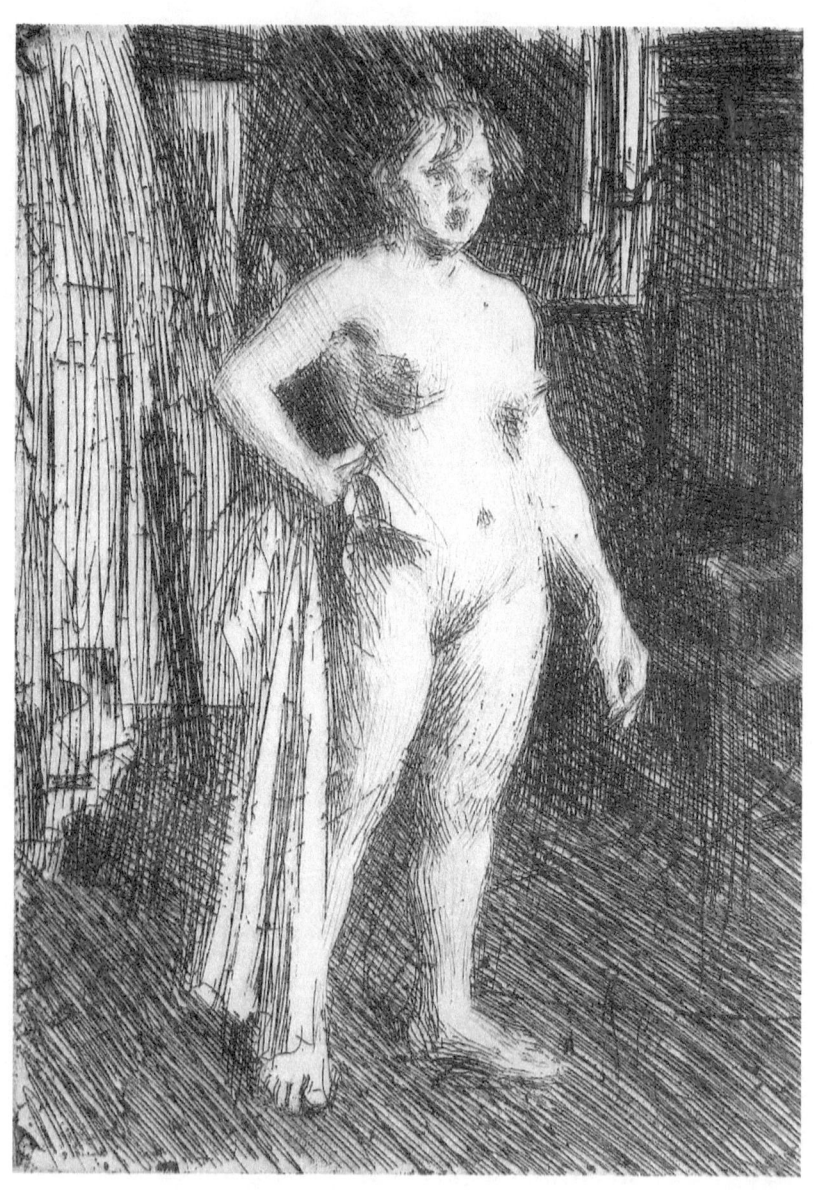

Venus de la Vilette, 1893, etching

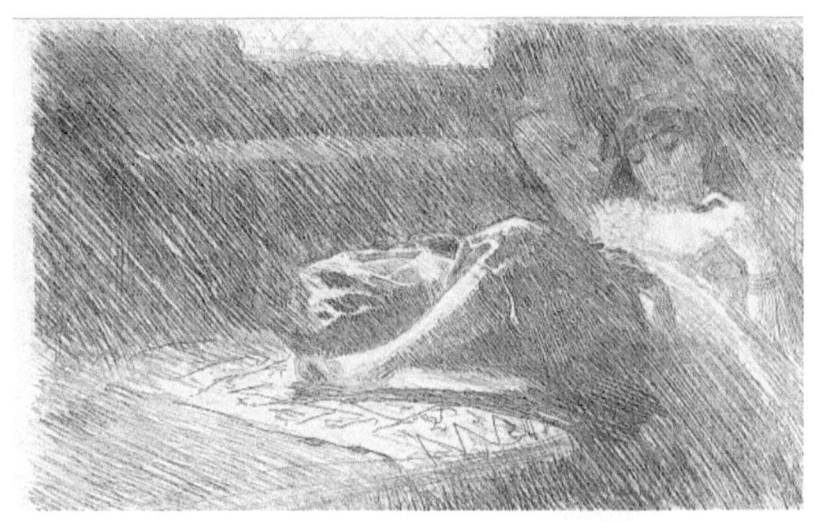

Sleeping Odalisque, 1886, etching

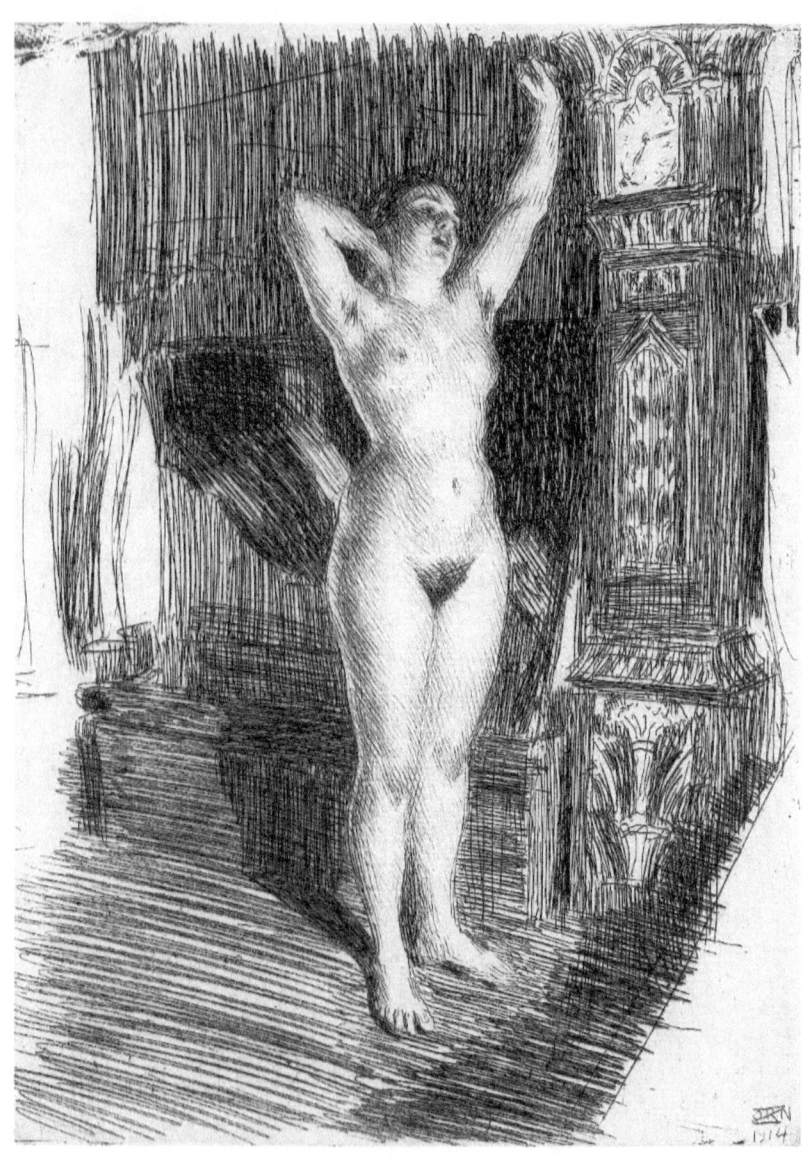

Early, 1904, etching

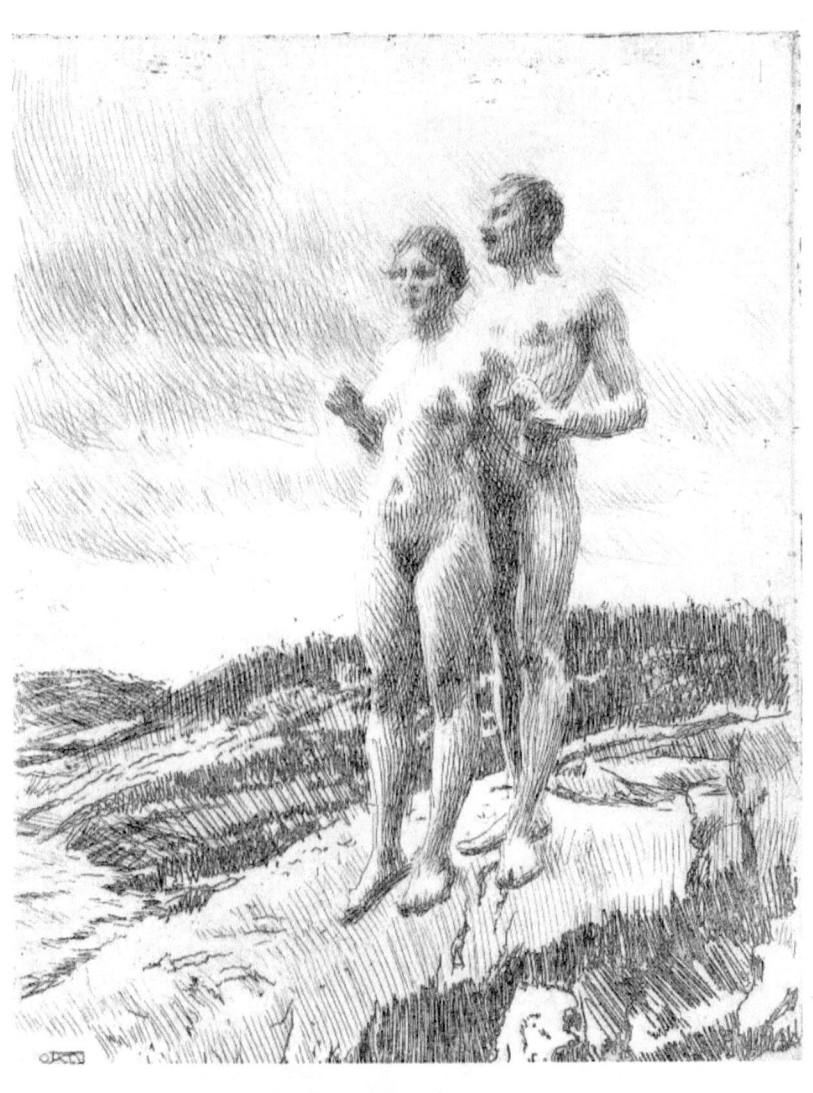

The Two, 1916, etching

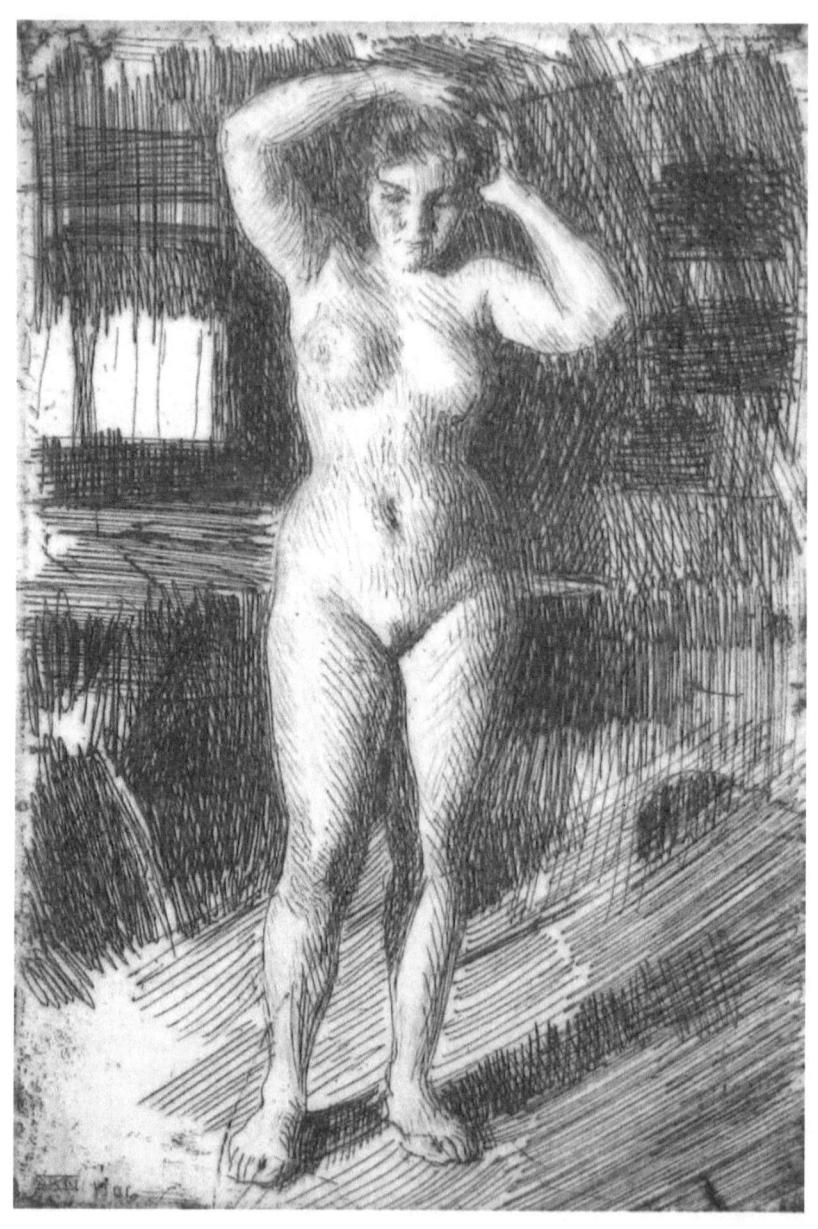

Anna doing her hair, 1906, etching

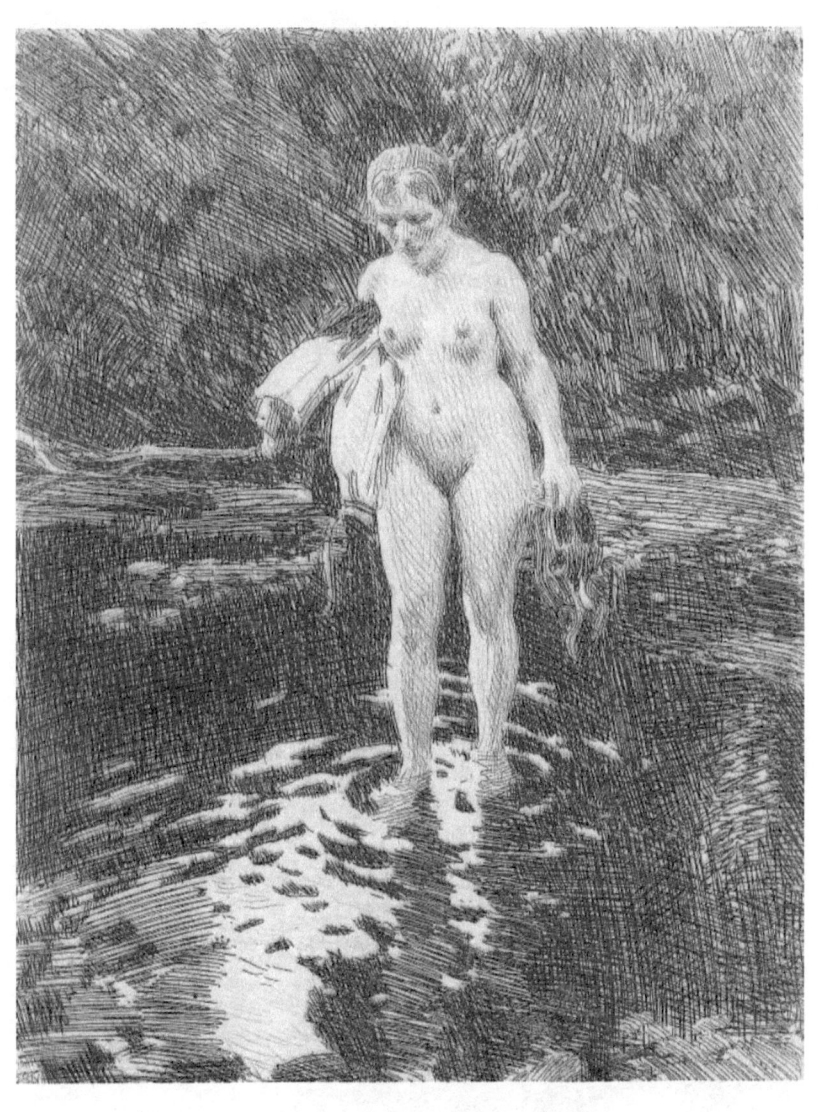

A Place to Wade, 1912, etching

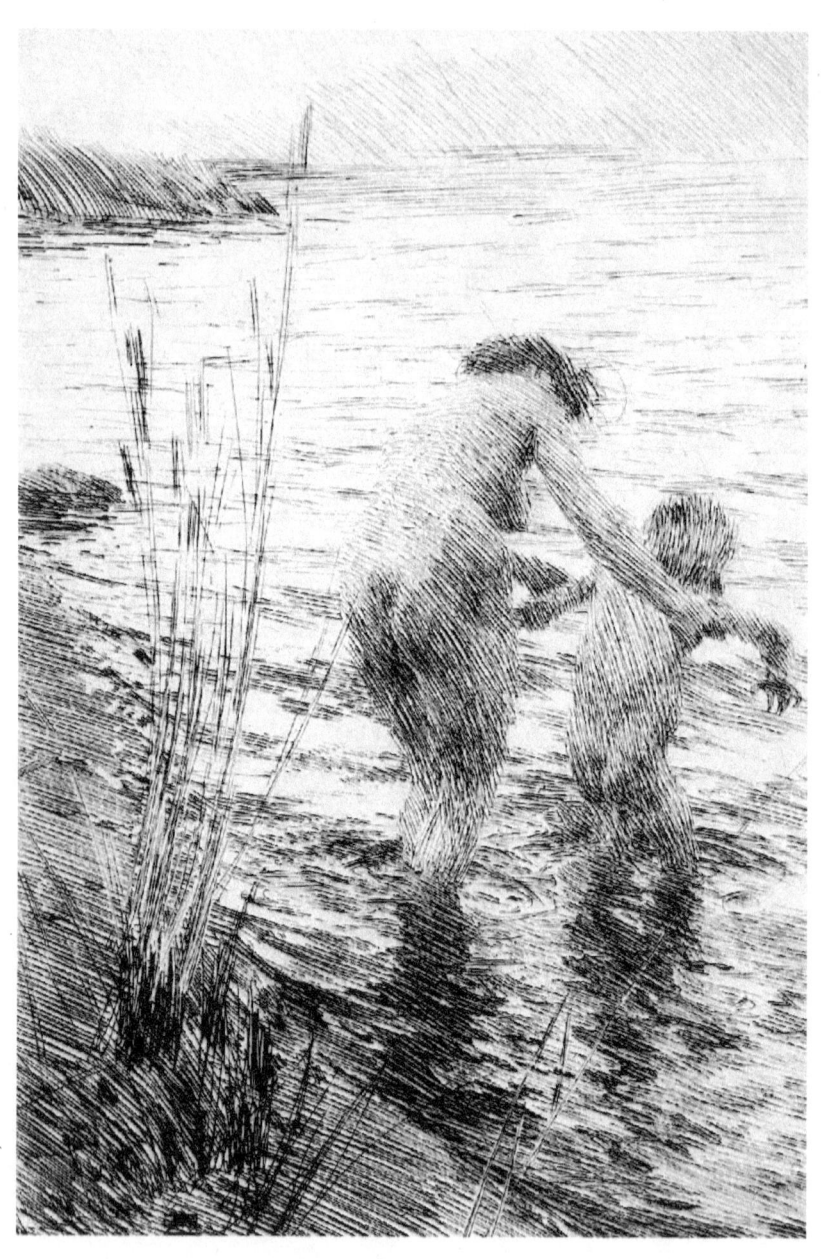

A Première, 1890, etching

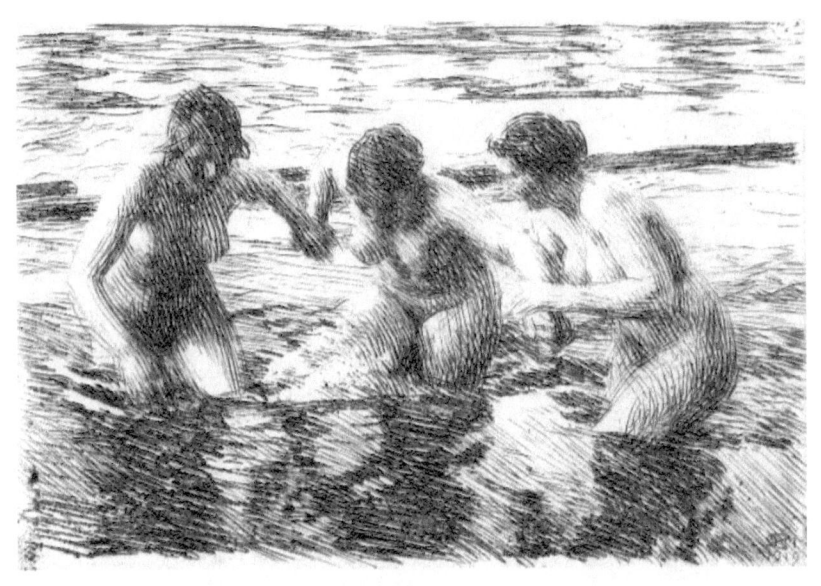

Against the Current, 1919, etching

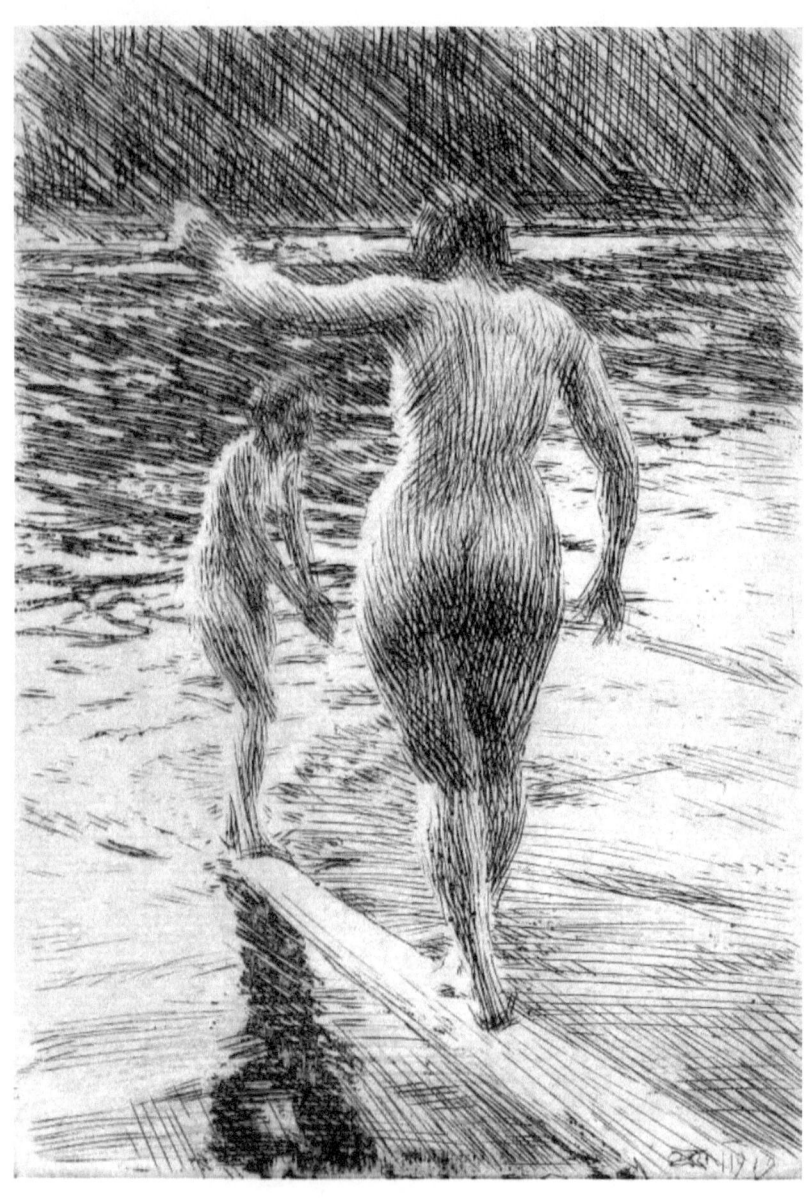

Balance, 1919, etching

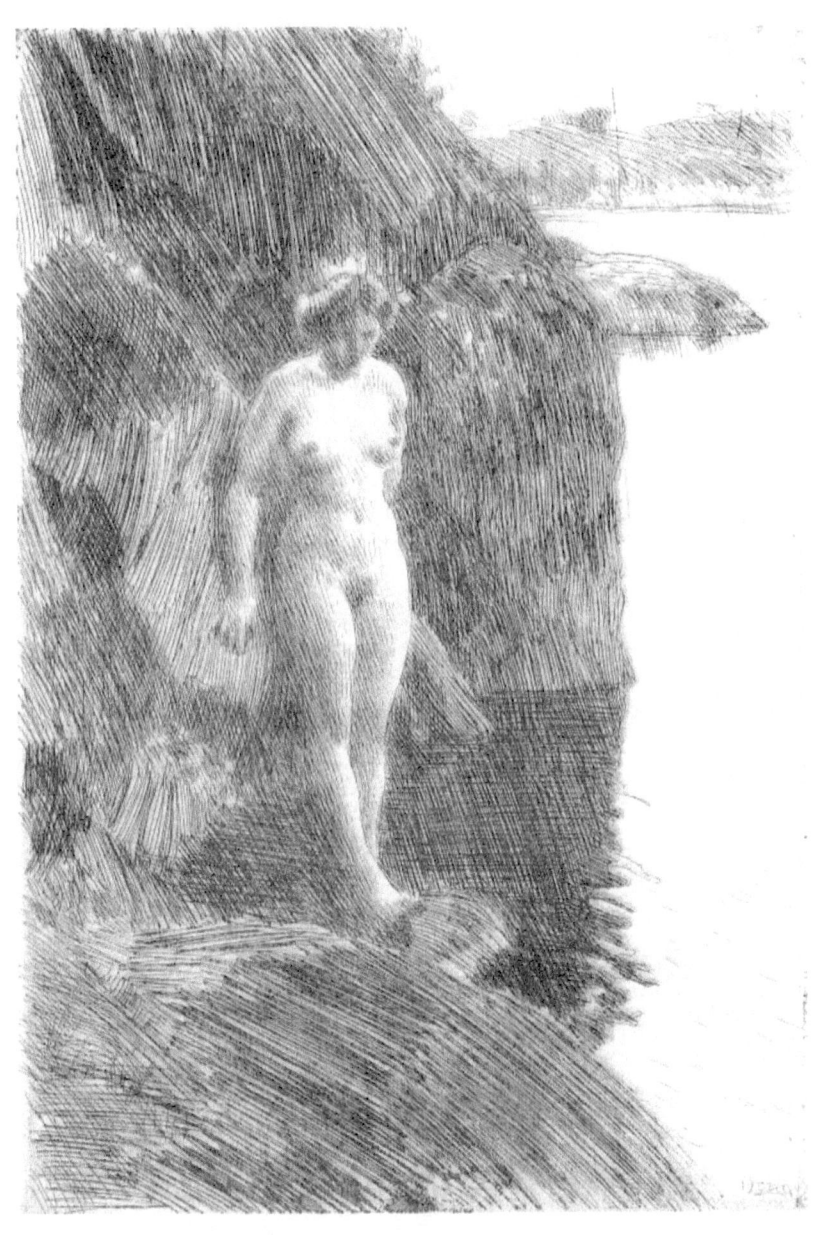

Dagmar, 1909, etching

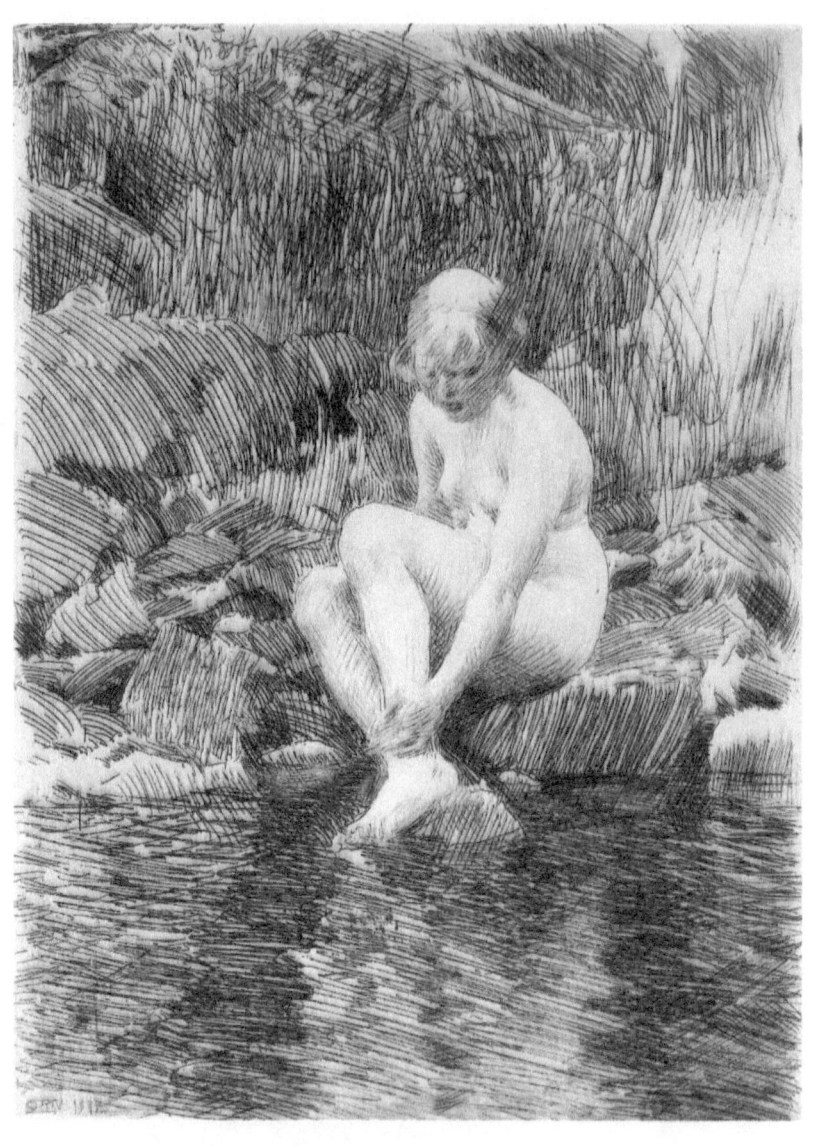

Dagmar, 1912, etching

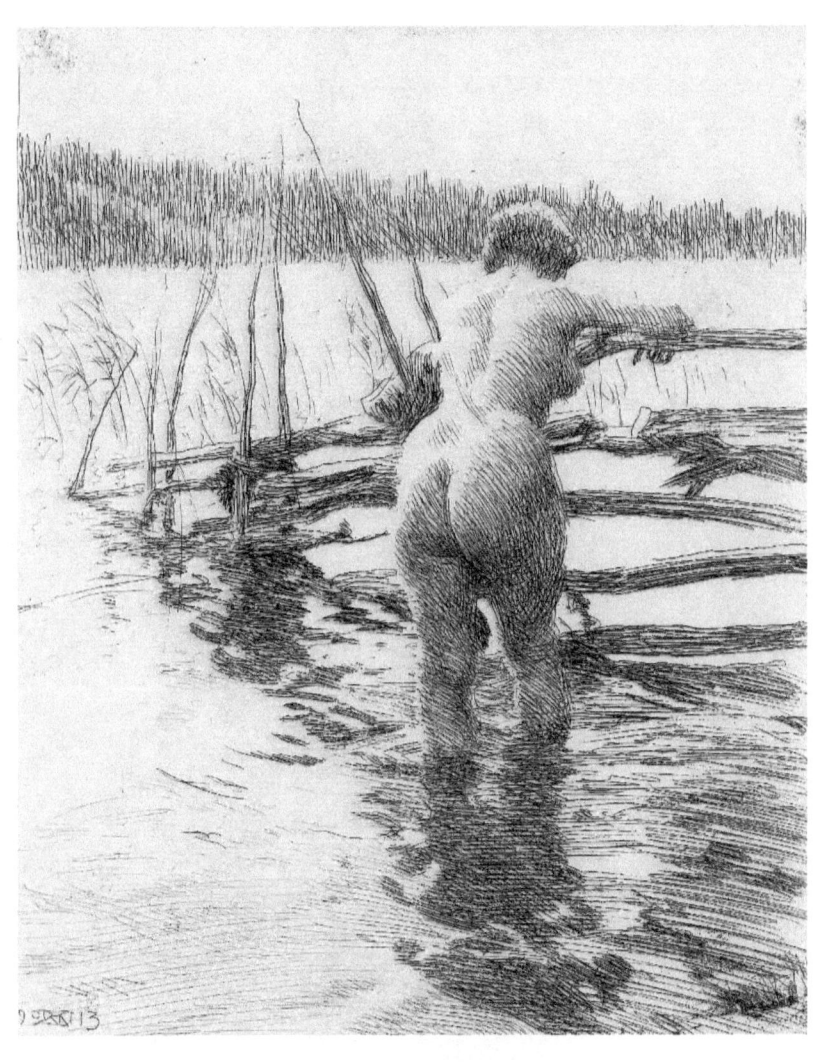

Fence, 1913, etching

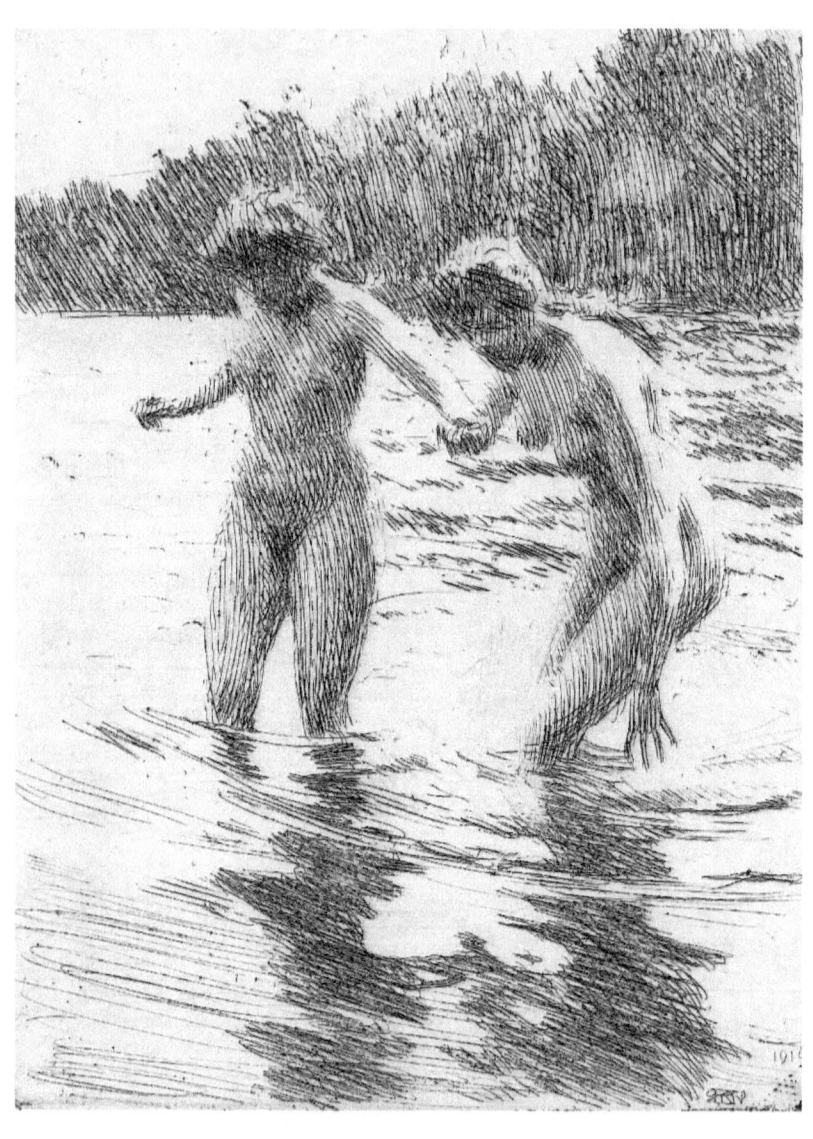

Stony Ground, 1910, etching

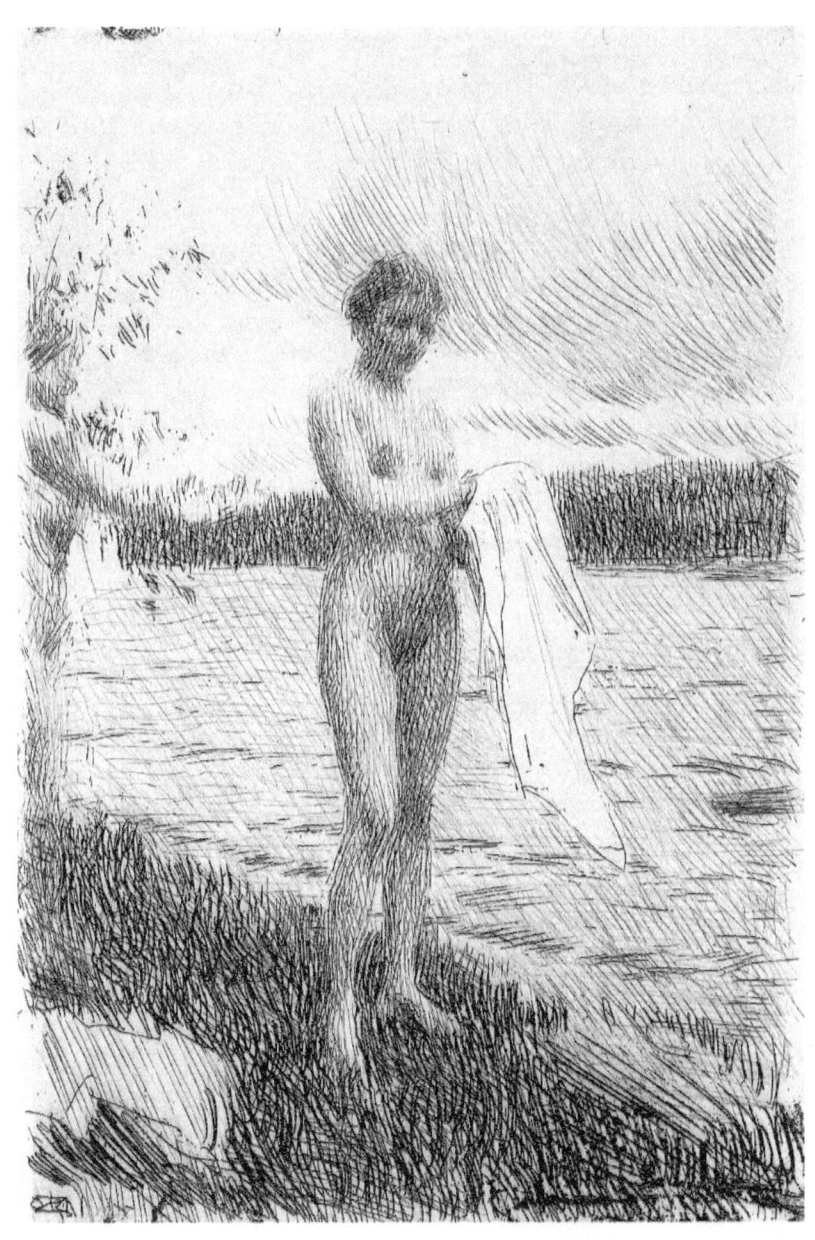

The Dal River, 1919, etching

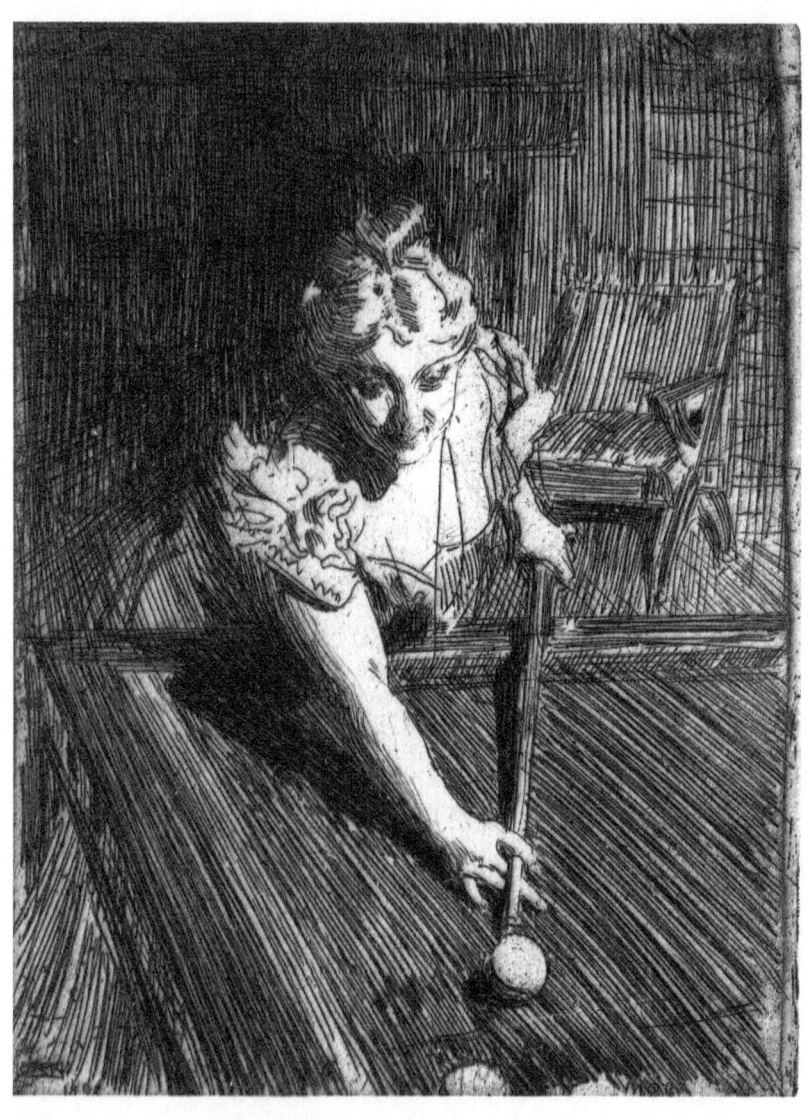

Billiards, 1898, etching

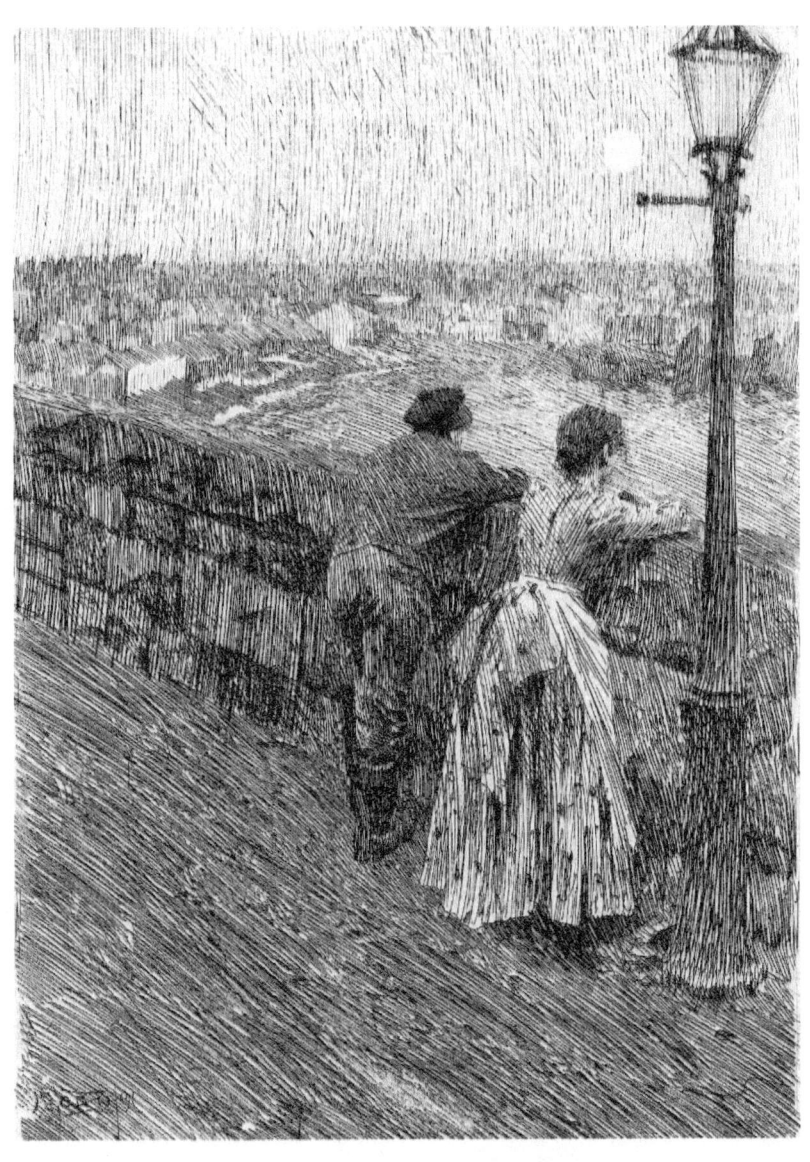

Fisherman in Saint Ives, 1891, etching

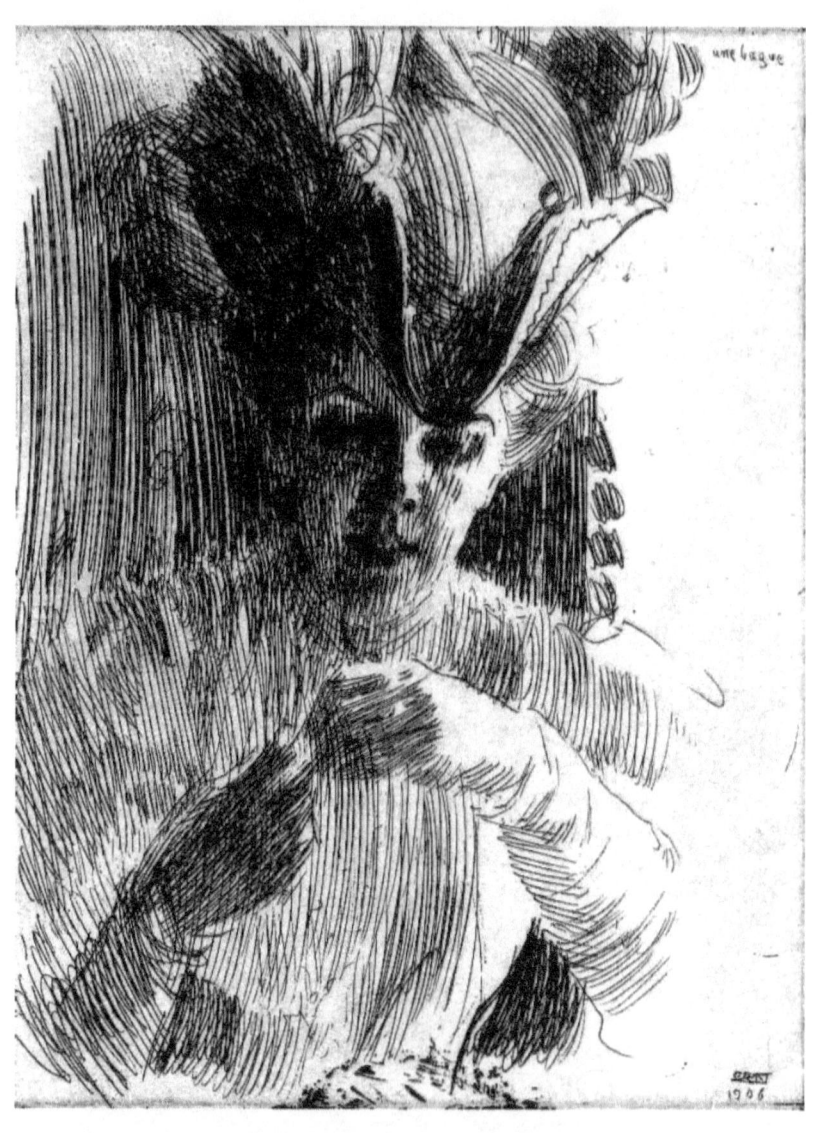

A ring, 1906, etching

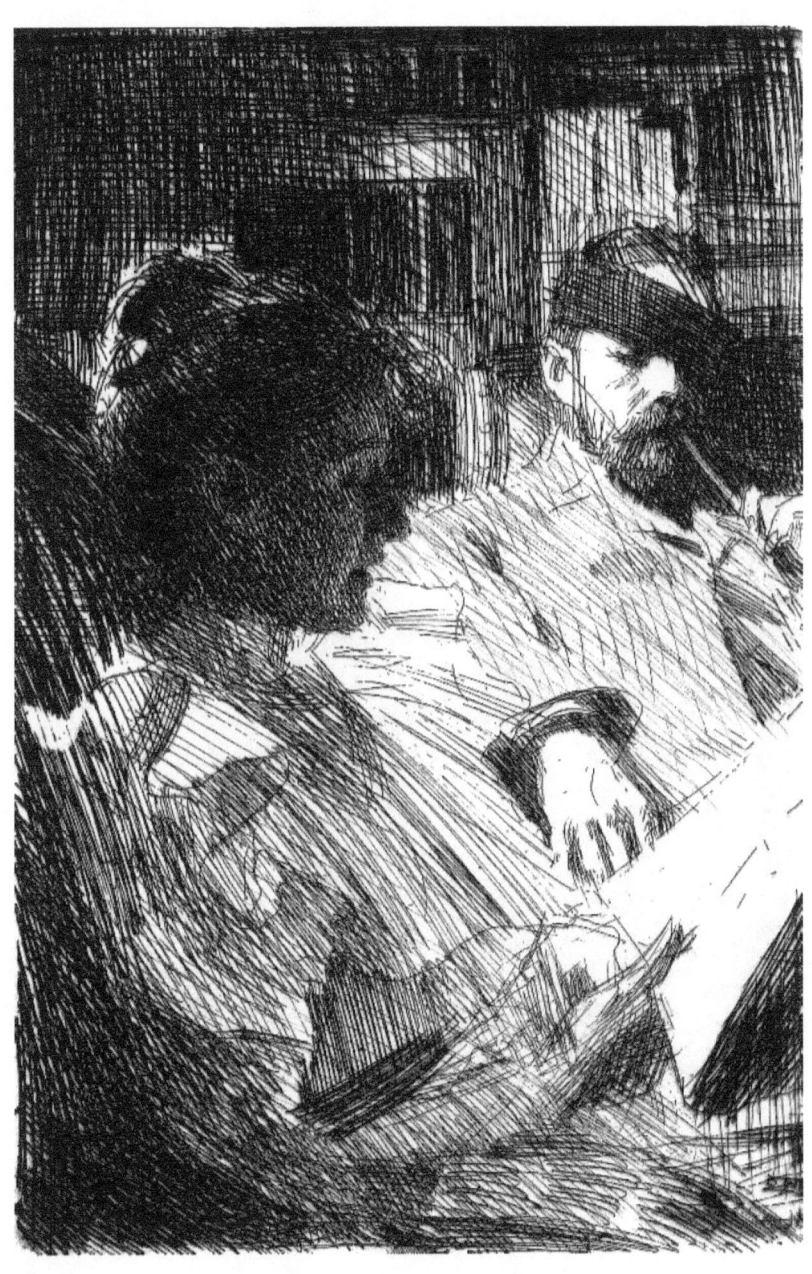

Reading, 1893, etching

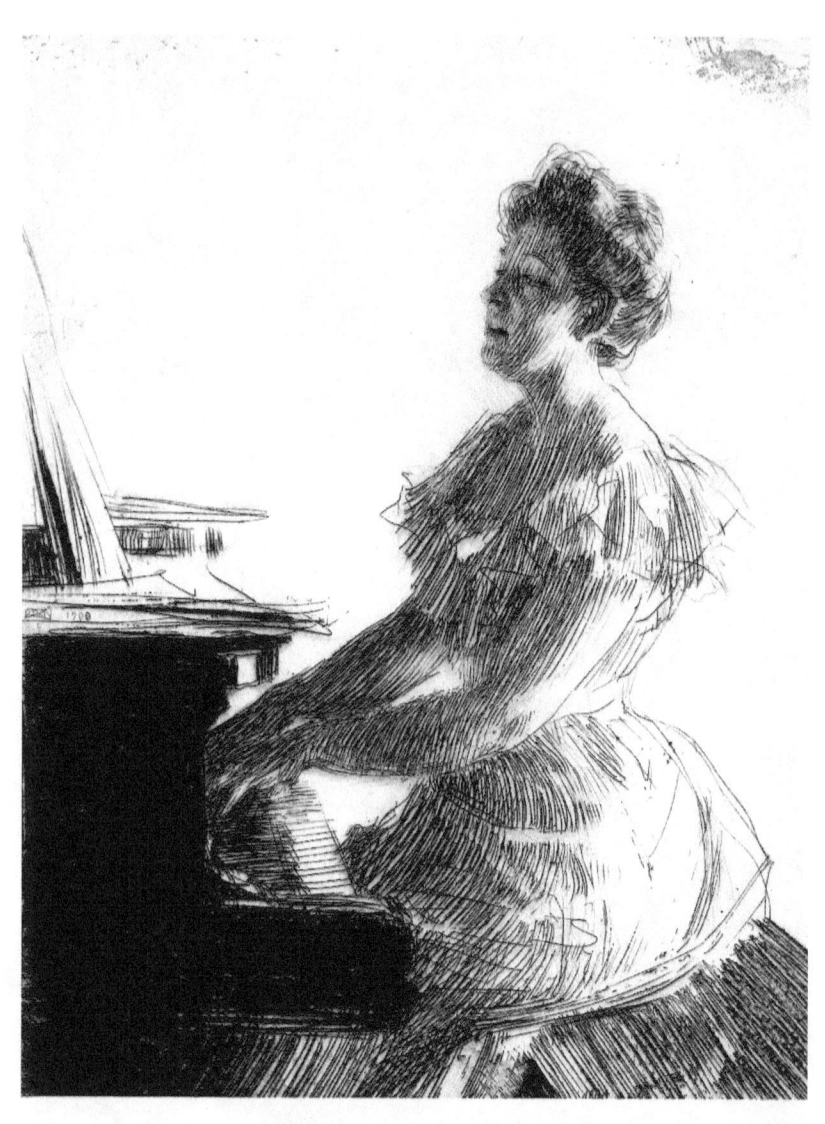

At the Piano, 1900, etching

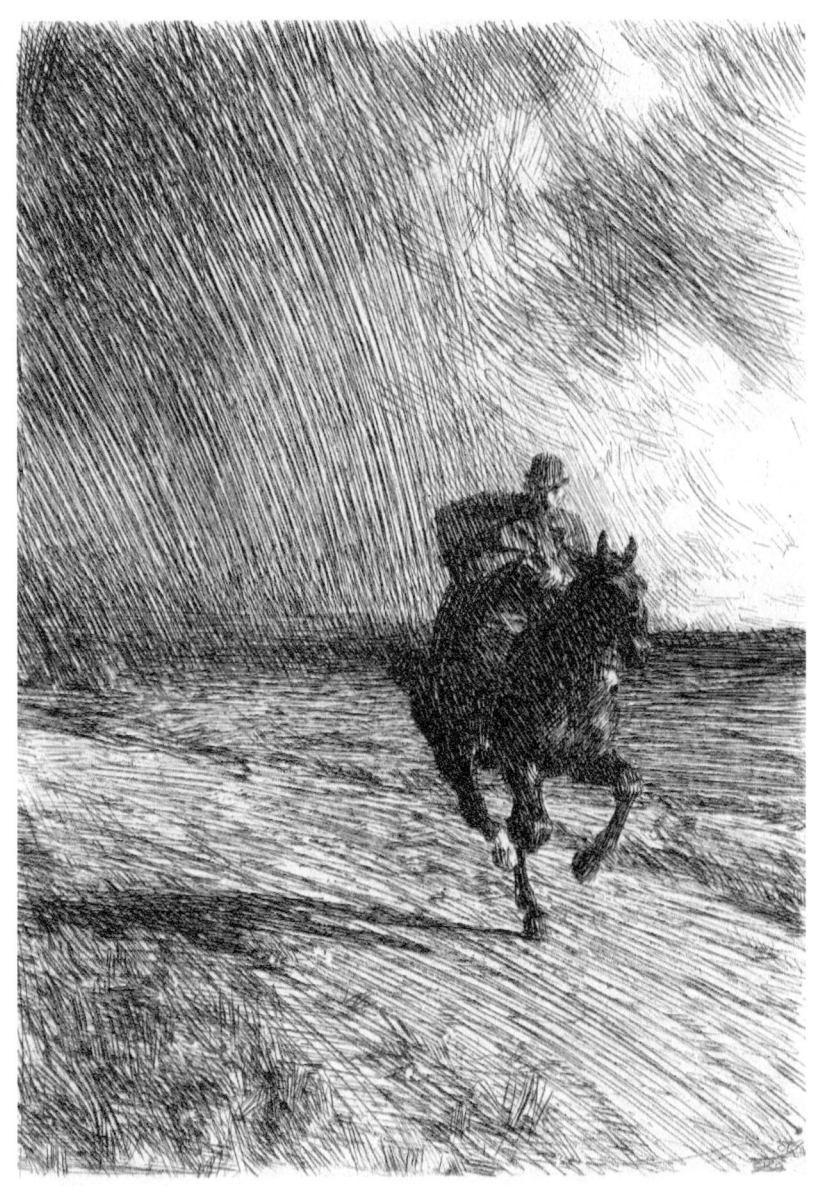

The Storm, 1891, etching

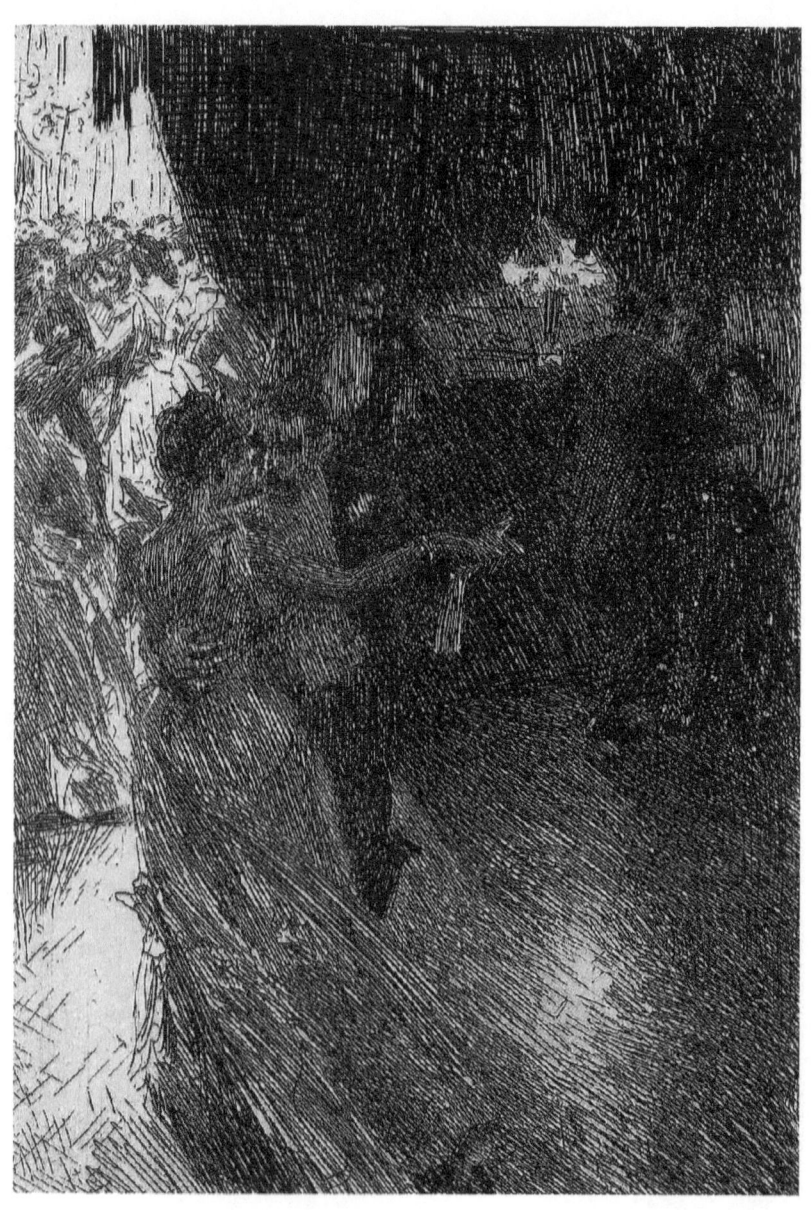

The Waltz, 1891, etching

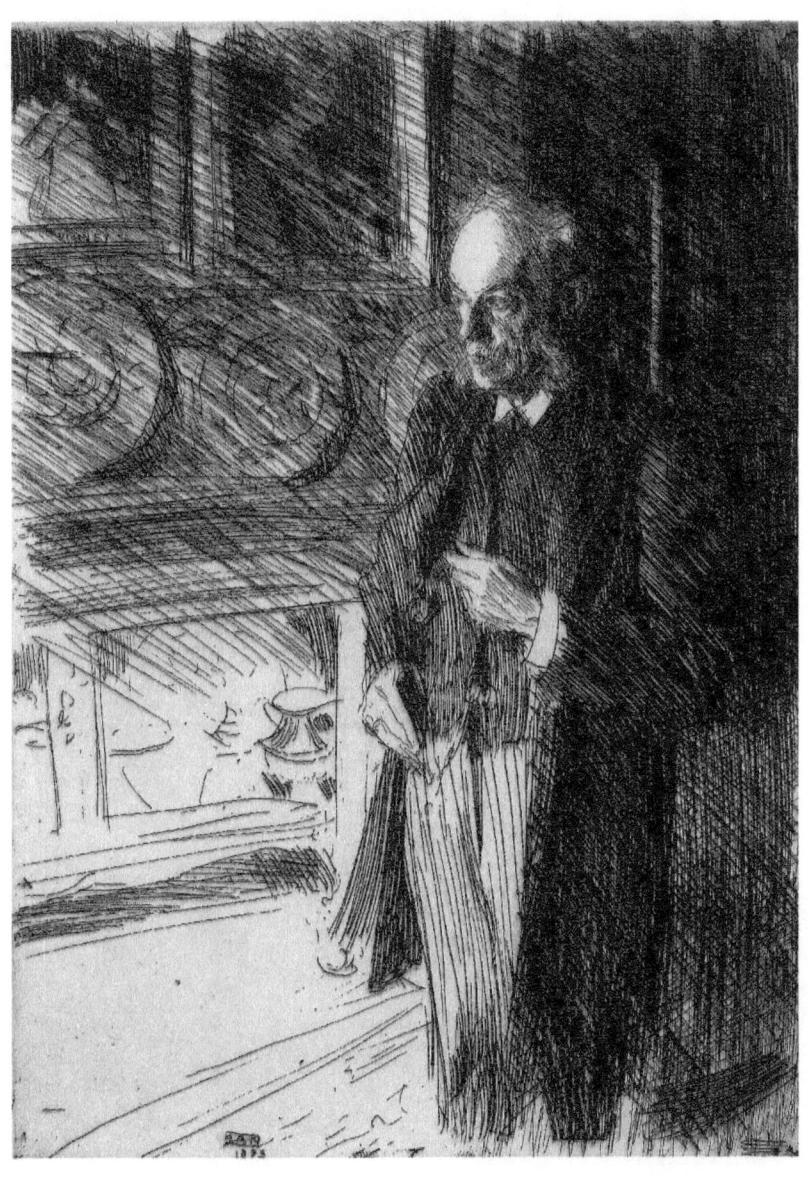

Henry Gurdon Marquand, 1893, etching

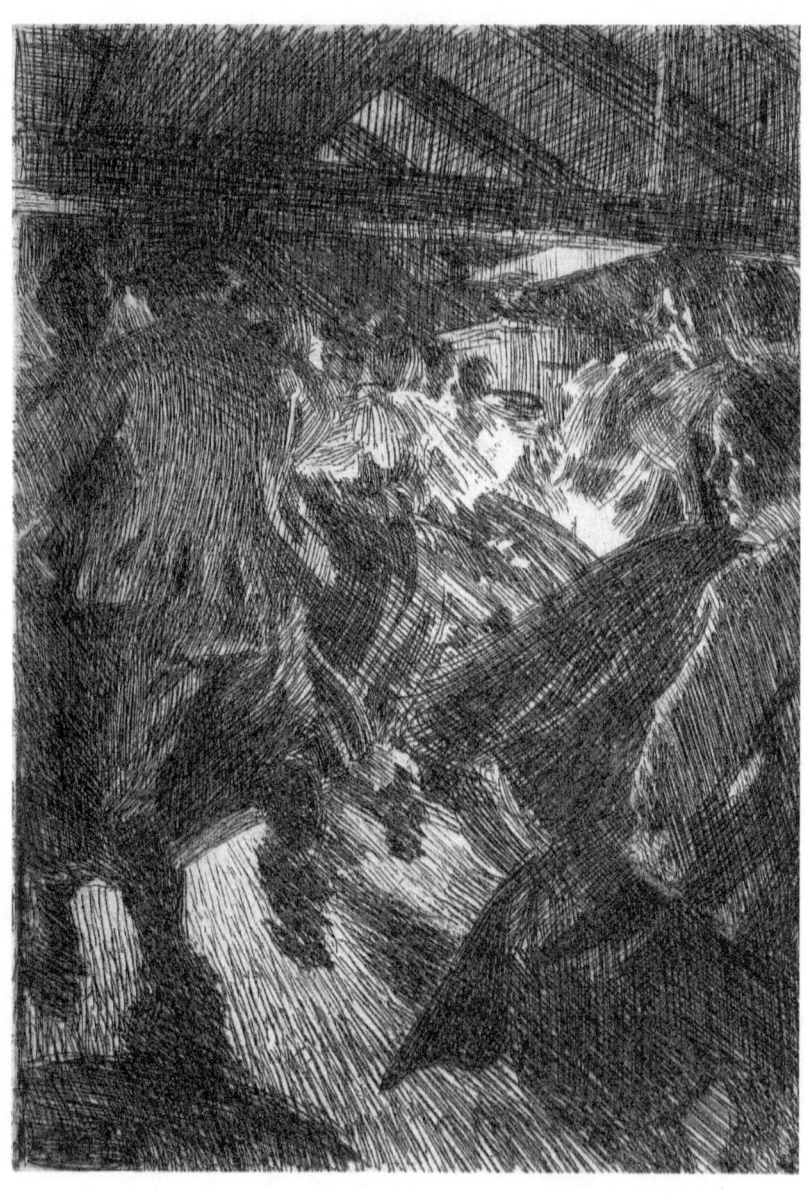

Gopsmor Cottage, 1917, etching

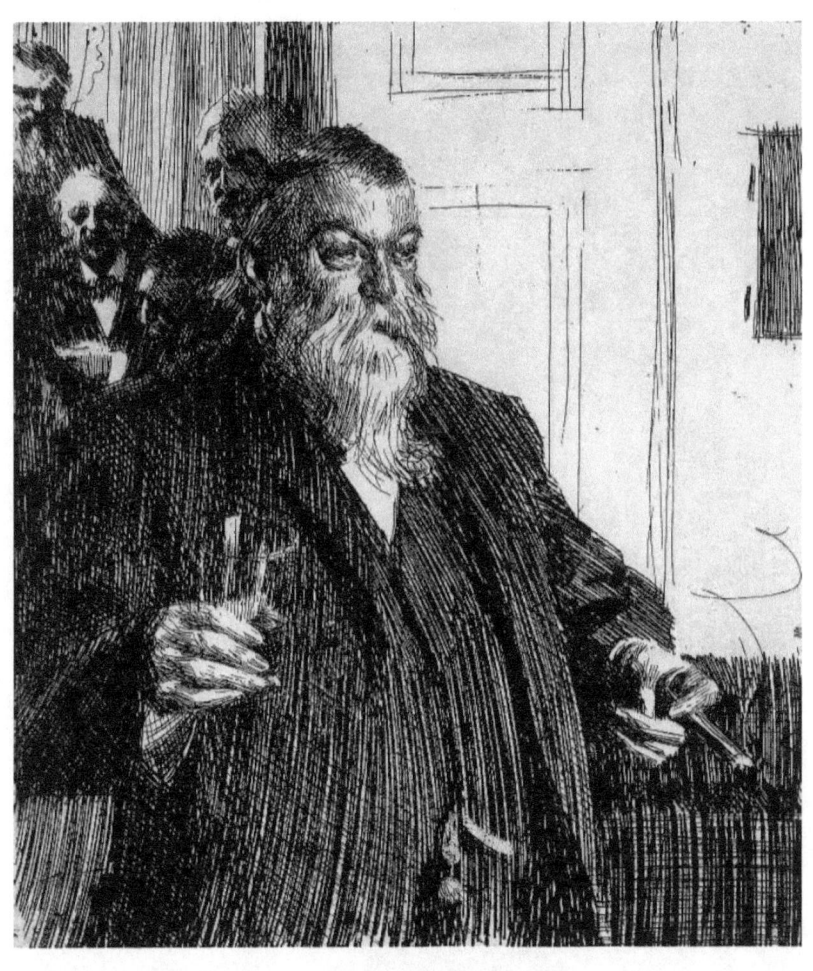

A Toast (Idun) II, 1893, etching

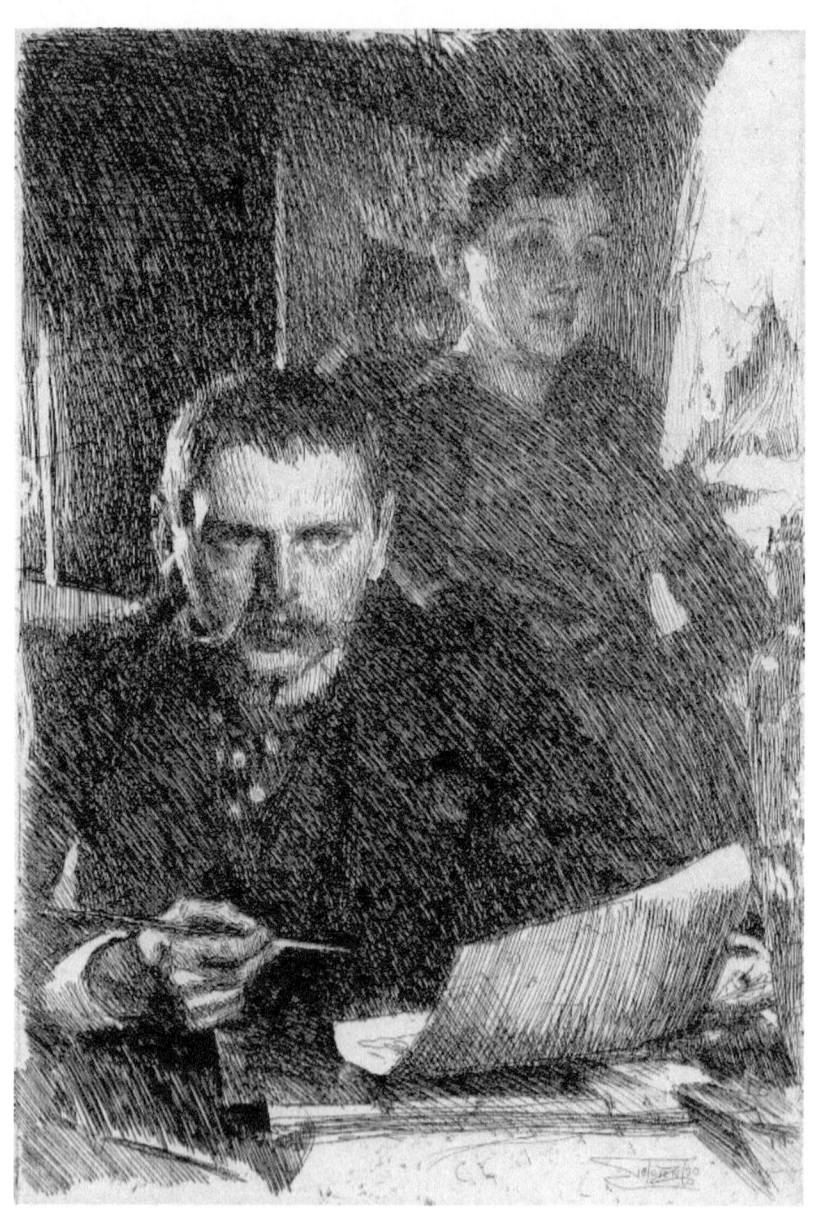

Zorn and his Wife, 1890, etching

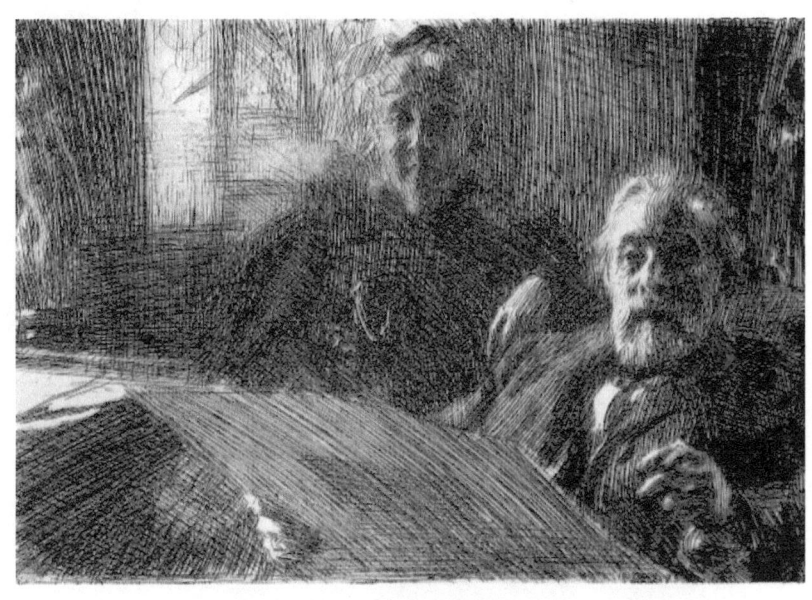

Mr. and Mrs. Fürstenberg, 1895, etching

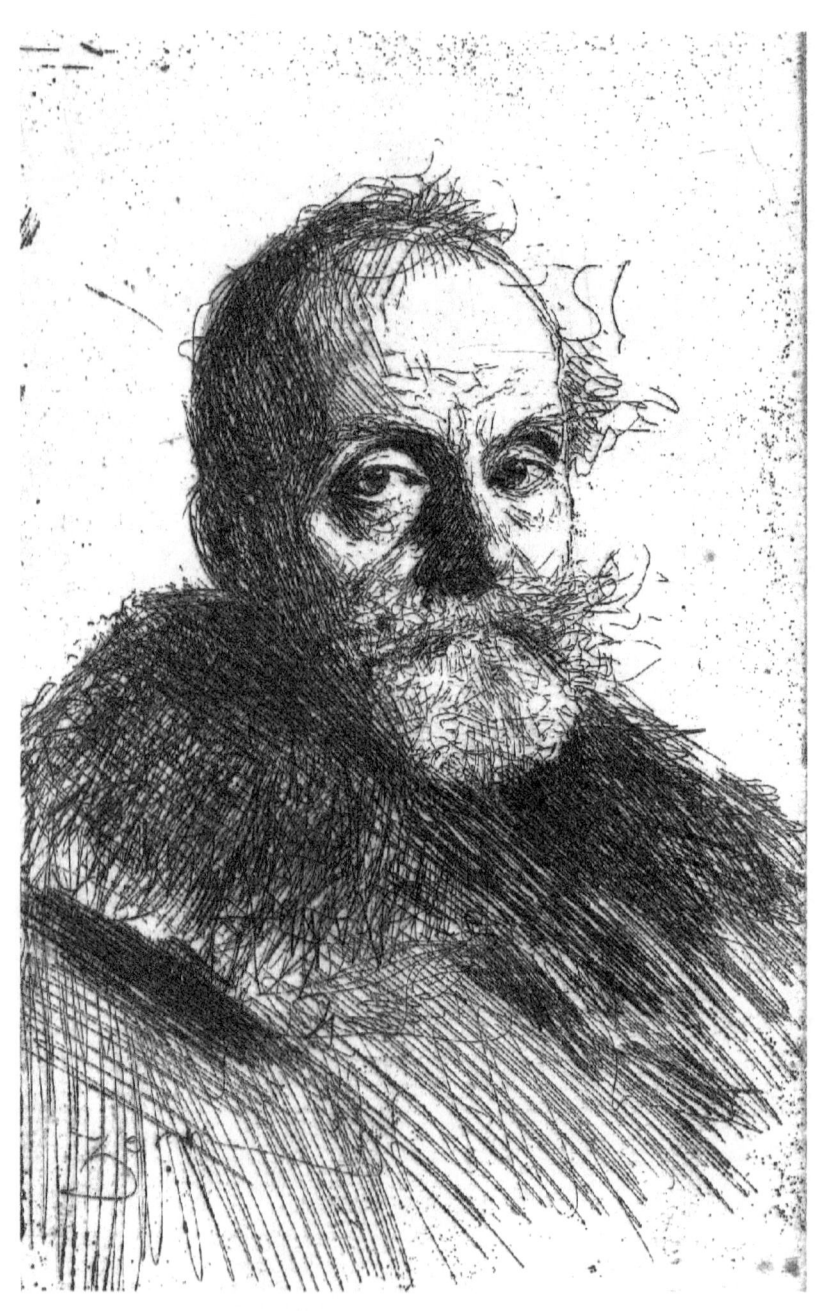

Christian Aspelin, 1884, etching

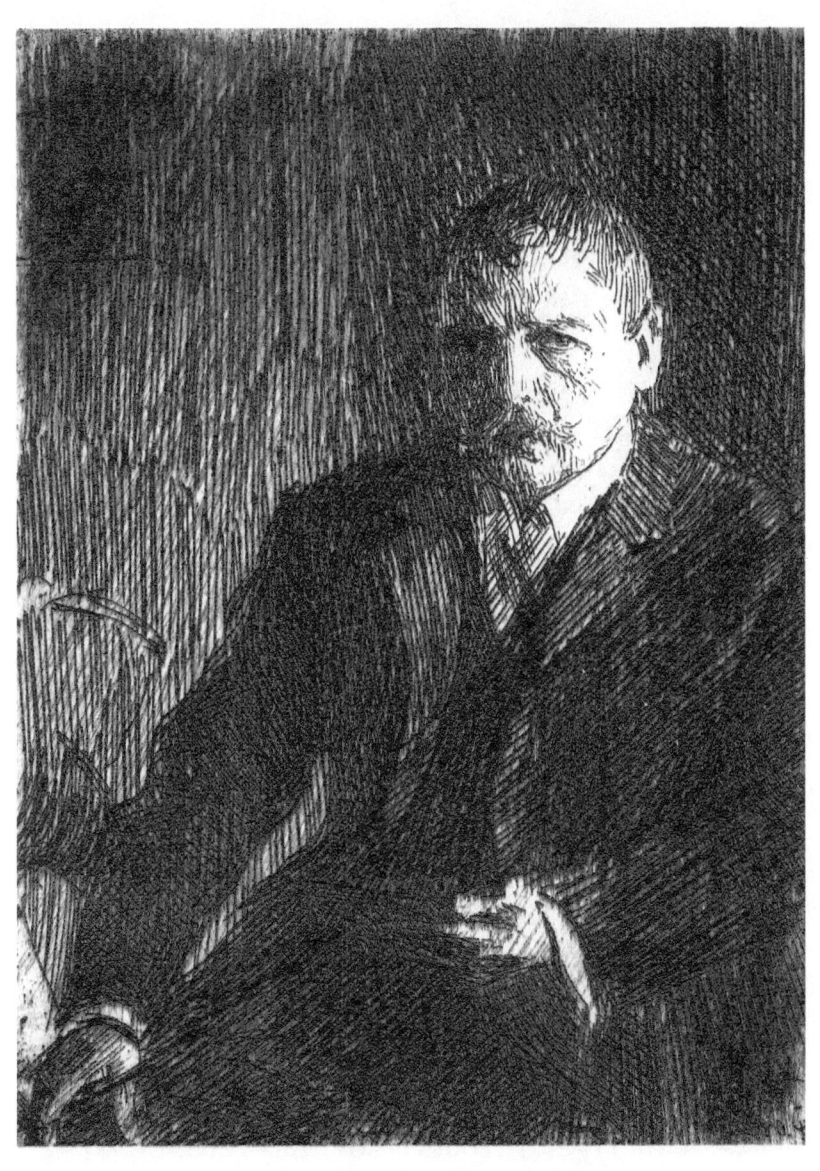

Selfportrait, 1904, etching

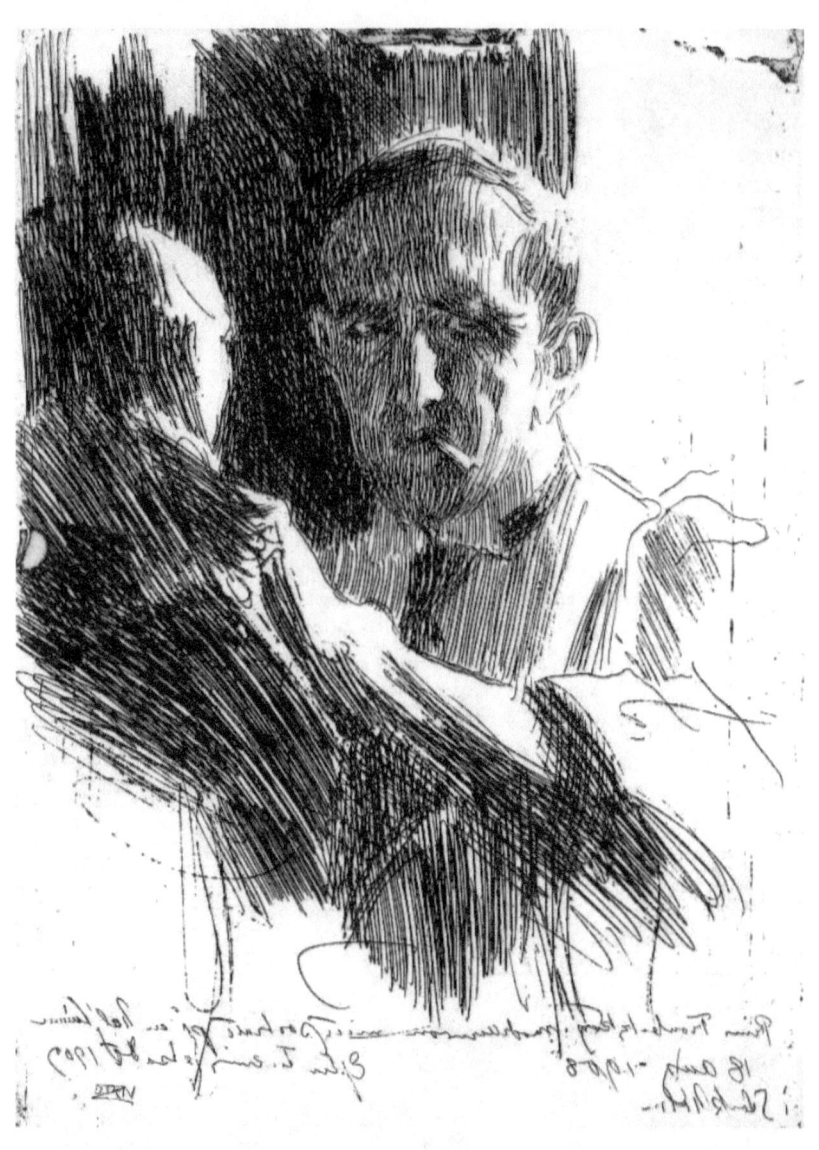

Paolo (Paul) Troubetzkoy, 1909, etching

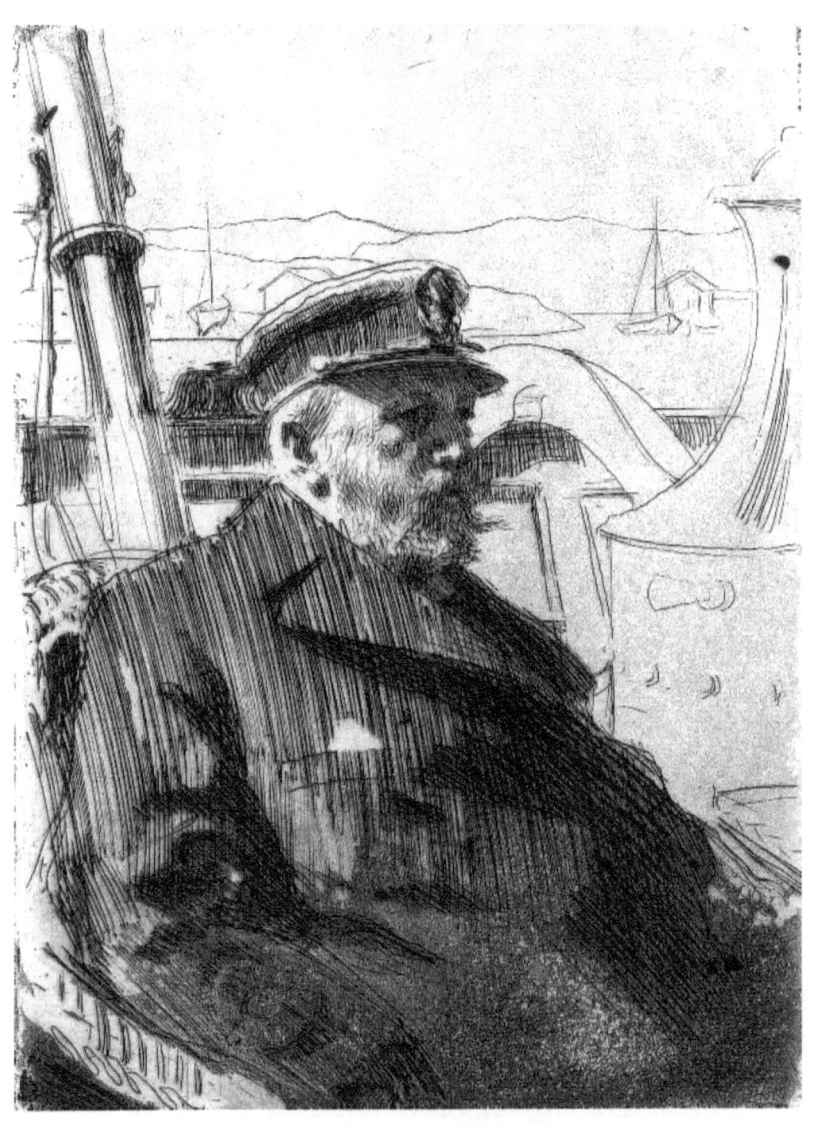

King Oscar II of Sweden, etching

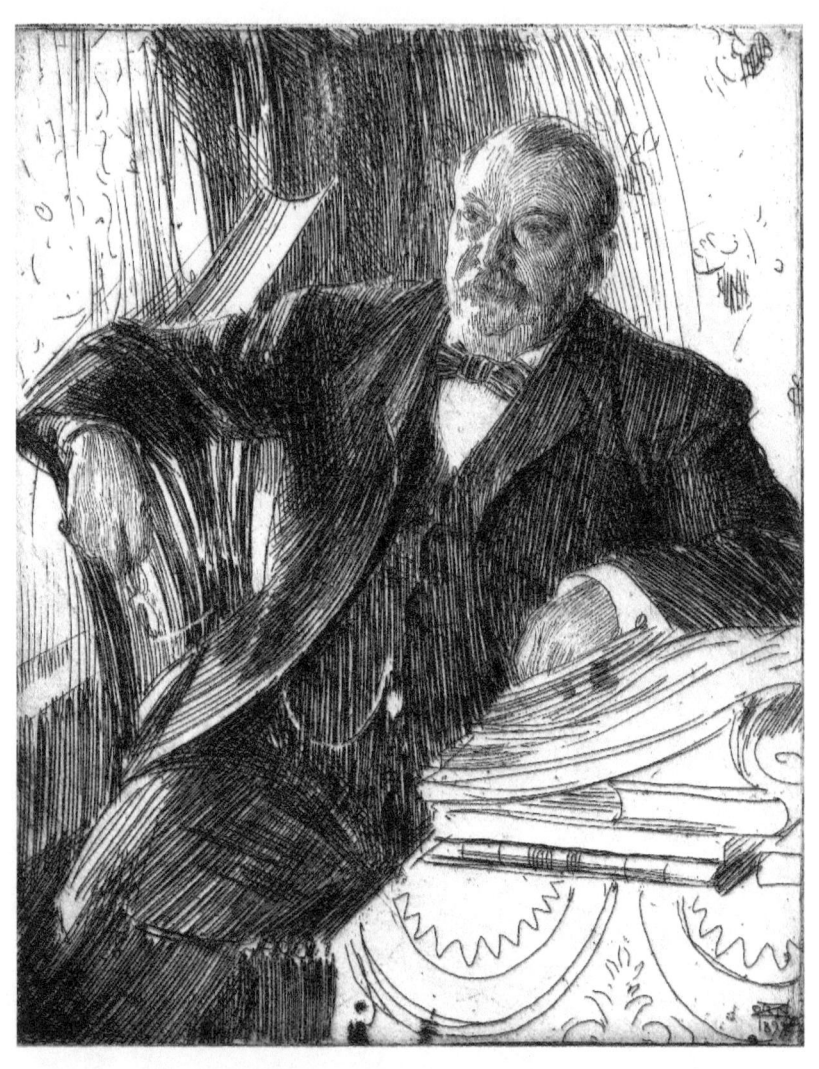

President Grover Cleveland II, 1899, etching

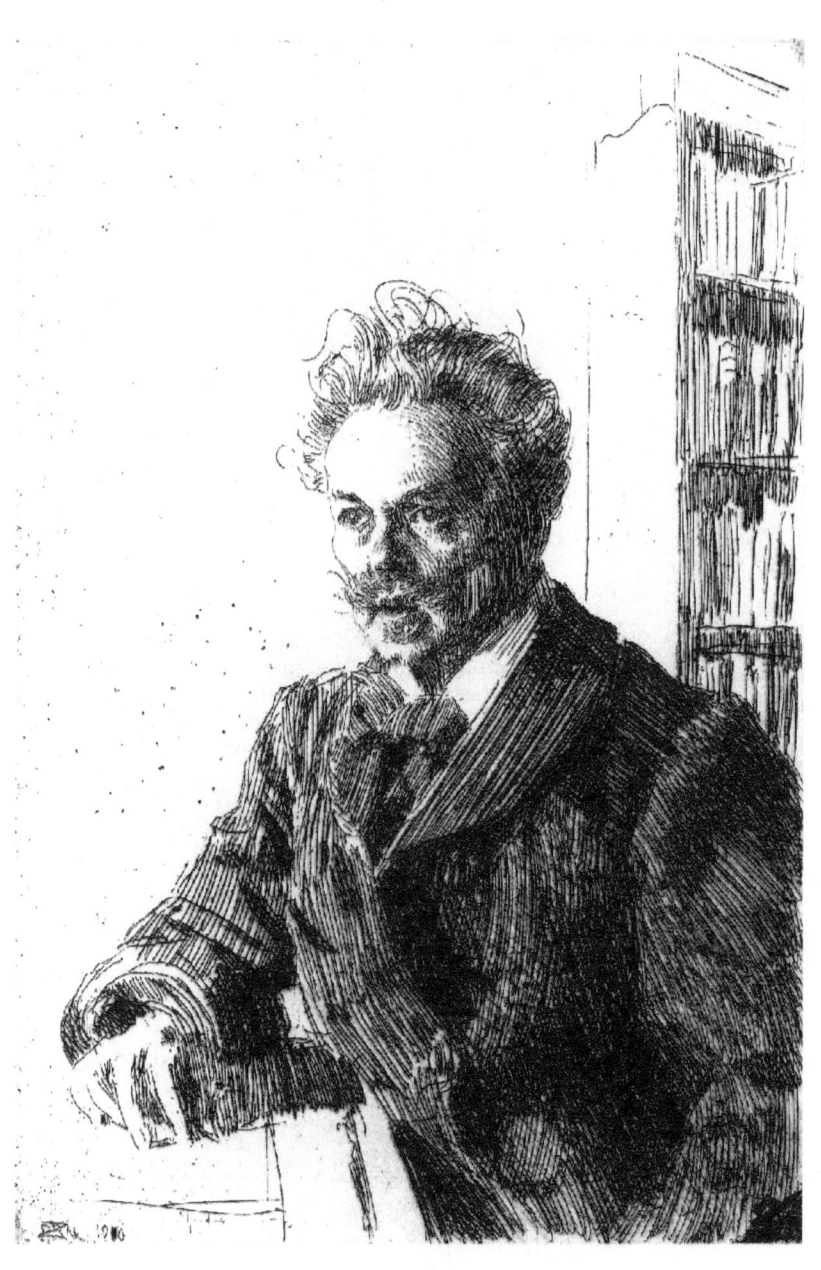

Portrait of August Strindberg, 1910, etching

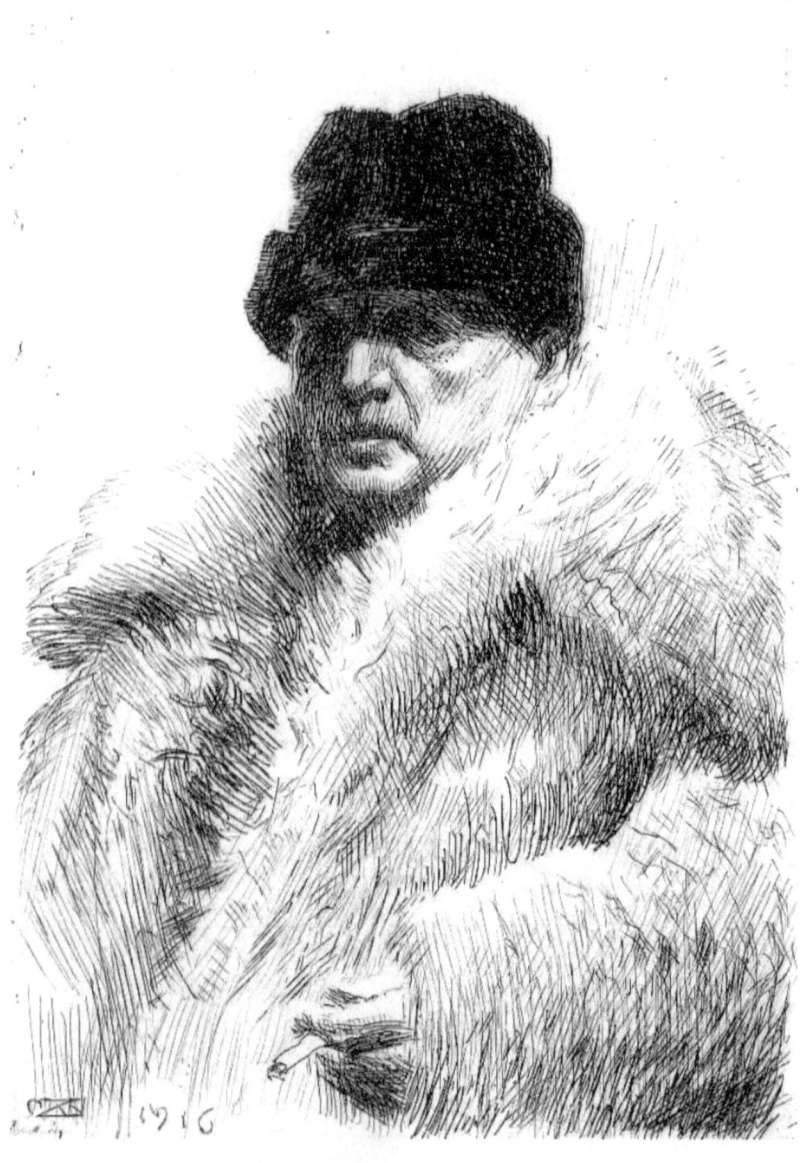

Self-Portrait in a Fur Coat, 1916, etching

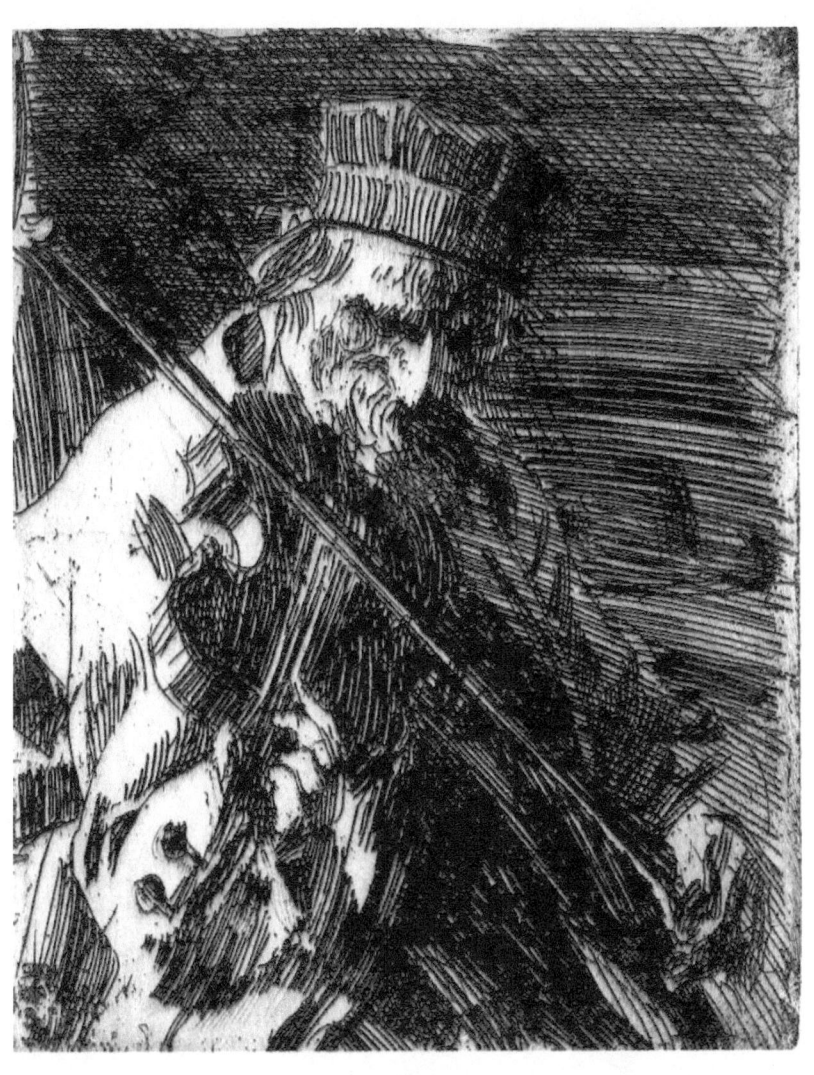

Village folk musician, 1904, etching

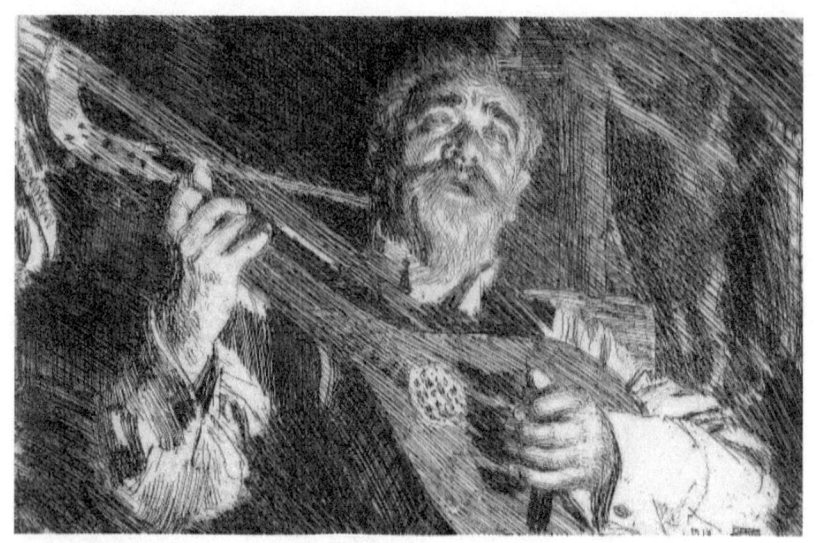

Vicke, 1918, etching

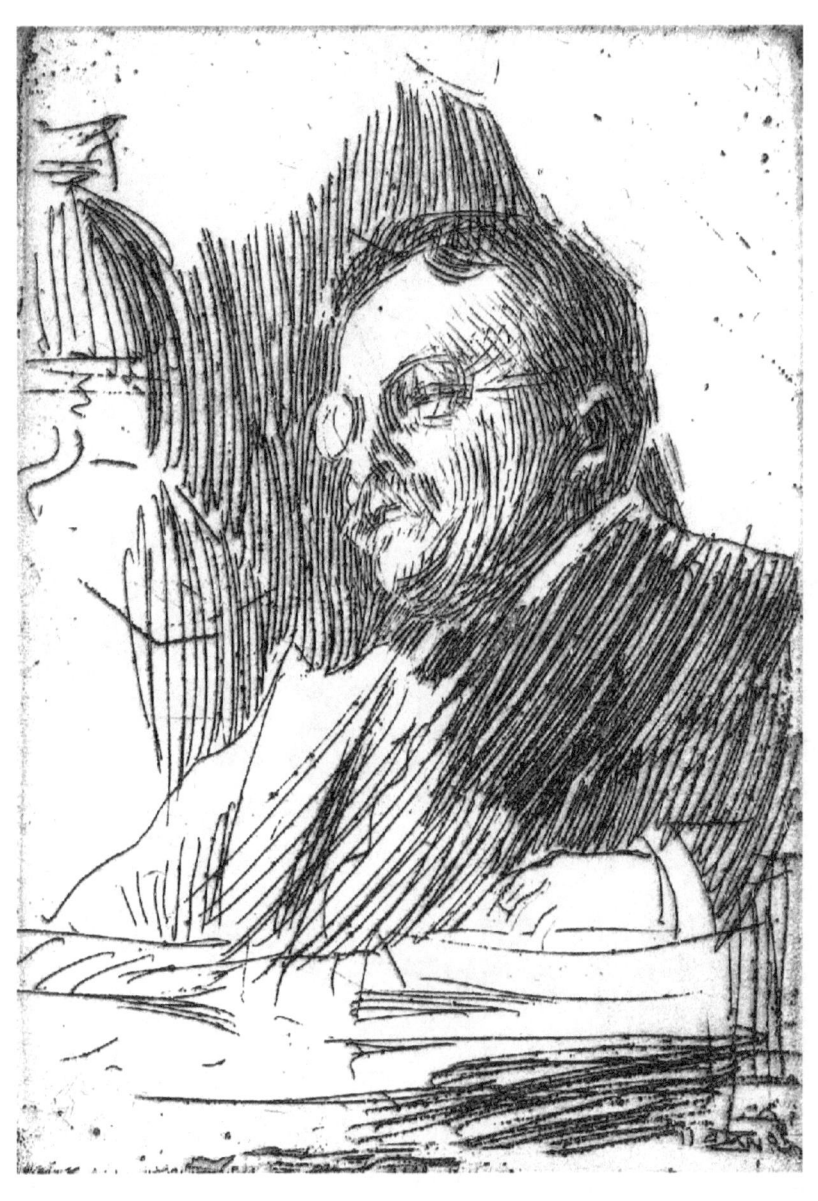

Theodore Roosevelt, 1905, etching

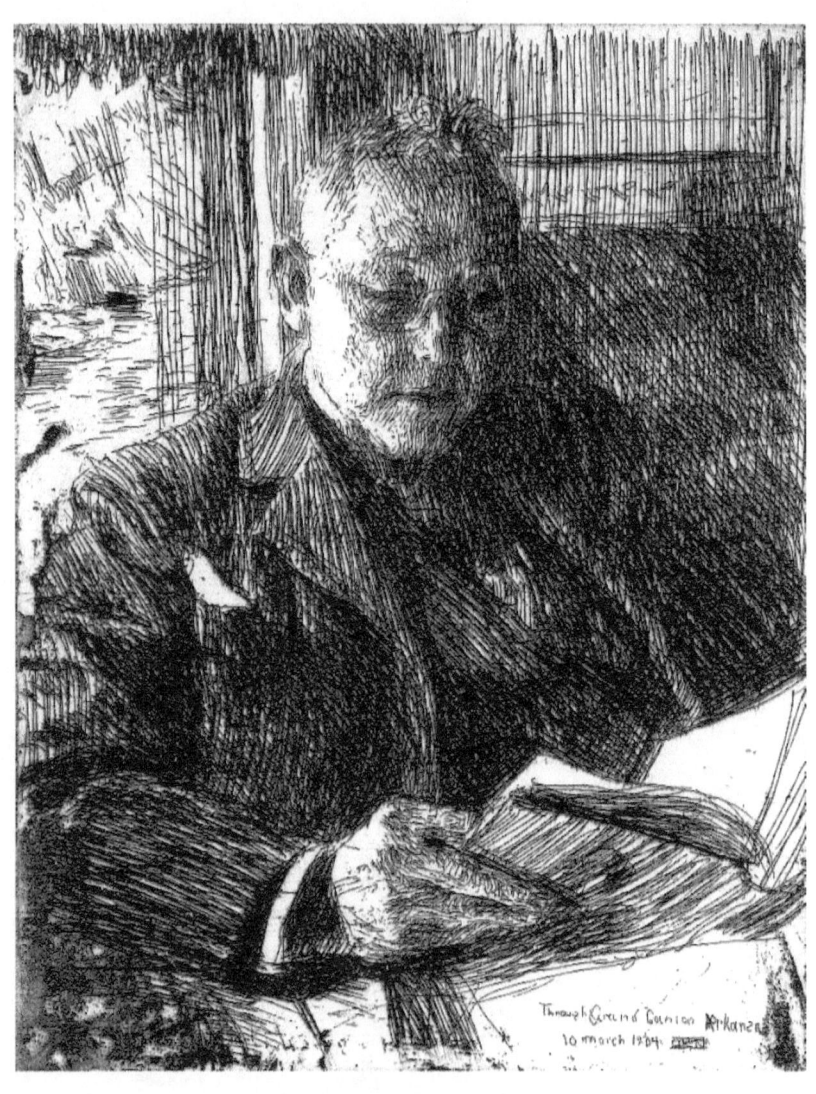

The travel companion (Mr. Charles Deering), 1904,
etching

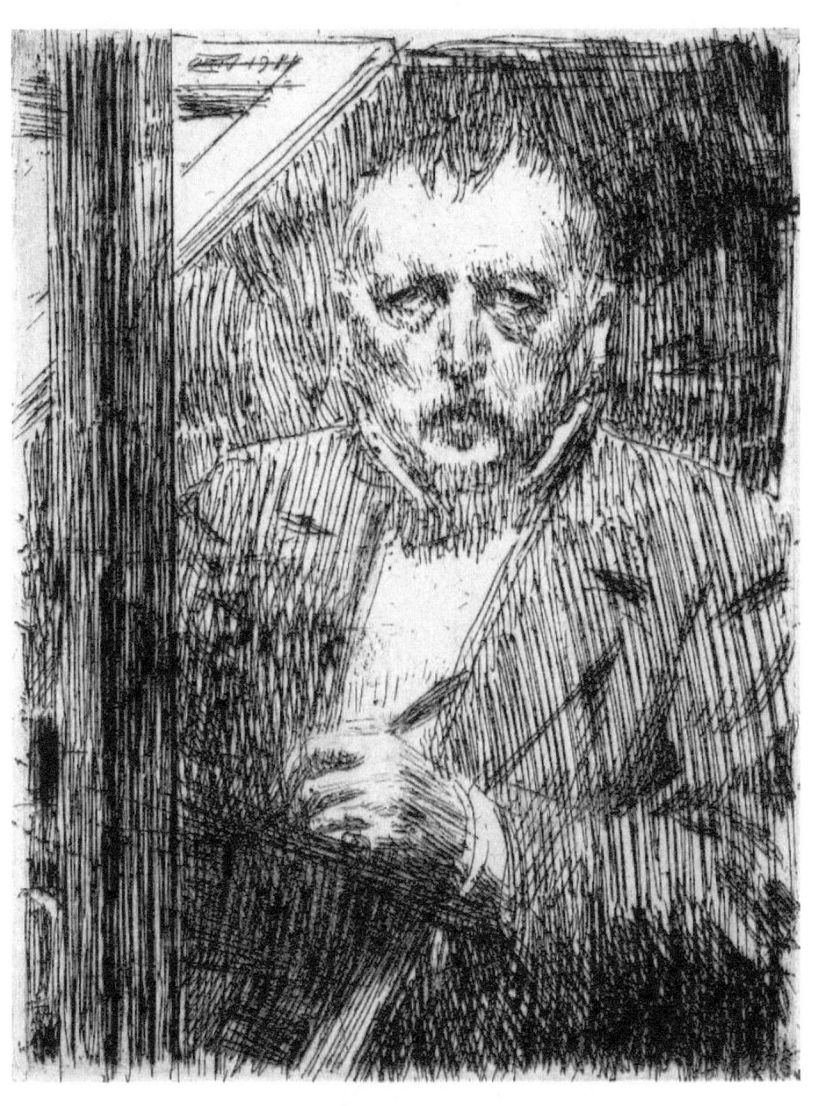

Self-portrait, 1911, etching

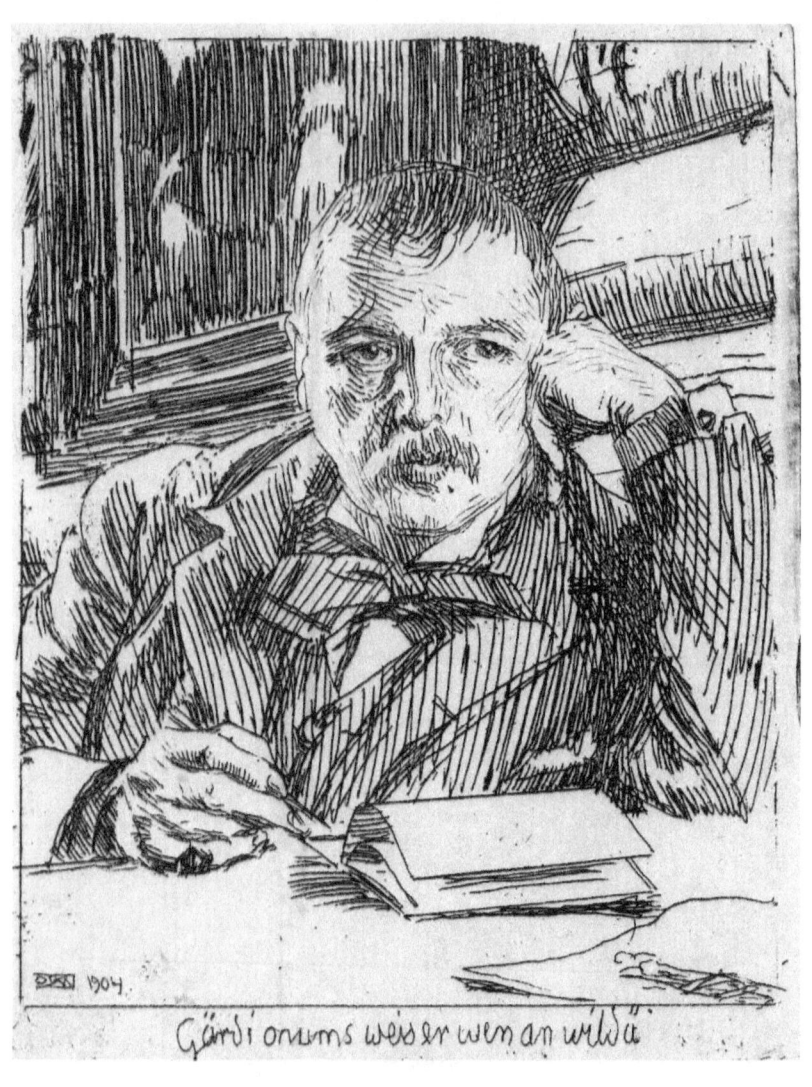

Self-portrait, 1904, etching

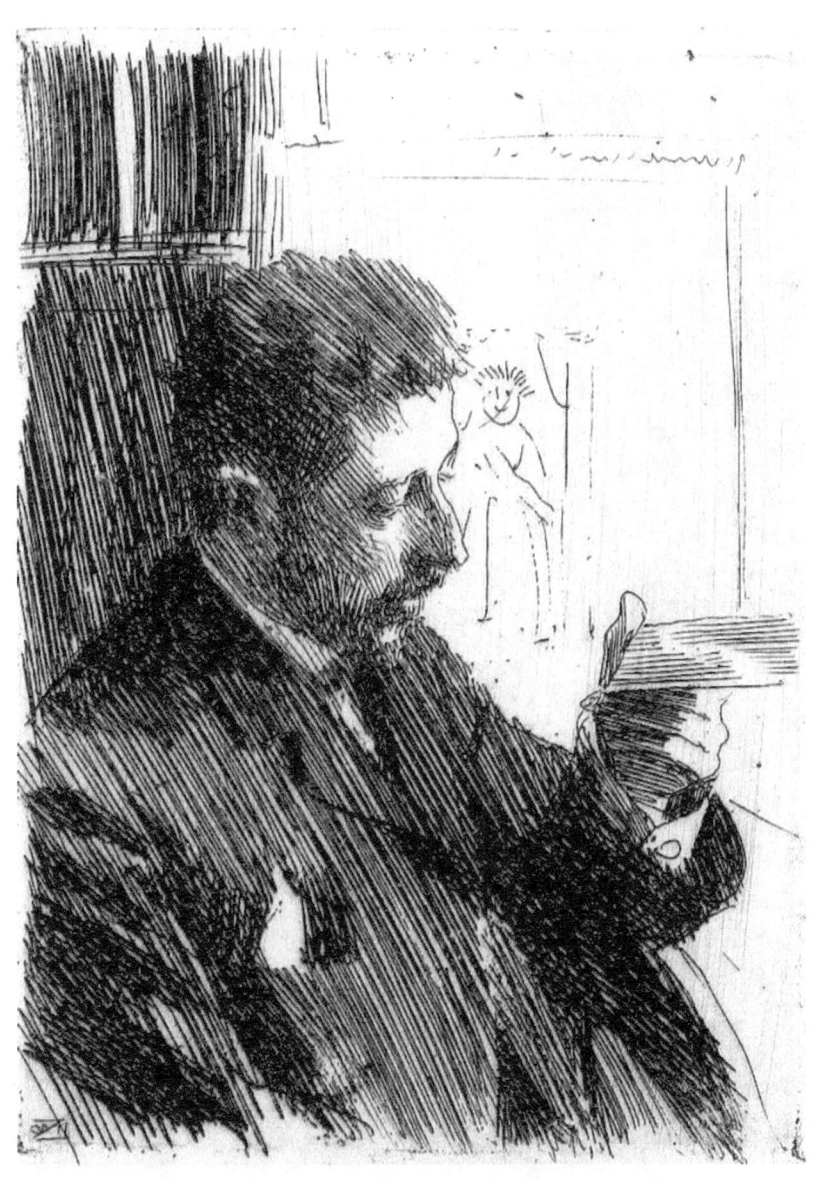

Prince Eugen of Sweden, 1904, etching

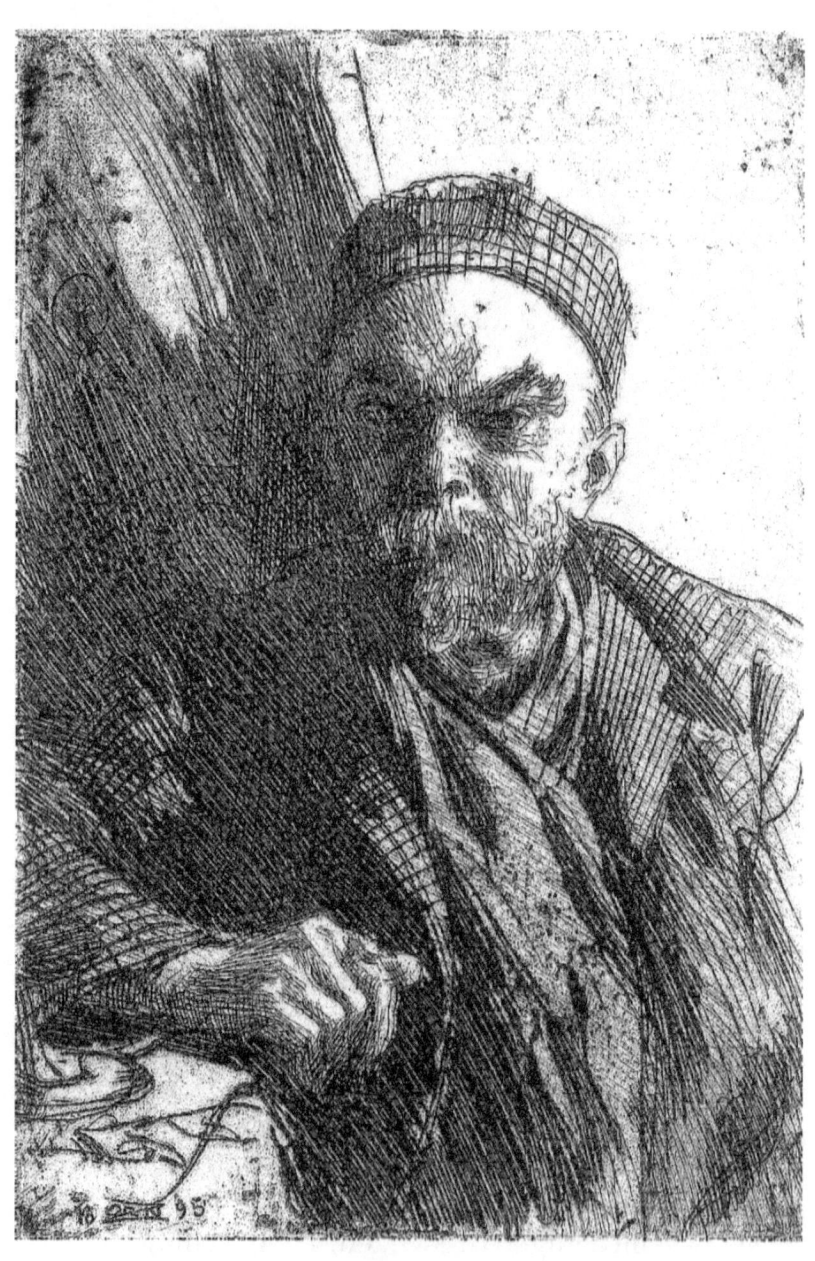

Paul Verlaine (1844-1896), 1895, etching

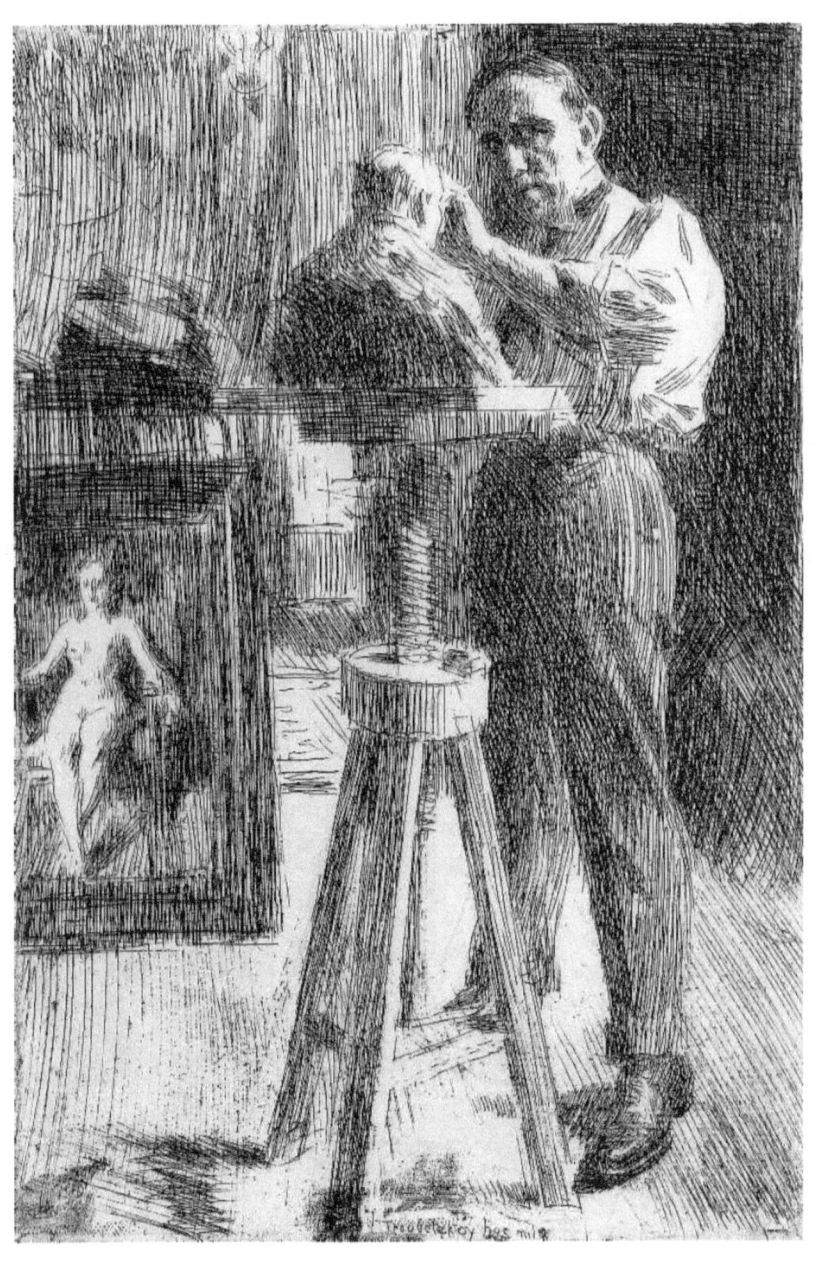

Sculptor Prince Paolo (Paul) Troubetzkoy (1866-1938),
1908, etching

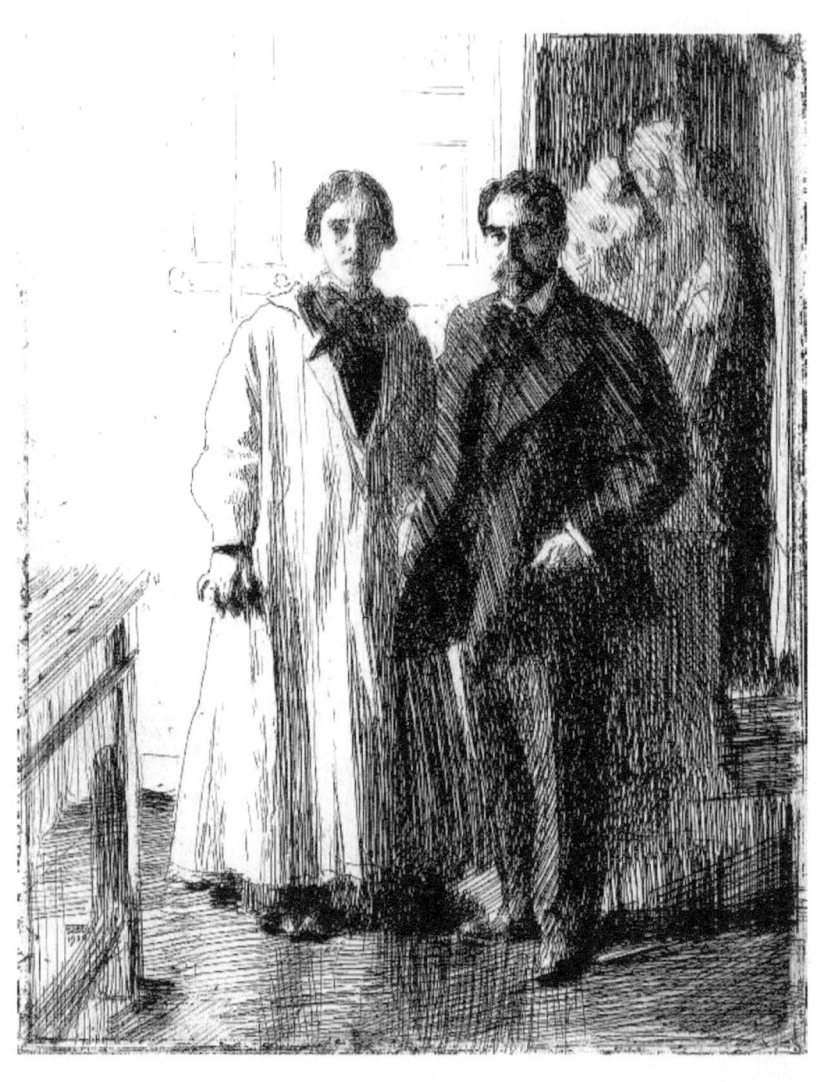

Mr. and Mrs Atherton Curtis, 1906, etching

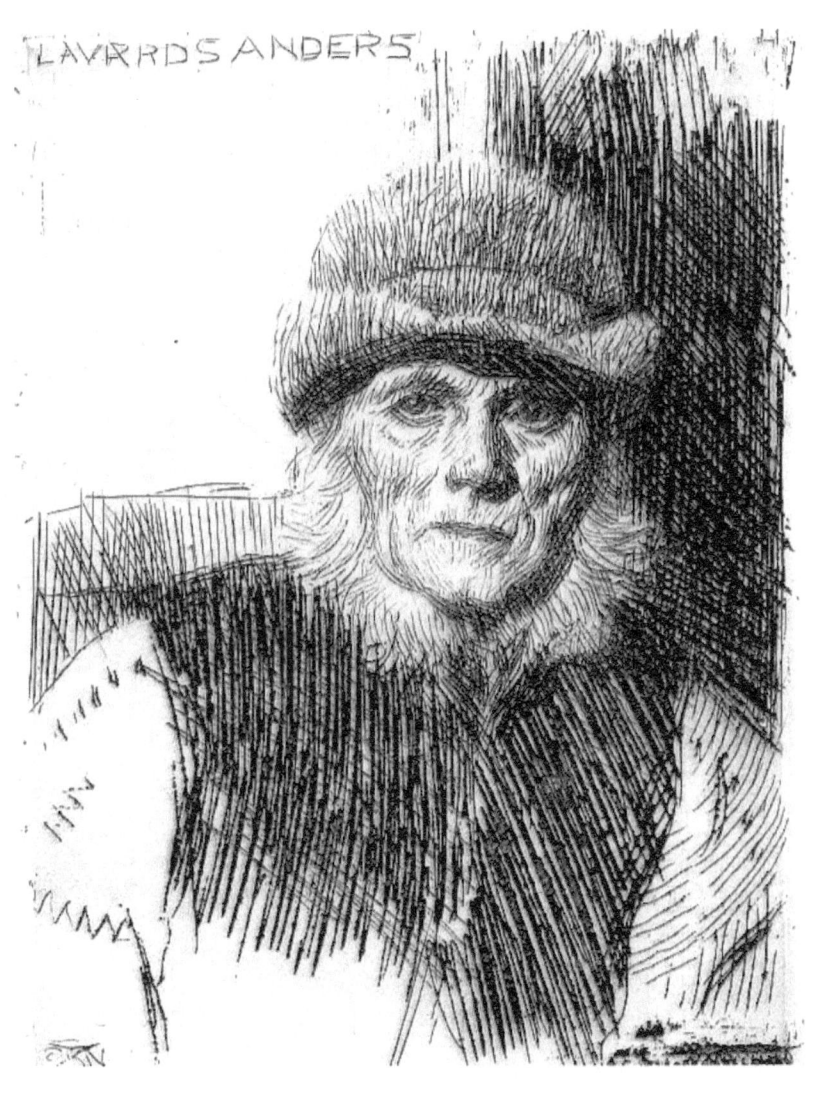

Lavards Anders, 1919, etching

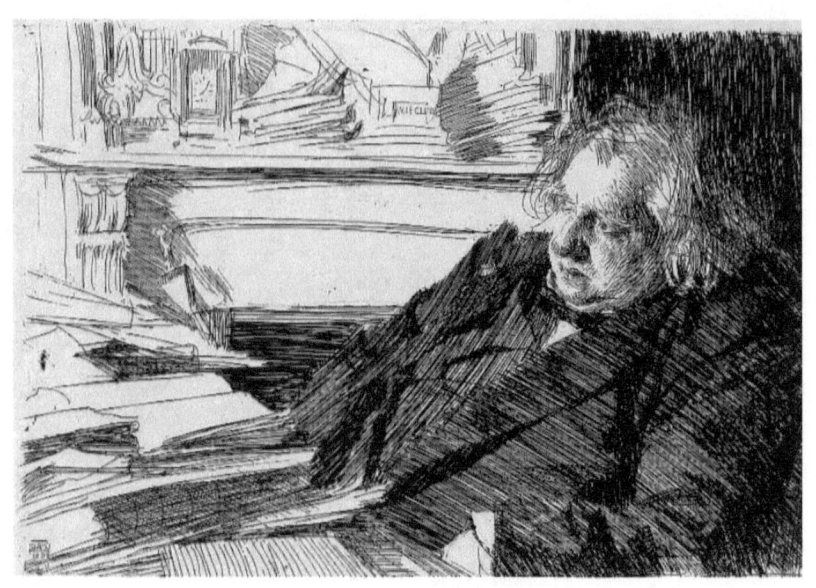

Ernest Renan, 1892, etching

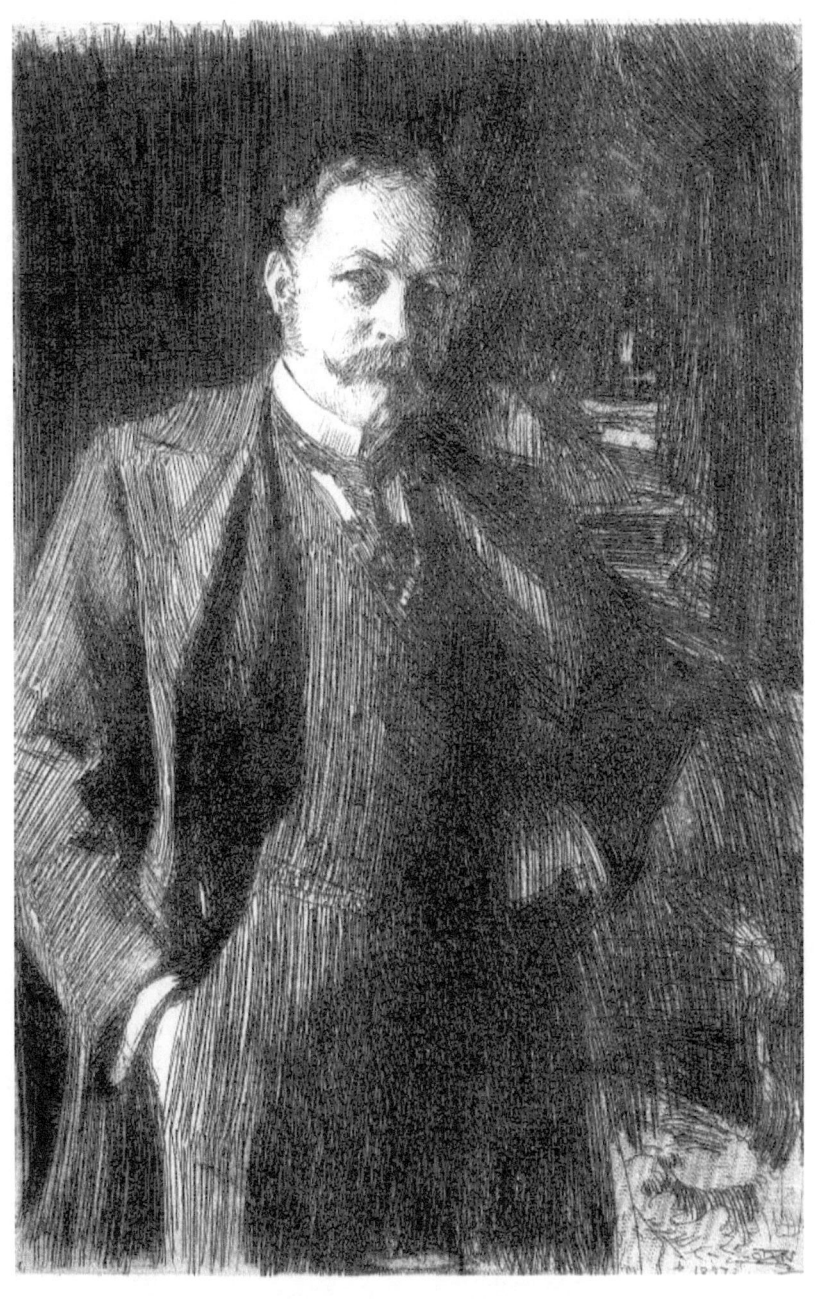

E. R. Bacon, 1897, etching

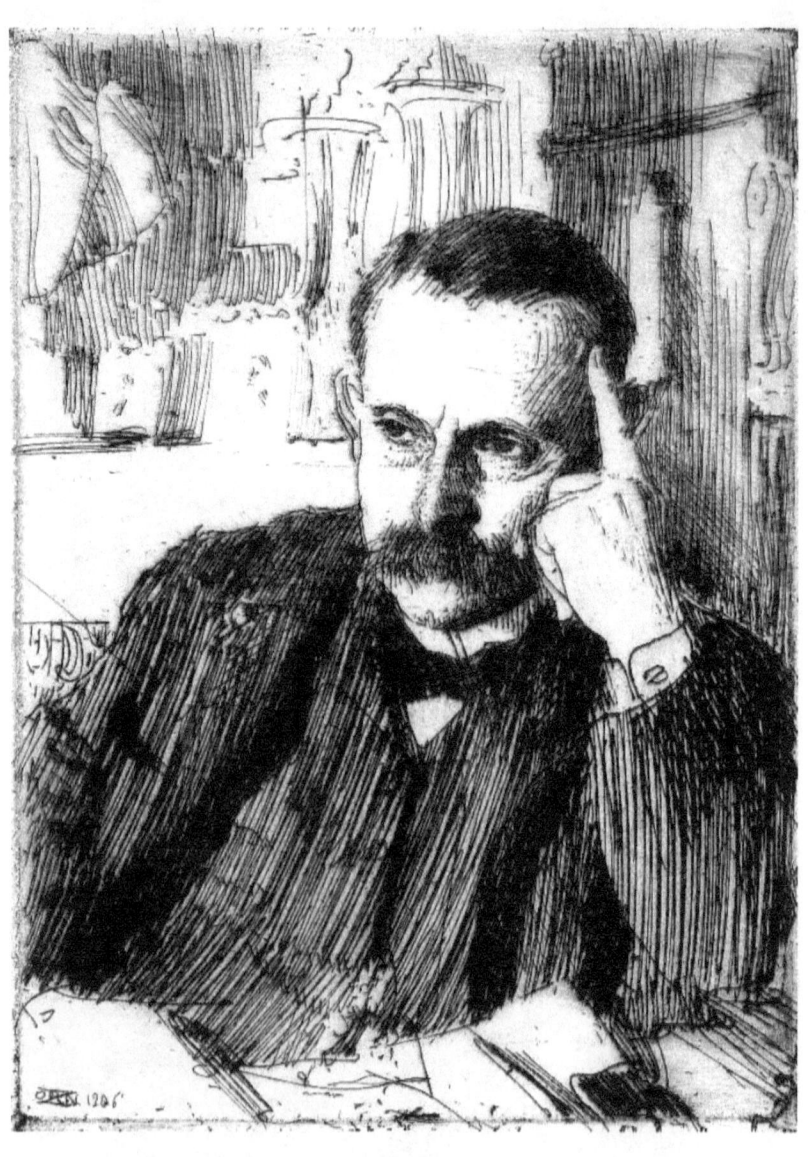

D'Estournelles de Constant, 1906, etching

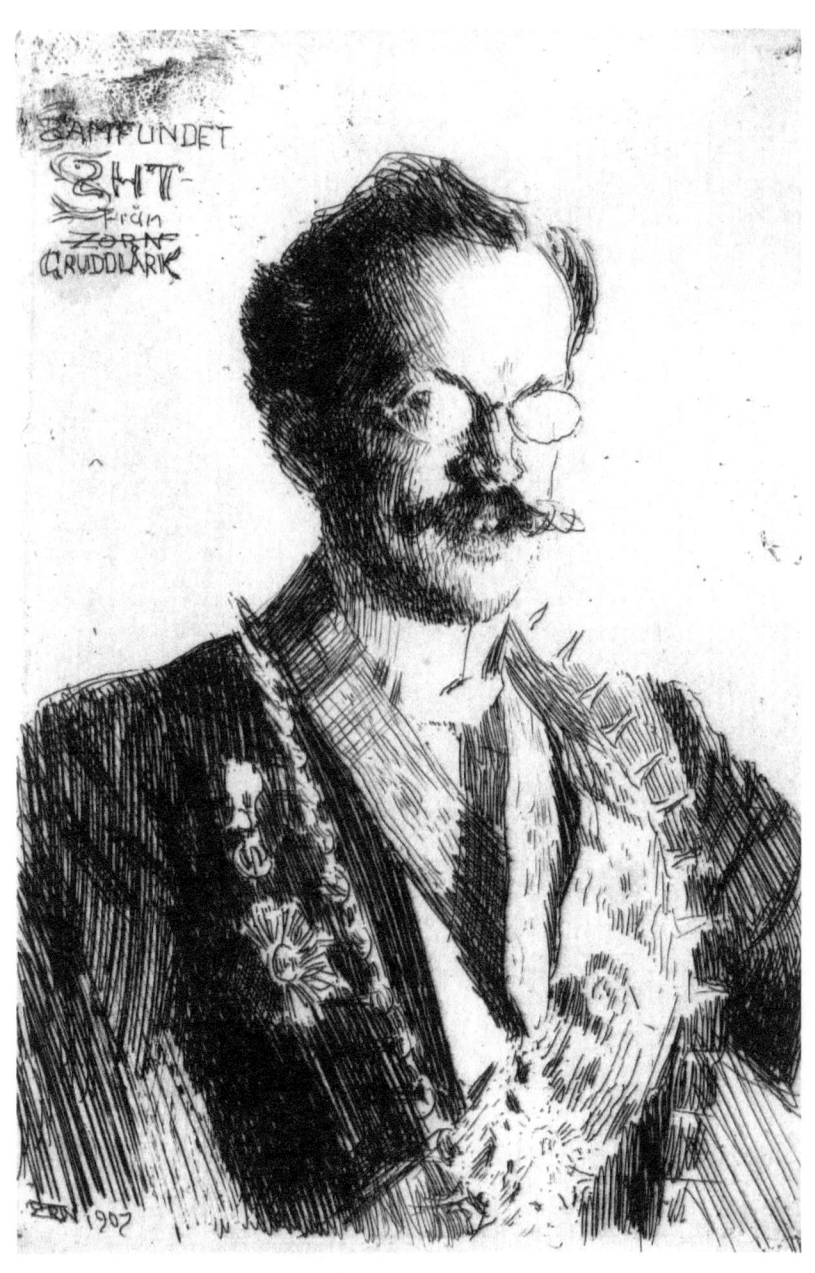

Knut Kjellberg, 1907, etching

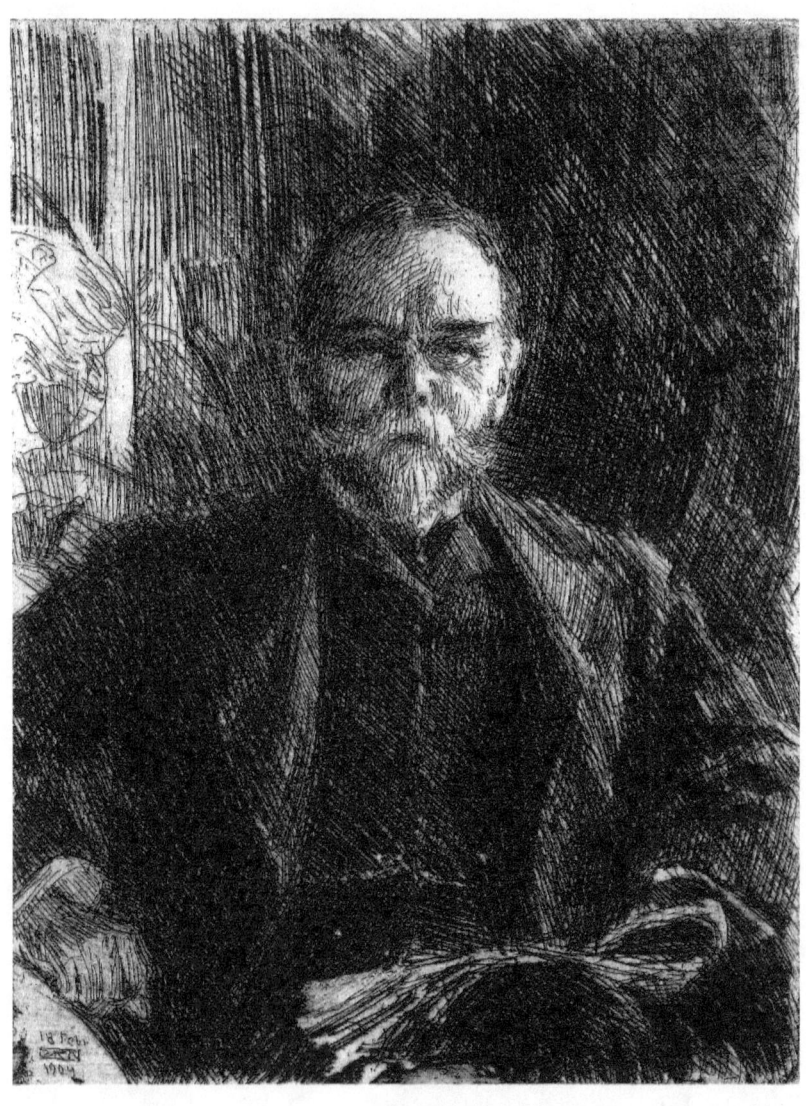

United States Secretary of State John Hay, 1904, etching

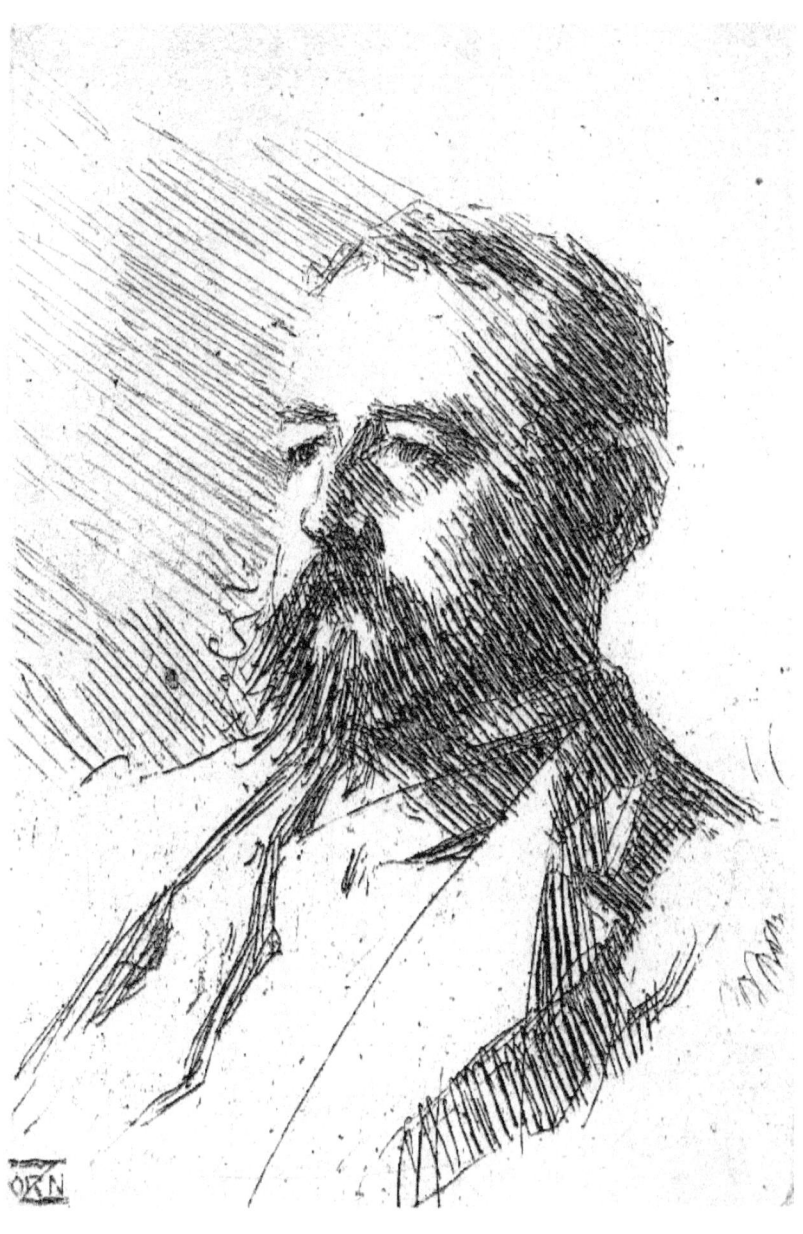

Swedish poet Carl Snoilsky (1841-1903), 1888, etching

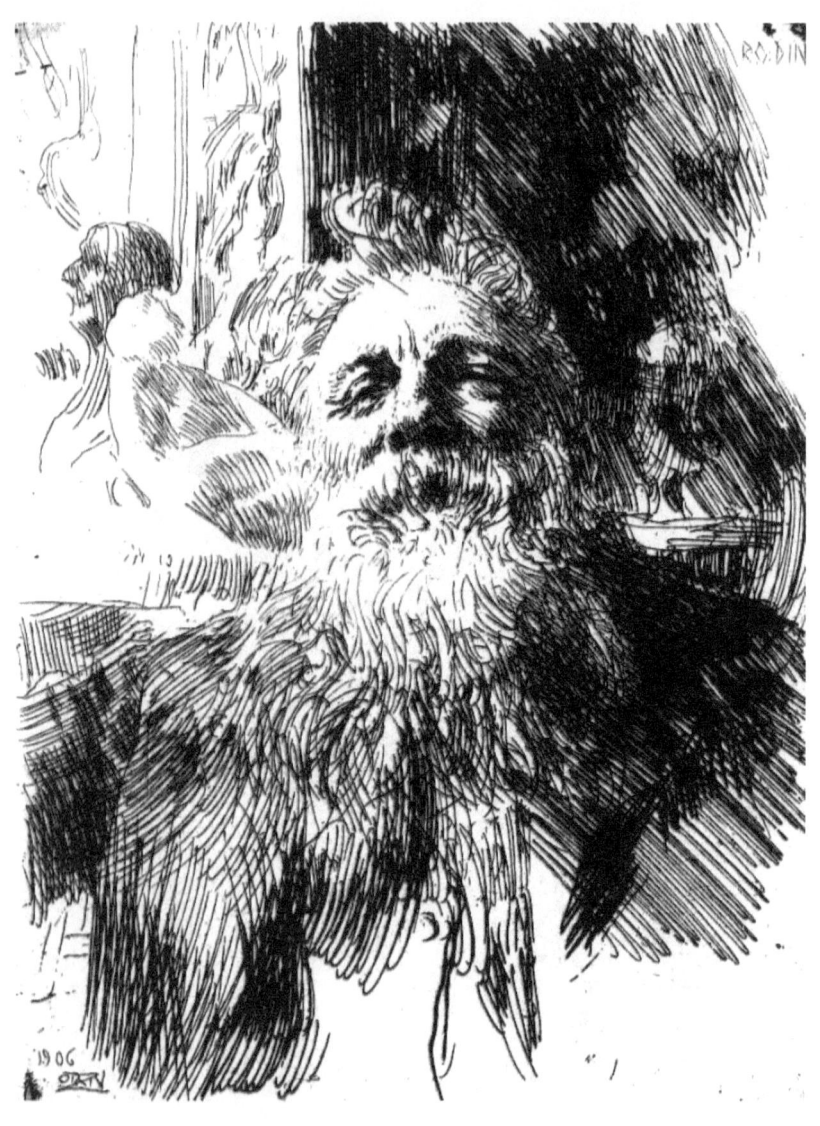

Auguste Rodin, 1906, etching

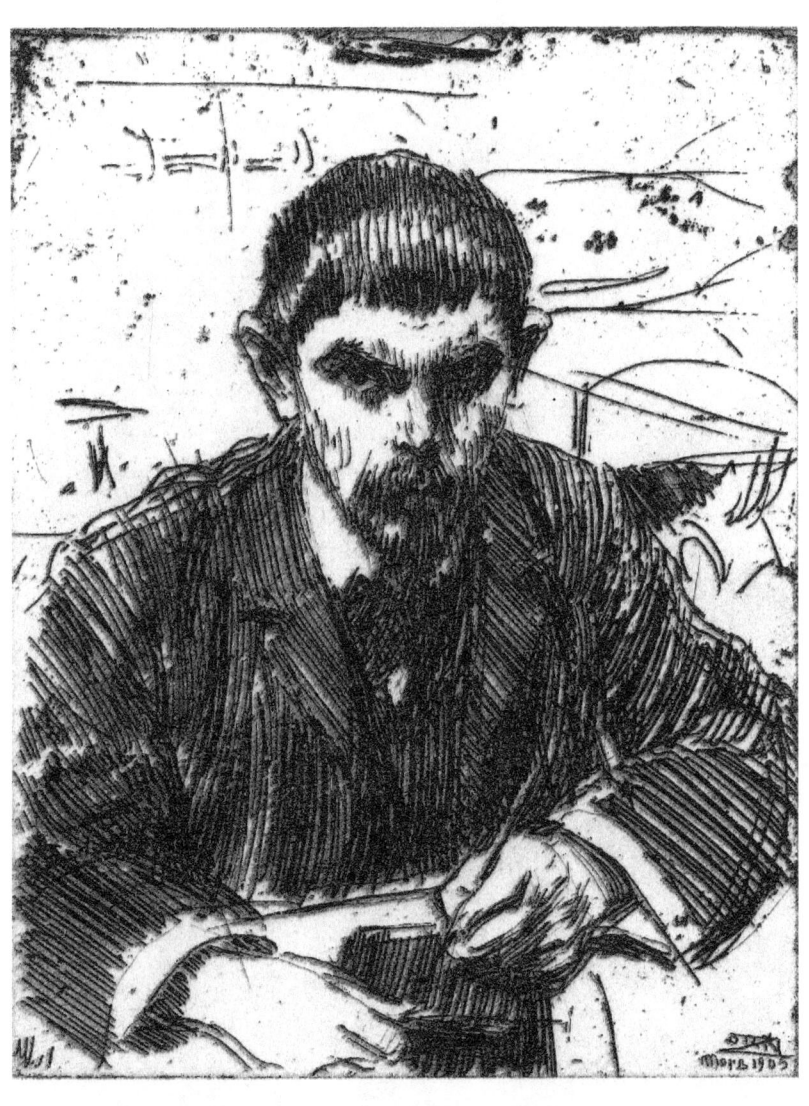

Swedish Academy member Albert Engström, 1905,
etching

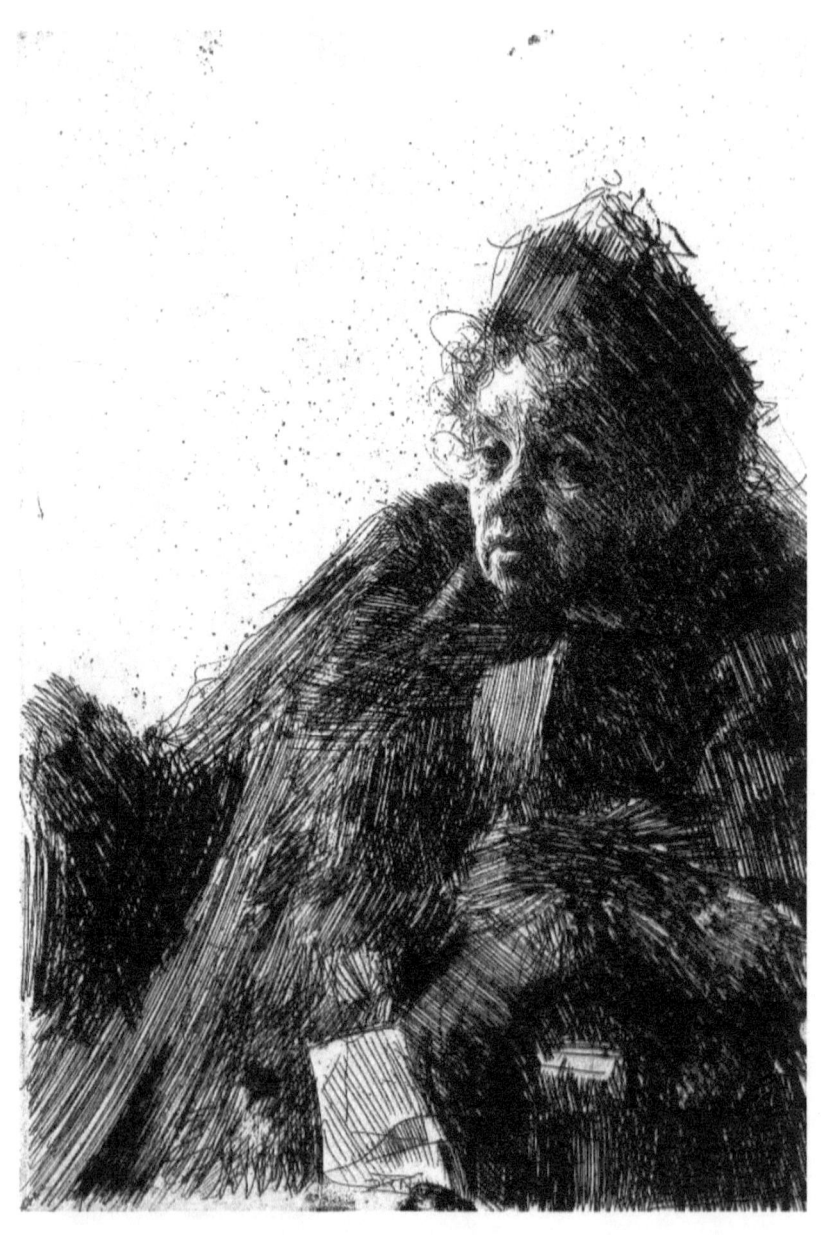

Madam Simon II, 1891, etching

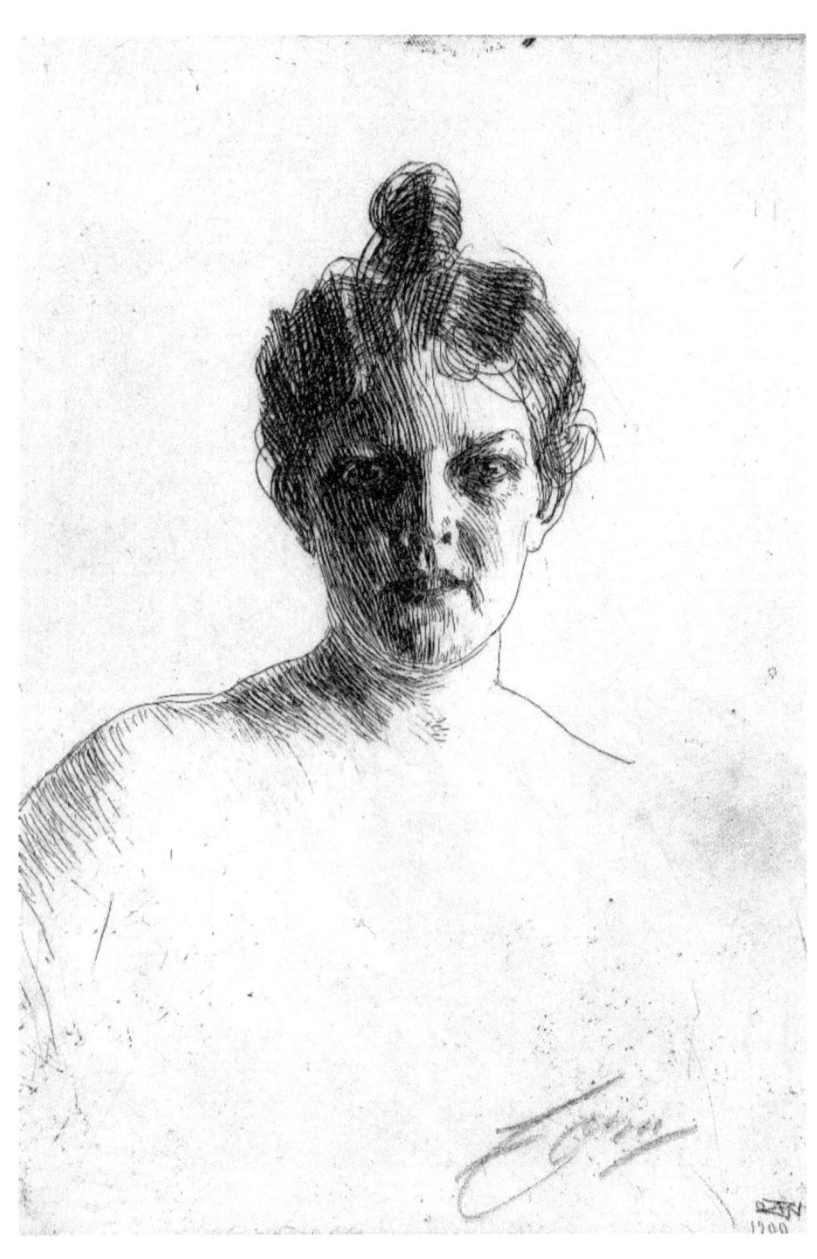

Mrs Runeberg, 1900, etching

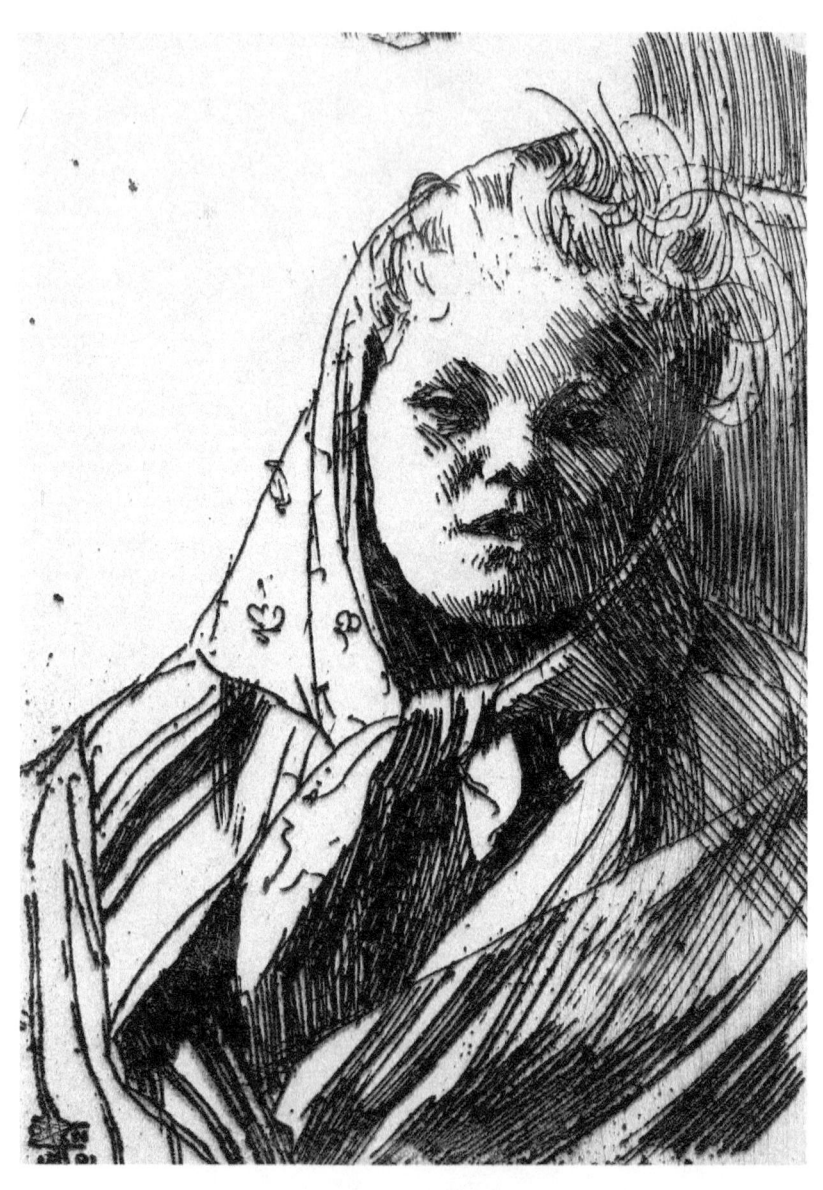

Dalkulla, 1891, etching

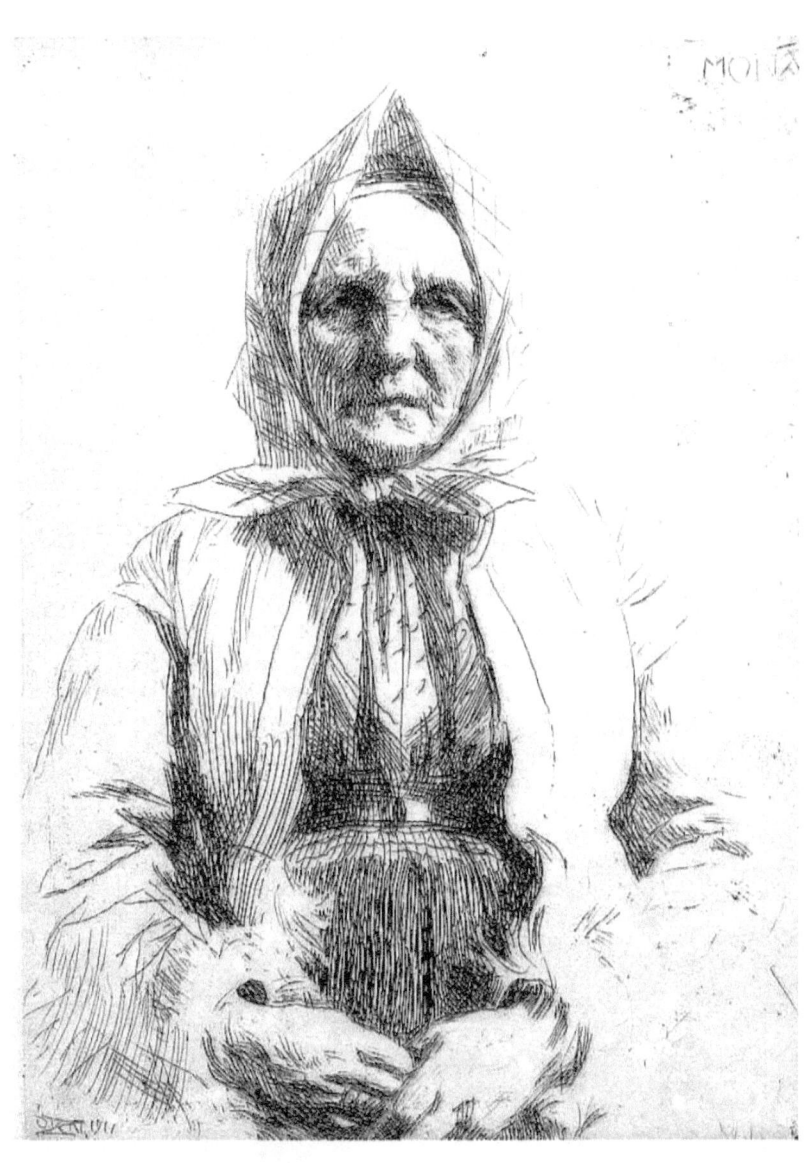

Mona, 1911, etching

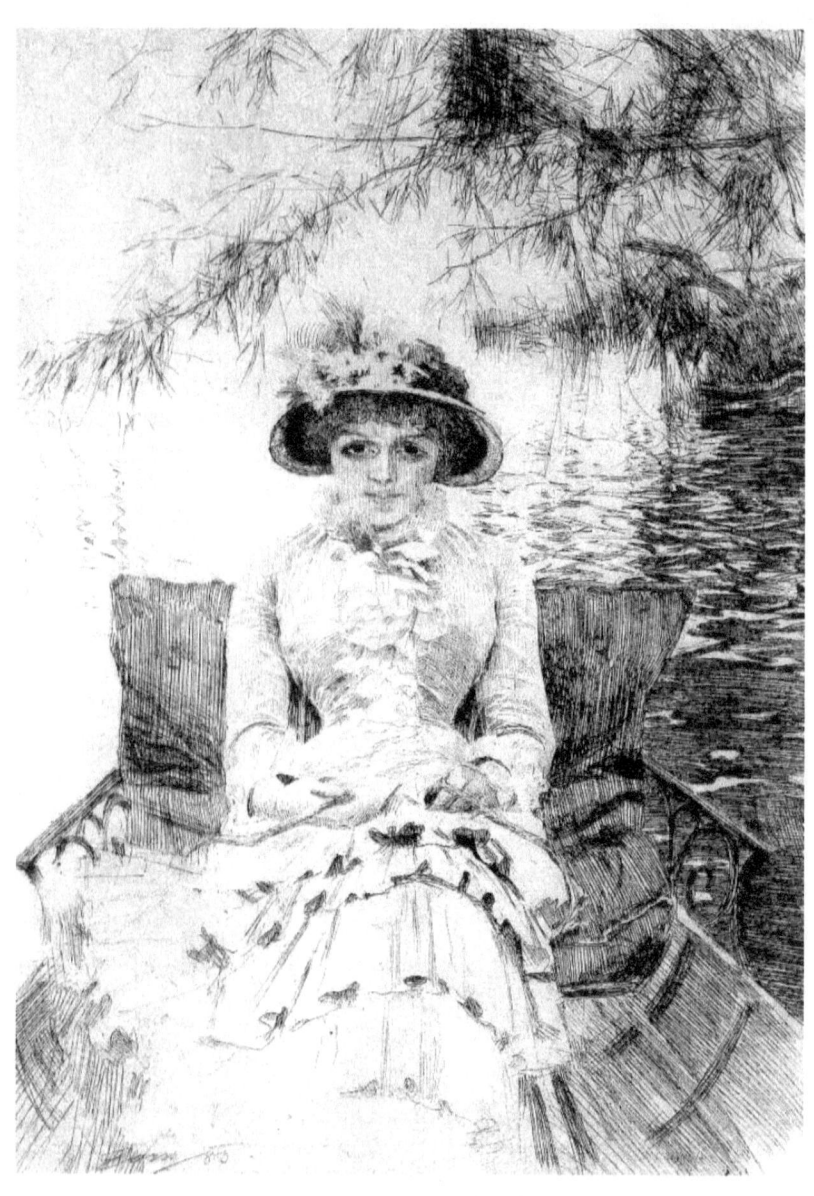

On the Thames, 1883, etching

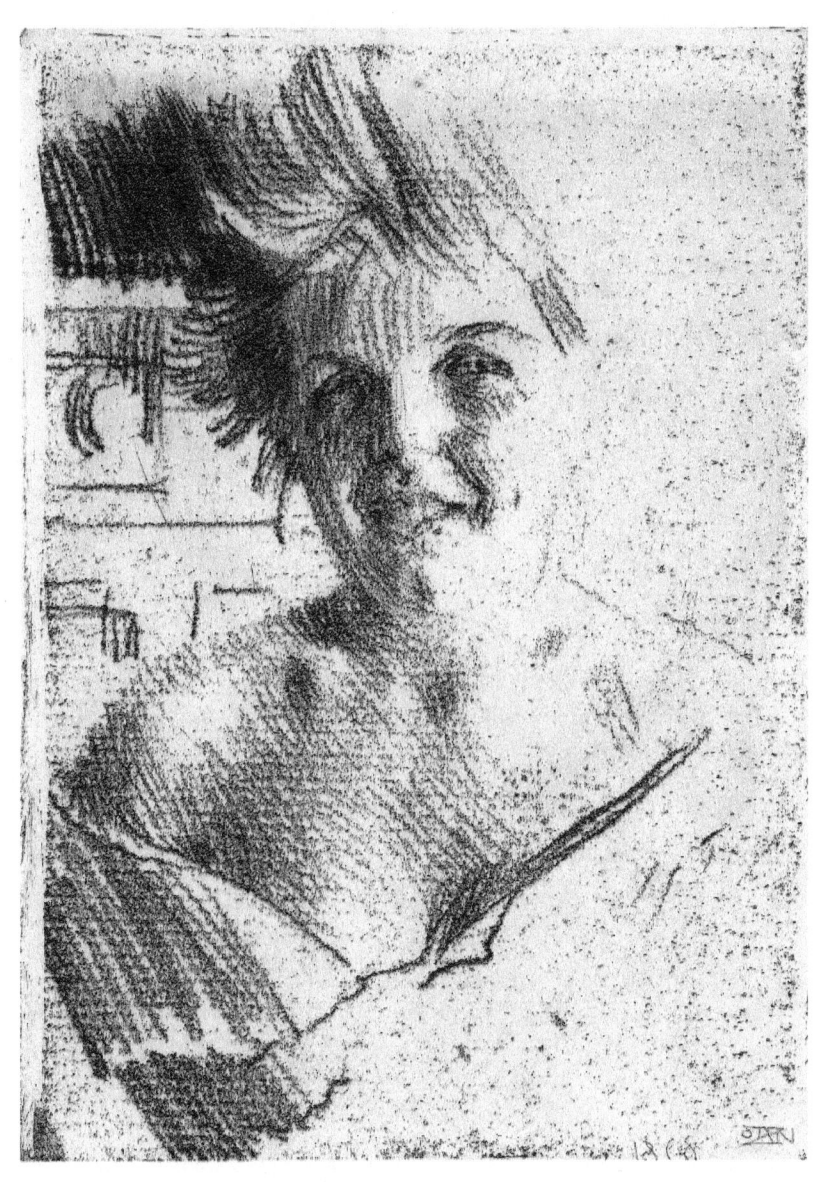

Laughing Model, 1898, etching

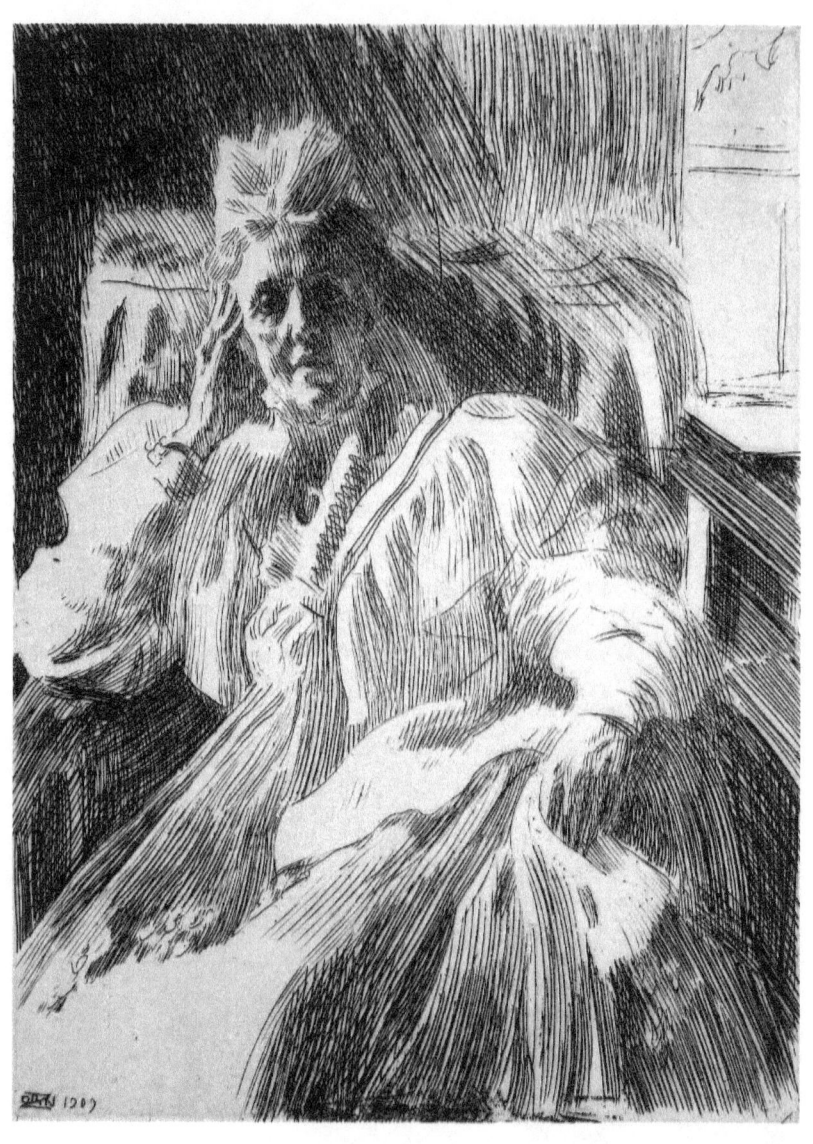

Queen Sofia, etching

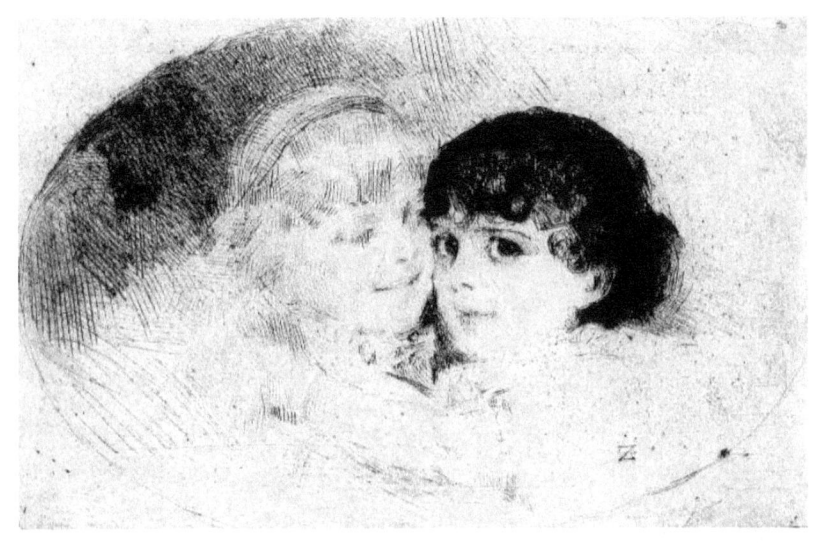

The Sisters, 1882, etching

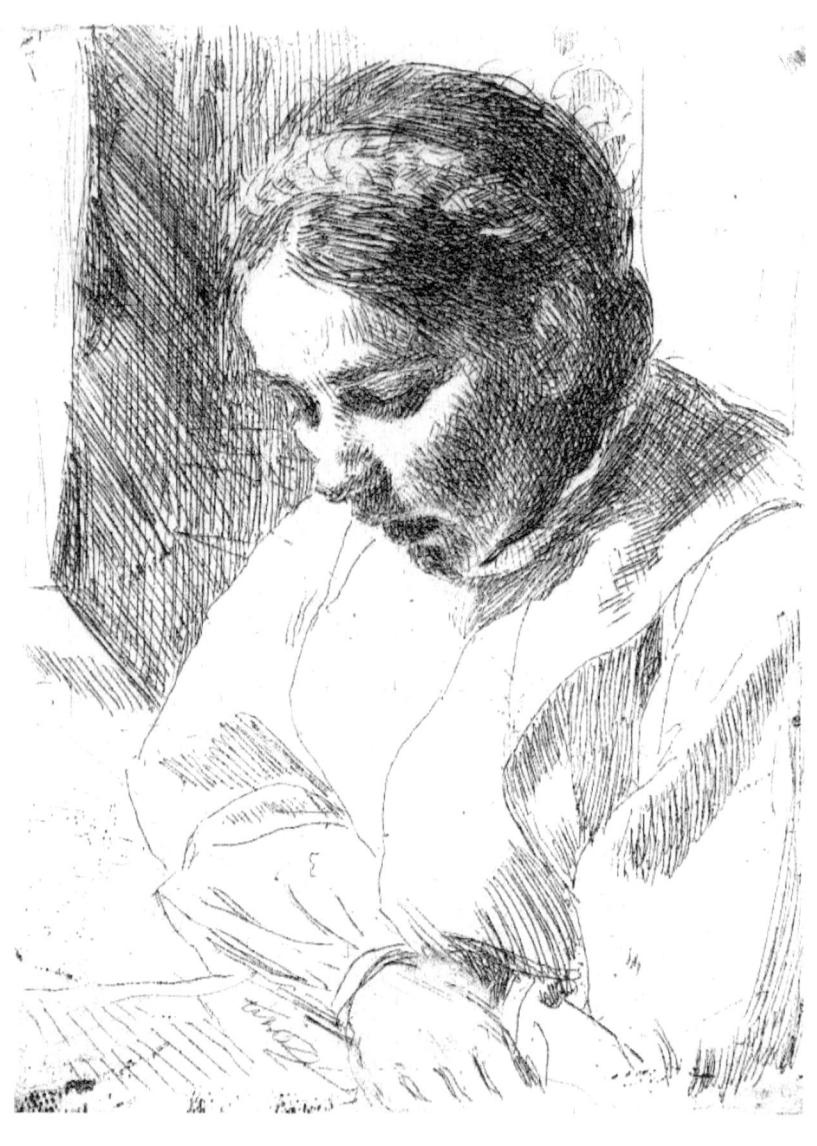

The Prayer, 1911, etching

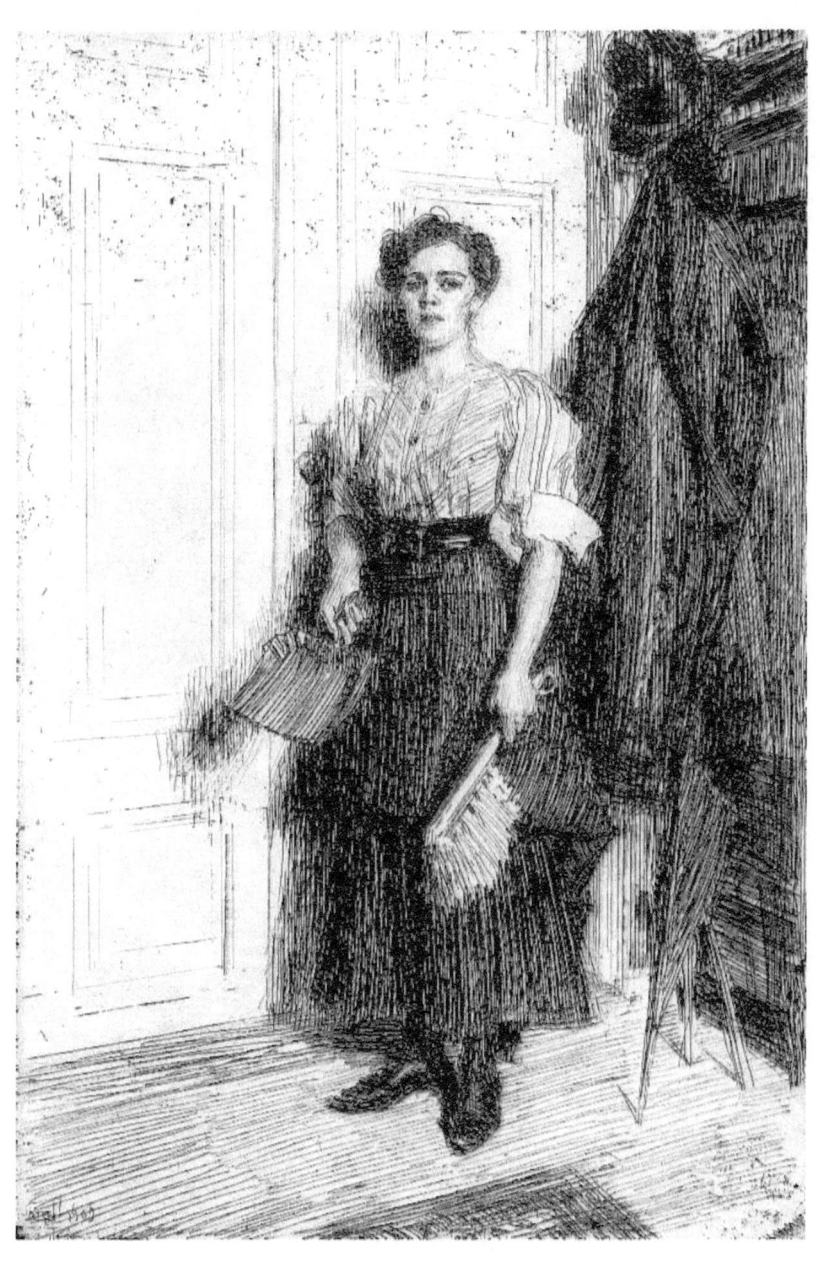

The New Maid, 1909, etching

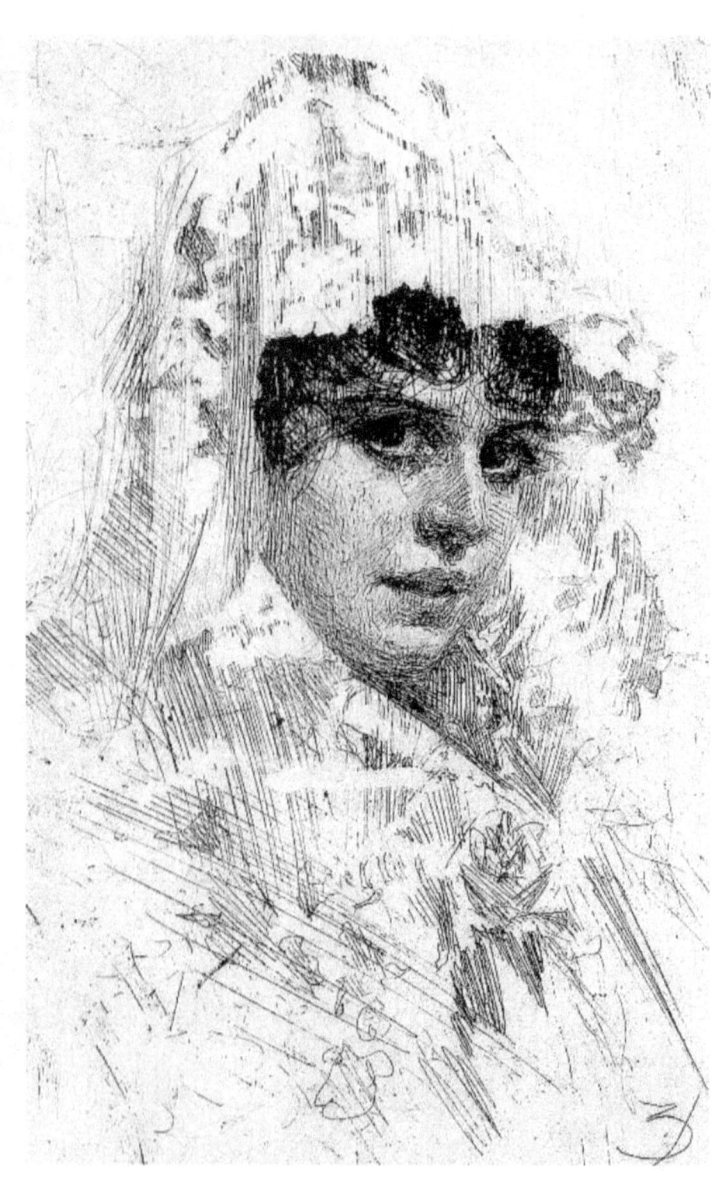

Spanish Lady, 1884, etching

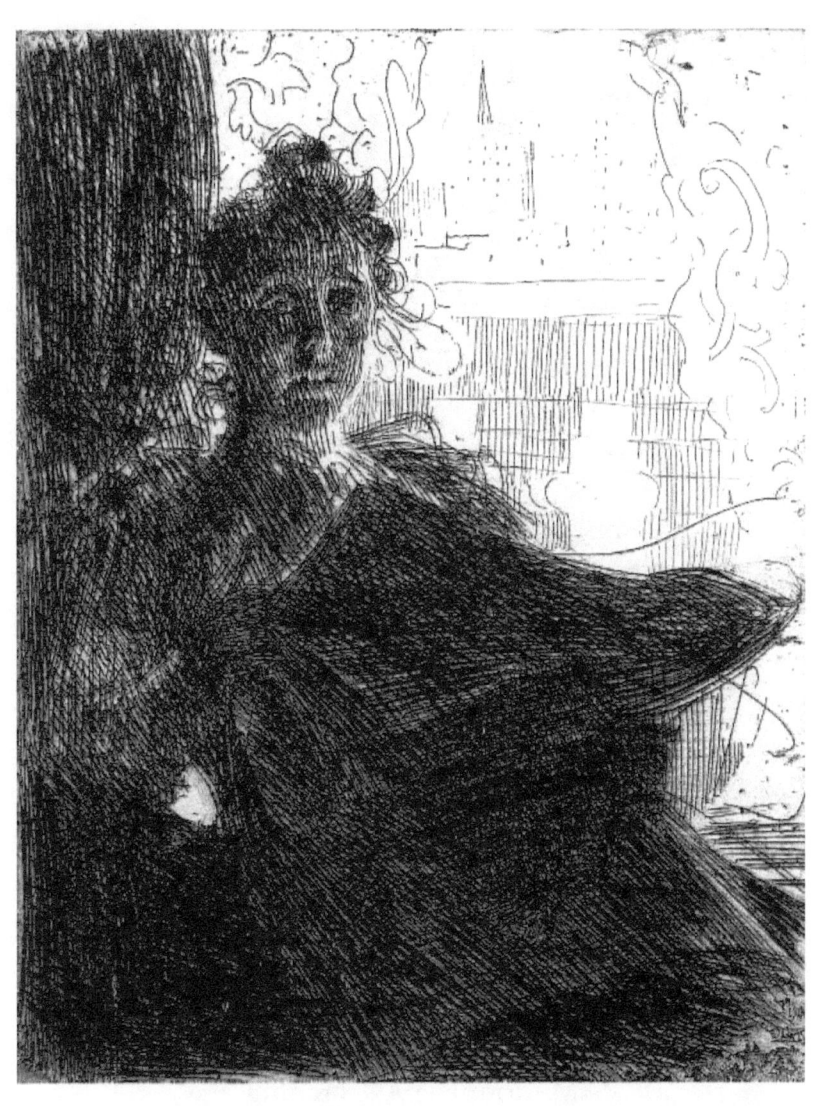

Mrs. Emma Zorn, 1900, etching

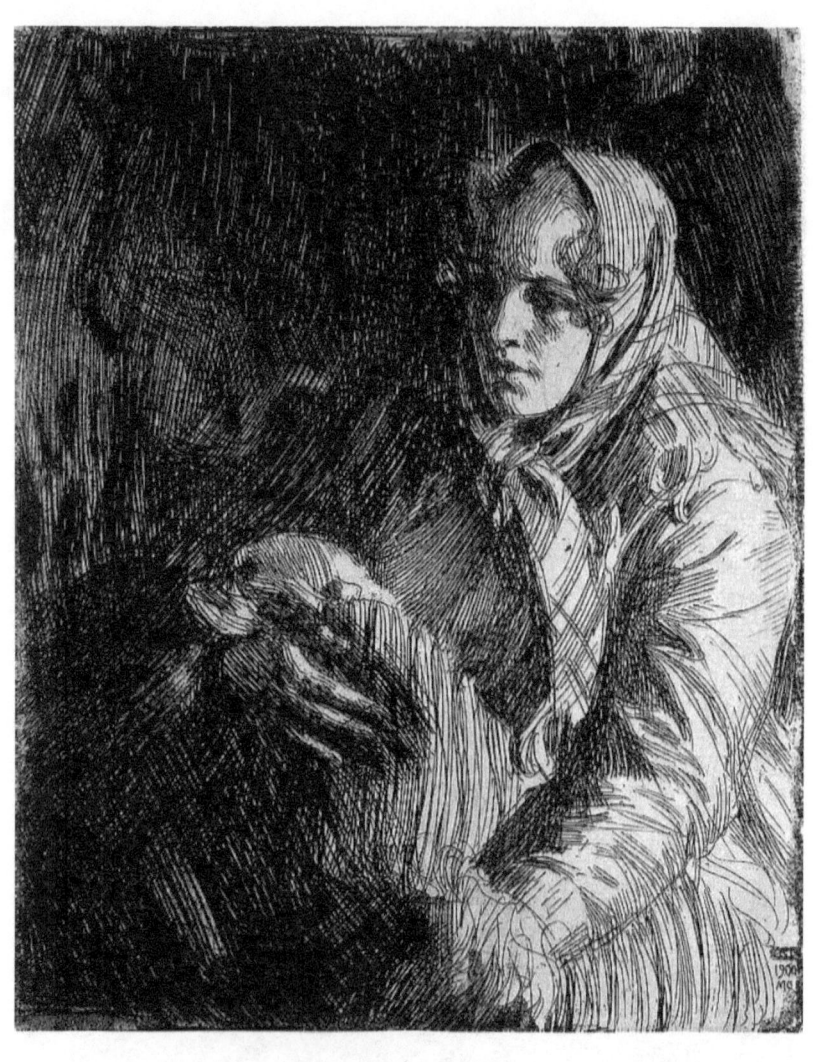

Madonna, 1900, etching

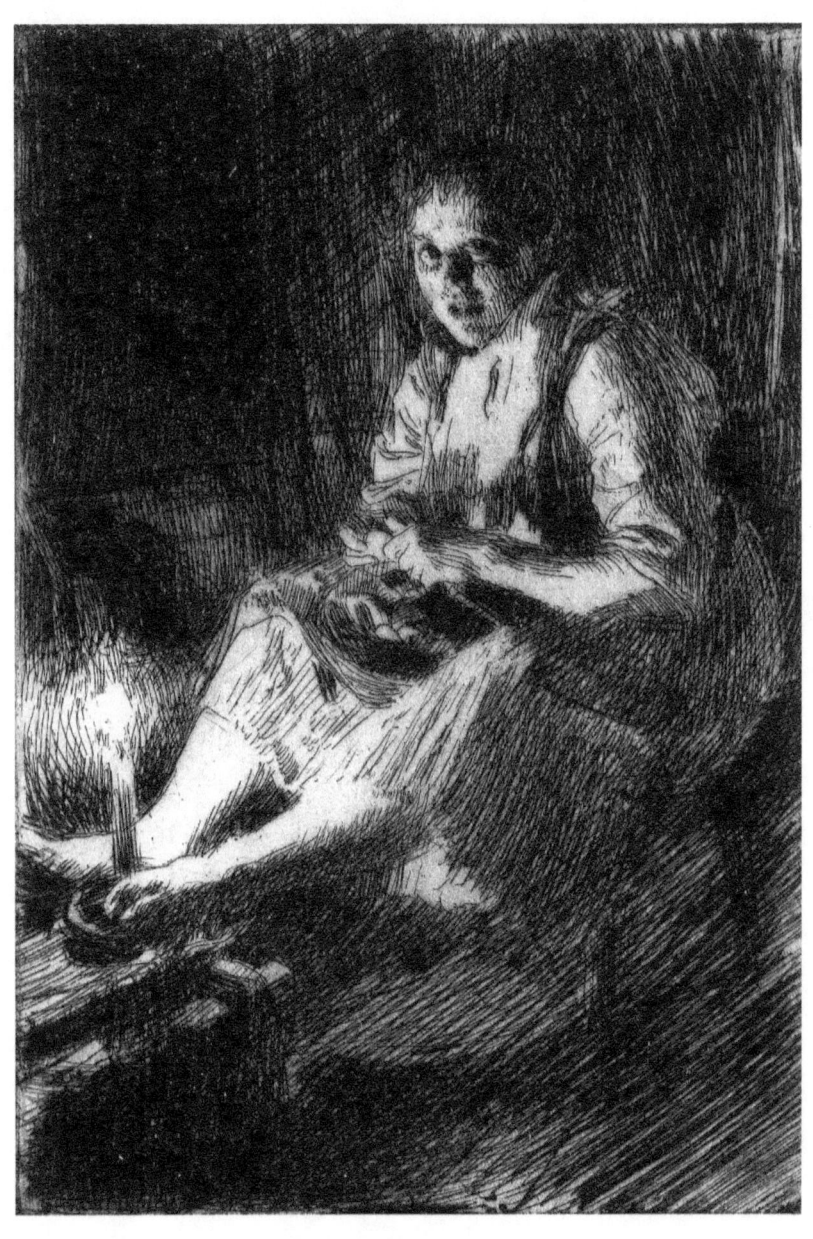

Ida, 1905, etching

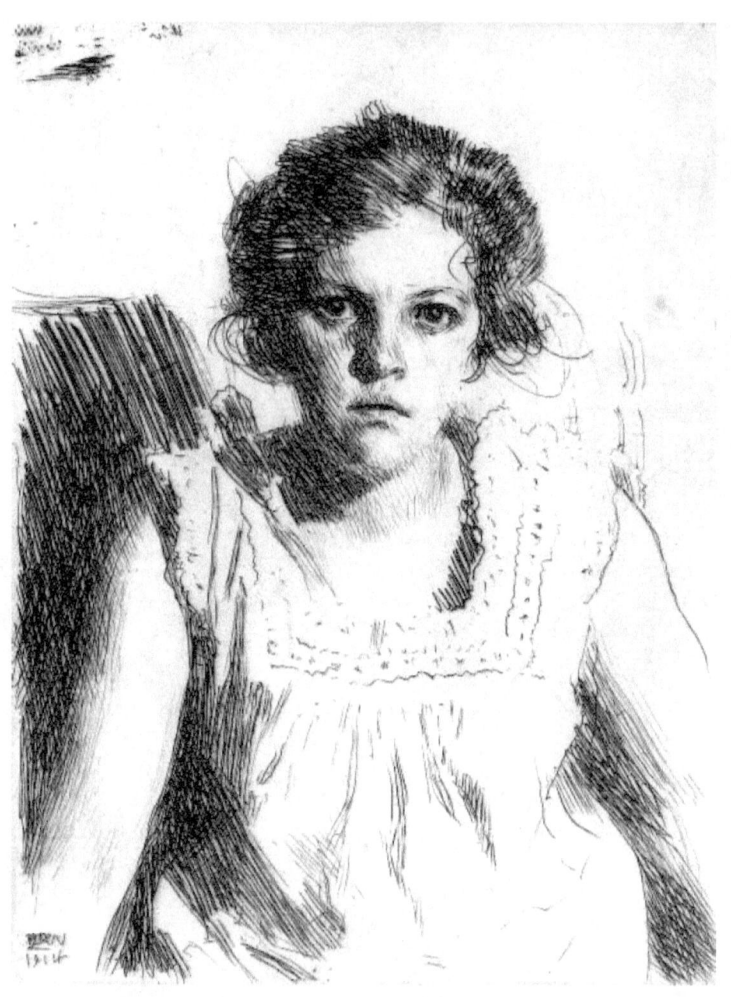

Frida, 1914, etching

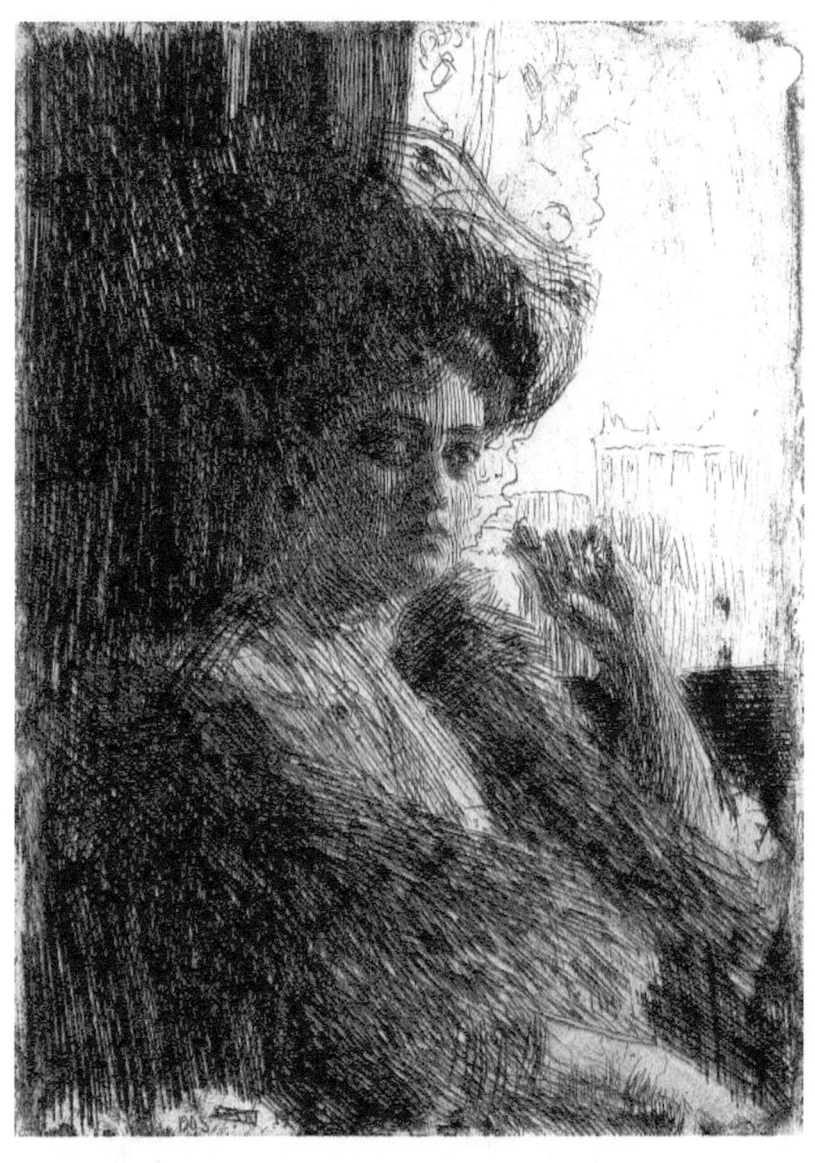

Danish actress Betty Nansen (1873-1943), 1905, etching

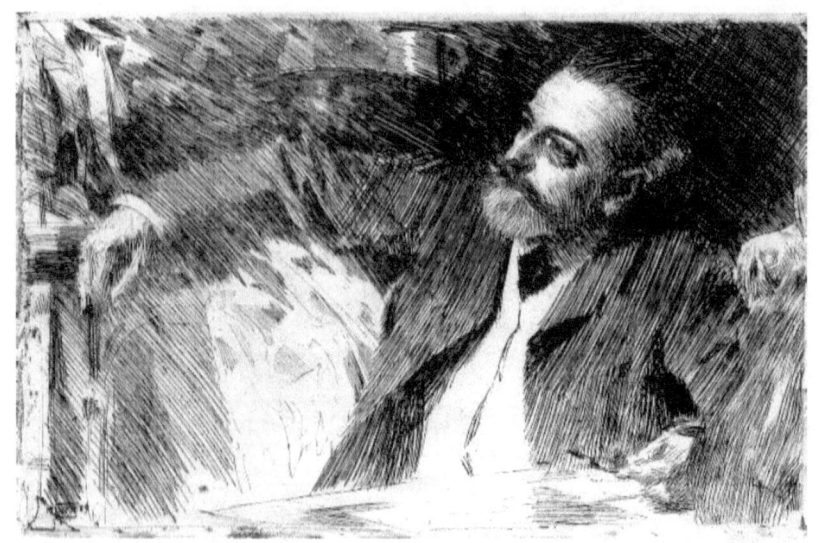

Antonin Proust, 1889, etching

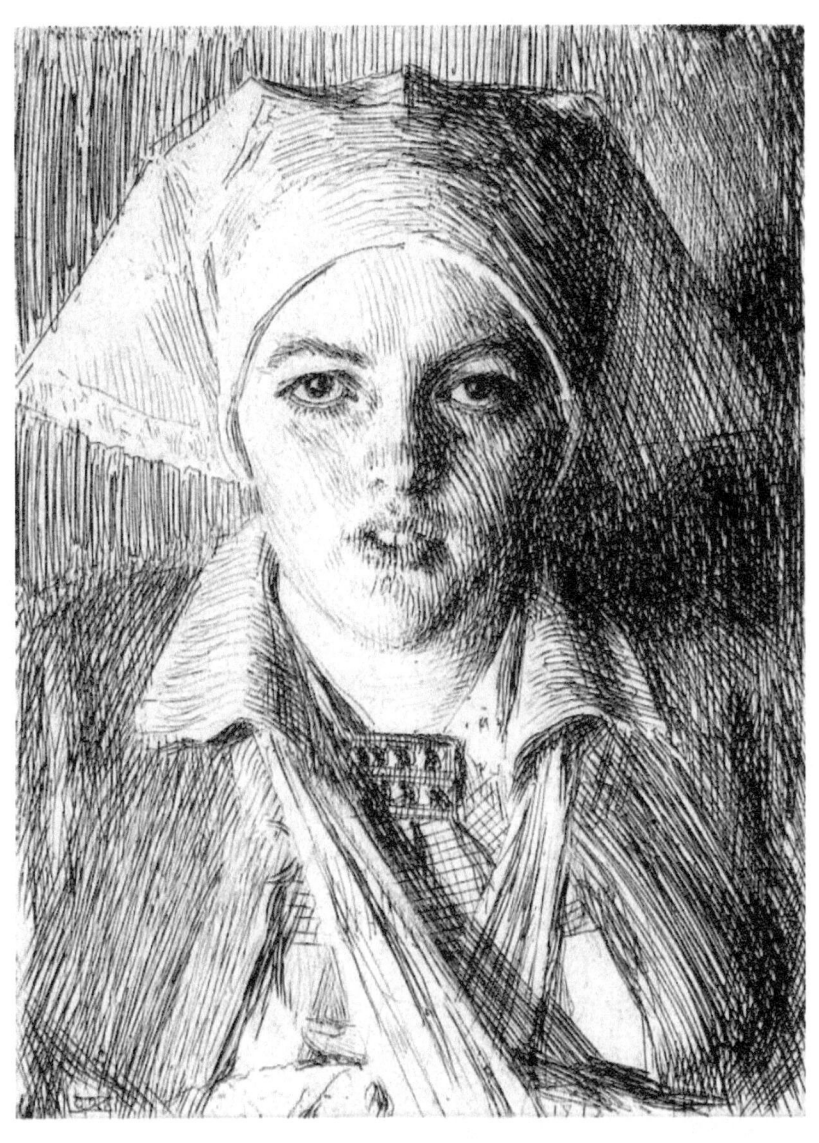

Gulli II, etching with drypoint on cream laid paper
with full margins

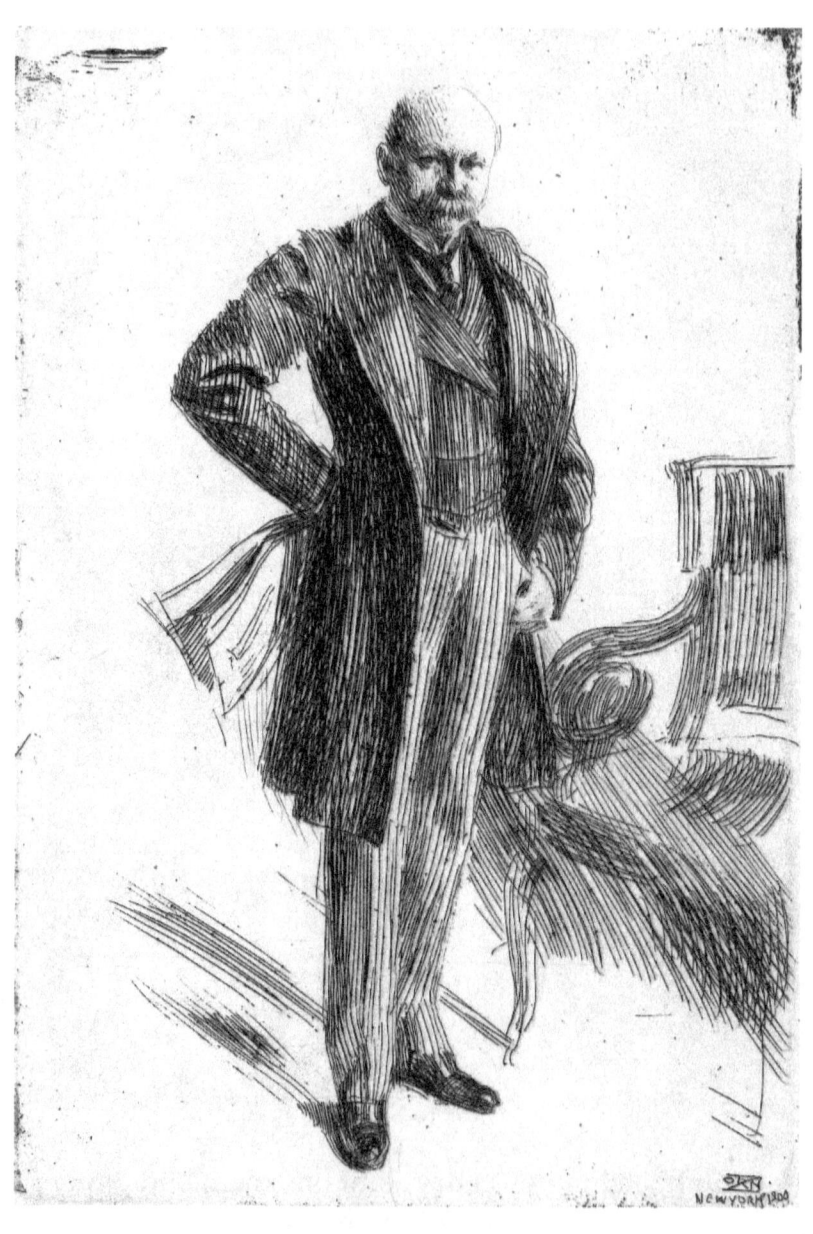

39th United States Secretary of War Daniel S. Lamont
(1851-1905), 1900, etching

Oil Paintings

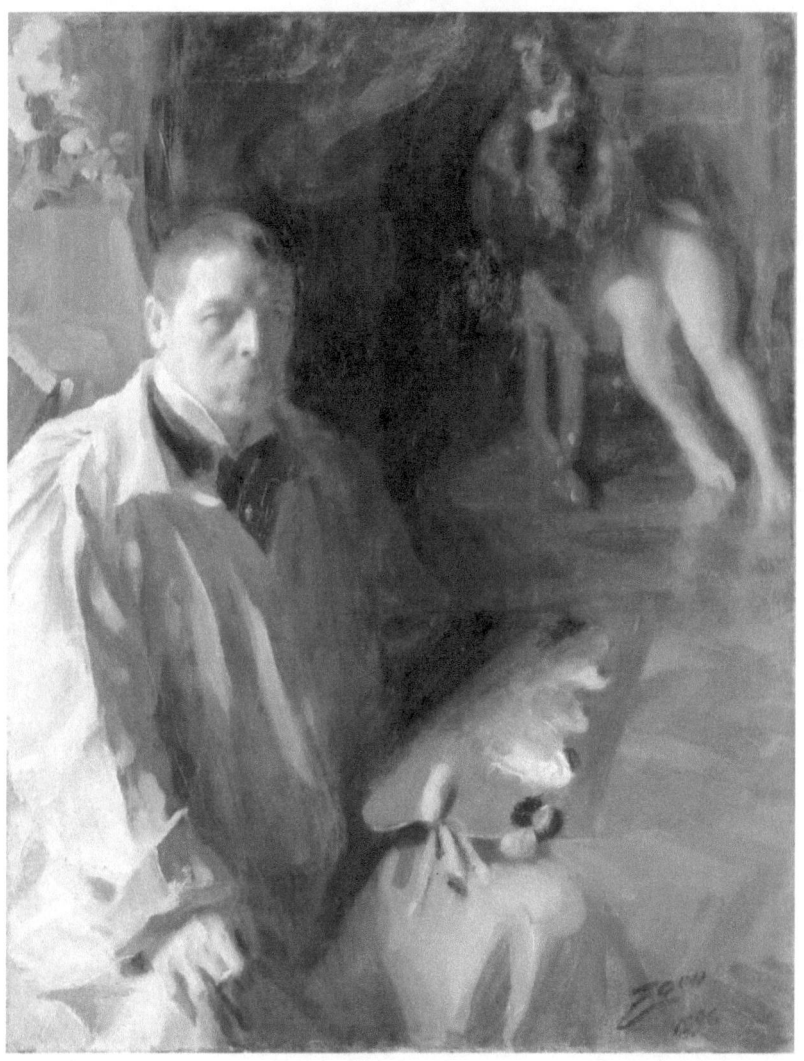

Self-Portrait with Model, 1896, Oil on canvas

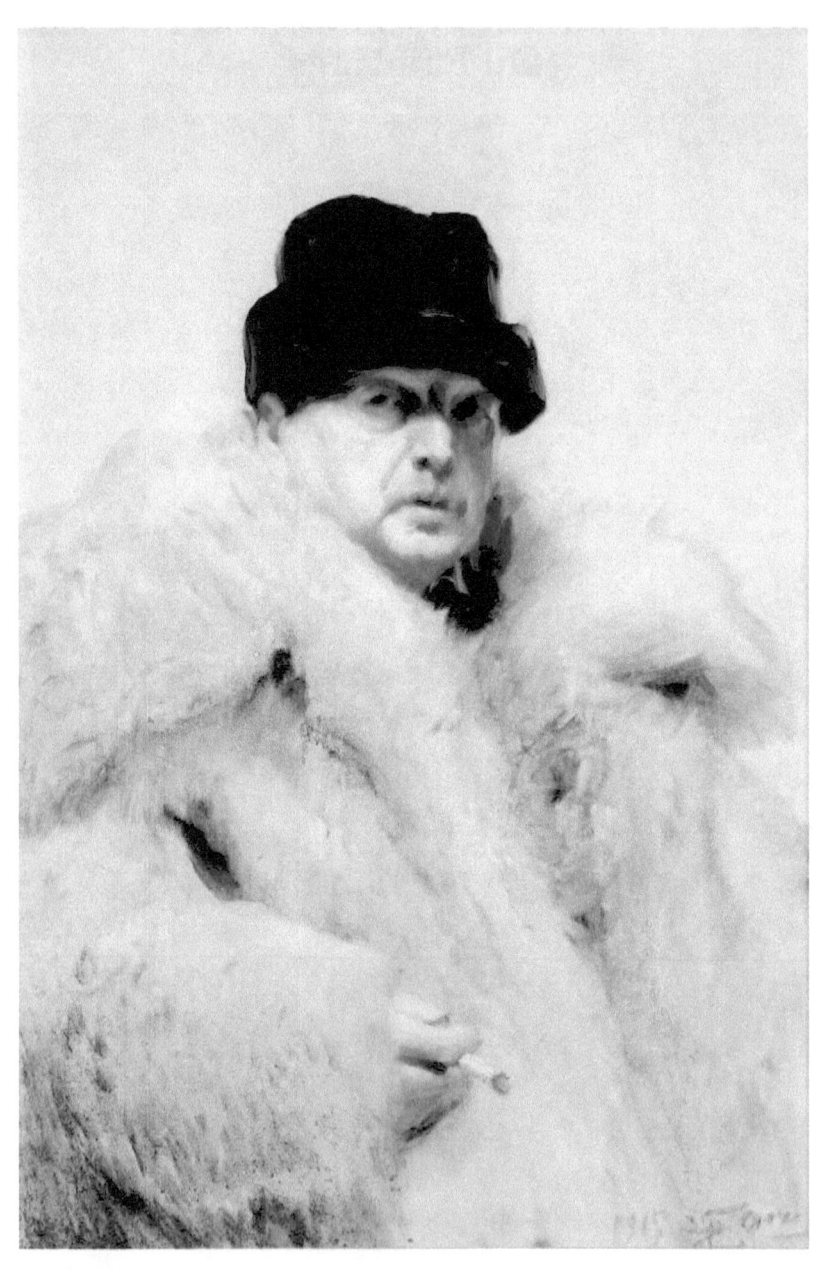

Self-portrait in a wolf skin, 1915, oil on canvas

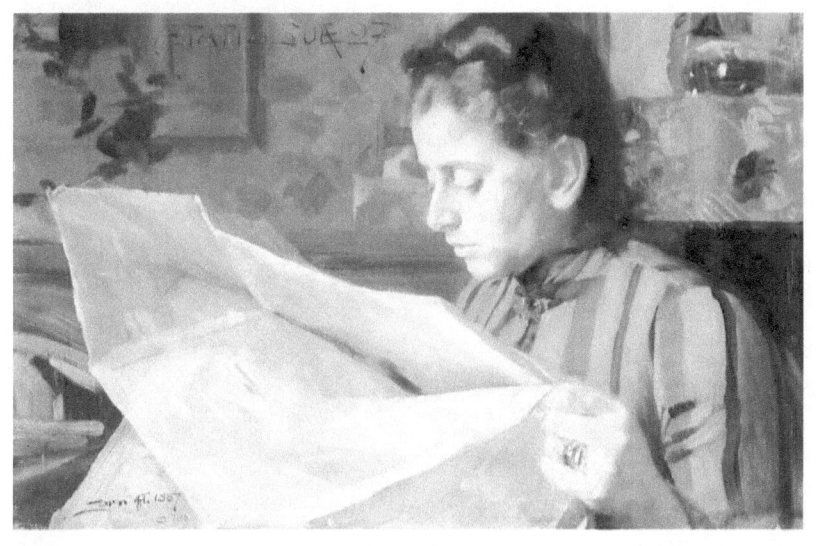

Portrait of Emma Zorn, 1887, Oil on canvas

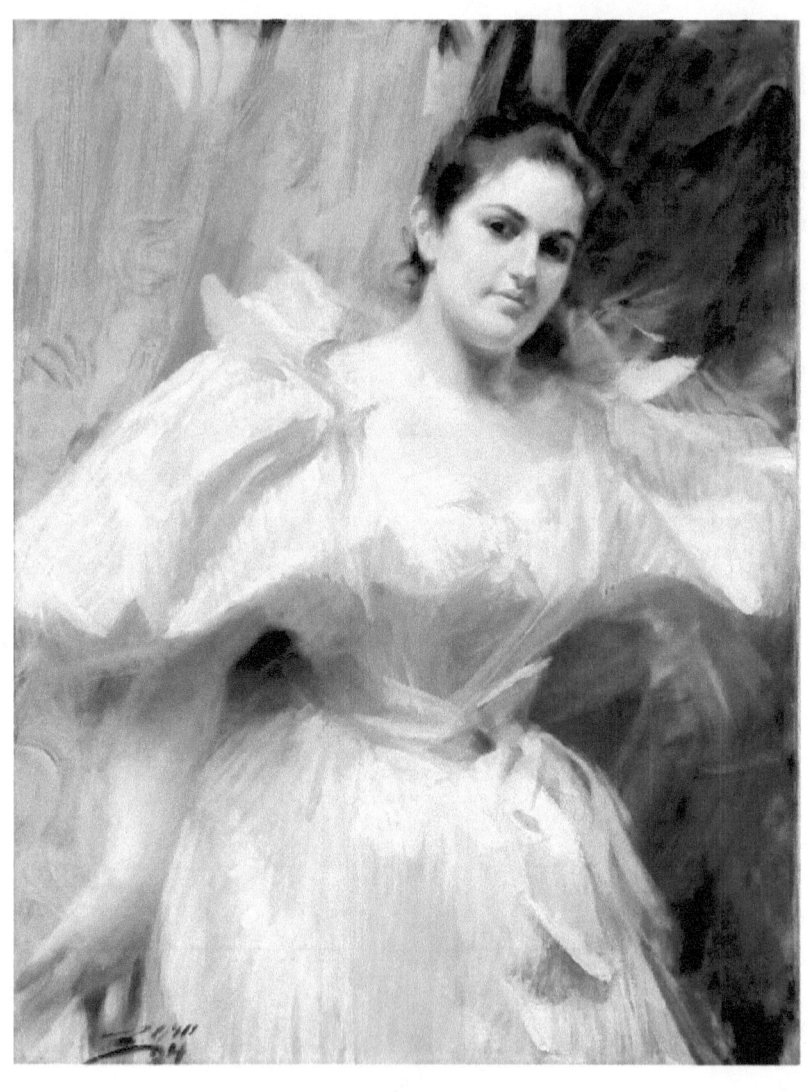

Frieda Schiff (1876–1958), Later Mrs. Felix M. Warburg
1894, Oil on canvas

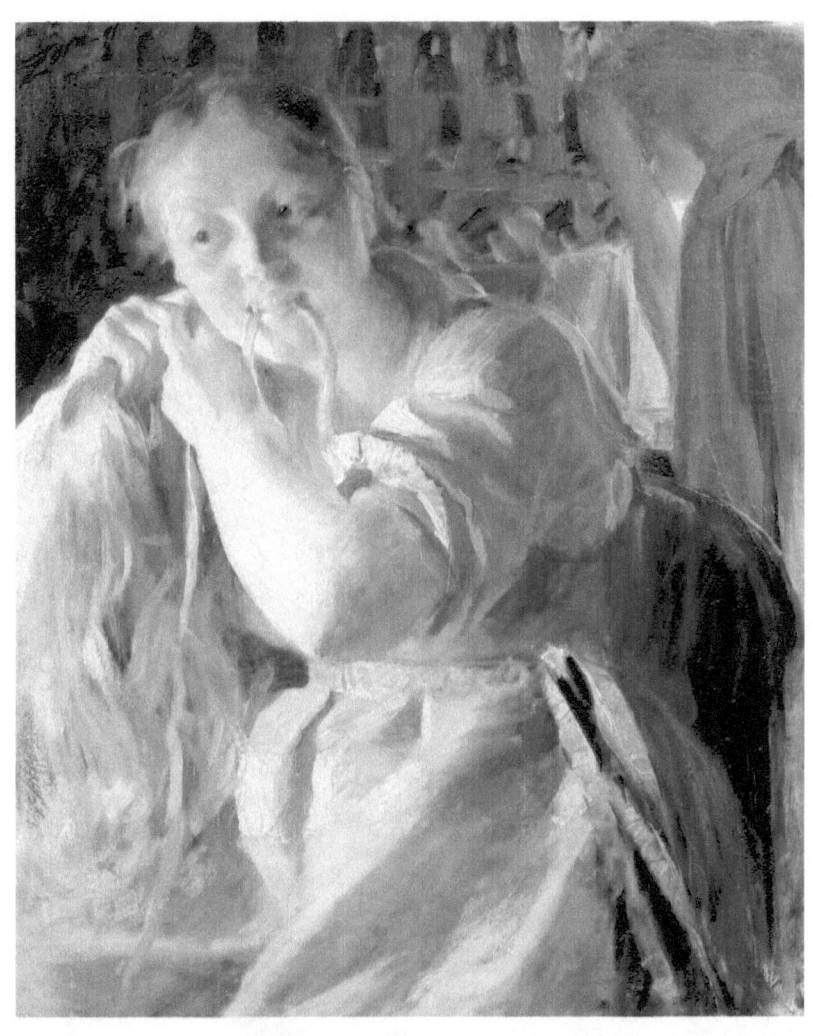

Margit, 1891, Oil on canvas

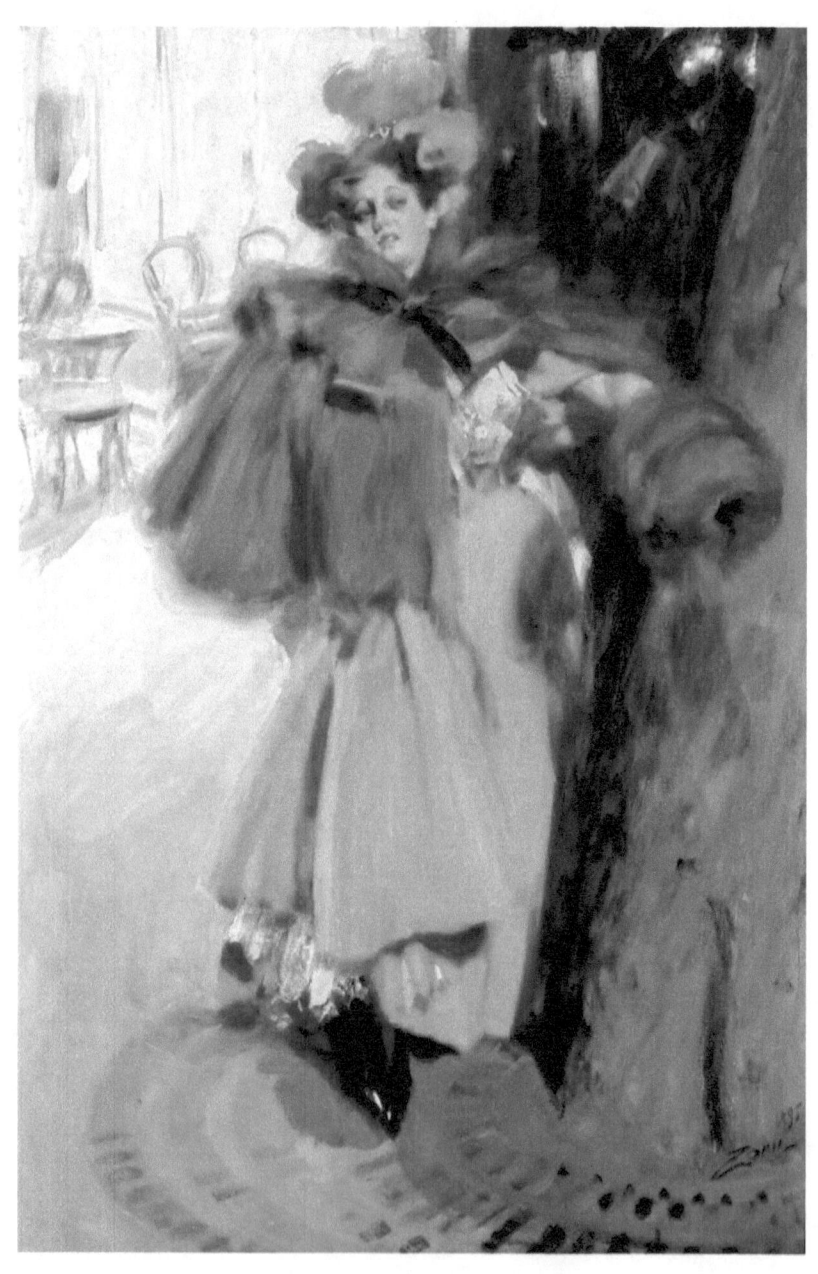

Night Effect, 1895, Oil on canvas

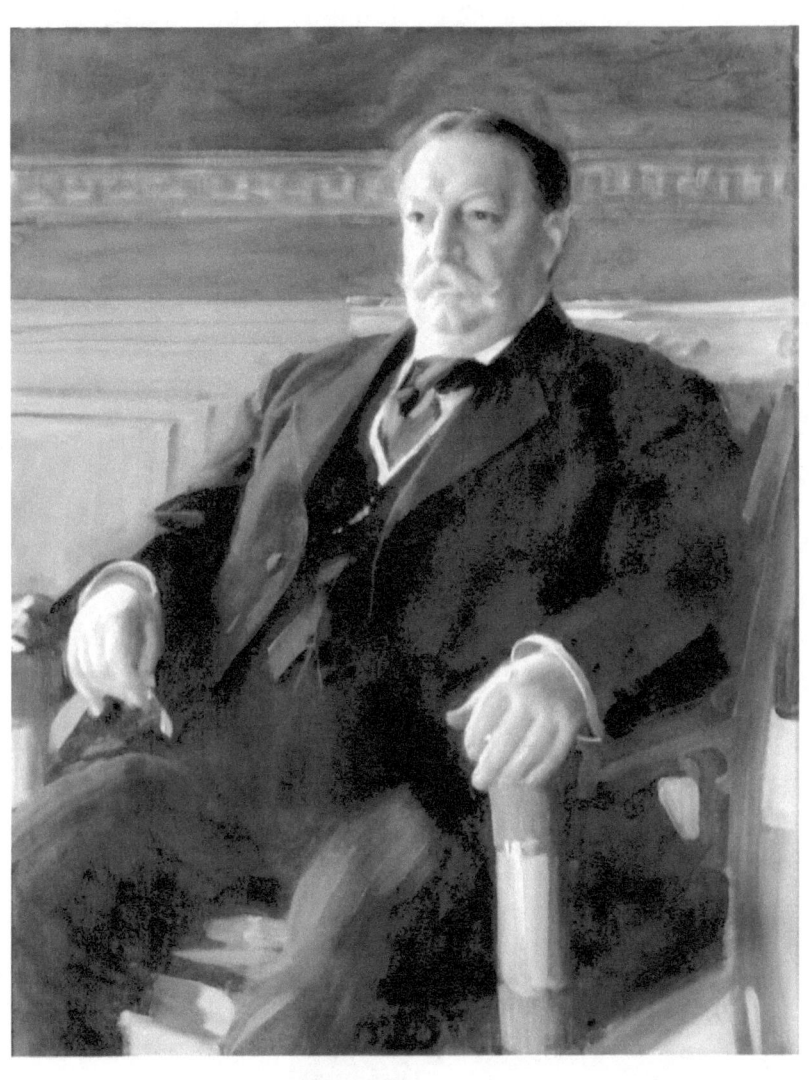

Official White House portrait of William Howard Taft,
1911, Oil on canvas

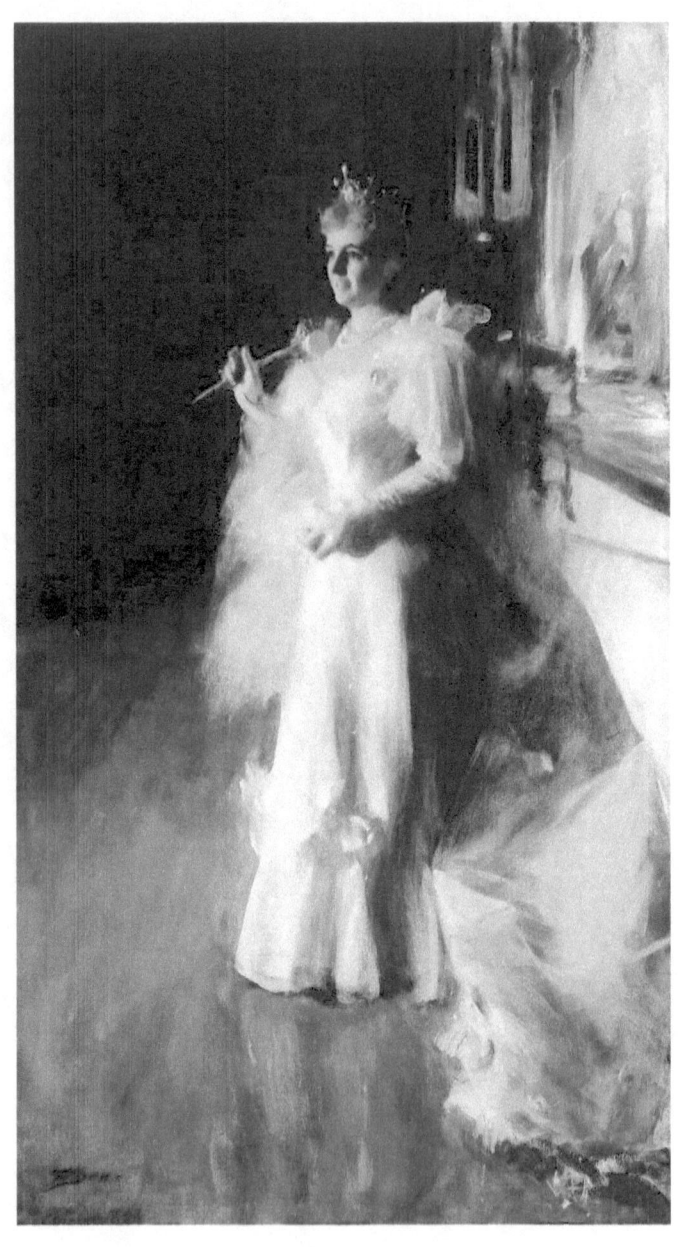

Portrait Mrs. Potter Palmer, 1893, Oil on canvas

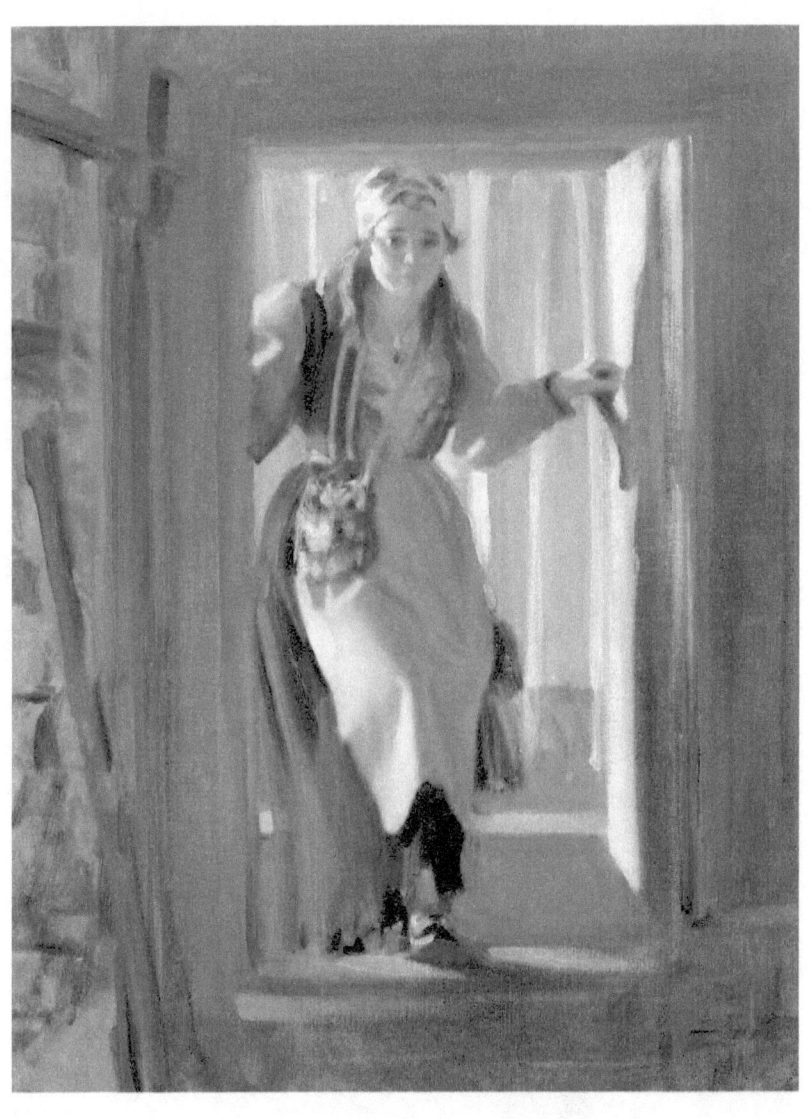

Maria, 1918, Oil on canvas

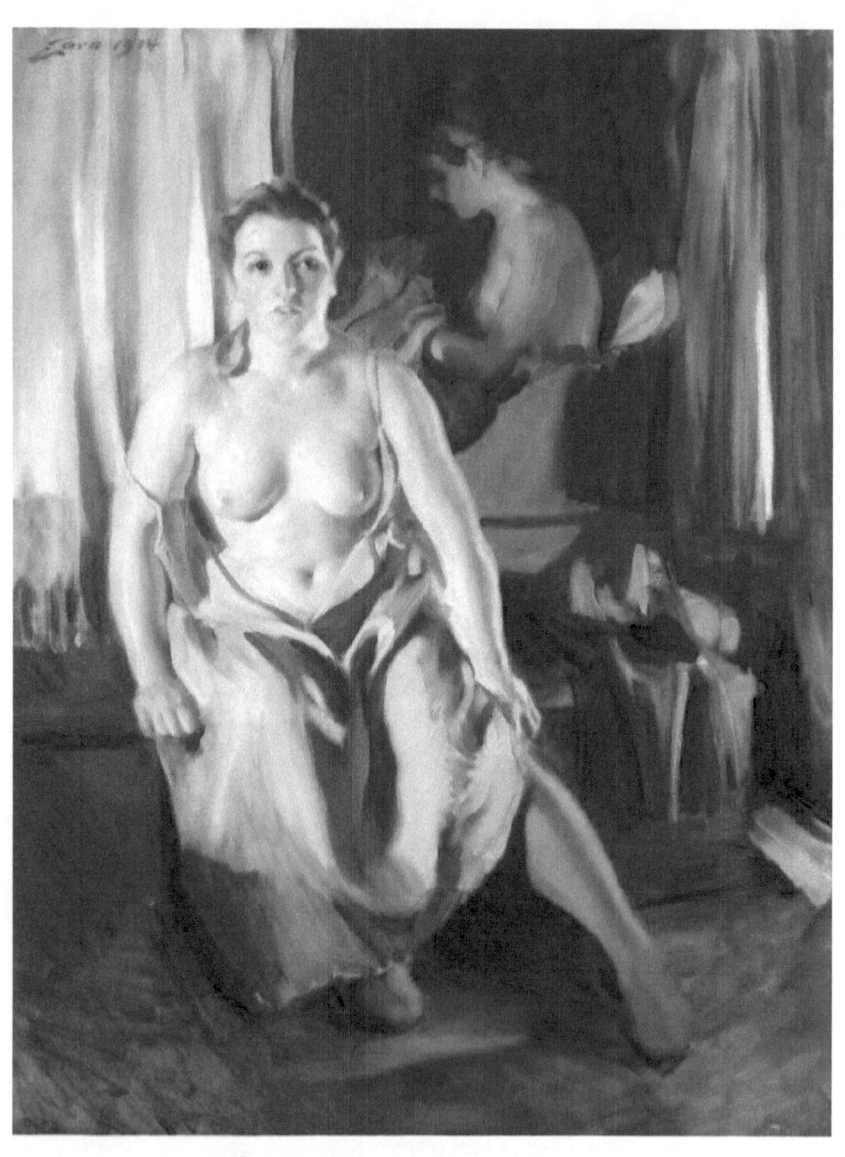

Red stockings, 1914, Oil on canvas

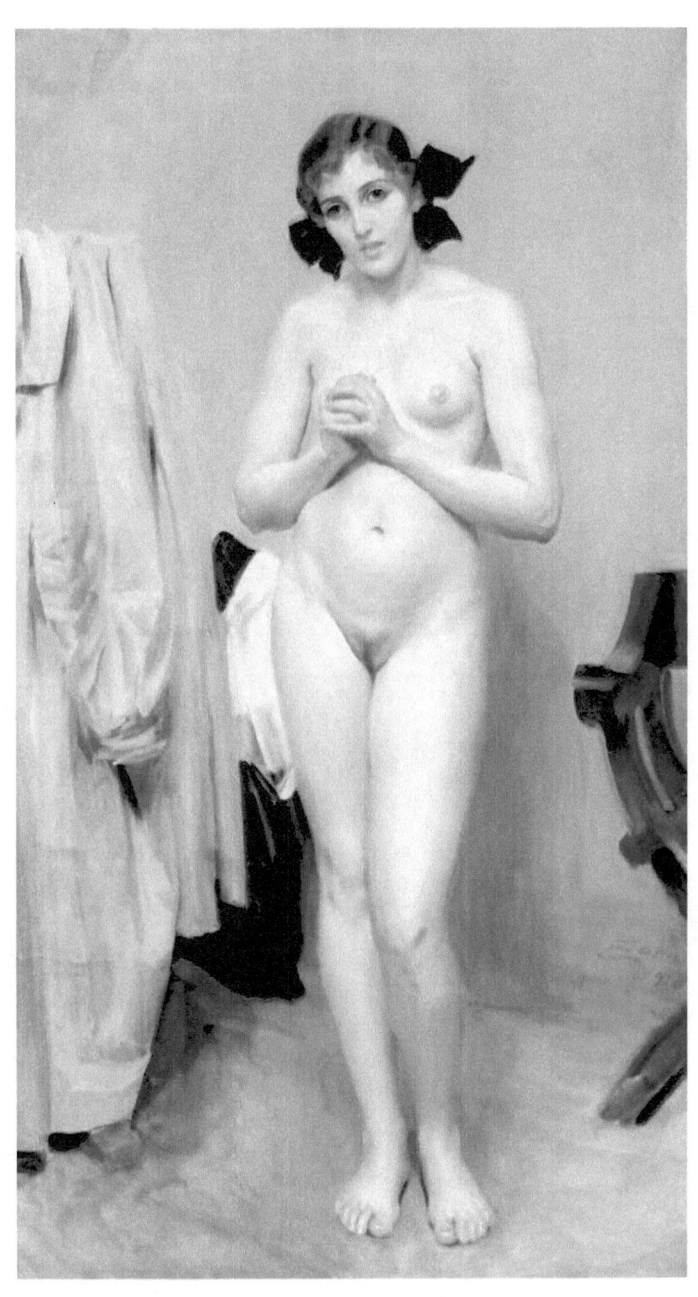

Painter's Model, 1916, Oil on canvas

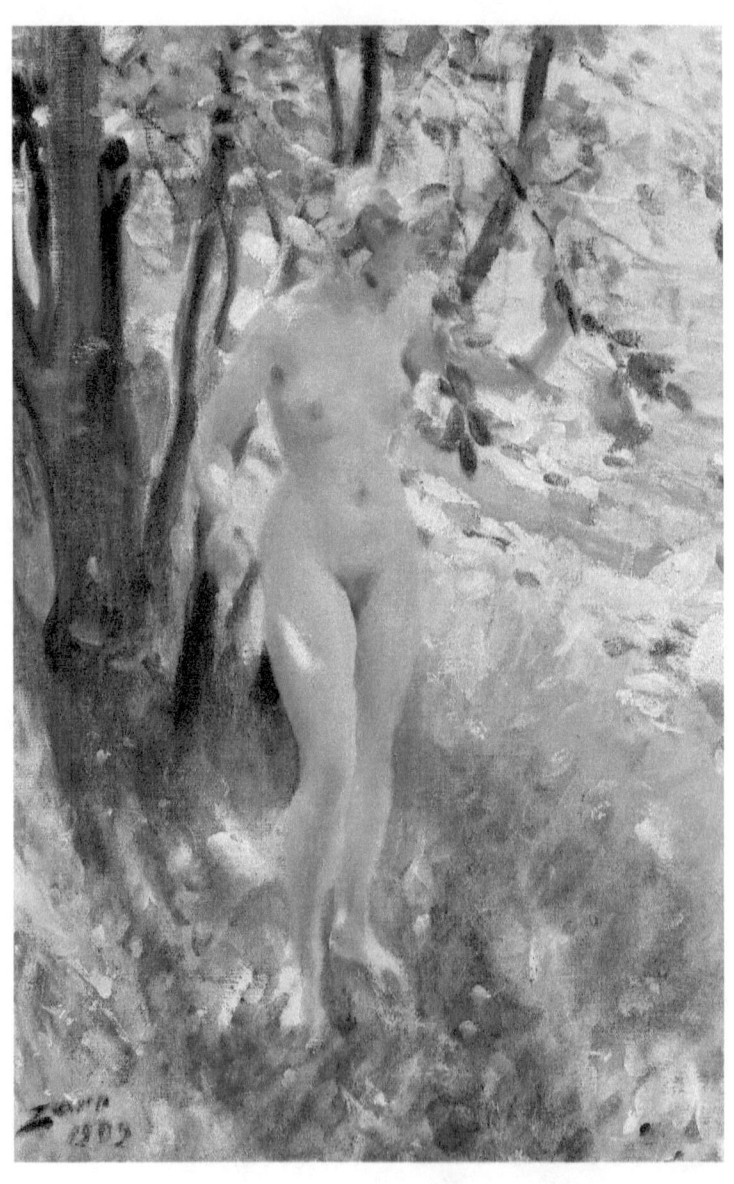

The Shadow, 1909, Oil on canvas

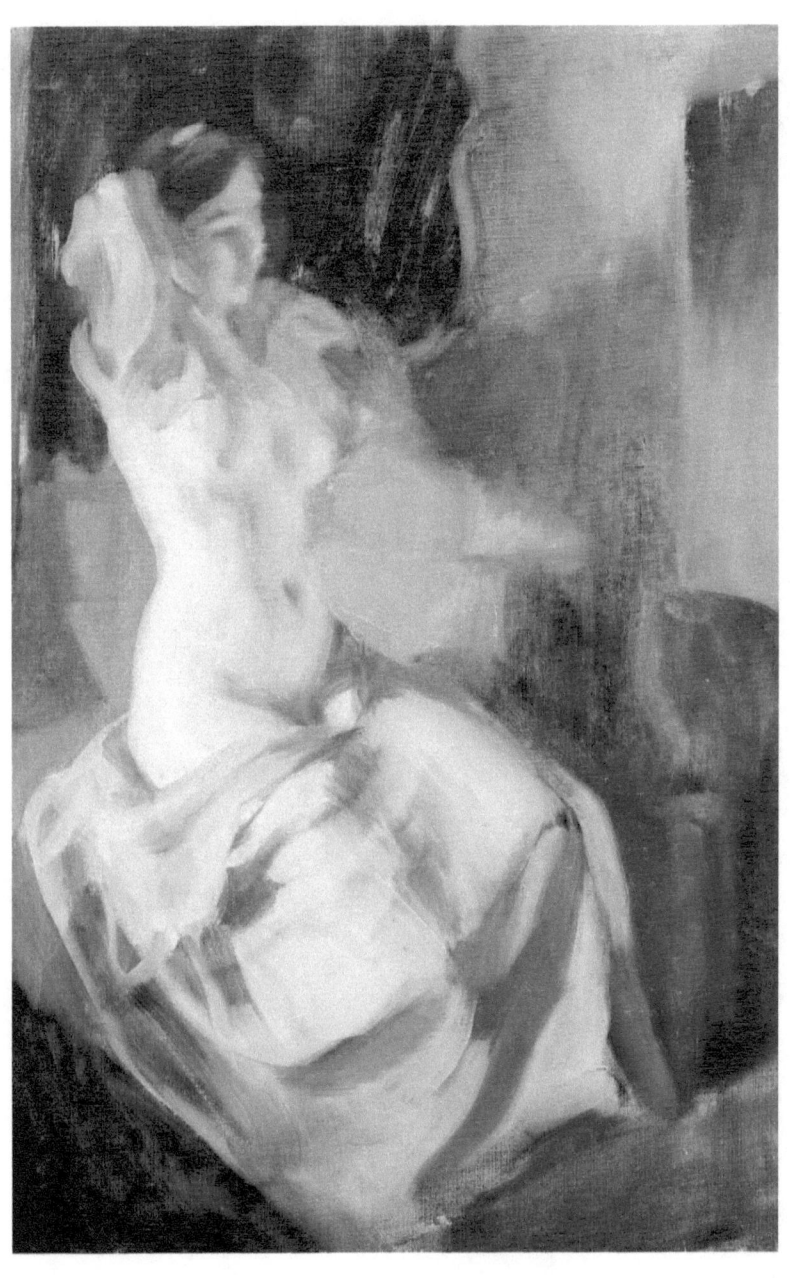

Nude in Fire Light, 1904, Oil on canvas

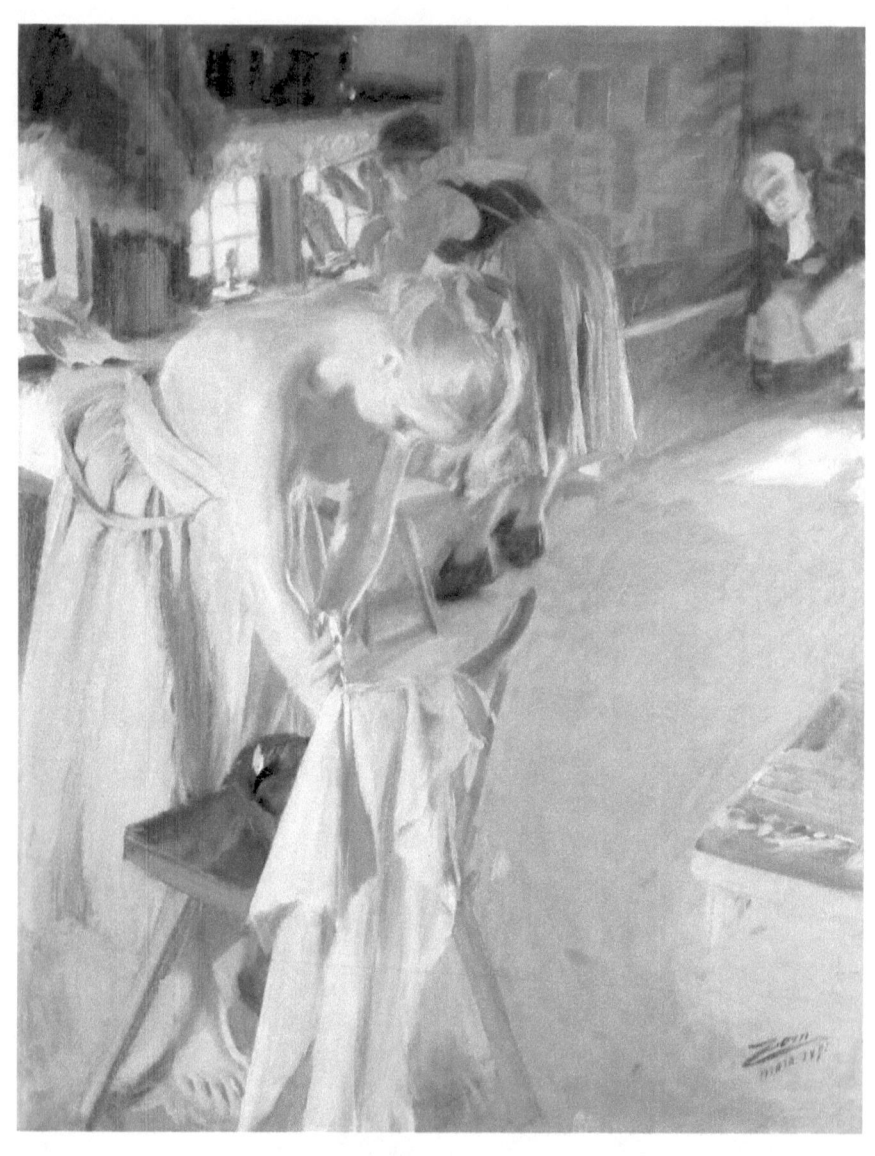

Sunday morning, 1891, Oil on canvas

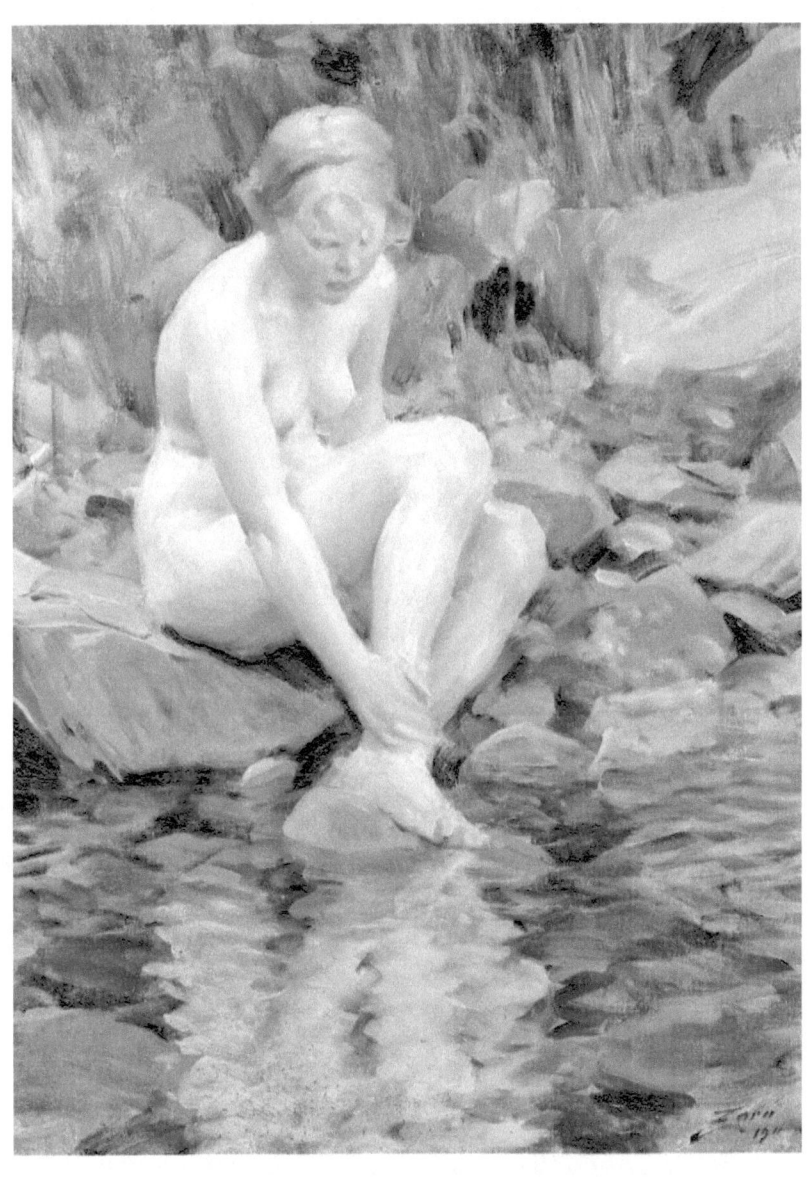

Dagmar, 1911, Oil on canvas

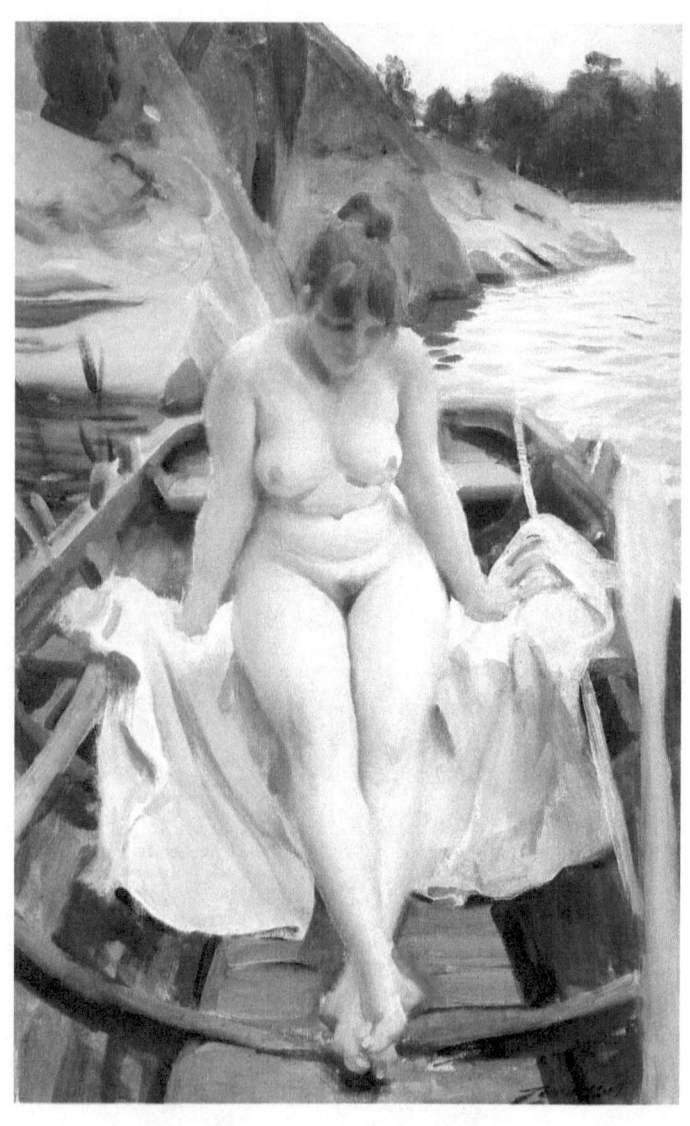

In Werner's Rowing Boat, 1917, Oil on canvas

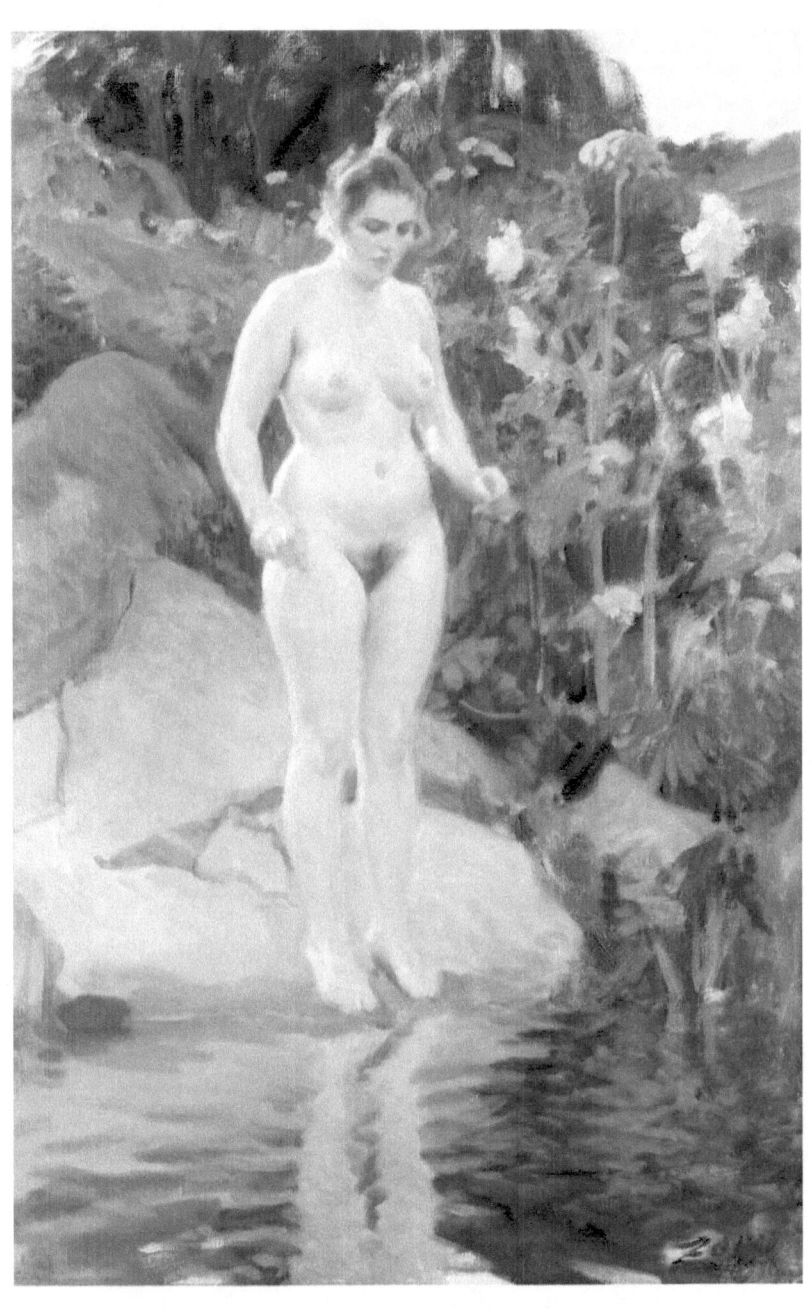

Archipelago flower, 1916, Oil on canvas

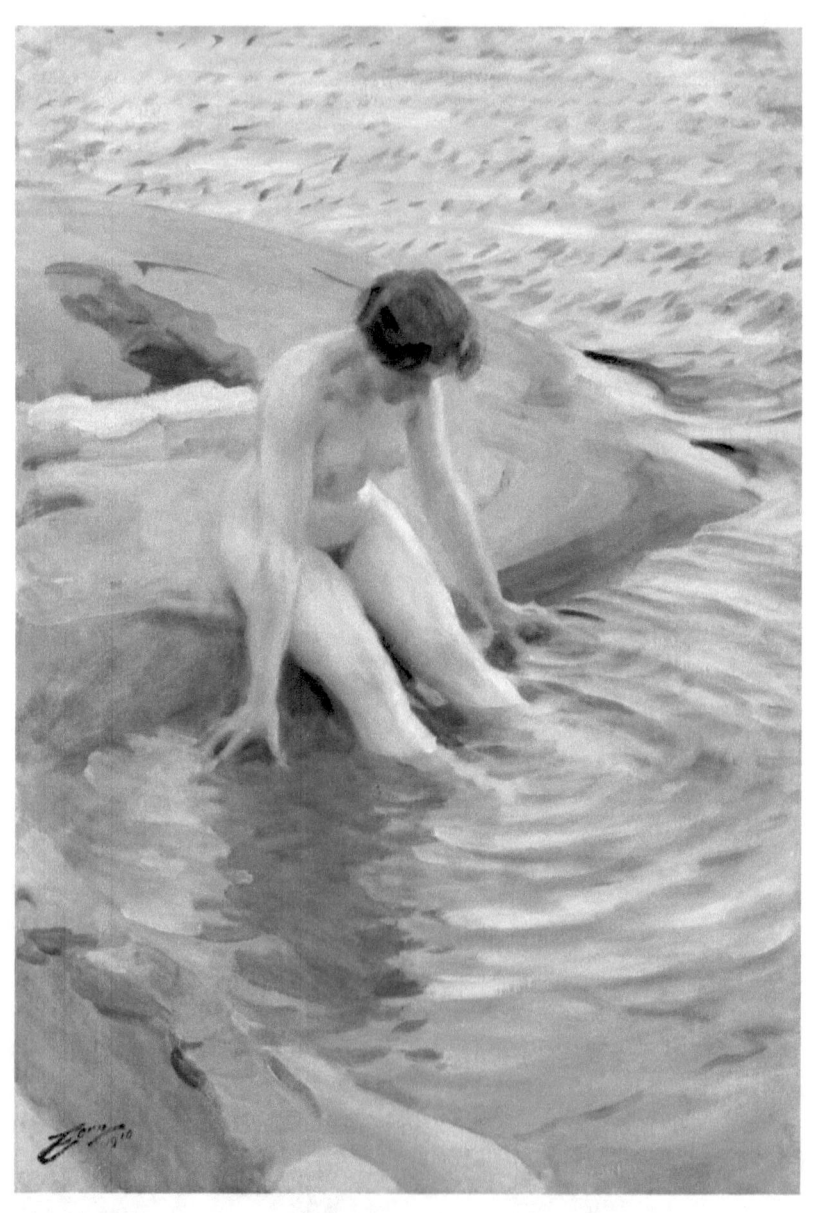

Wet, 1910, Oil on canvas

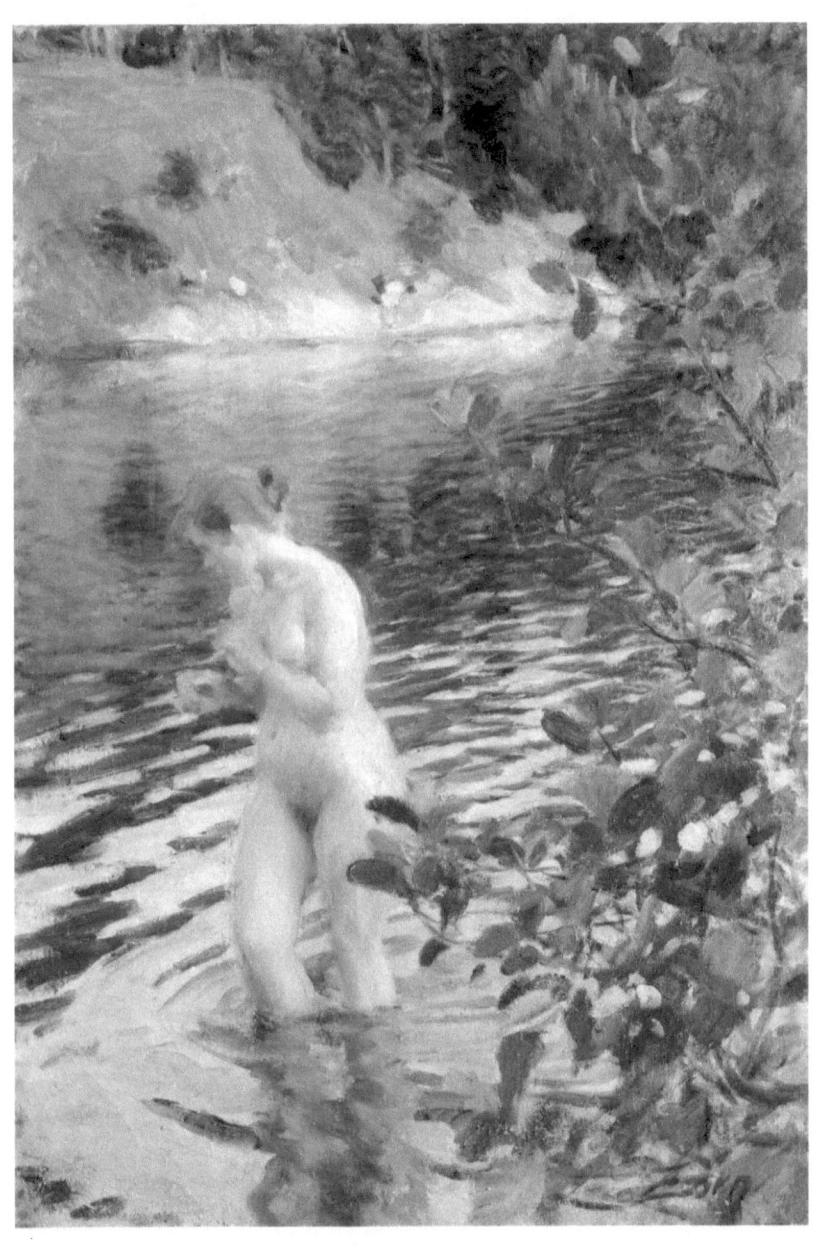

Frileuse, 1920, Oil on canvas

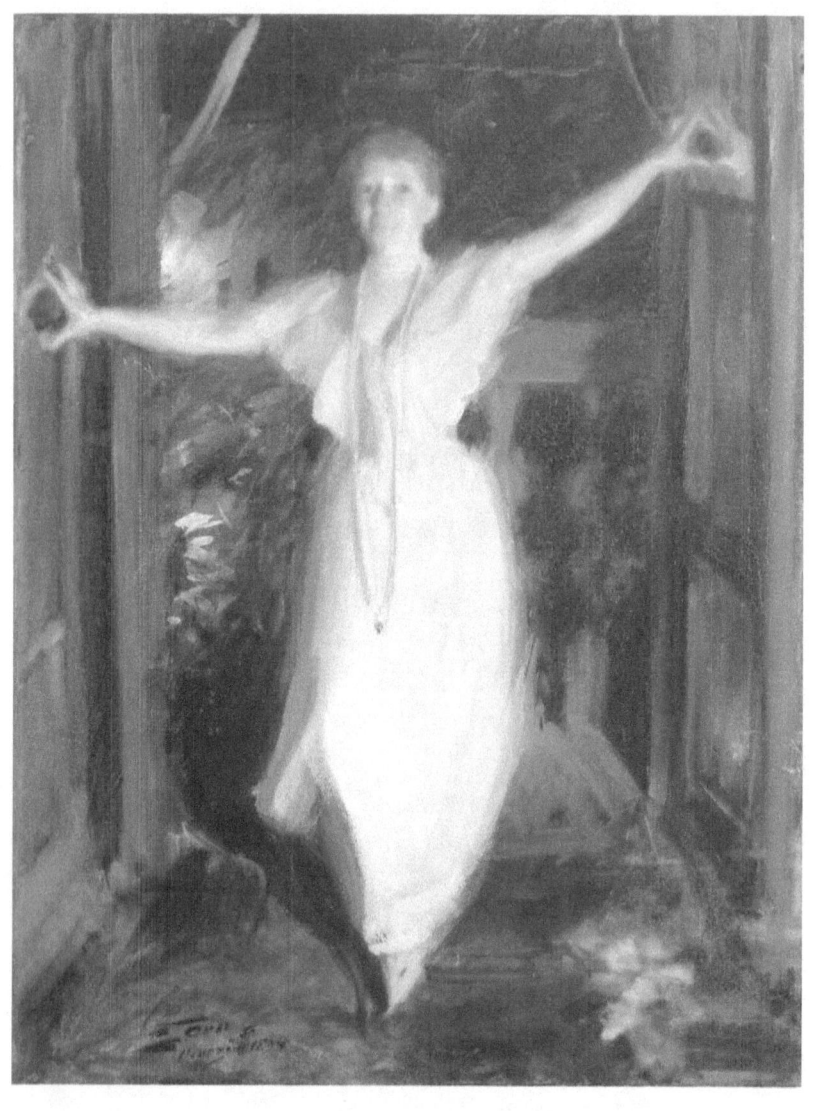

Isabella Stewart Gardner in Venice, 1894, oil on canvas

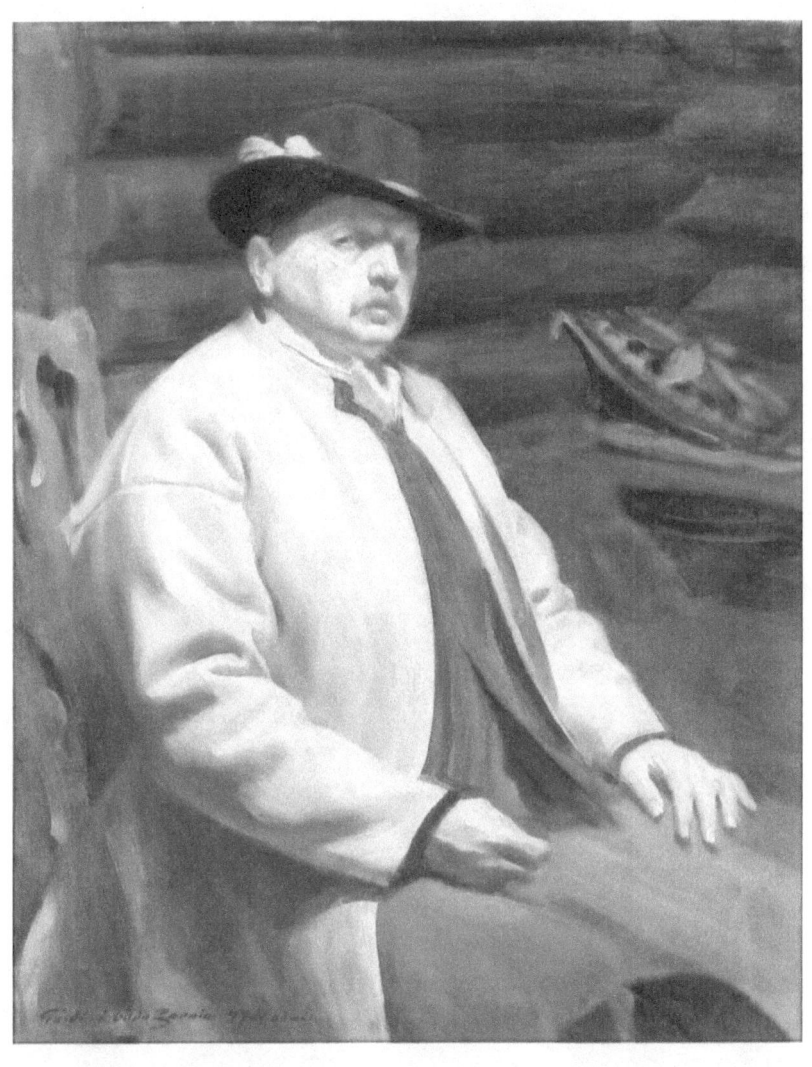

Self-Portrait, 1907, oil on canvas

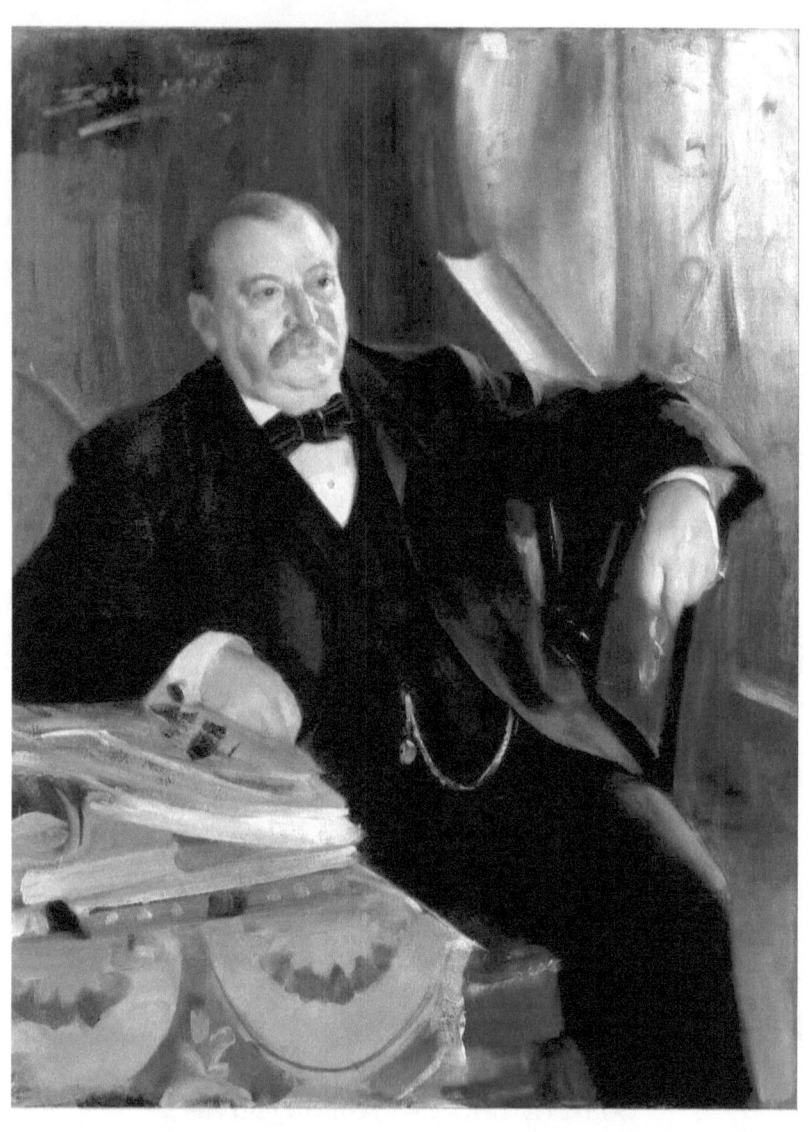

Grover Cleveland, 1899, oil on canvas

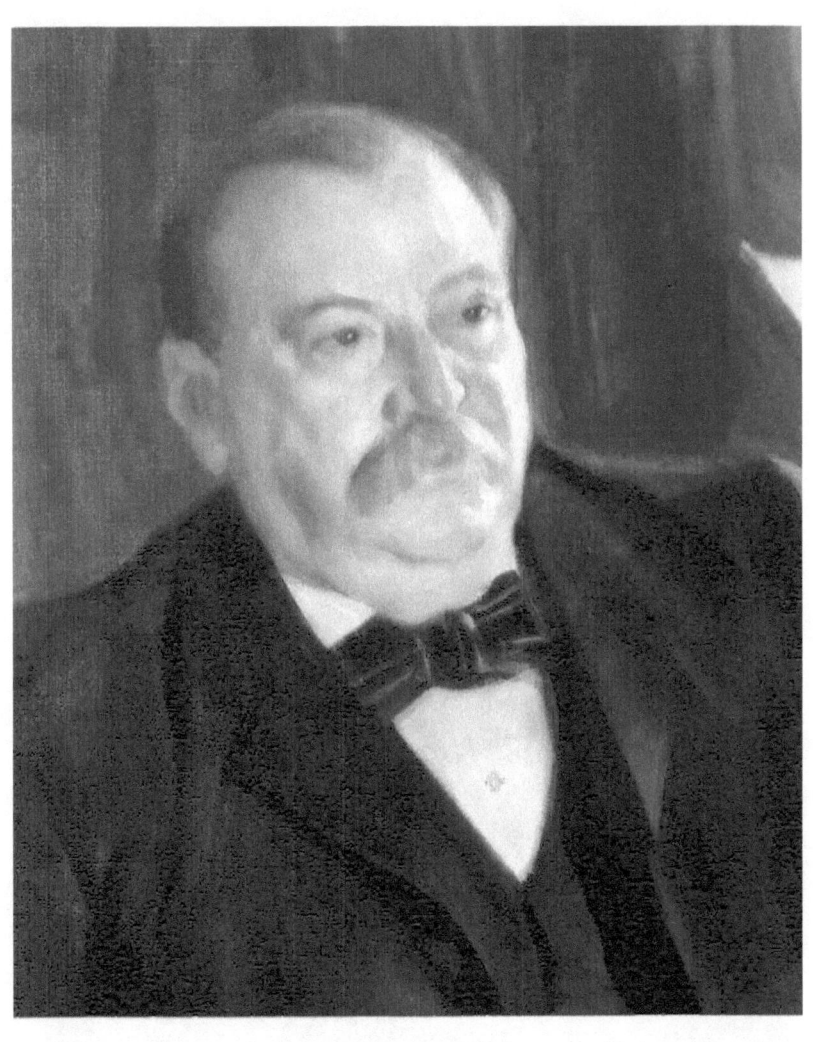

Grover Cleveland, Detail, 1899, oil on canvas

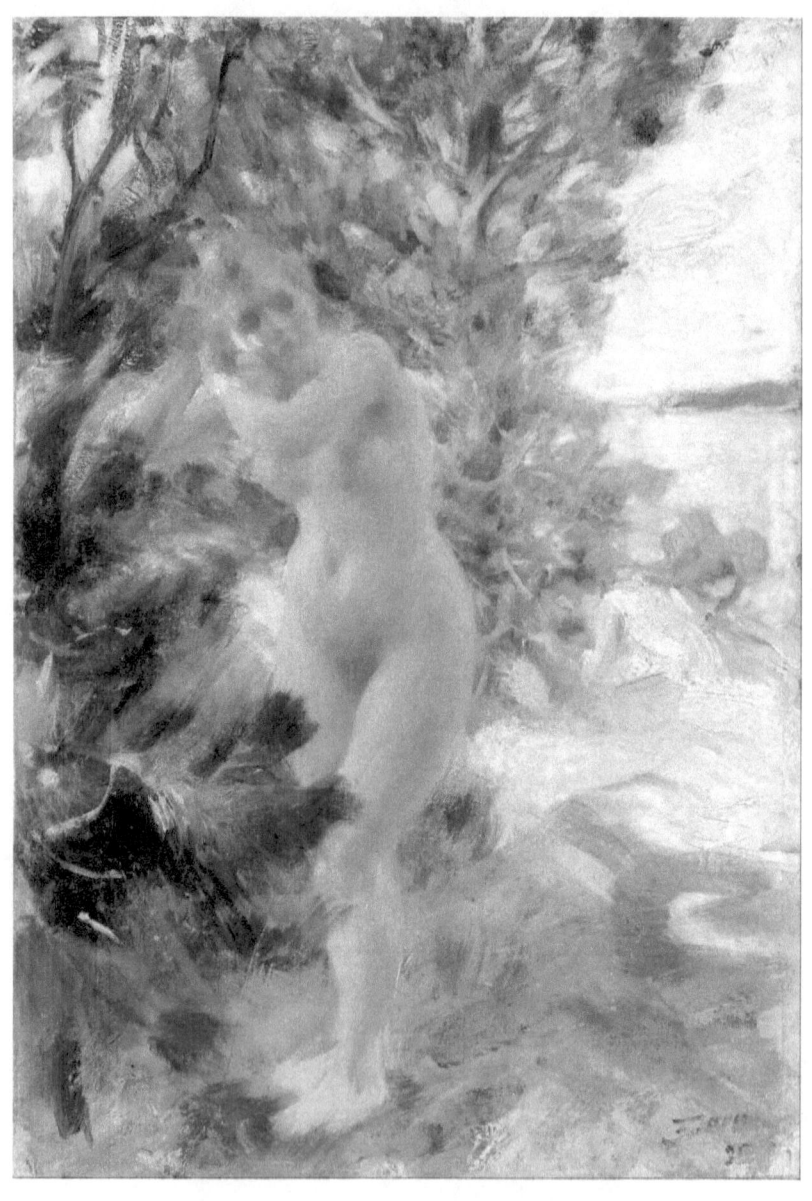

After the Bath, 1895, oil on canvas

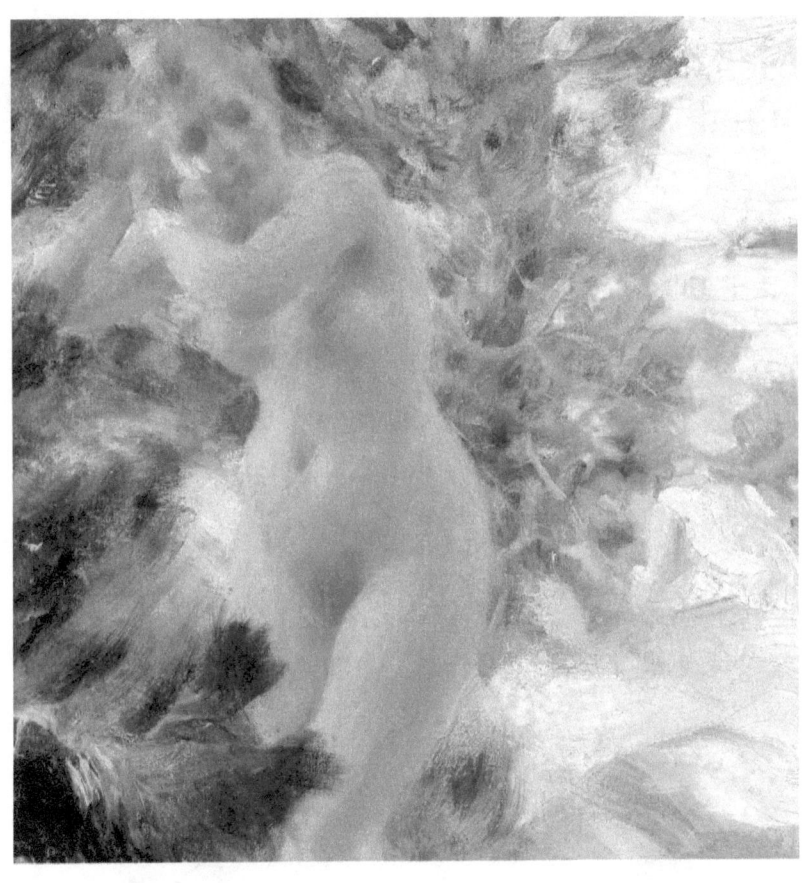

After the Bath, Detail, 1895, oil on canvas

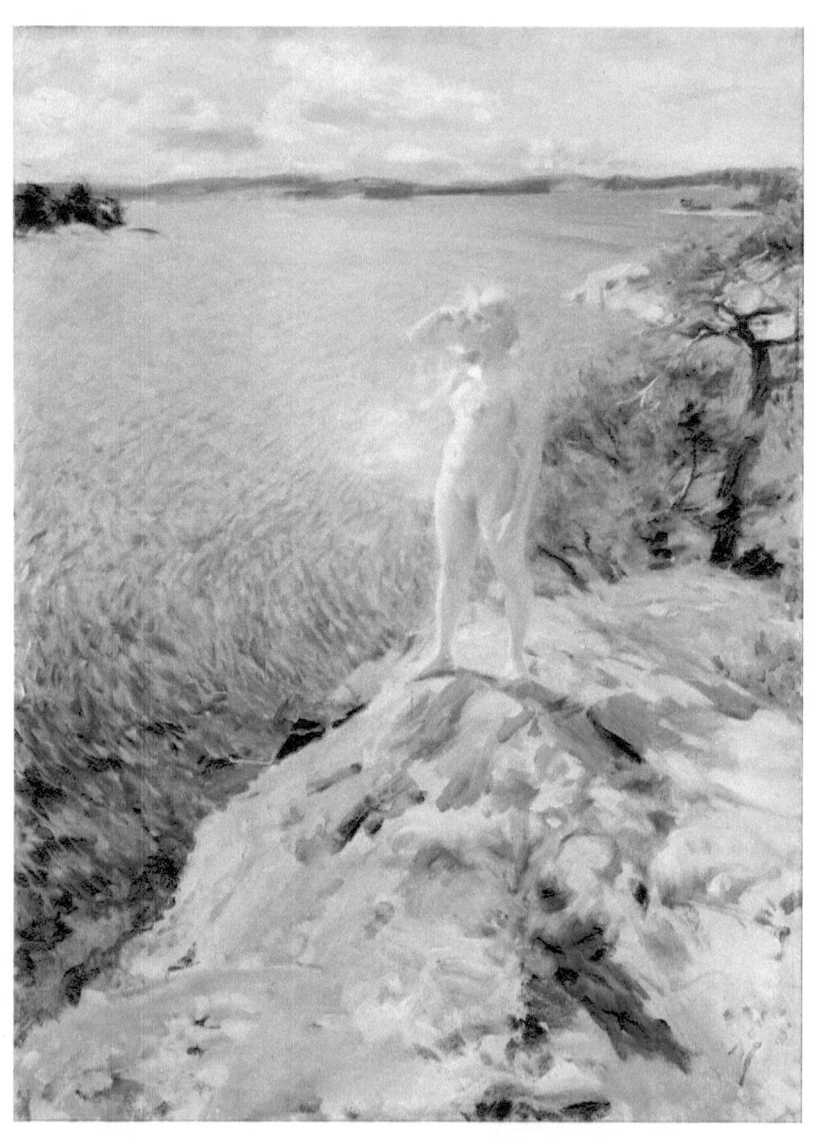

In the Skerries, 1894, oil on canvas

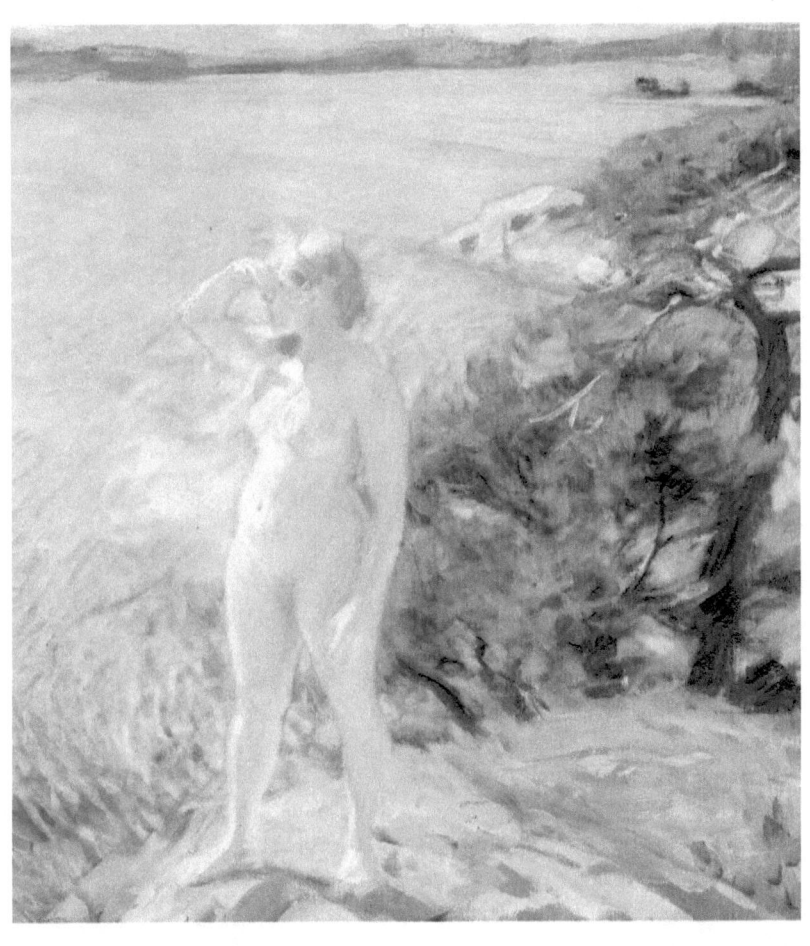

In the Skerries, Detail, 1894, oil on canvas

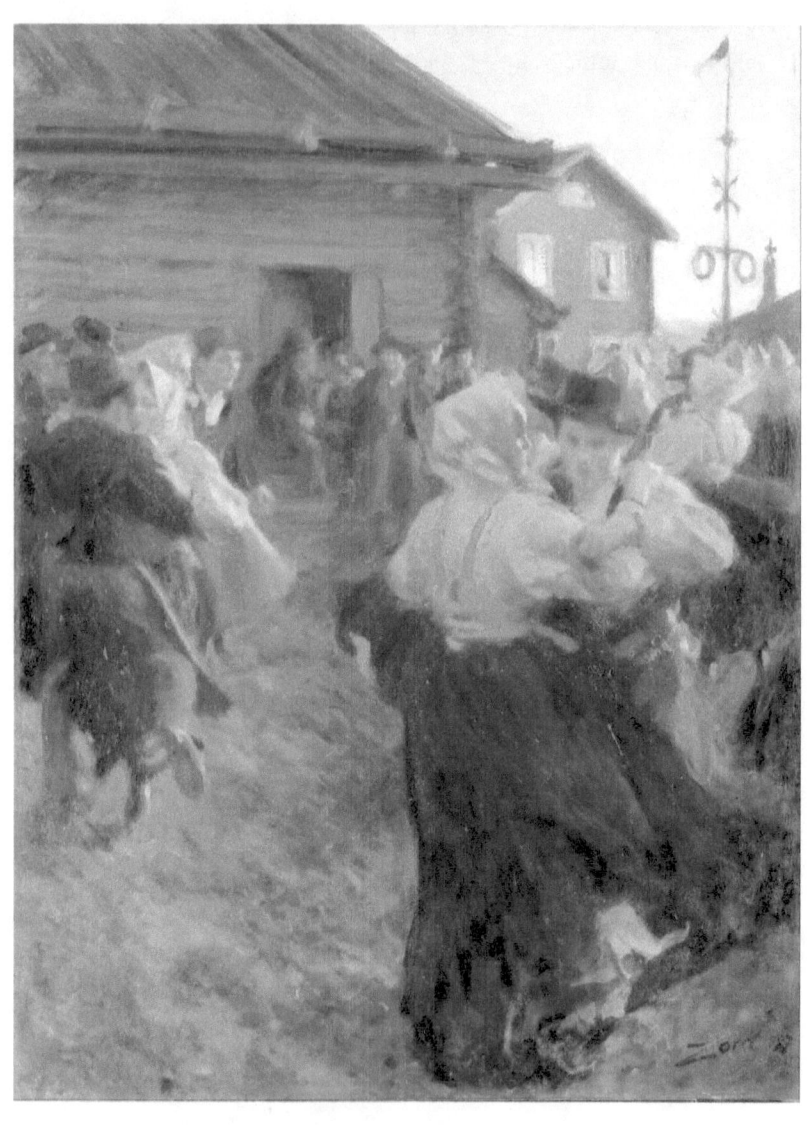

Midsummer Dance, 1897, oil on canvas

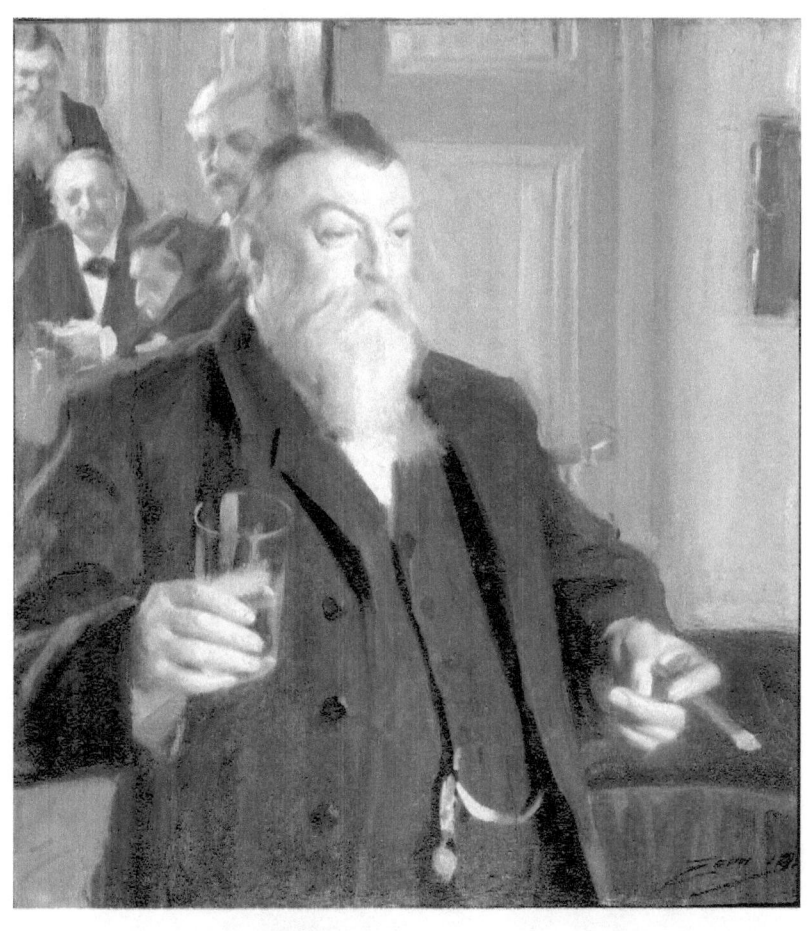

A Toast in the Idun Society, 1892, oil on canvas

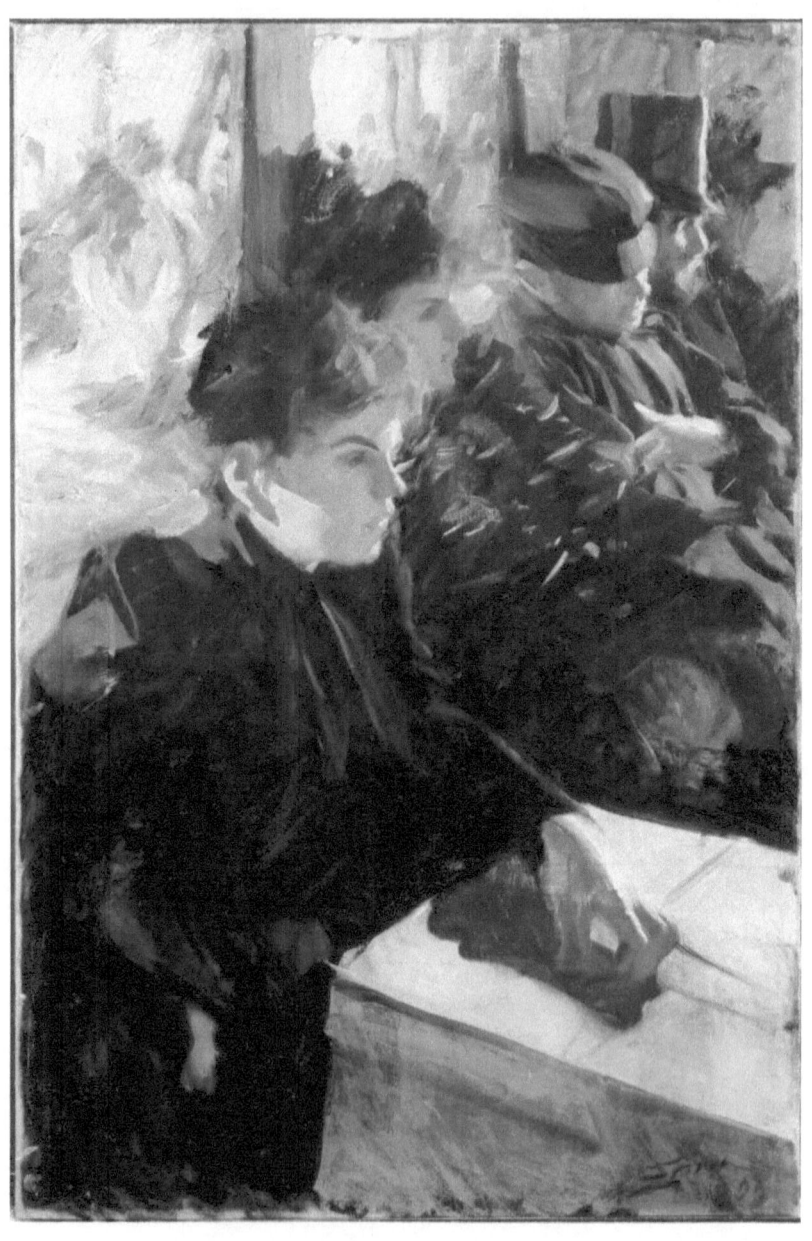

Omnibus, between 1891 and 1892, oil on canvas

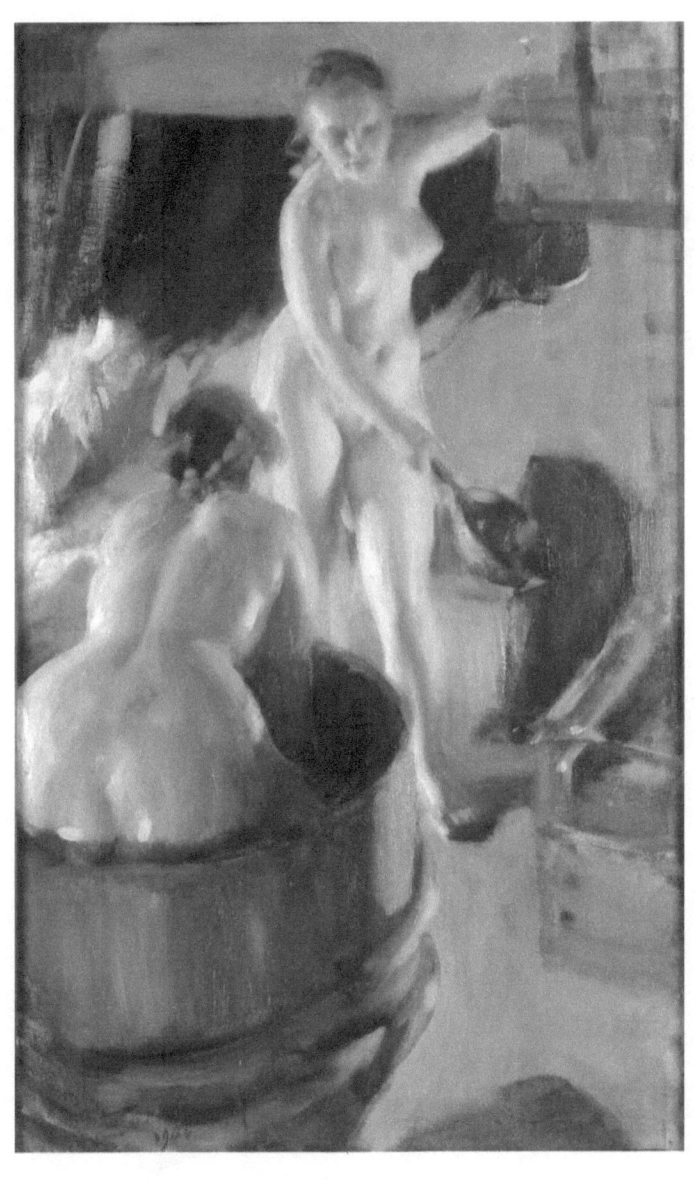

Girls from Dalarna Having a Bath, 1906, oil on canvas

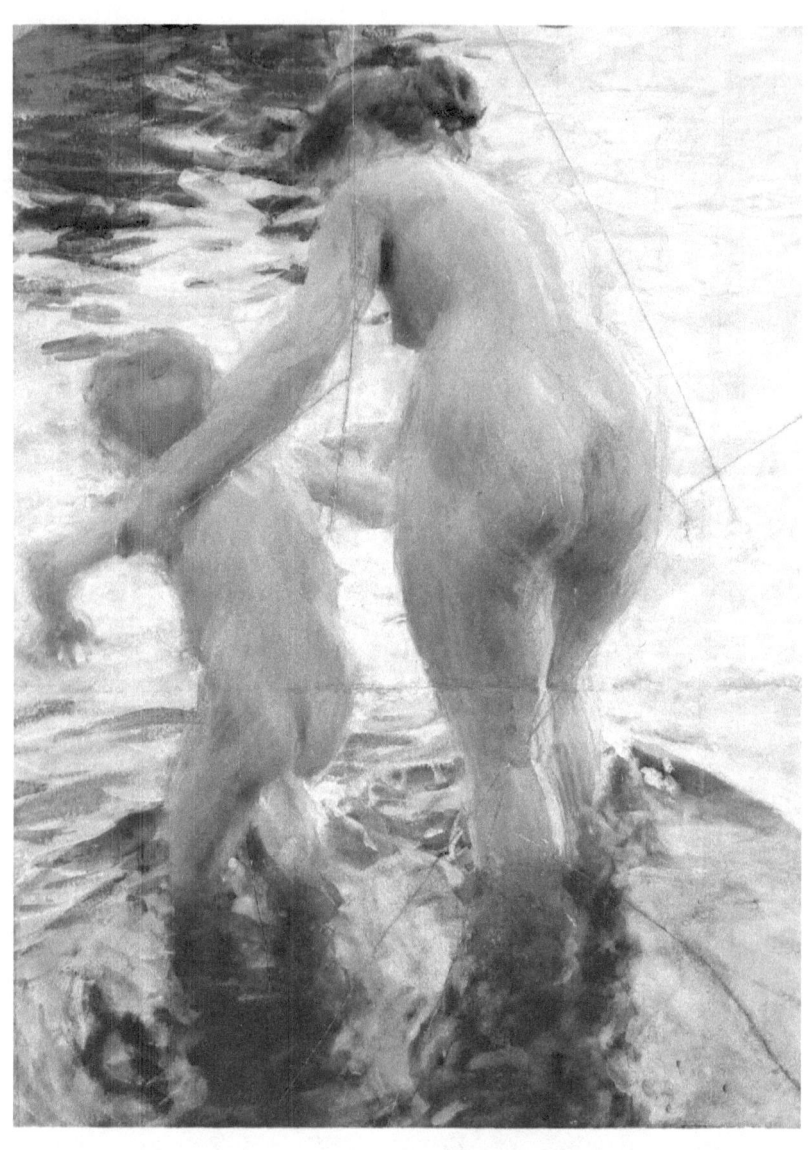

A premiere, 1888, gouache

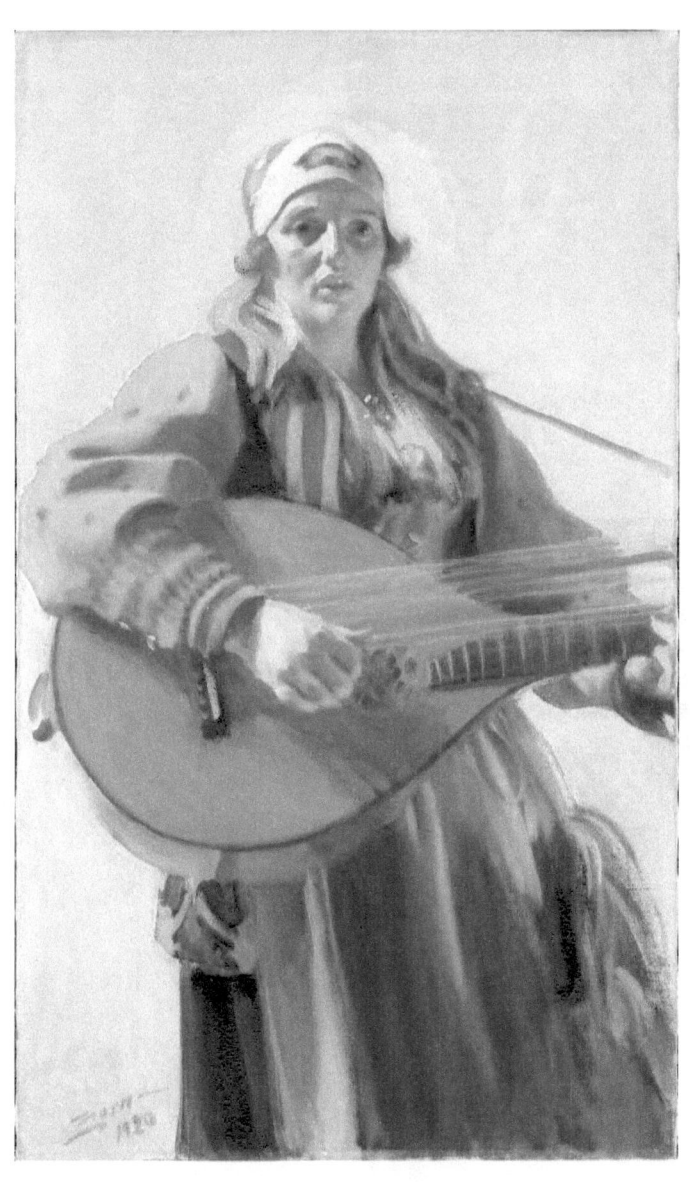

Home Tunes, 1920, oil on canvas

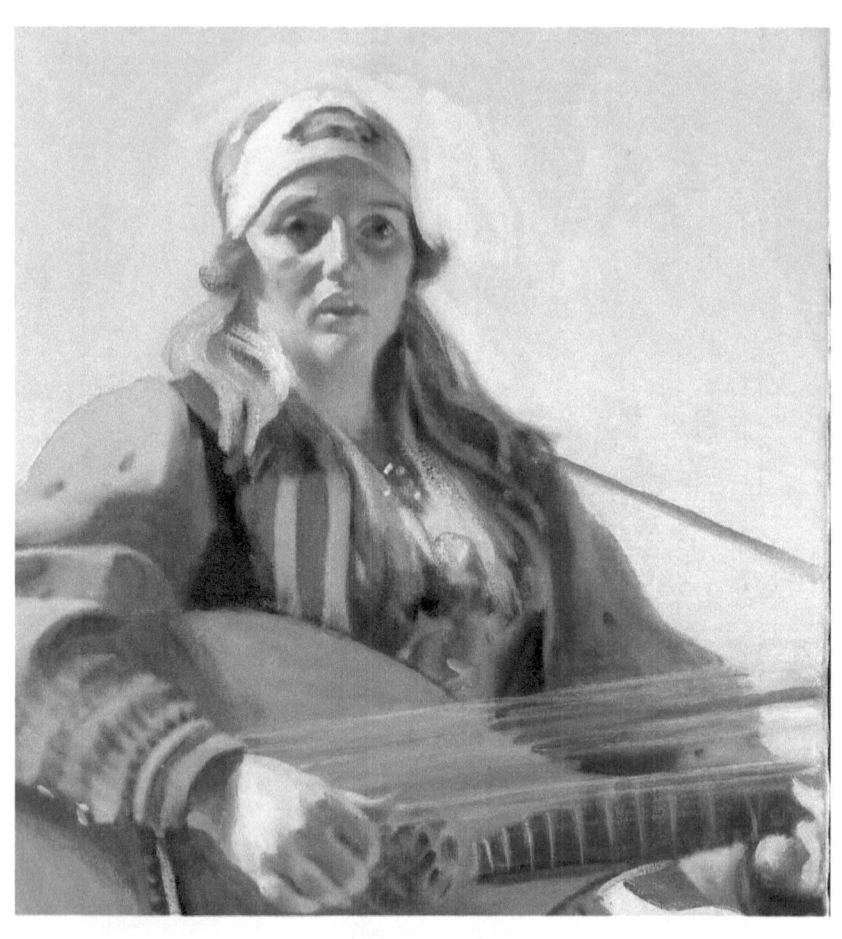

Home Tunes, Detail, 1920, oil on canvas

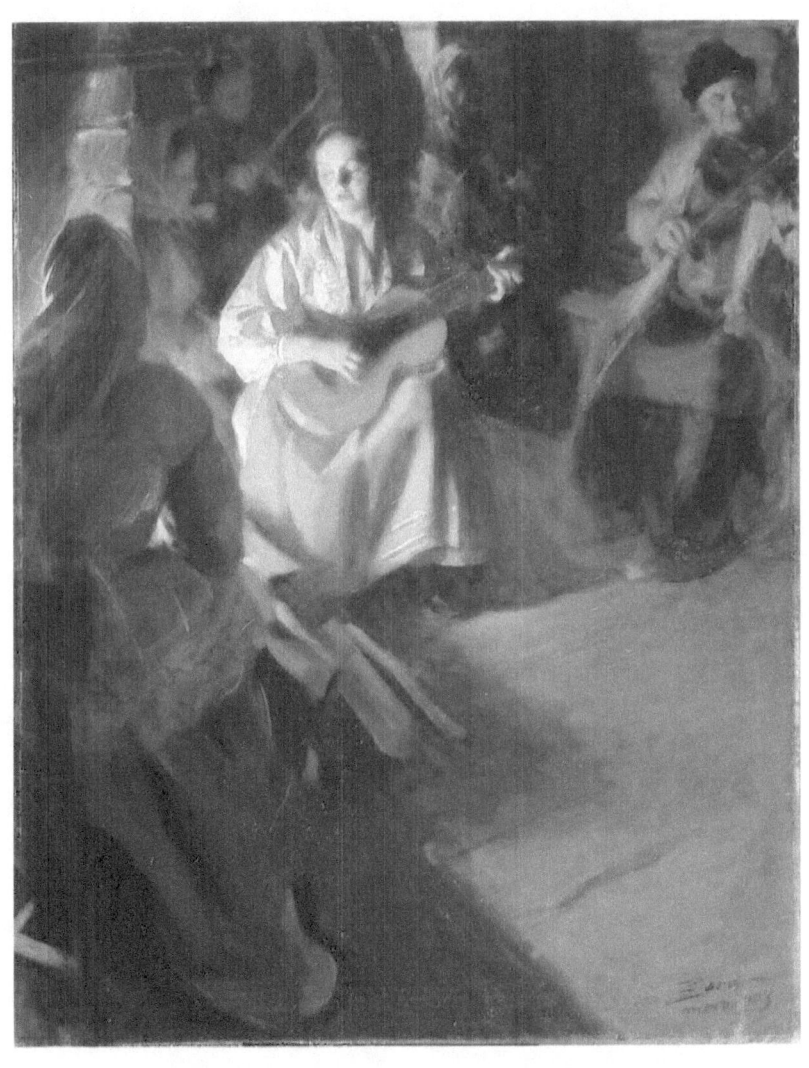

A Musical Family, 1905, oil on canvas

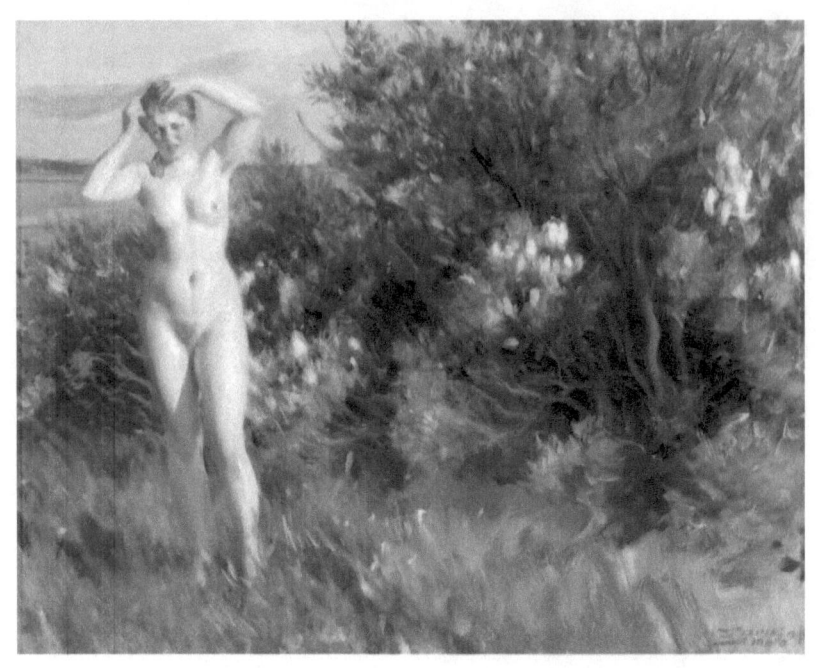

By Lake Siljan, 1905, oil on canvas

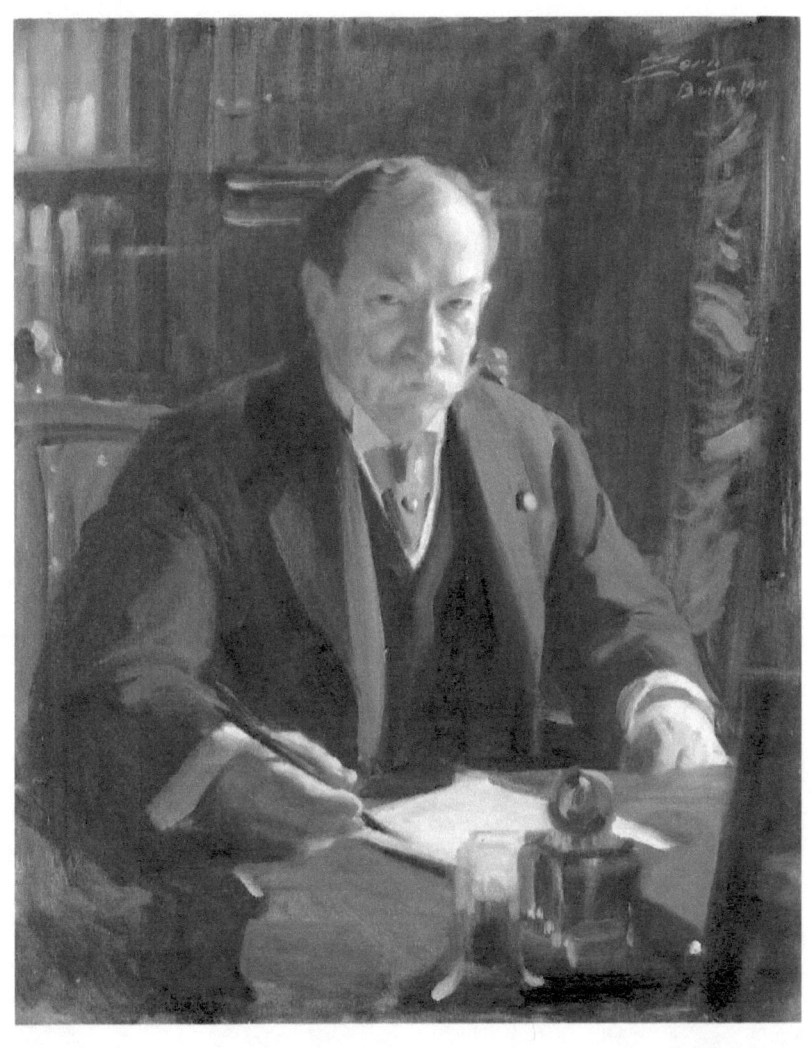

Ambassador David Jayne Hill, 1911, oil on canvas

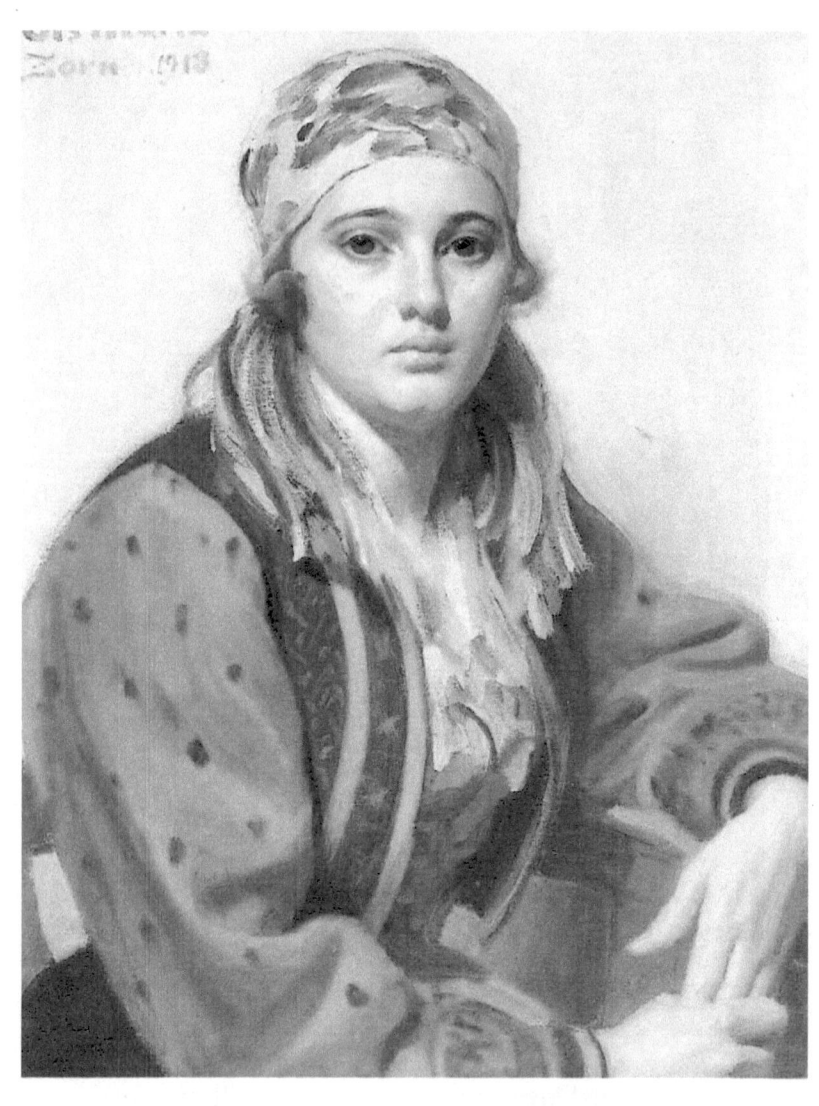

Ols Maria, 1918, oil on canvas

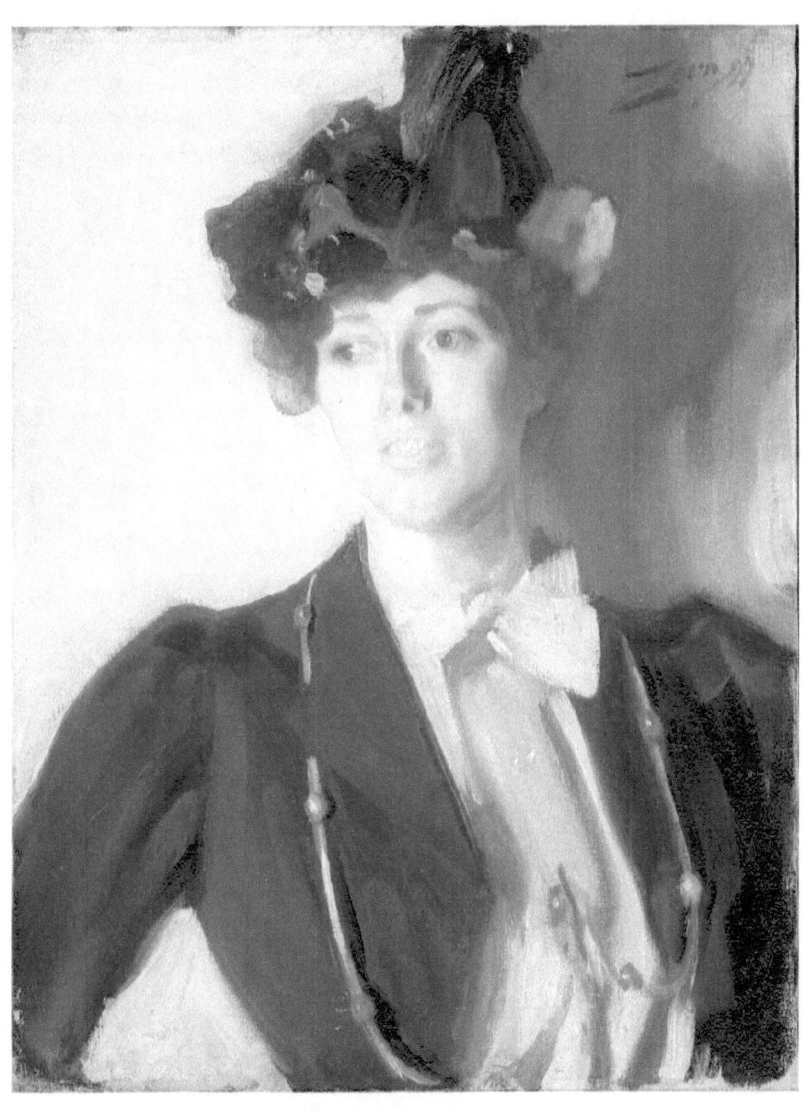

Martha Dana, 1899, oil on canvas

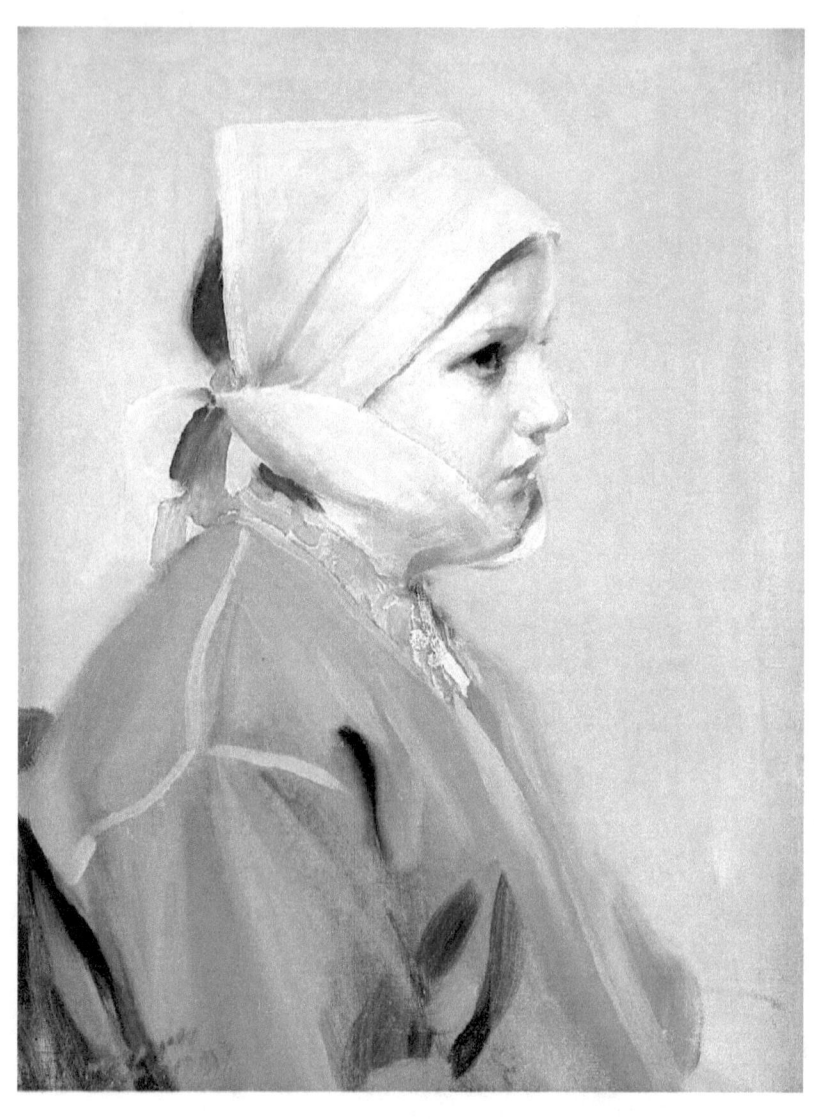

Confirmed, 1908, oil on canvas

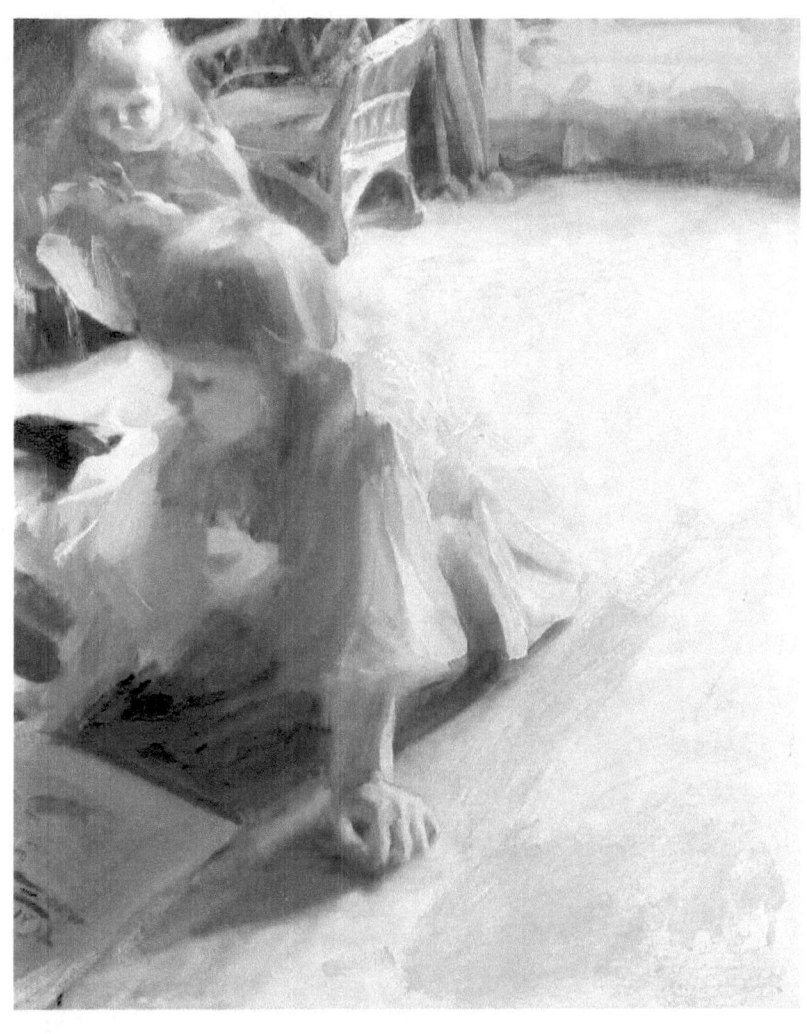

A Portrait of the Daughters of Ramon Subercasseaux,
1892, oil on canvas

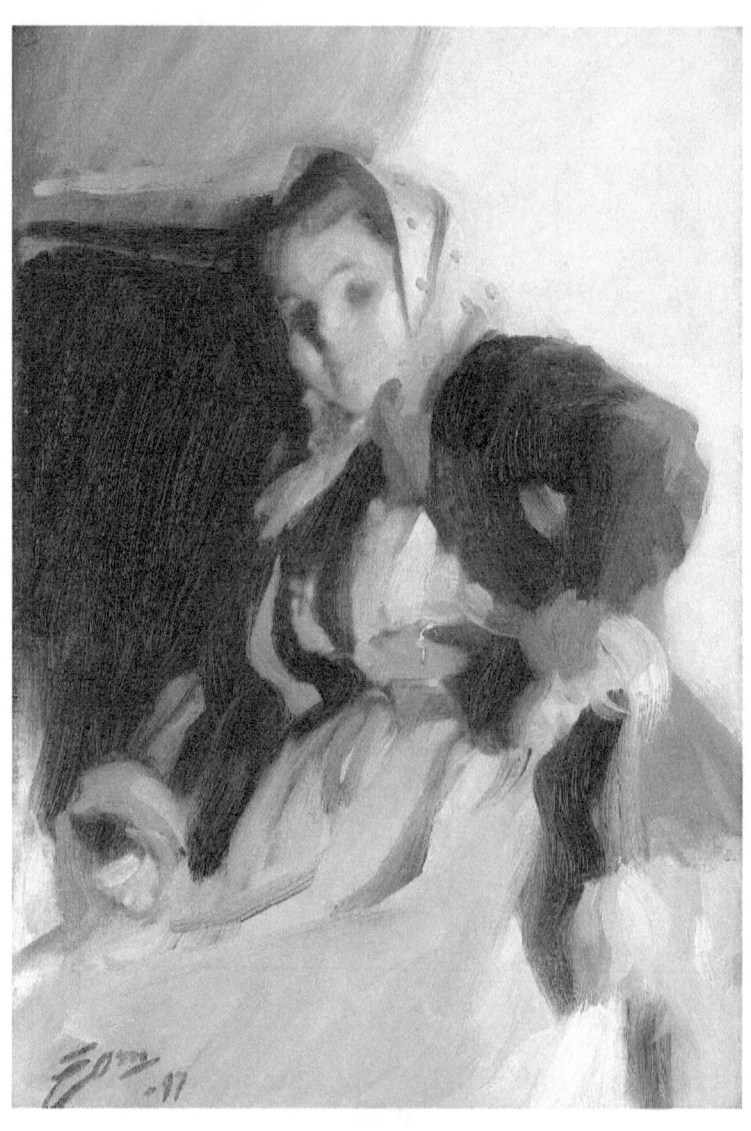

By the fireplace, 1897, oil on canvas

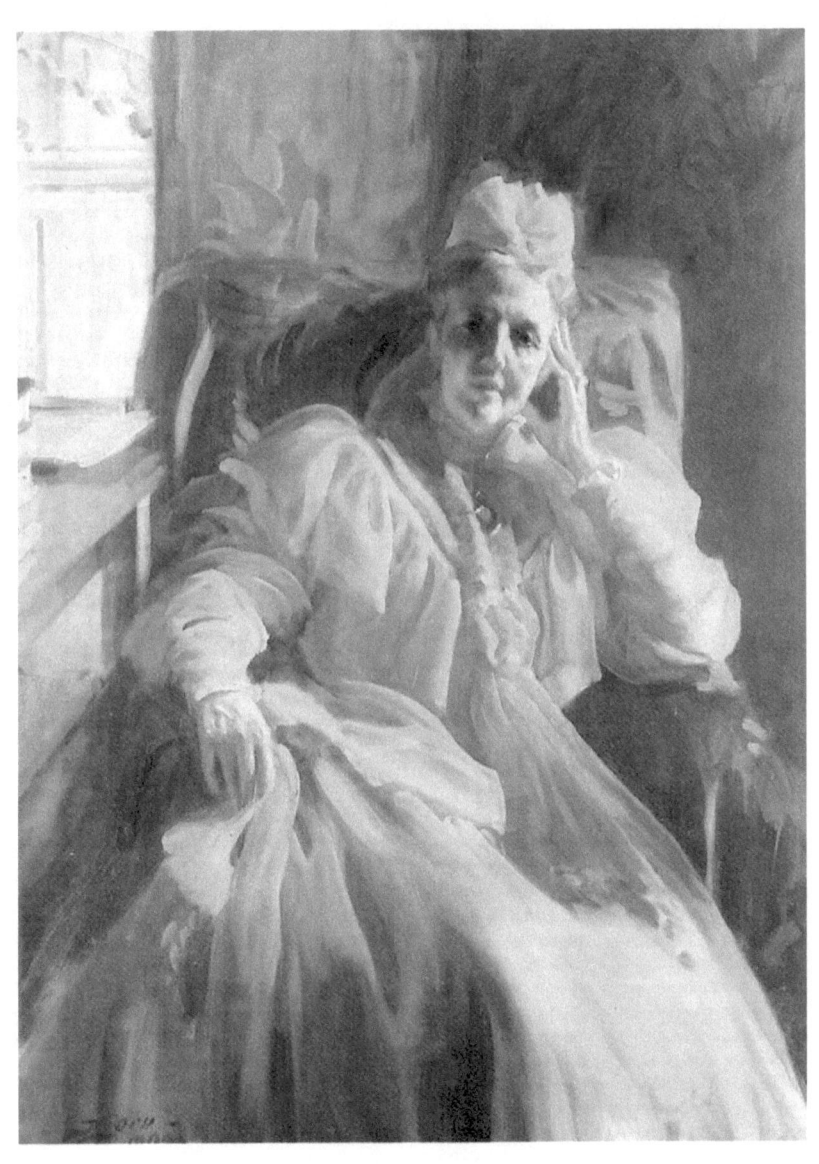

Queen Sophia, oil on canvas

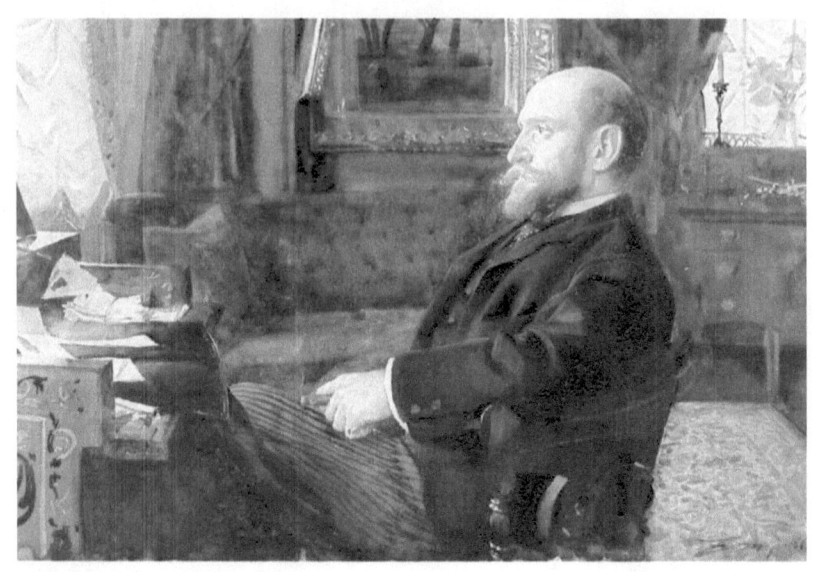

Ernest Cassel, 1886, oil on canvas

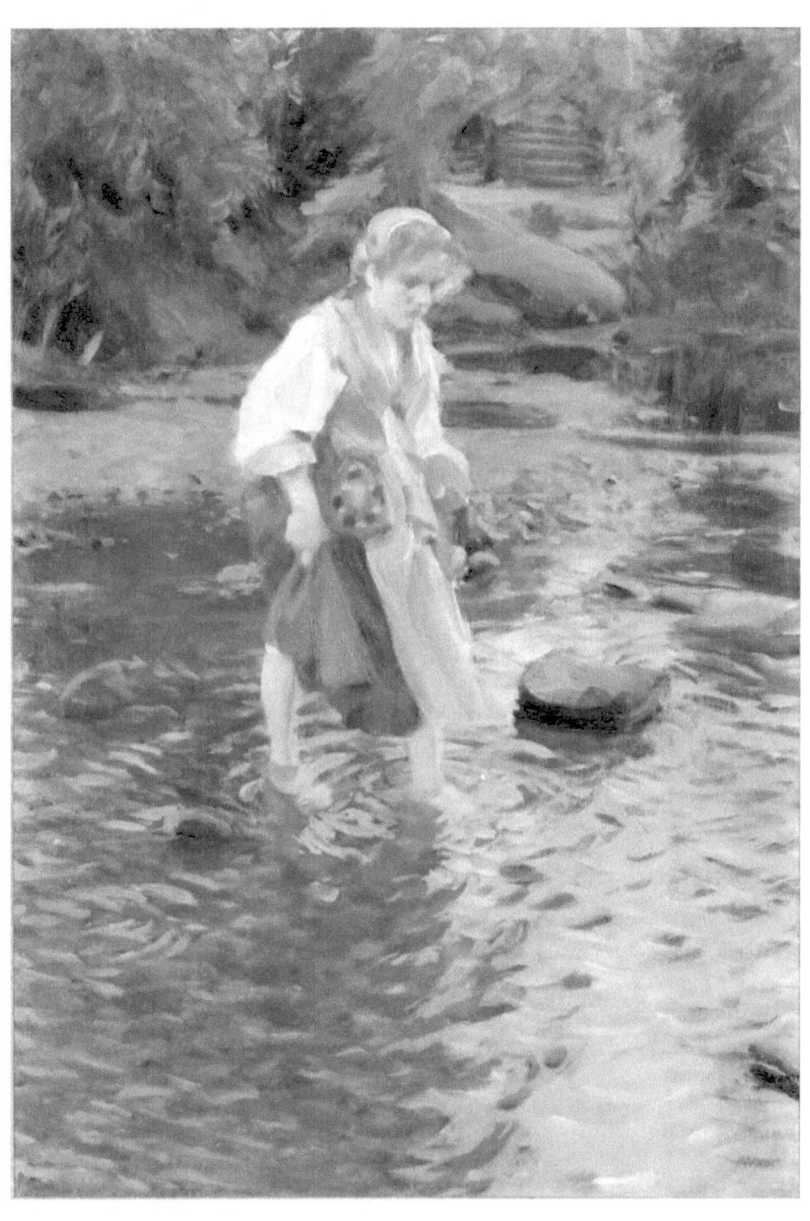

The Girl from Alvdalen, 1911, oil on canvas

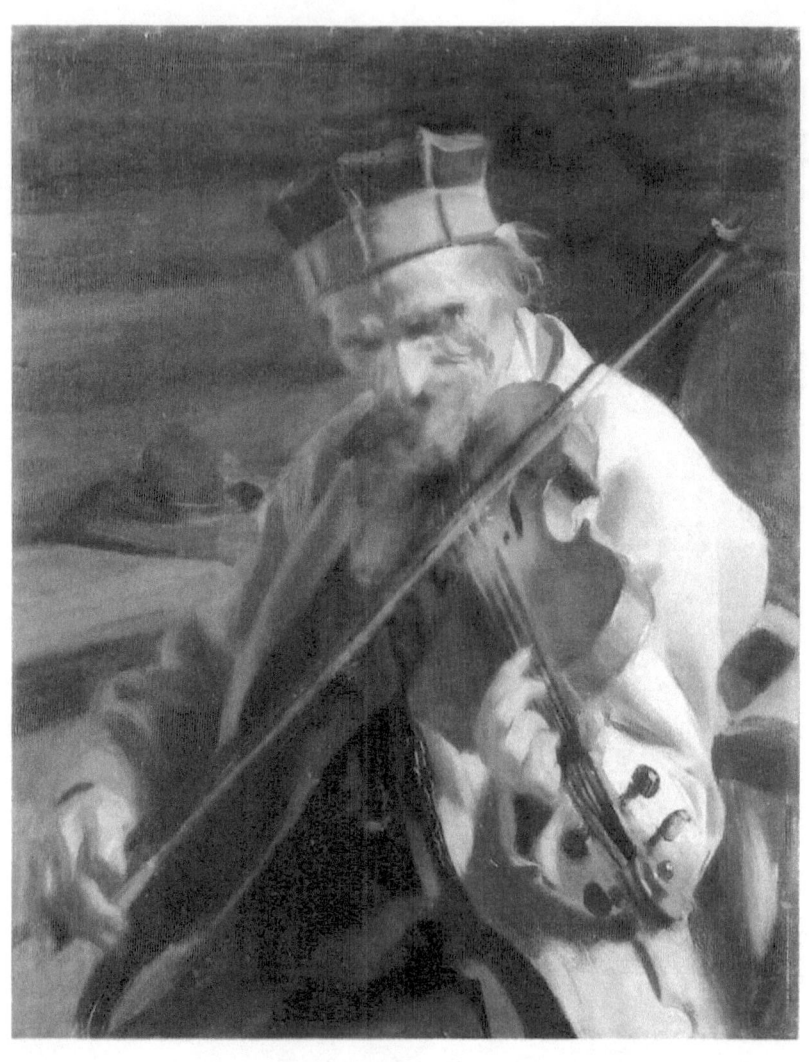

Hins Anders, 1904, oil on canvas

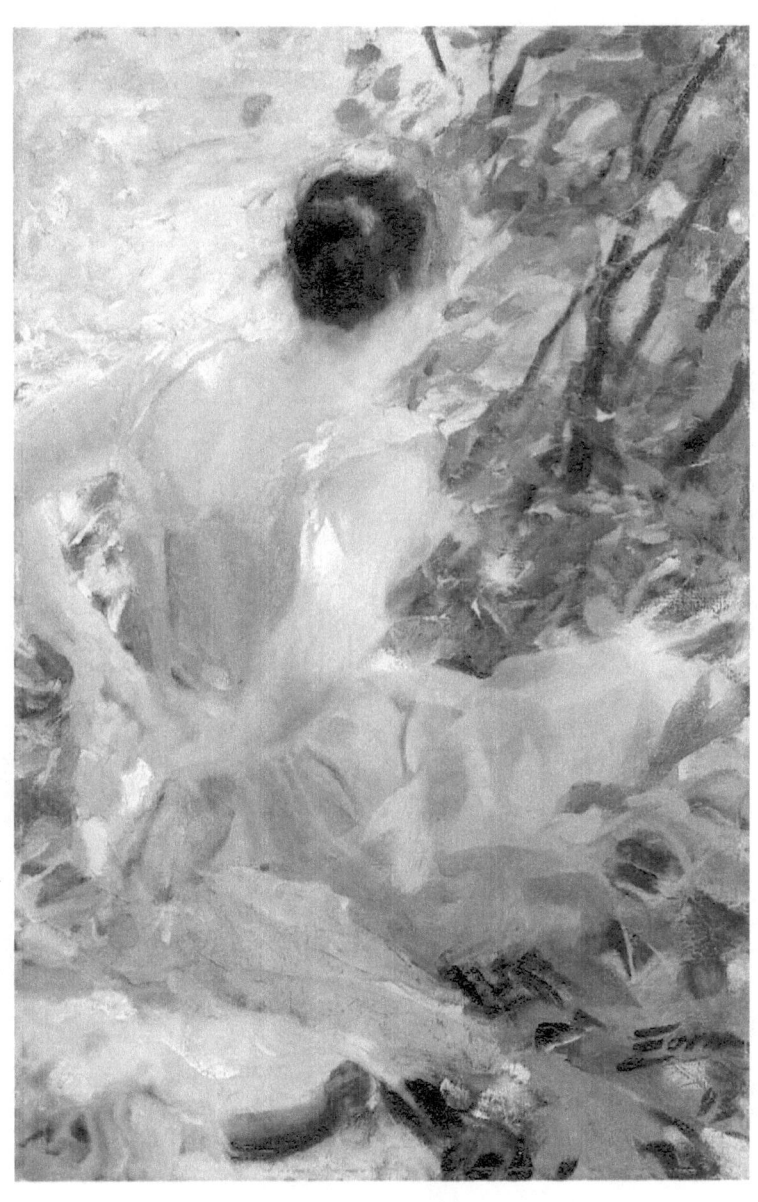

Woman getting dressed, 1893, oil on canvas

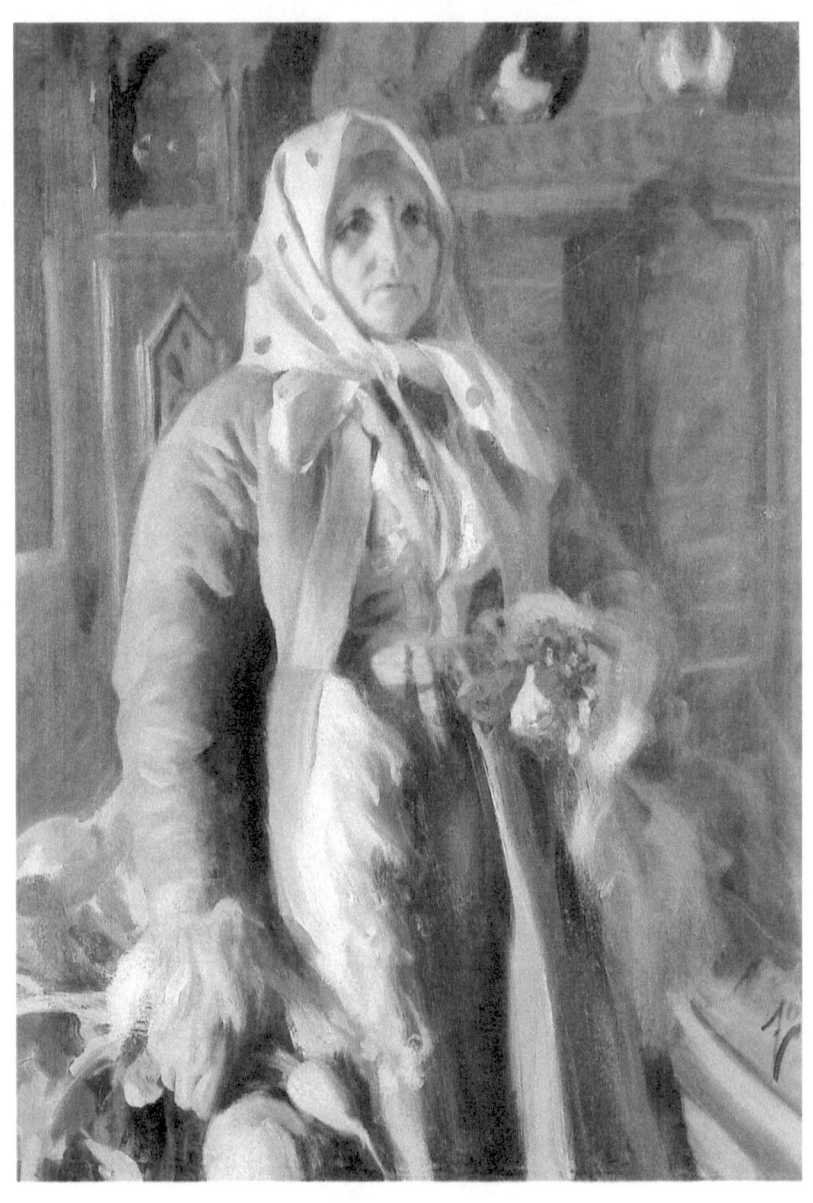

Mona, 1898, oil on canvas

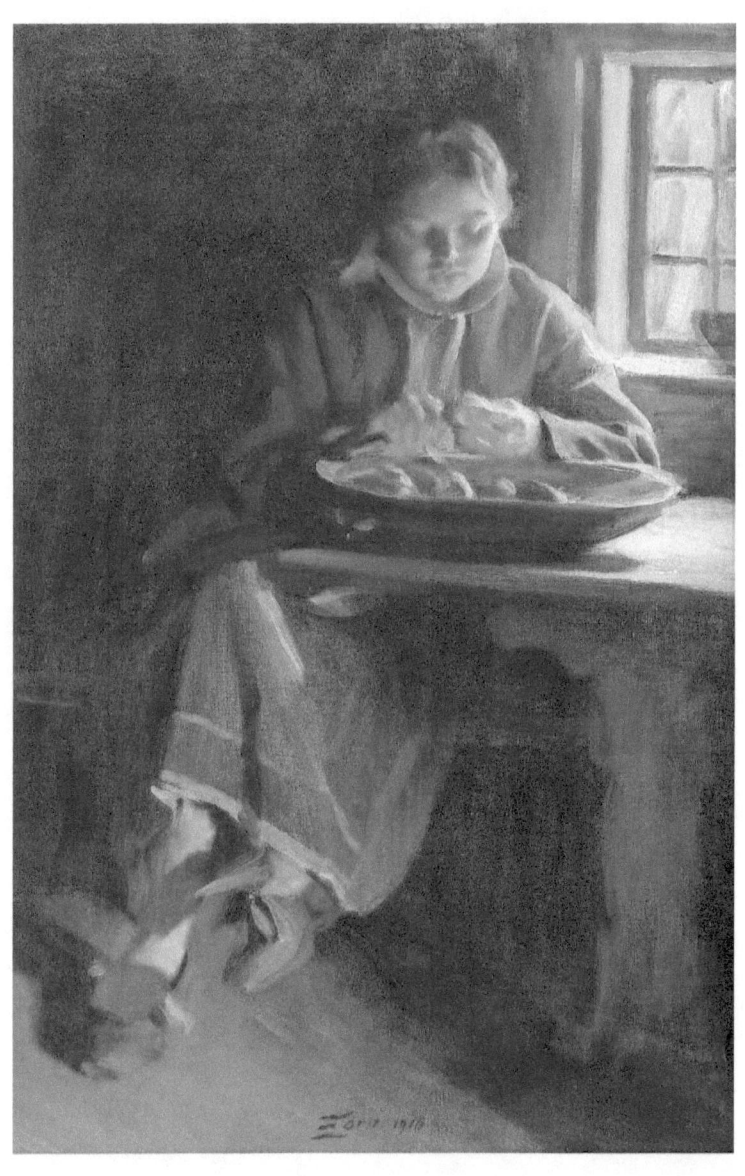

Peeling potatoes, 1916, oil on canvas

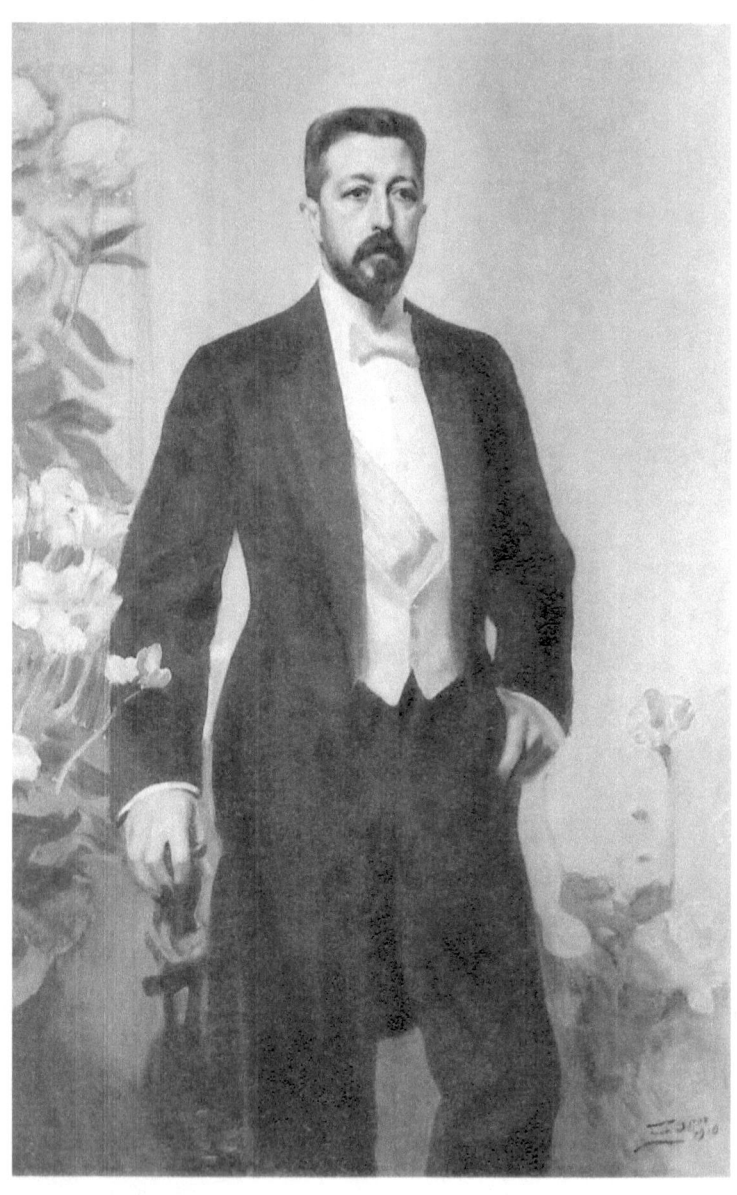

Prince Eugen, Duke of Narke, 1910, oil on canvas

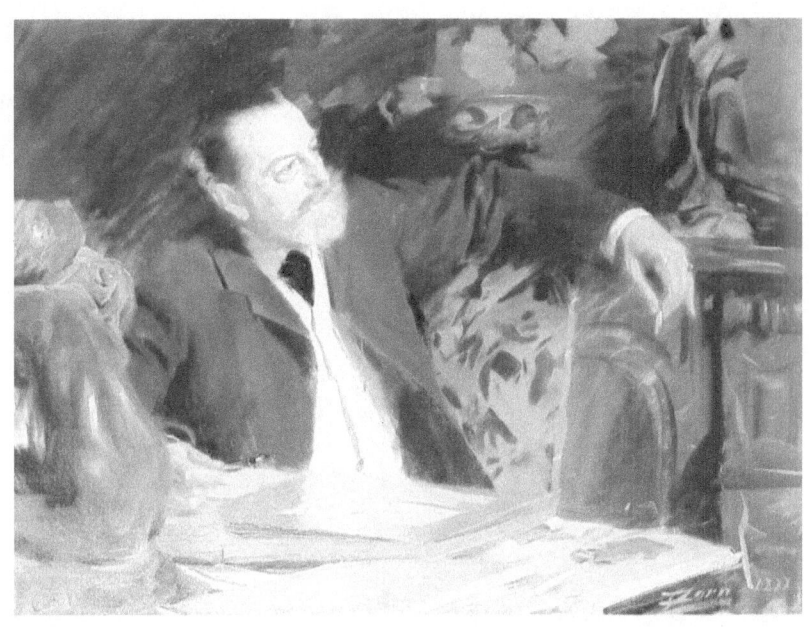

Portrait Antonin Proust, 1888, oil on canvas

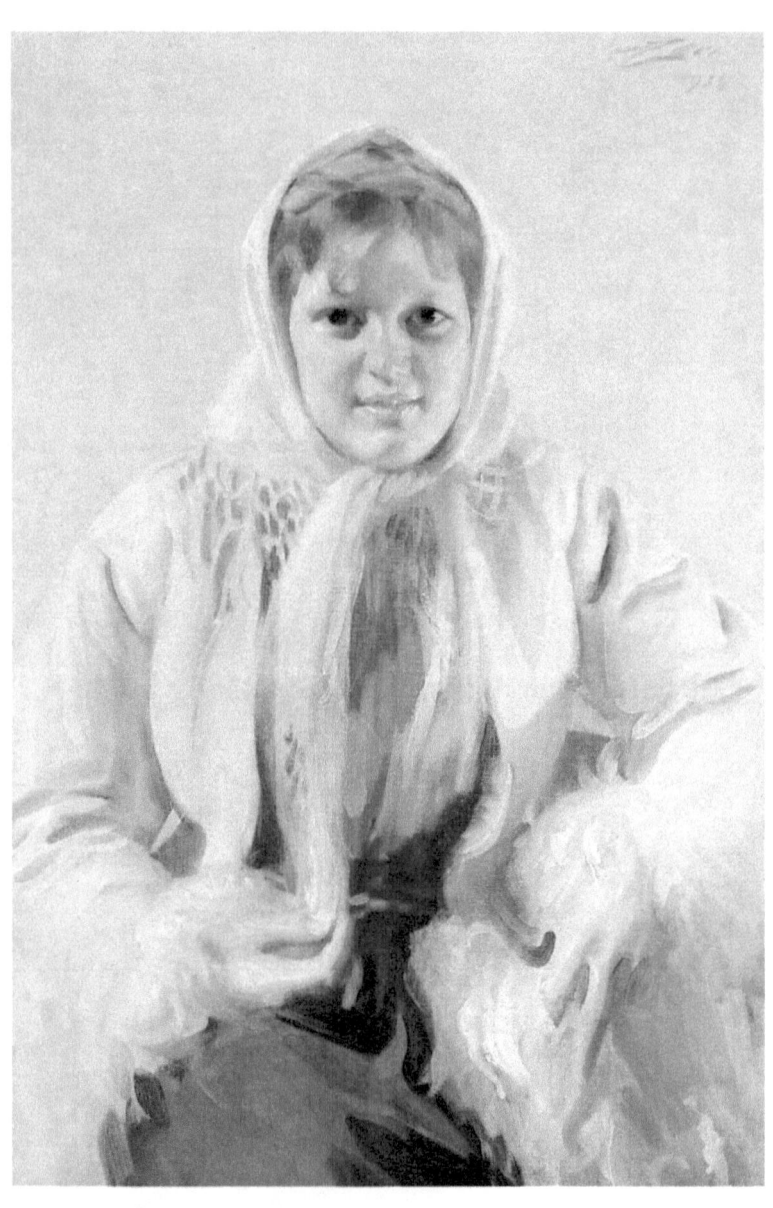

Lady from Mora, 1916, oil on canvas

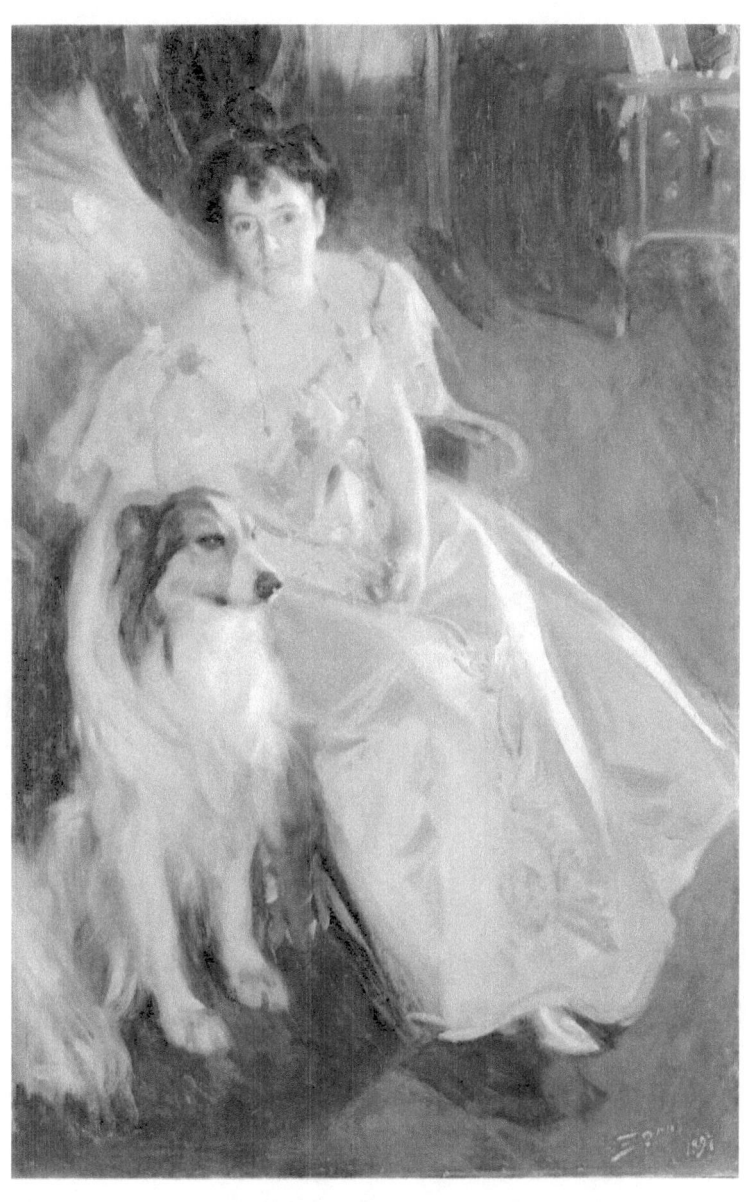

Portrait of Mrs Bacon, 1897, oil on canvas

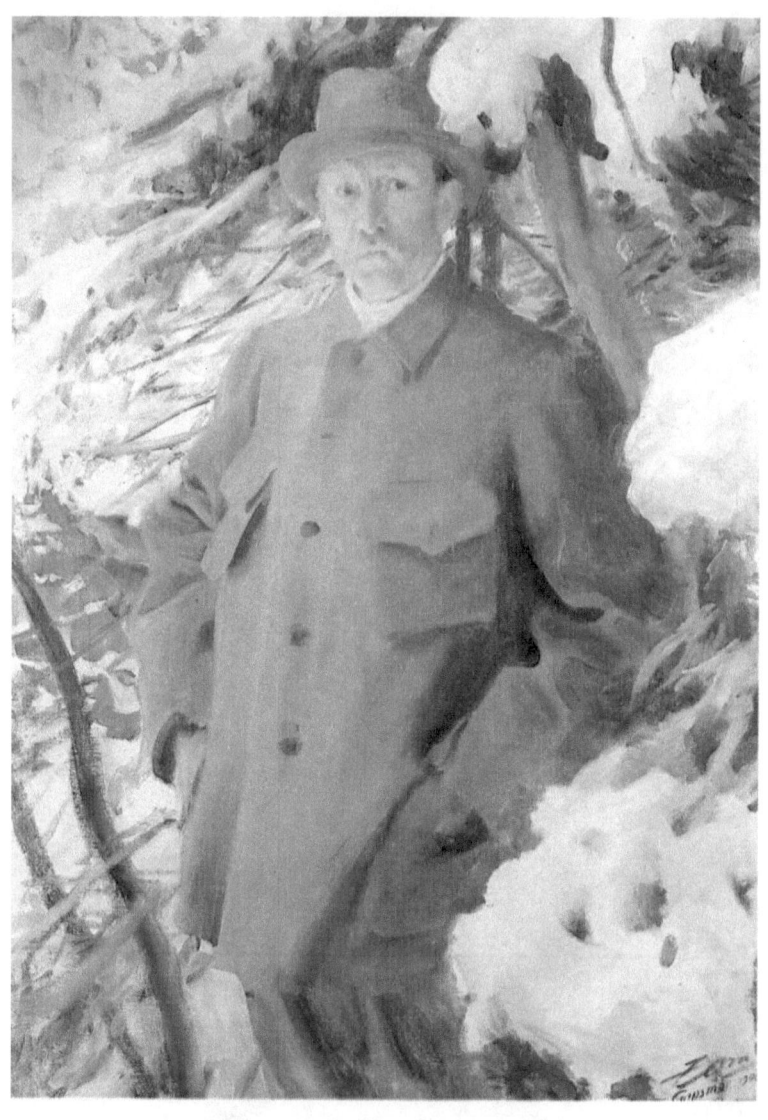

The Painter Bruno Liljefors, 1906, oil on canvas

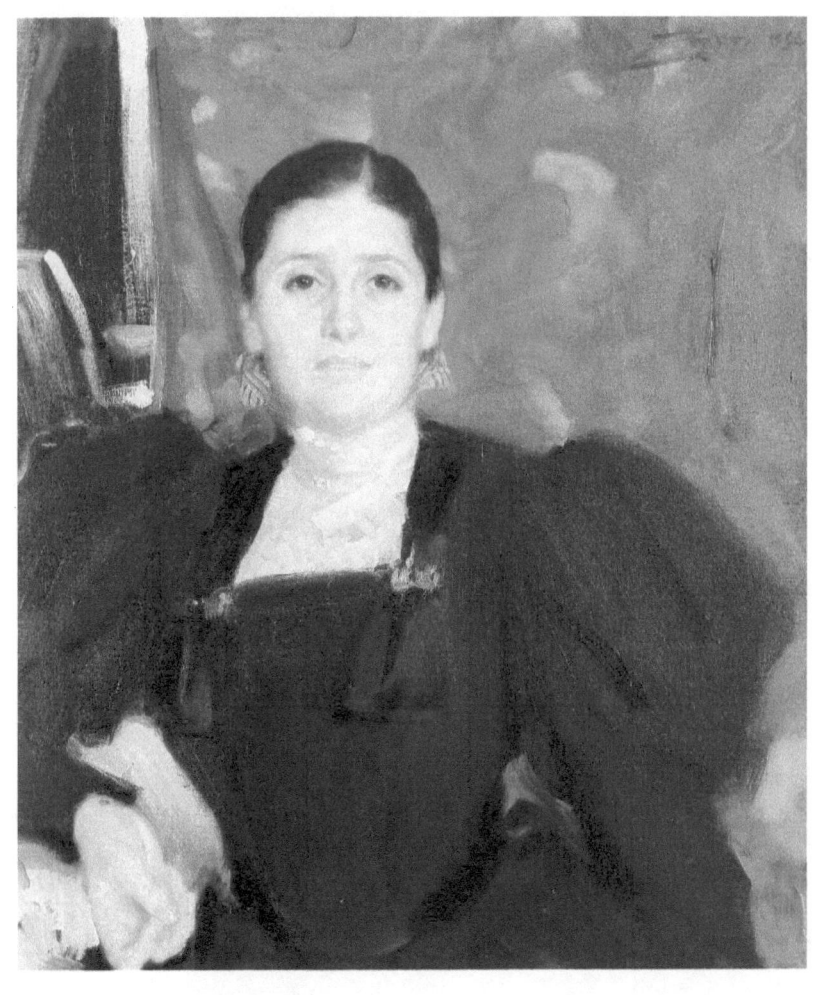

Portrait of Martha Marckwald, 1896, oil on canvas

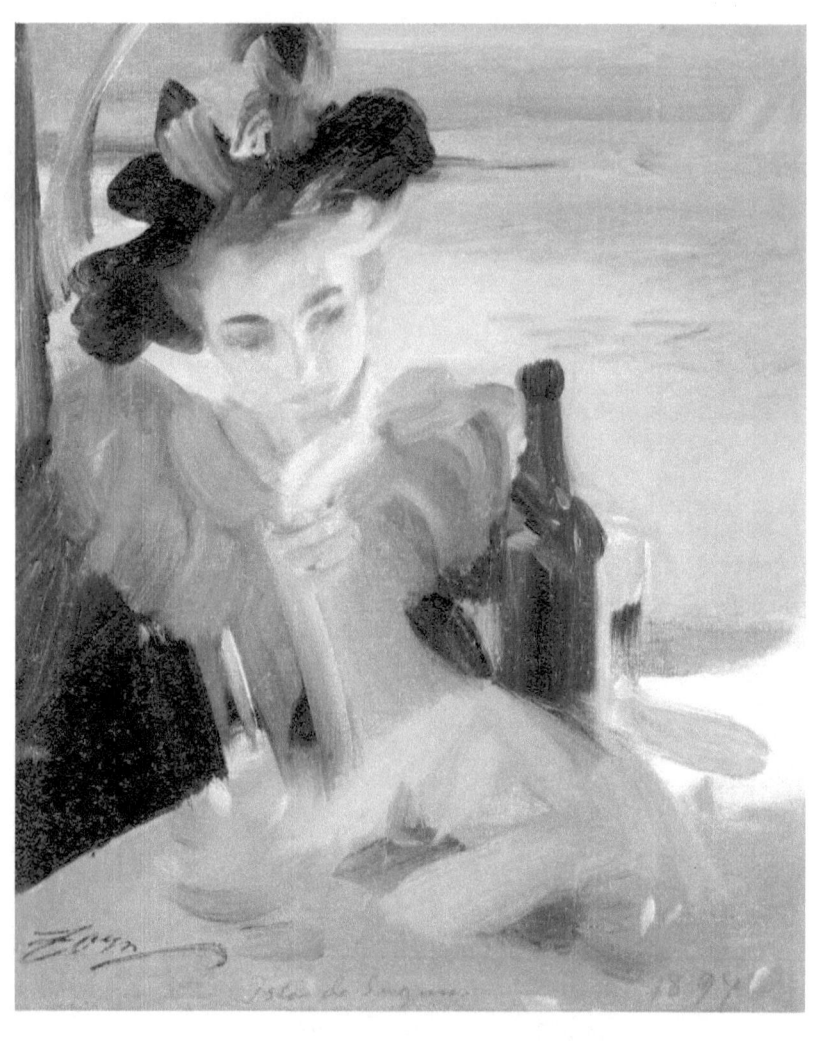

Women in the cafe, Isle de Seguin, 1894, oil on canvas

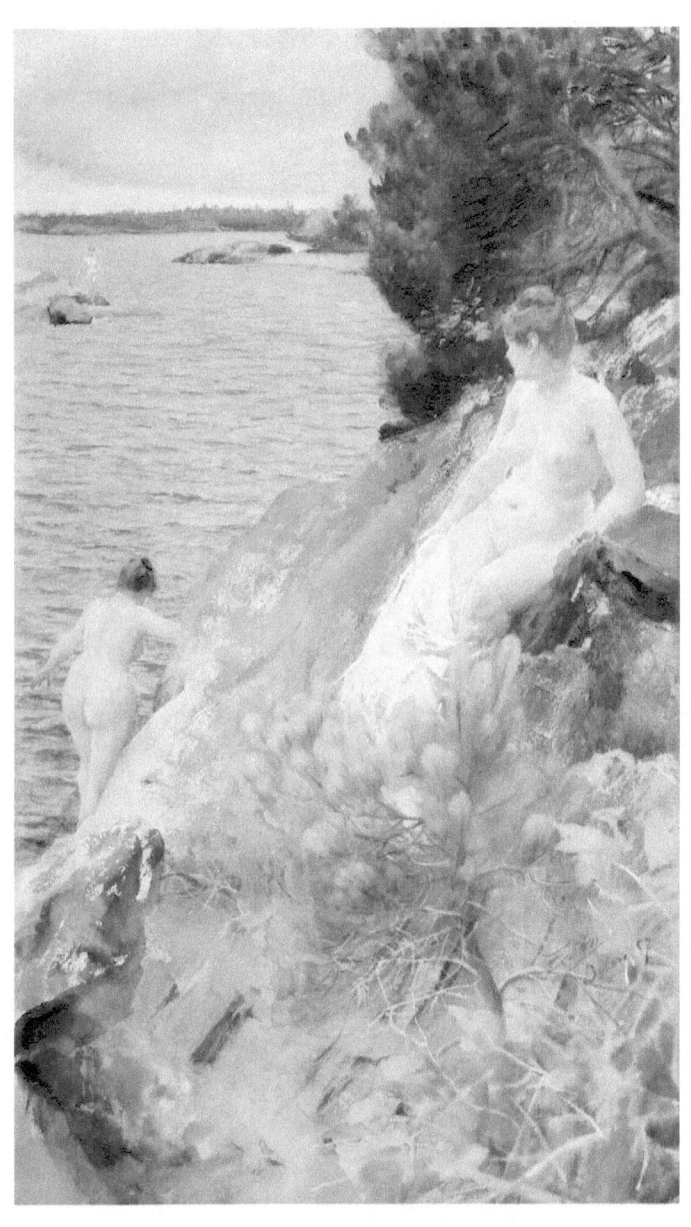

Summer, 1887, oil on canvas

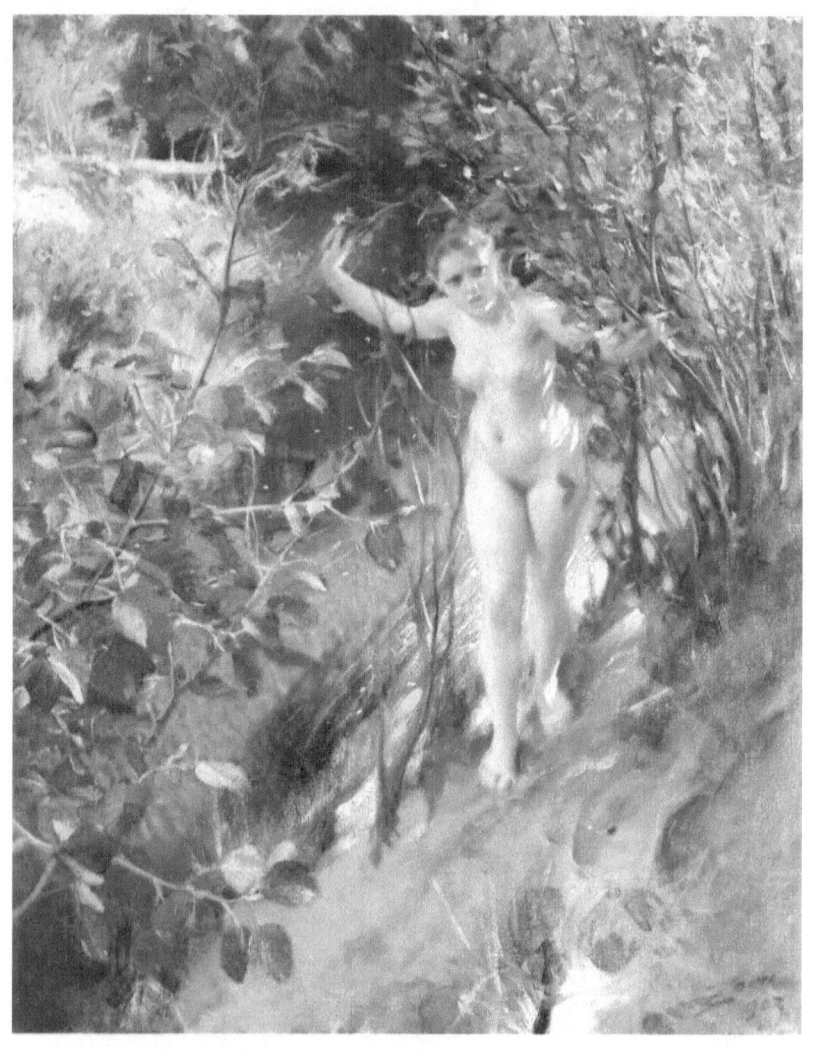

Red Sand, 1903, oil on canvas

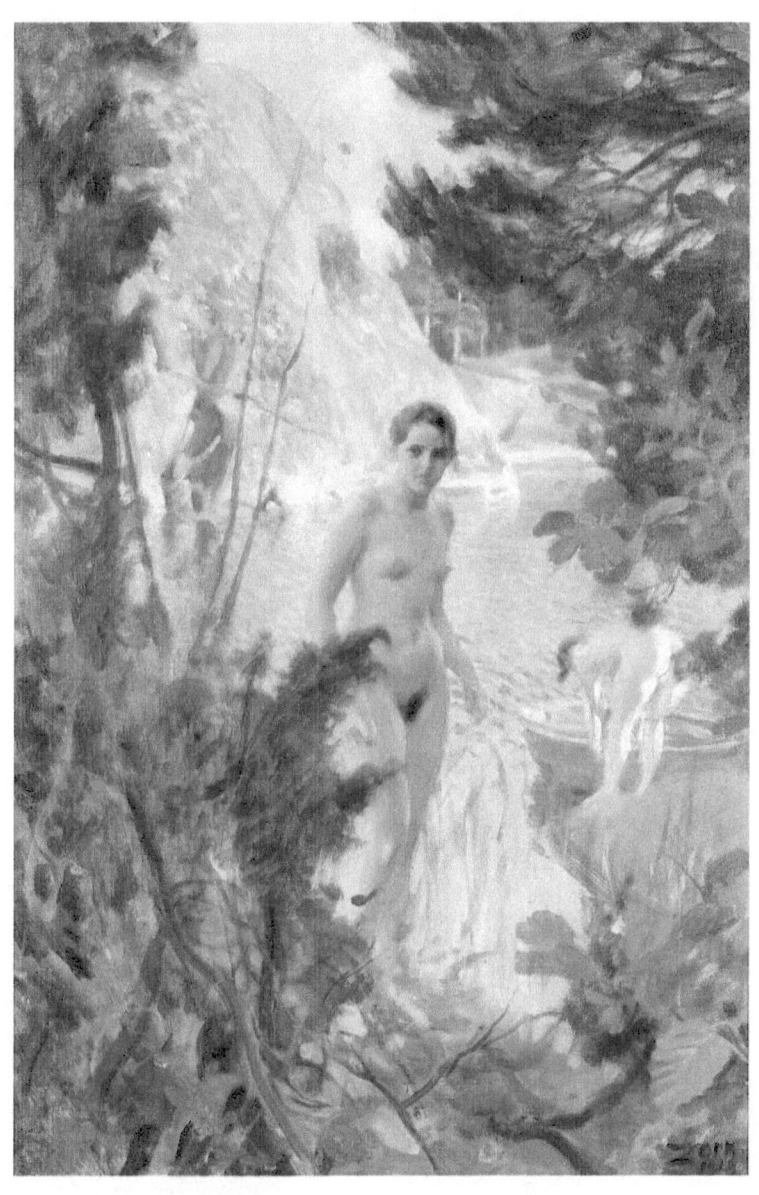

The dinghy, 1918, oil on canvas

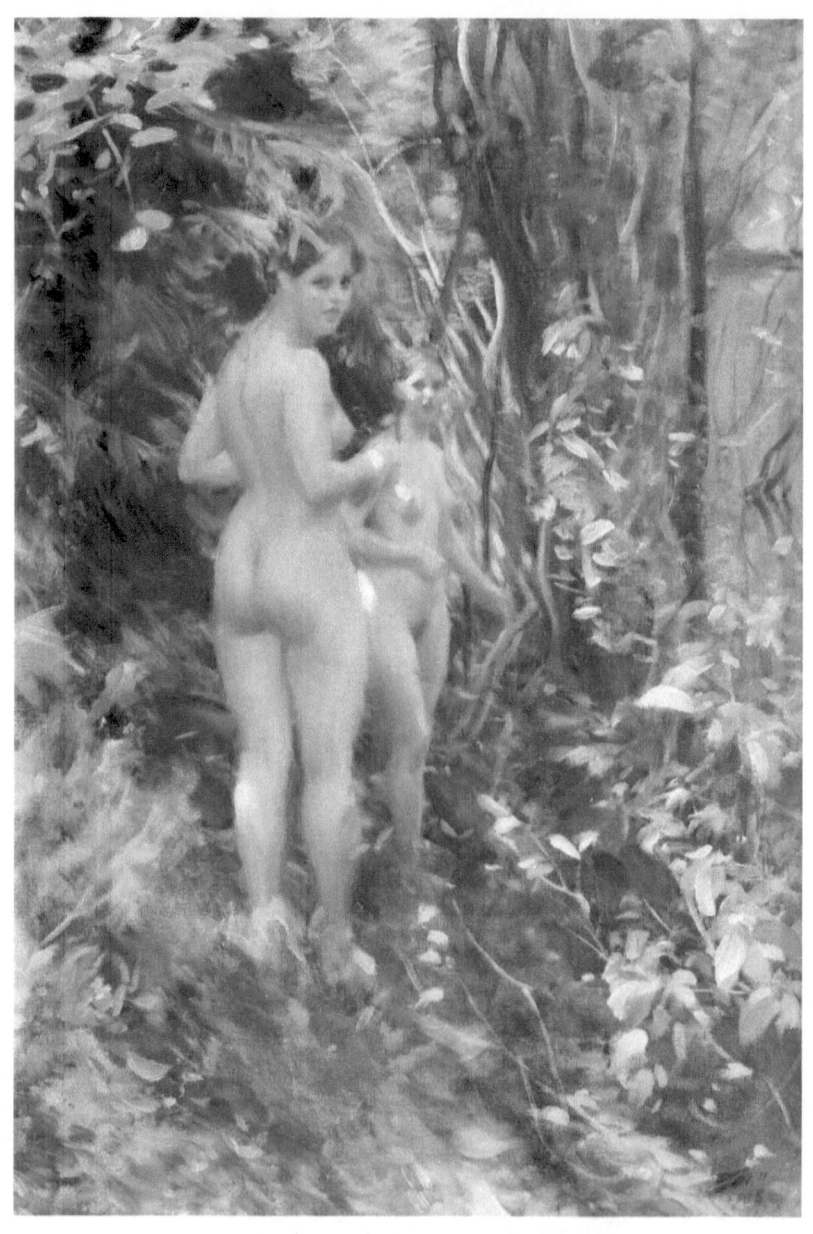

The Hinds, 1908, oil on canvas

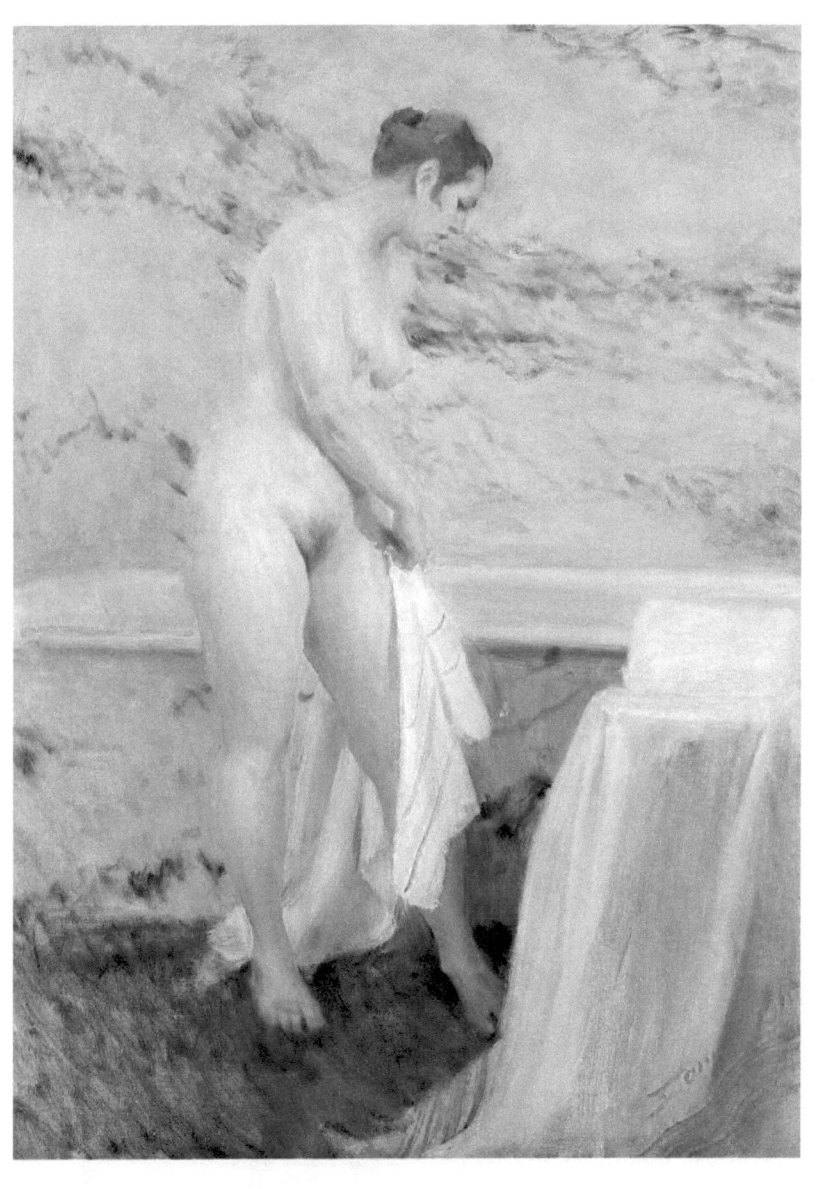

In the tub, 1915, oil on canvas

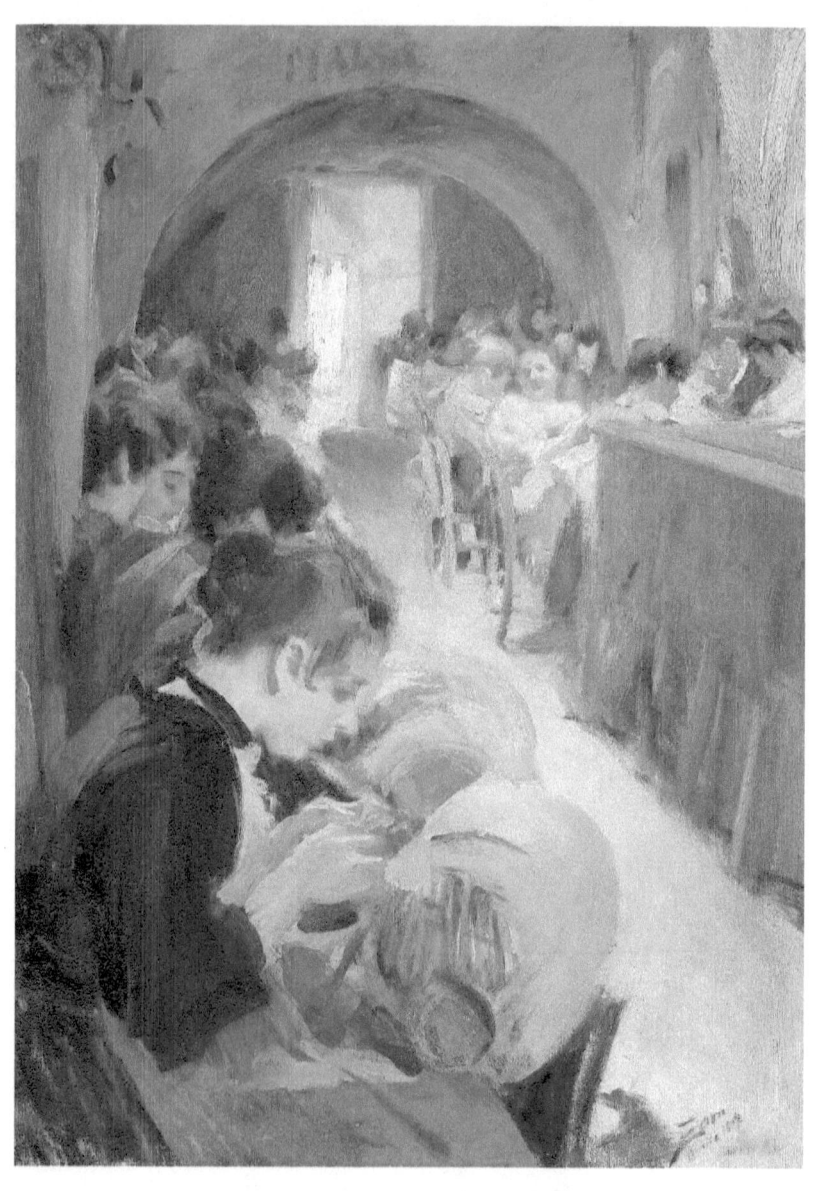

Lace-making in Venice, 1894, oil on canvas

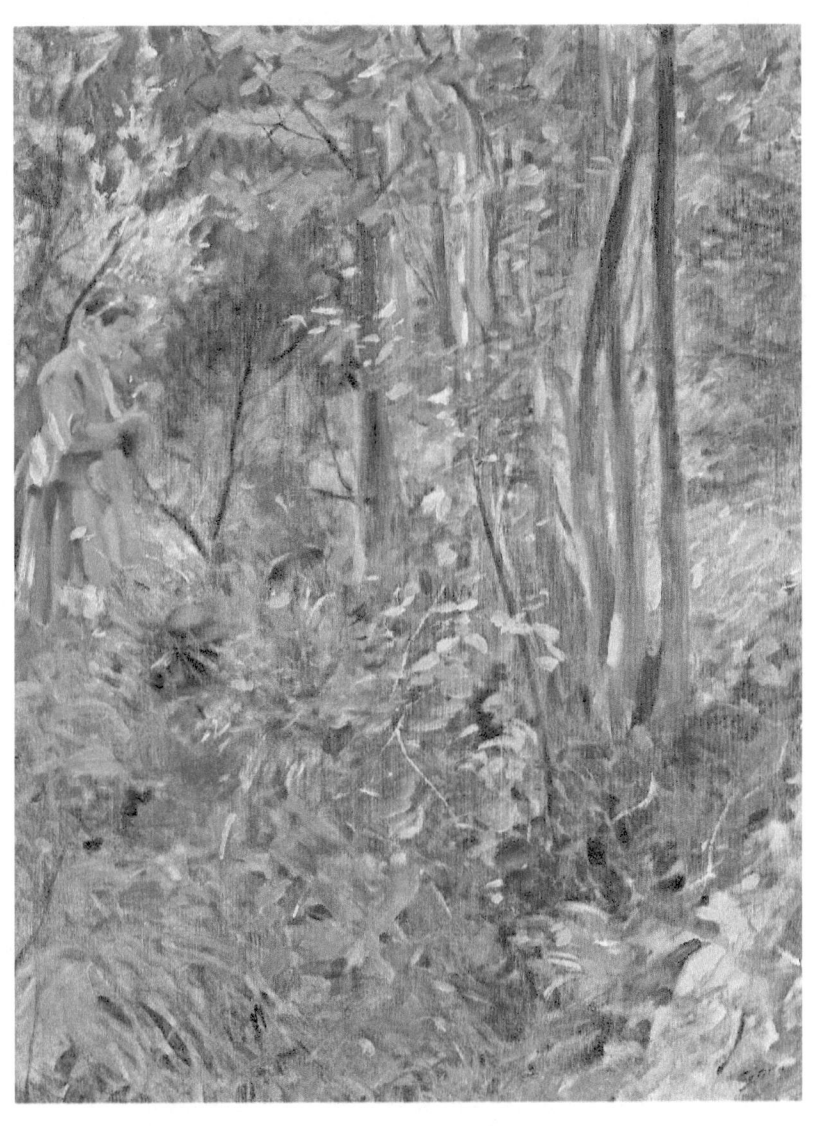

Sun in the forest, 1907, oil on canvas

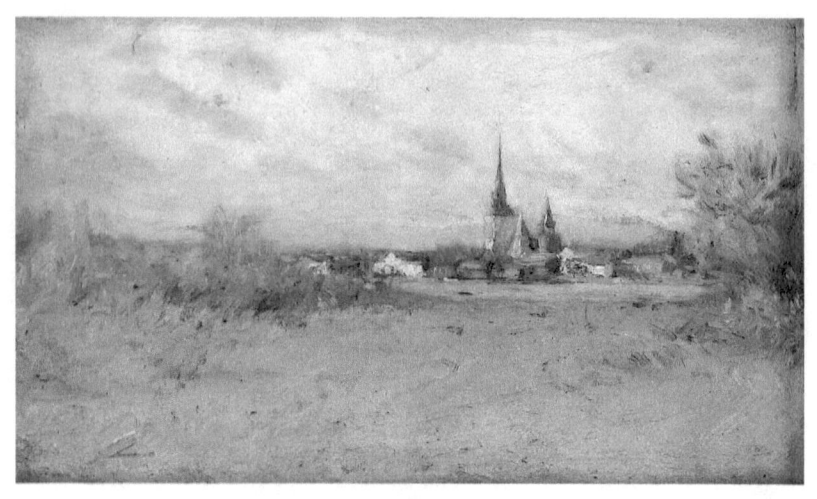

Mora Church, 1890, oil

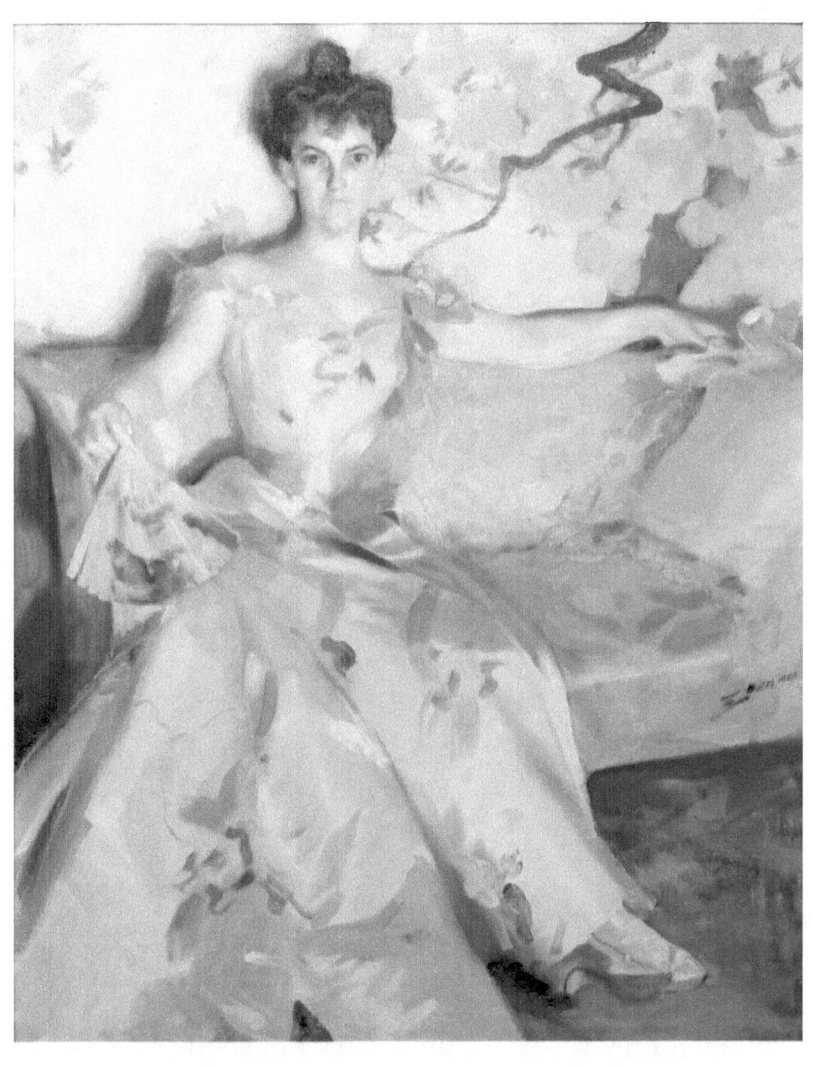

Portrait of Elizabeth Sherman Cameron, 1900, oil on canvas

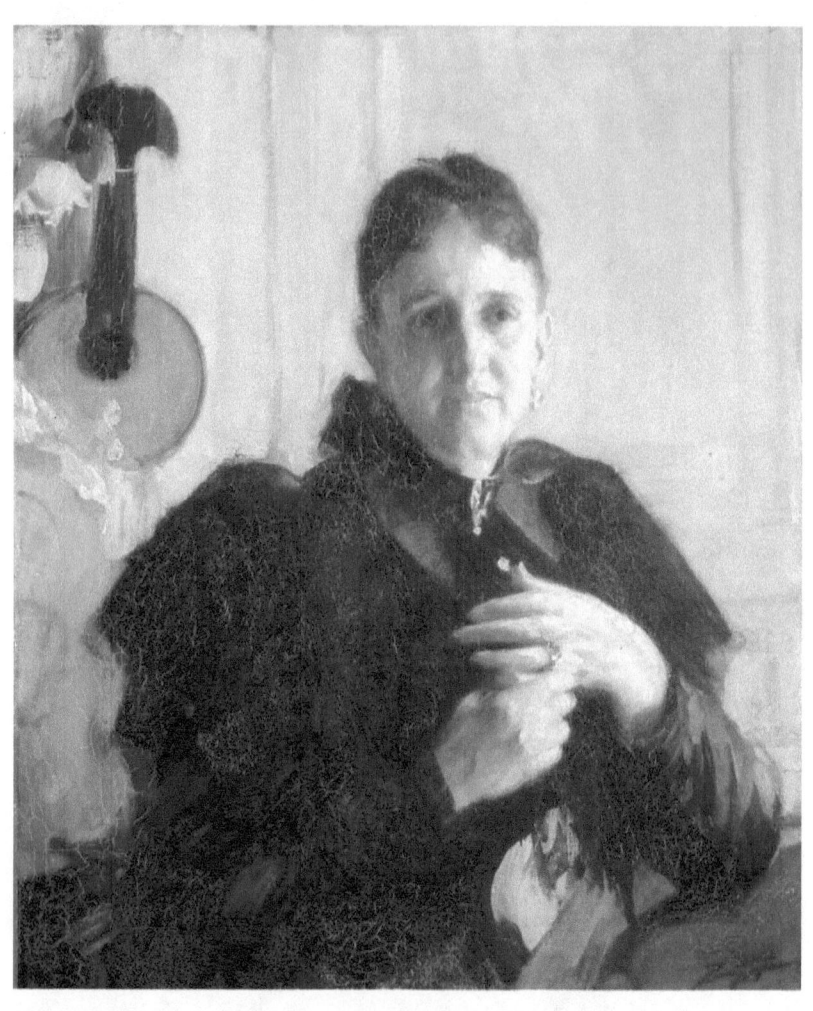

Mrs. John Crosby Brown (Mary Elizabeth Adams,
1842–1918), 1900, oil on canvas

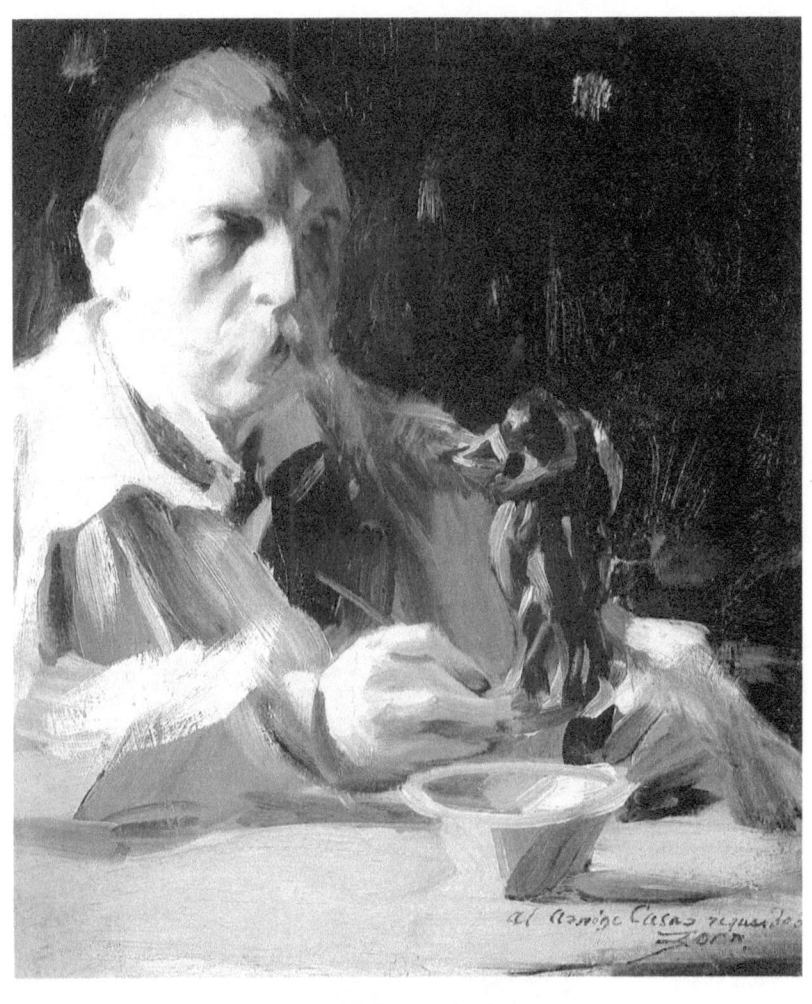

Self-Portrait with Faun and Nymph, oil on canvas

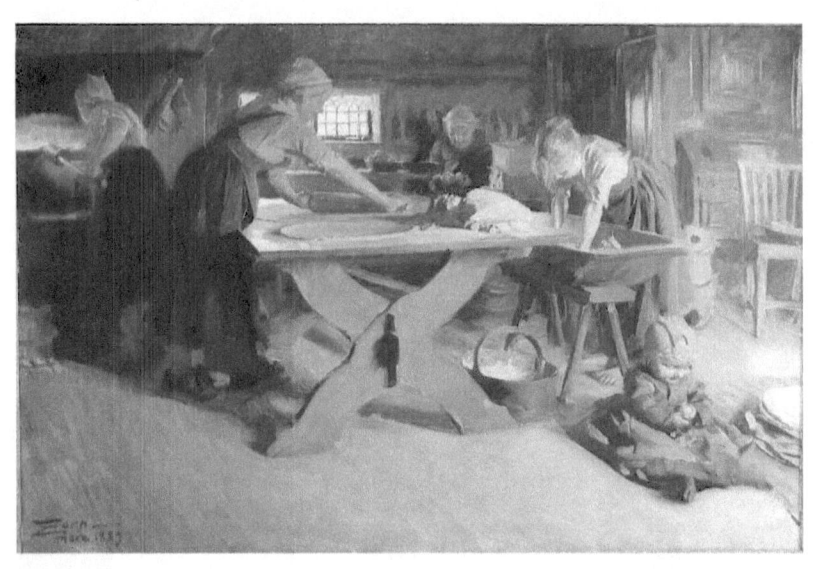

Baking bread, oil on canvas

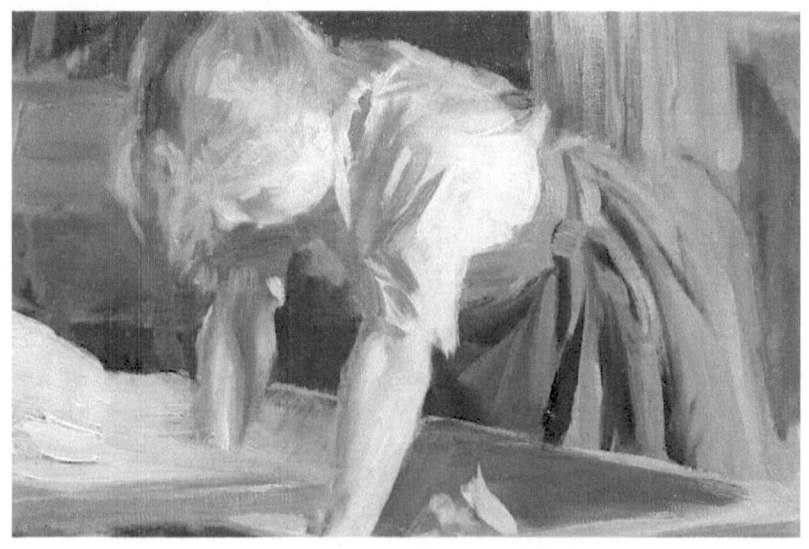

Baking bread, Detail, oil on canvas

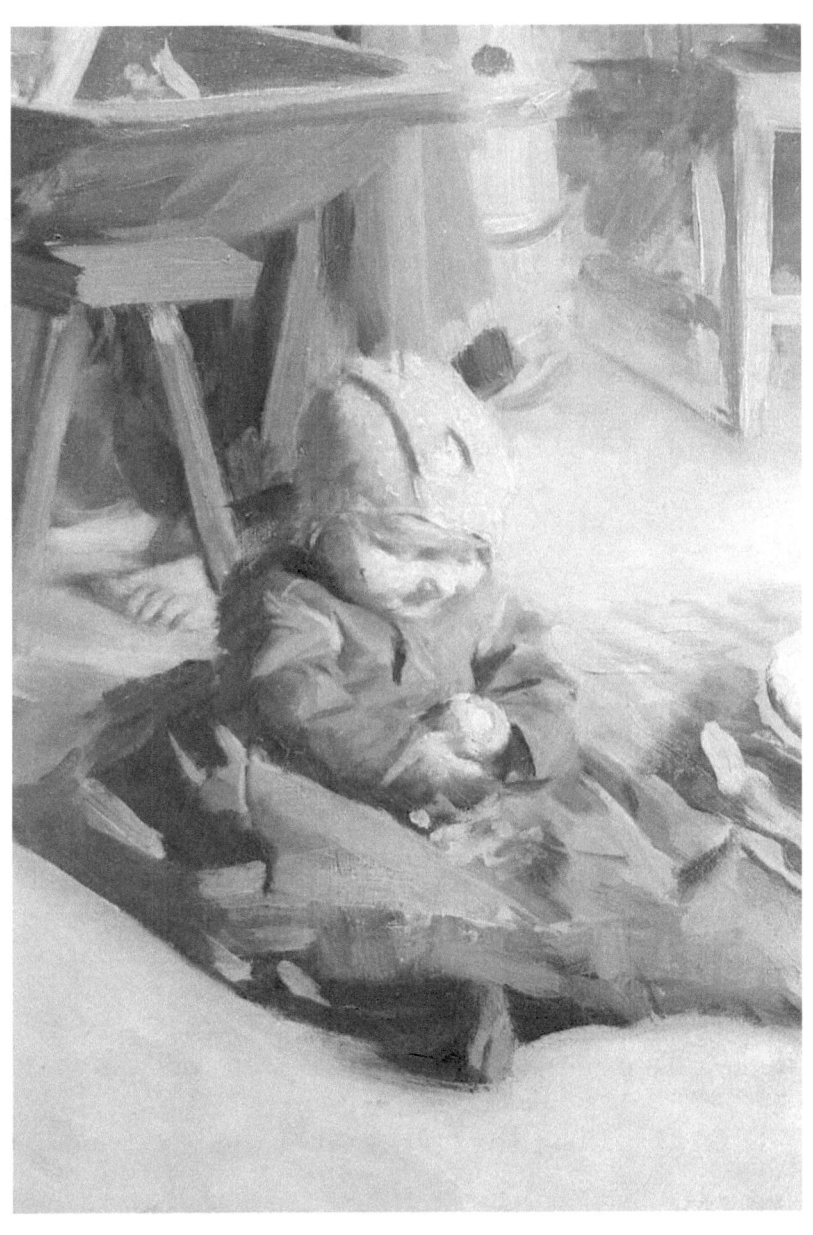

Baking bread, Detail, oil on canvas

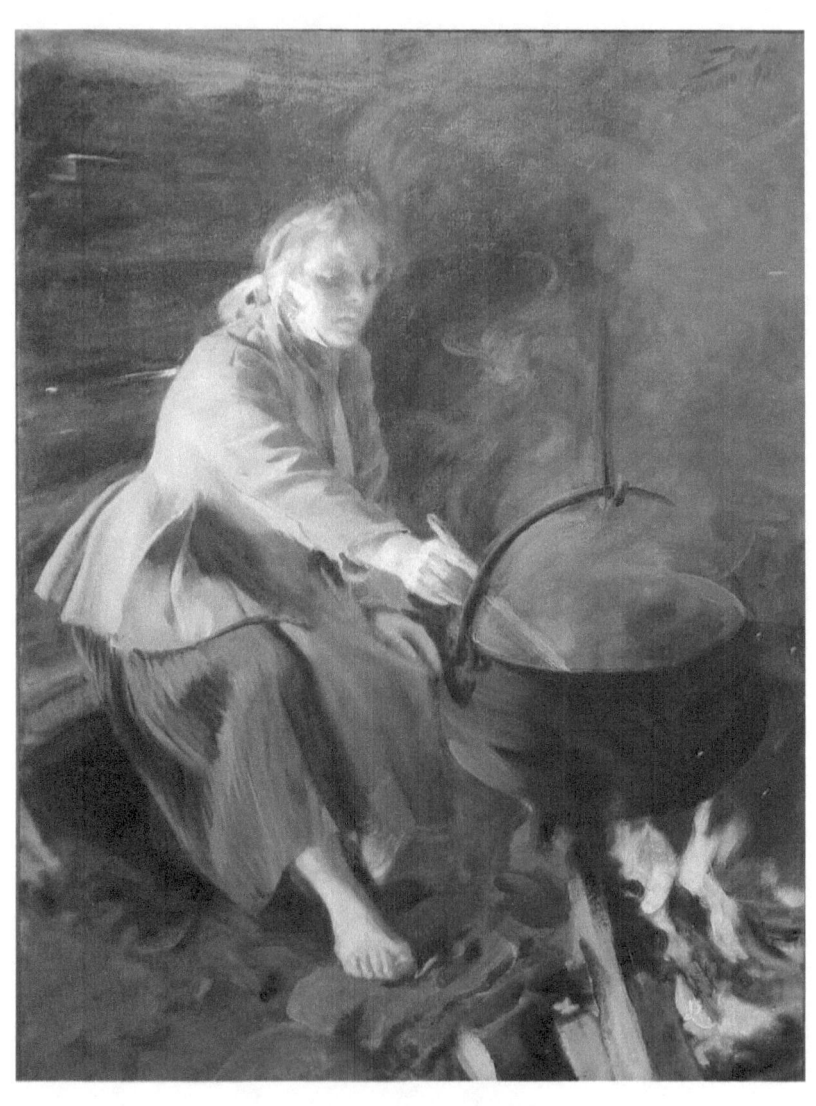

In the fire hut, oil on canvas

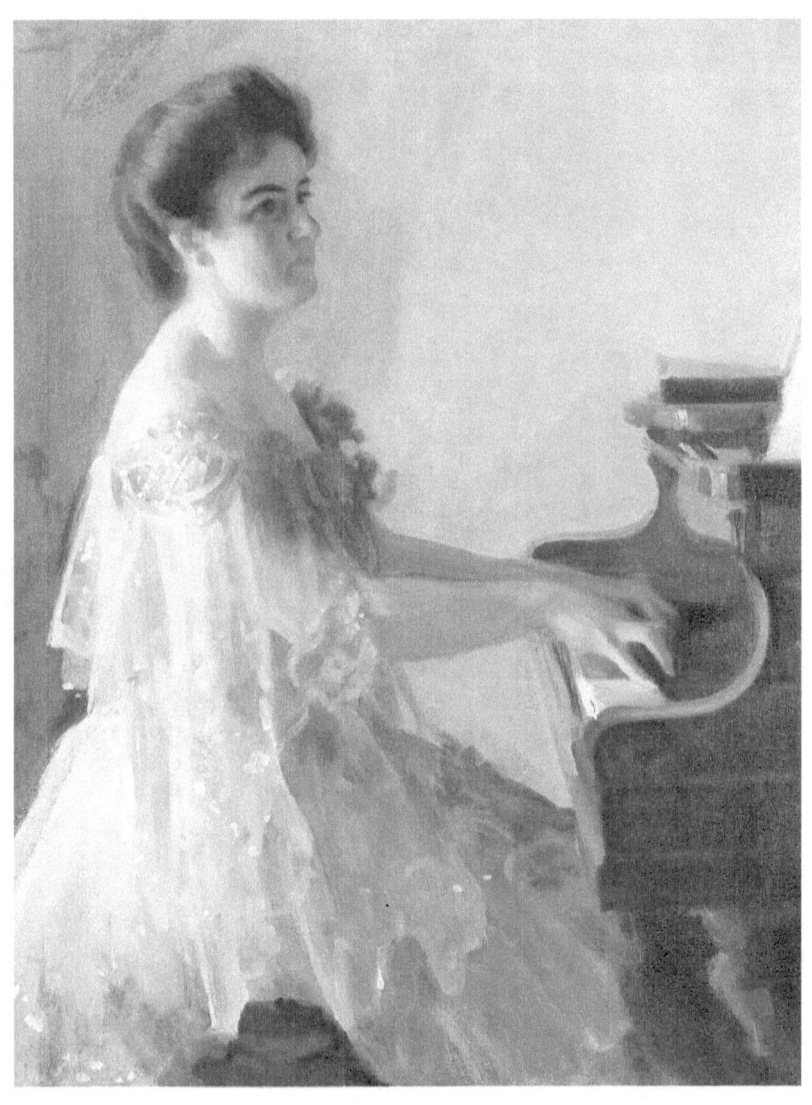

Mrs Emily Crane, 1904, Oil on canvas

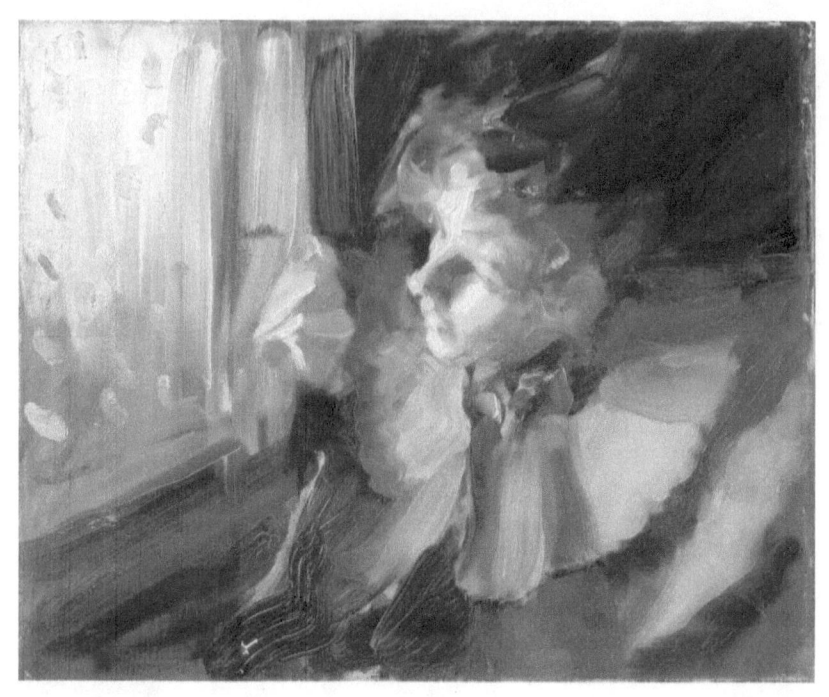

Omnibus (study) – oil sketch, 1892

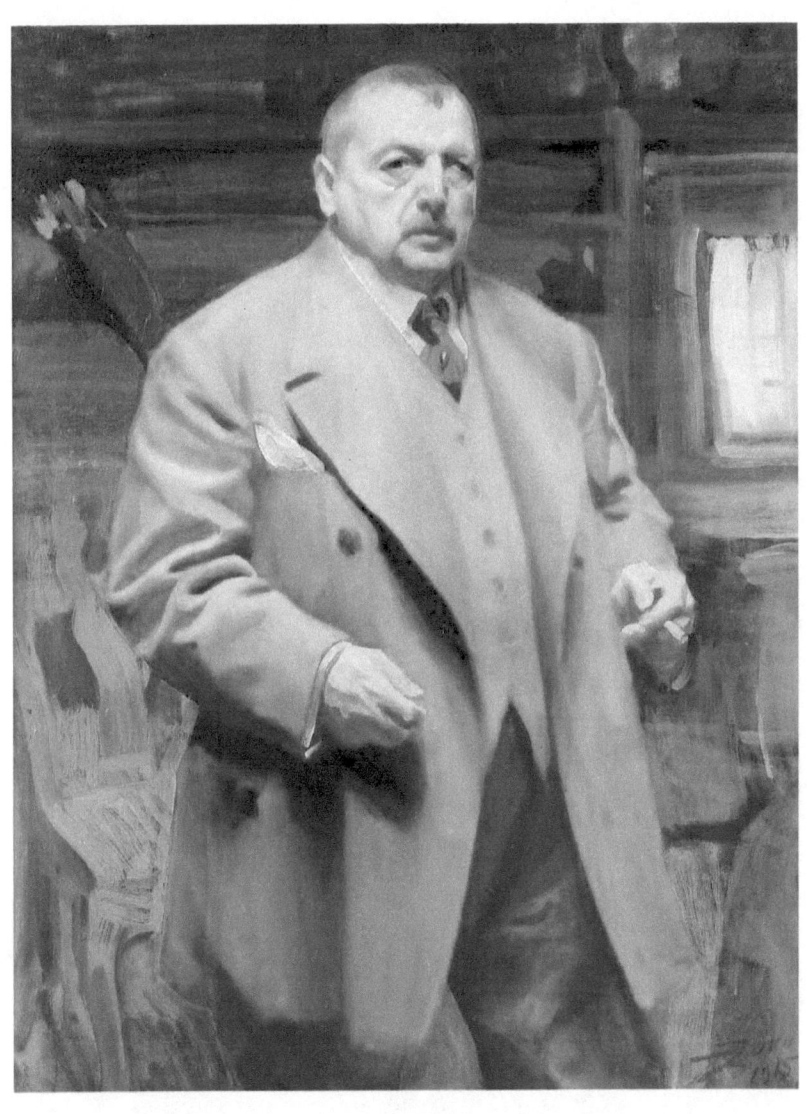

Self Portrait in Red, 1915, oil on canvas

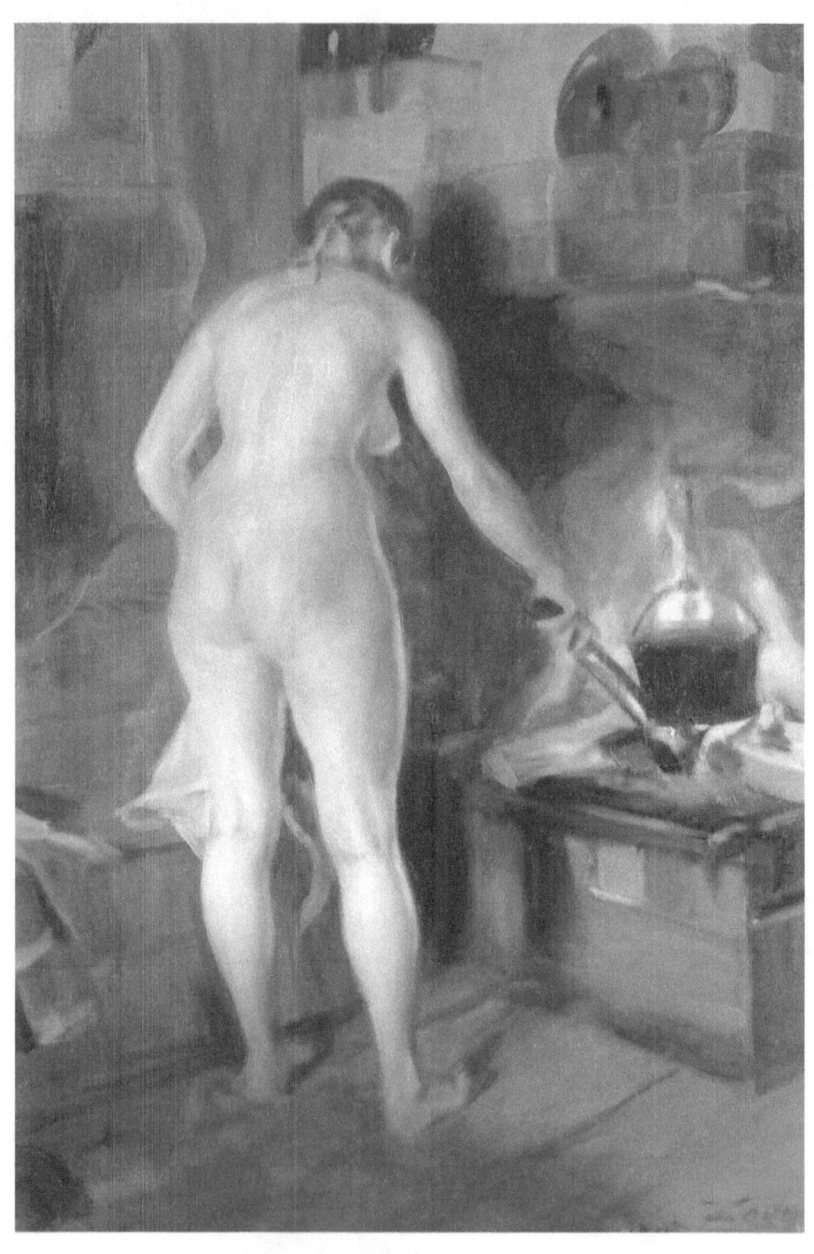

Cooking Potatoes, oil on canvas

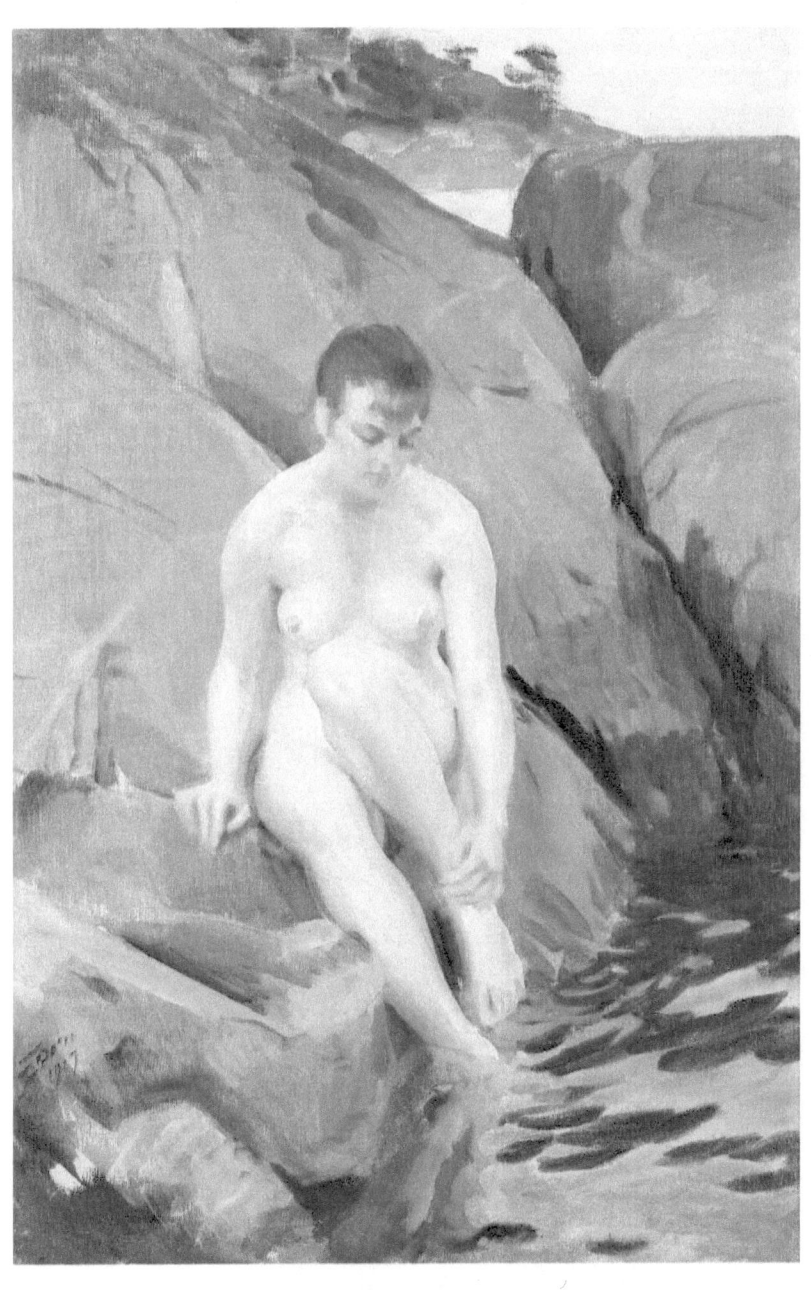

Märta, 1917, oil on canvas

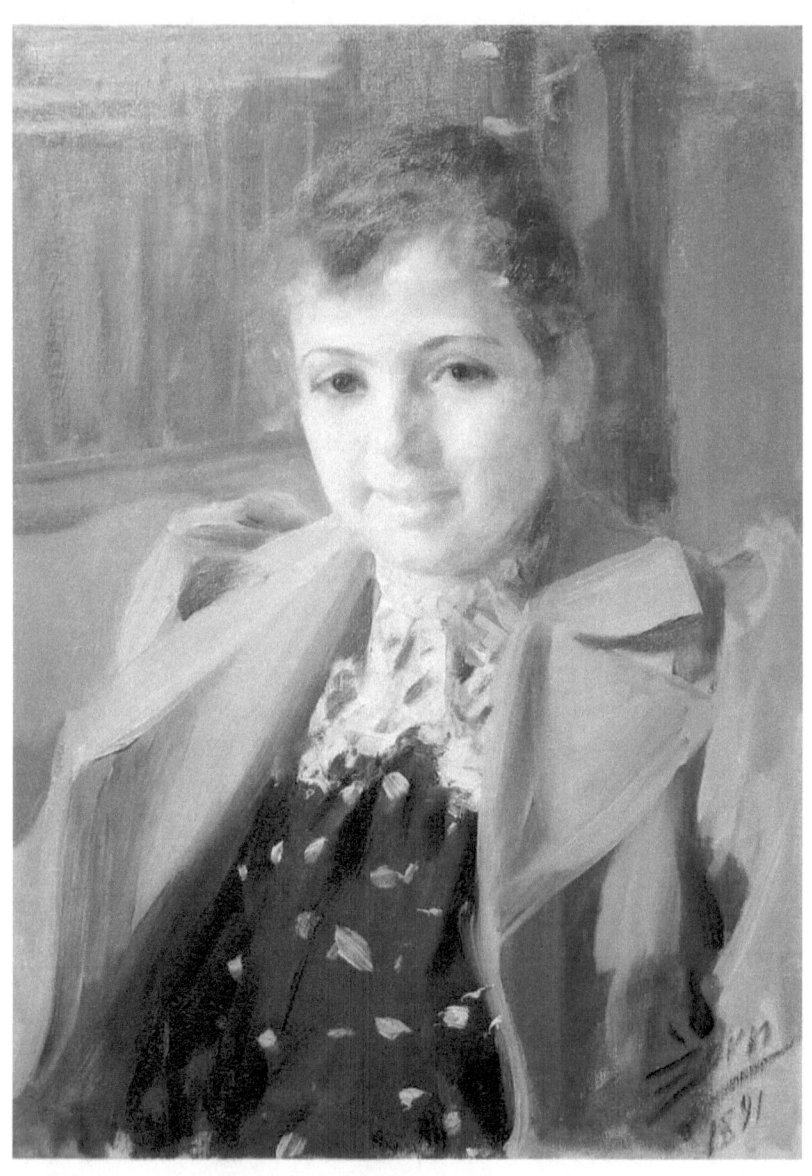

Magda Geber, oil on canvas

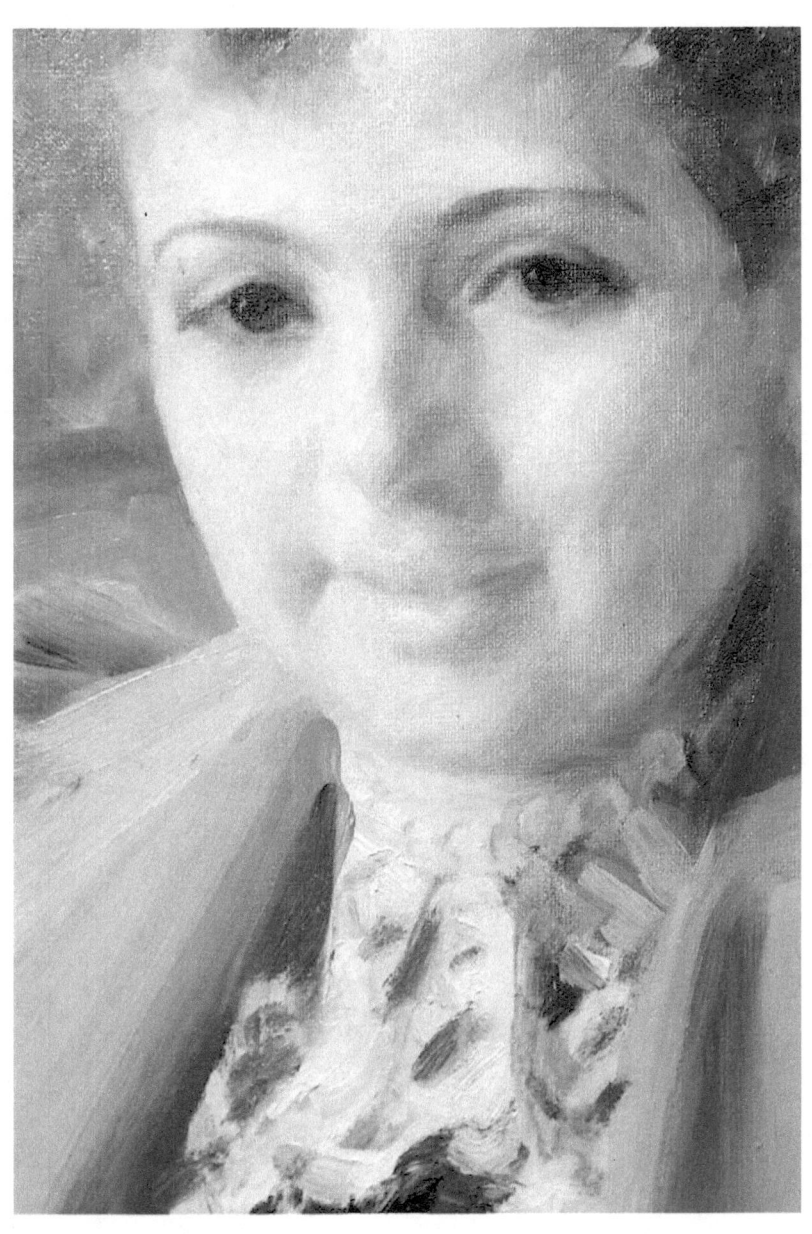

Magda Geber, Detail, oil on canvas

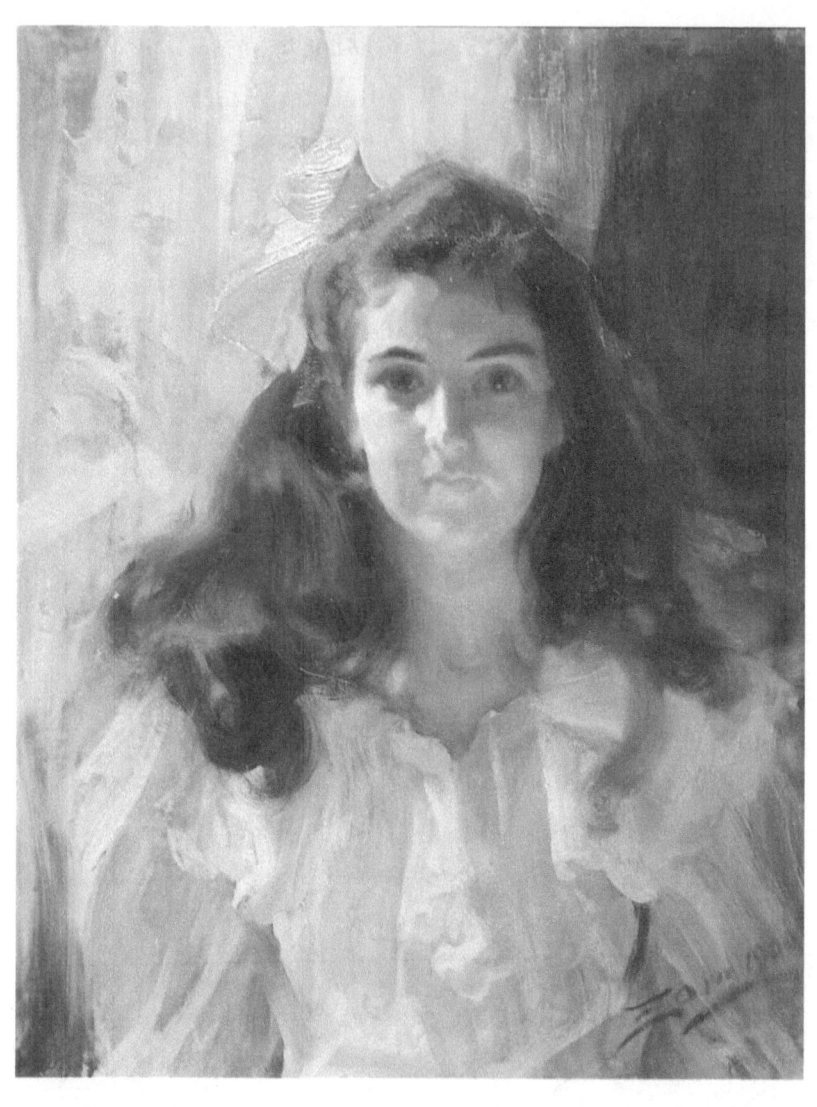

Marie Cohn, oil on canvas

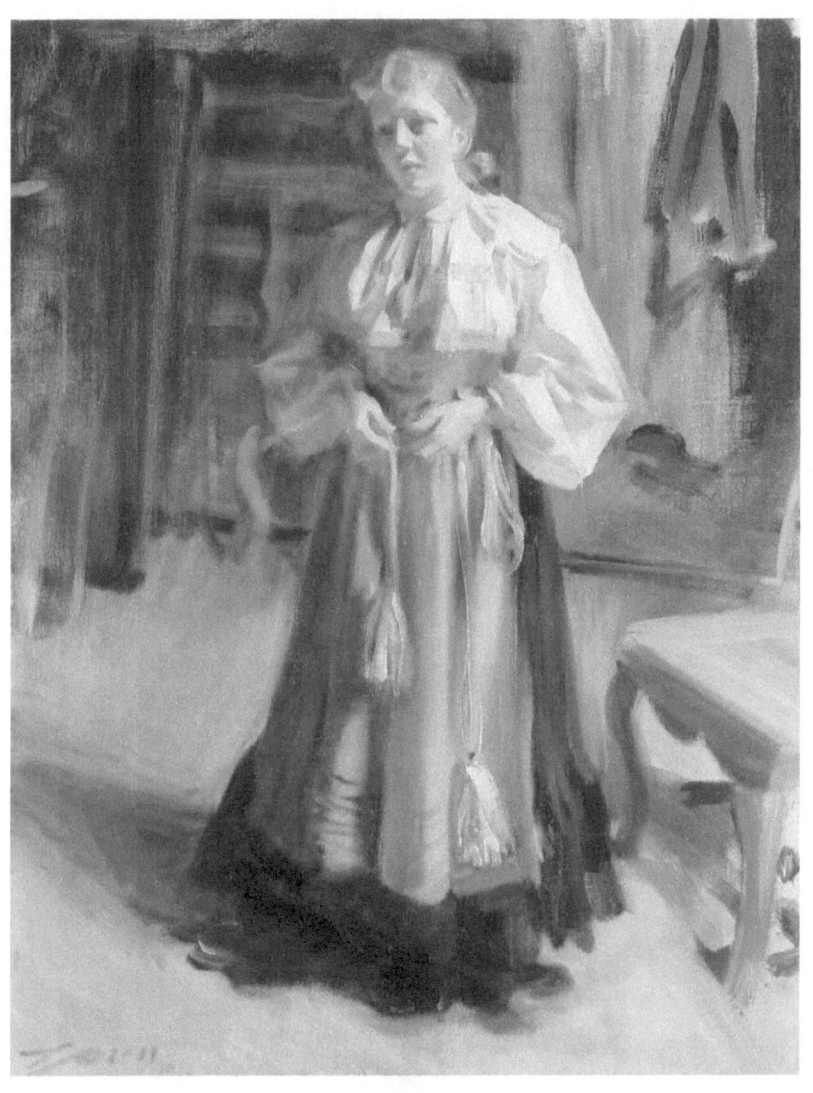

Girl in an Orsa Costume, 1911, oil on canvas

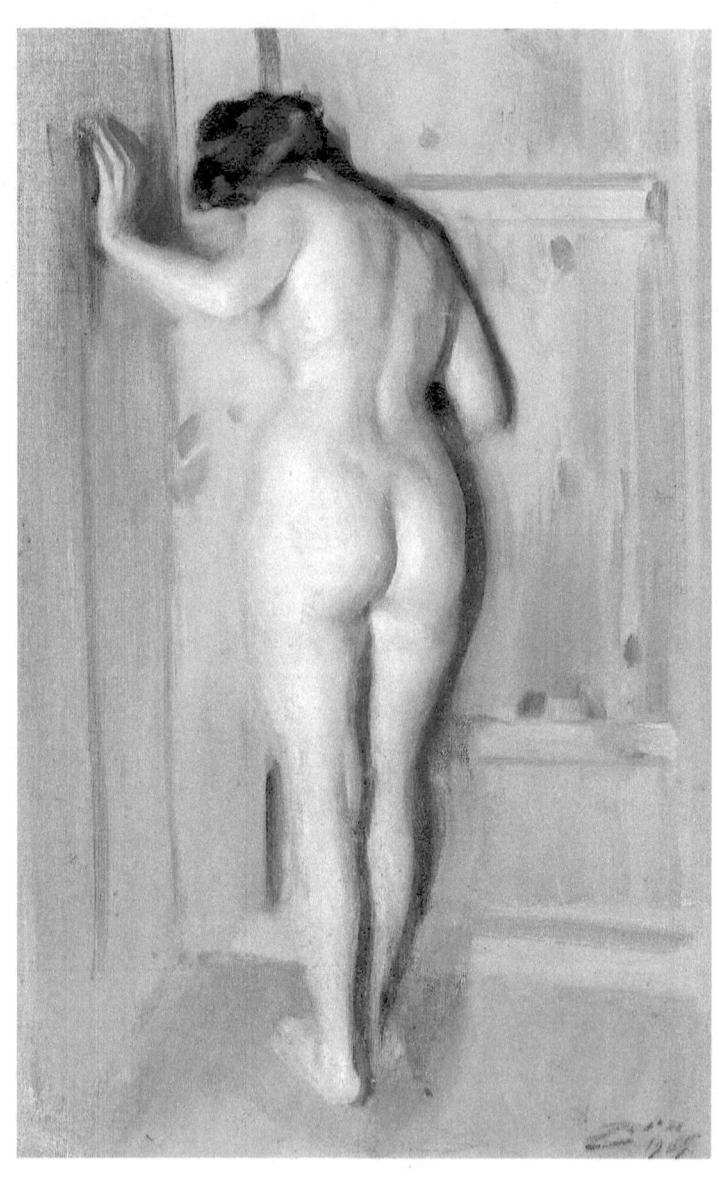

The Chamber Door, 1905, oil on canvas

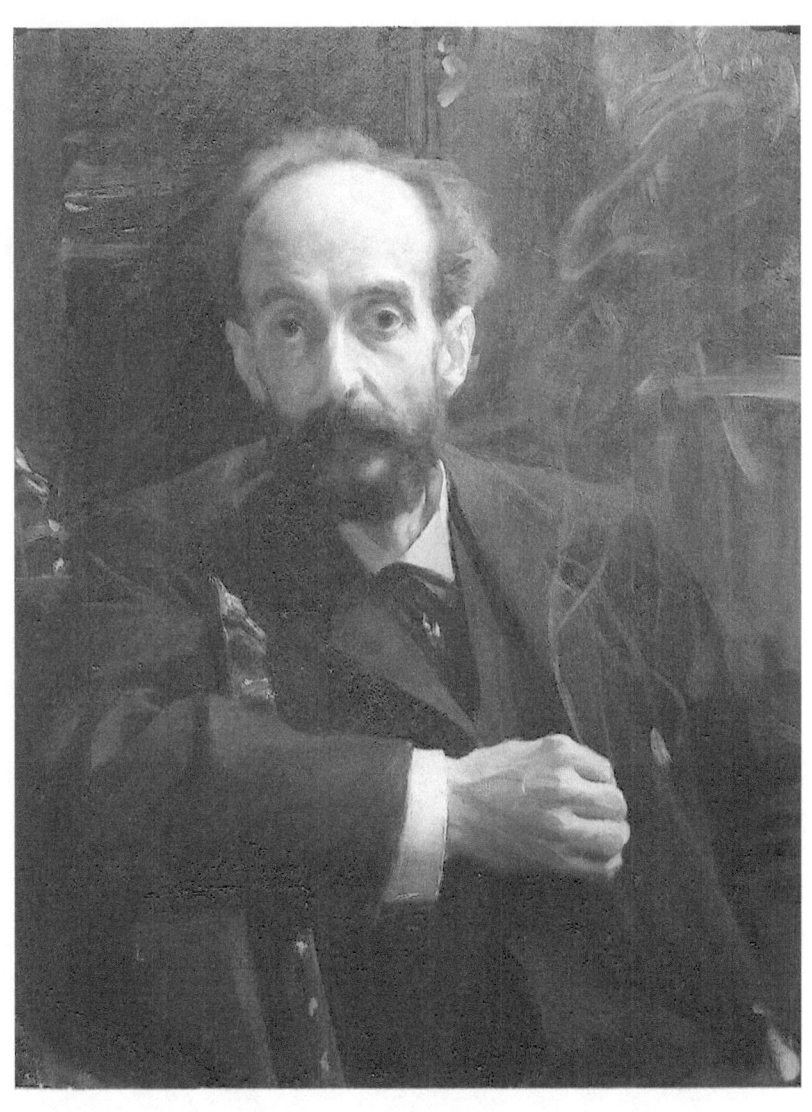

Monsieur Mauri, oil on canvas

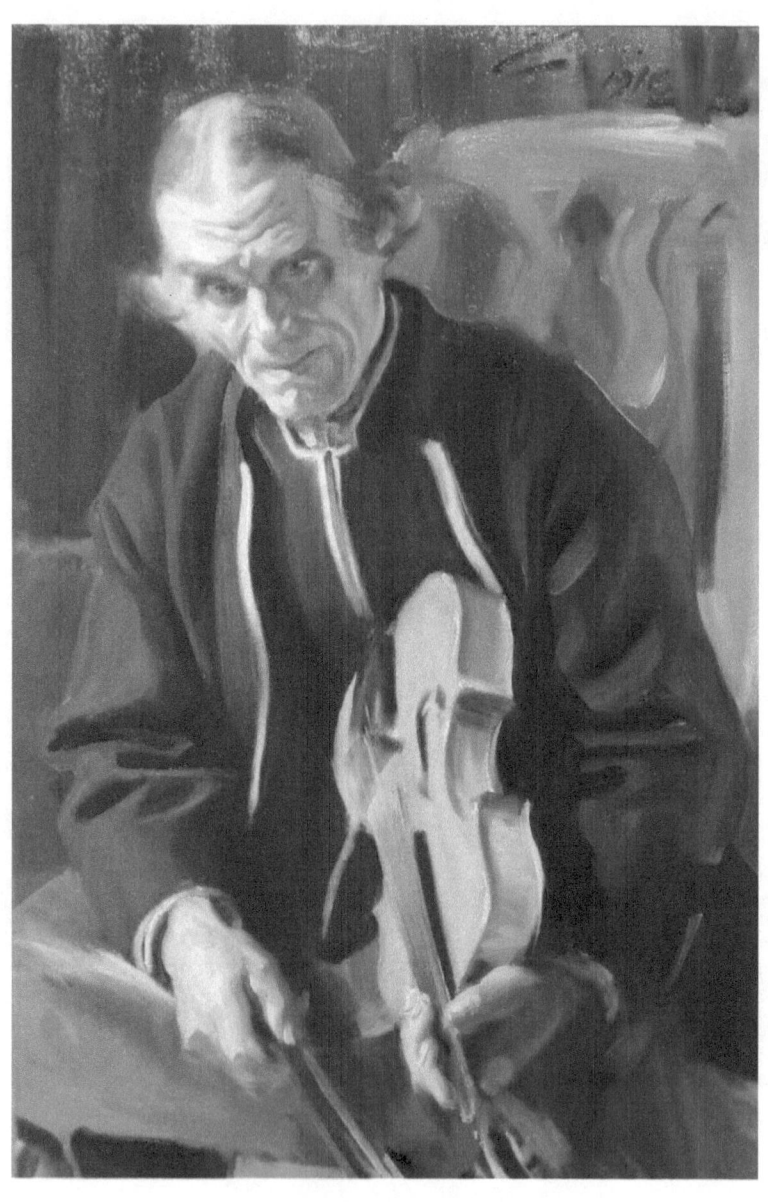

Sparf Anders, oil on canvas

Watercolors

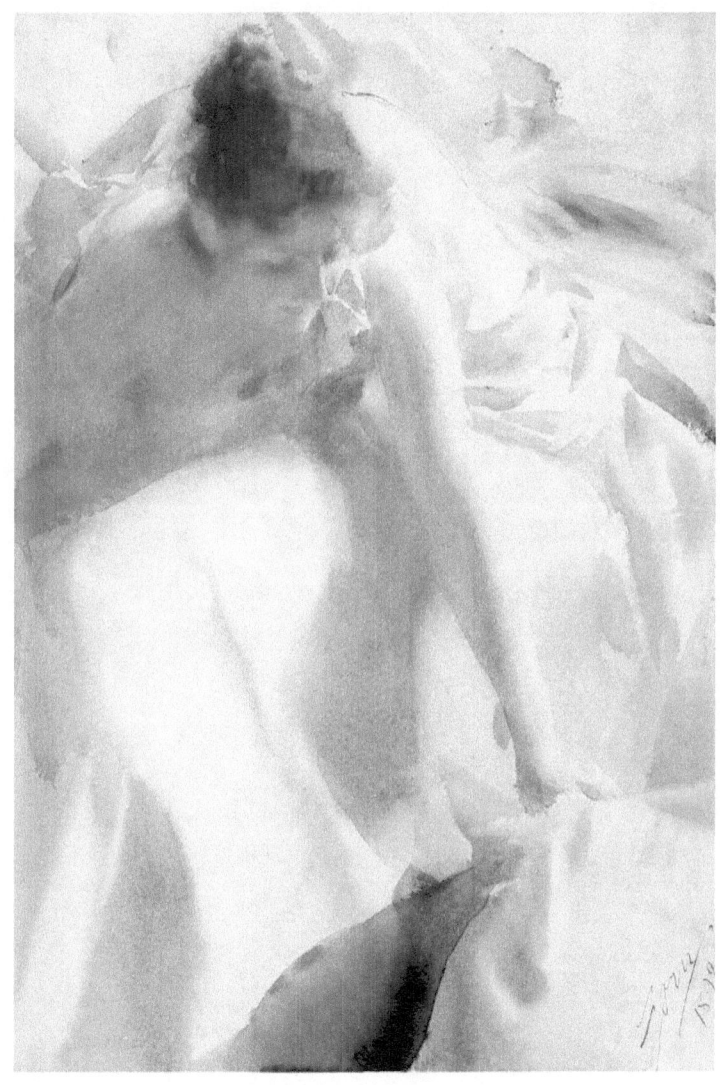

Reveil, the artist's wife, before 1920, Watercolor

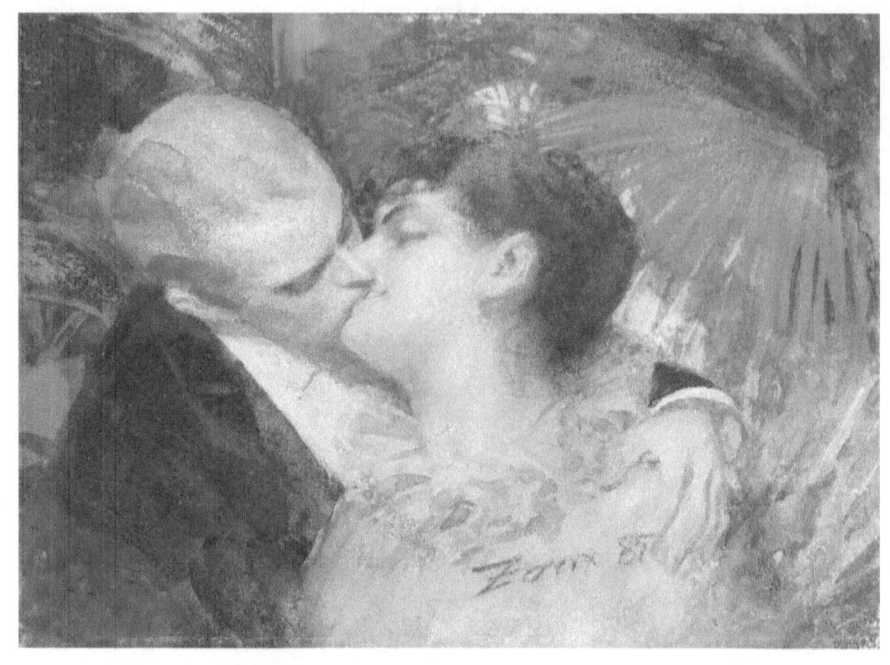

The Embrace, 1885, Watercolor

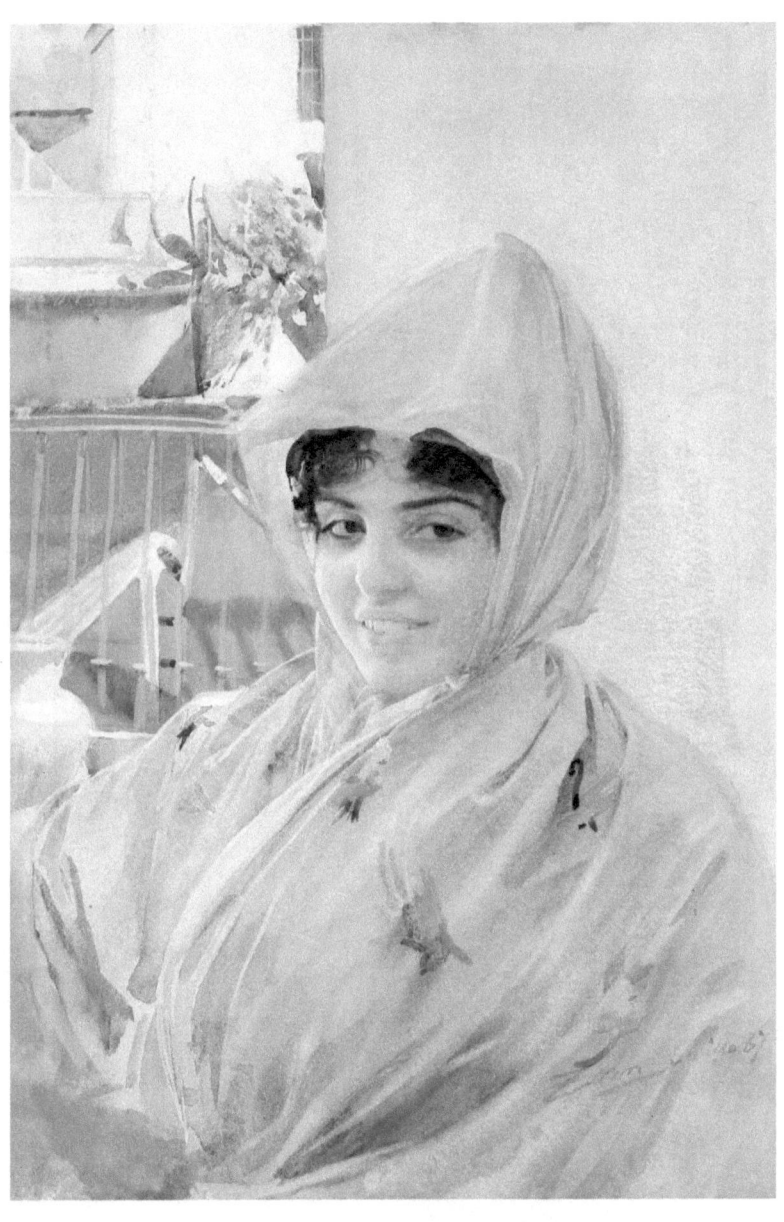

Mathilde, 1887, watercolor and gouache

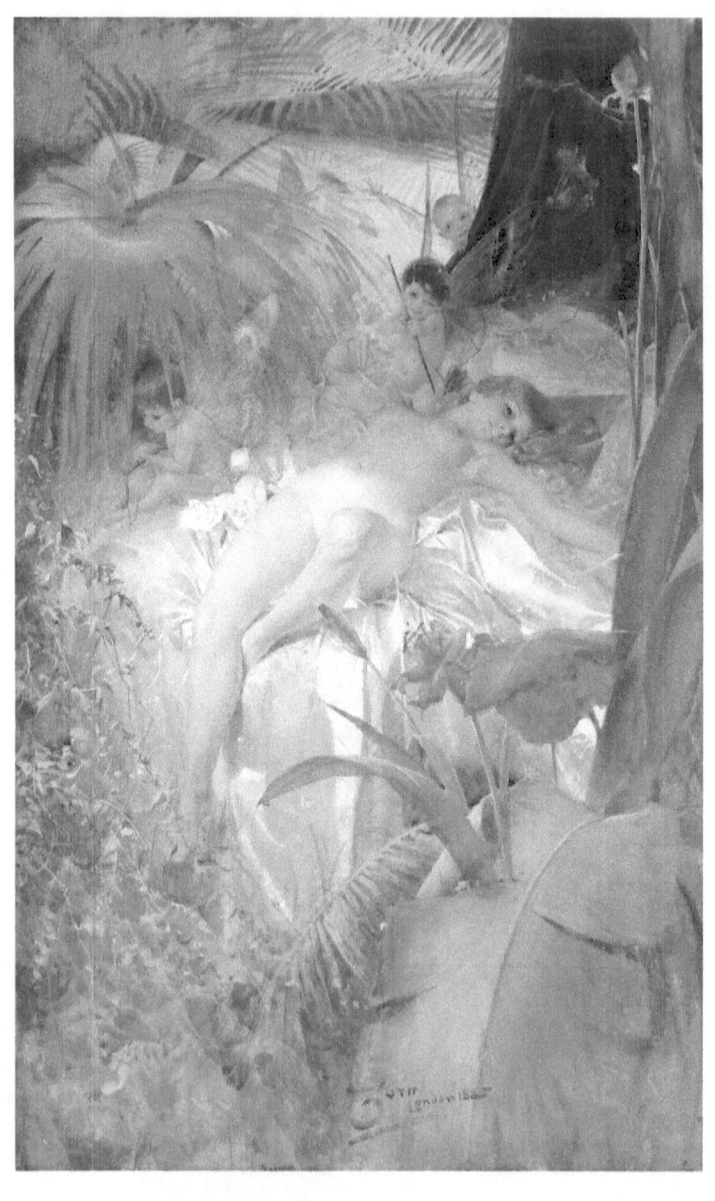

The Love Nymph, 1895, watercolor and gouache on paper

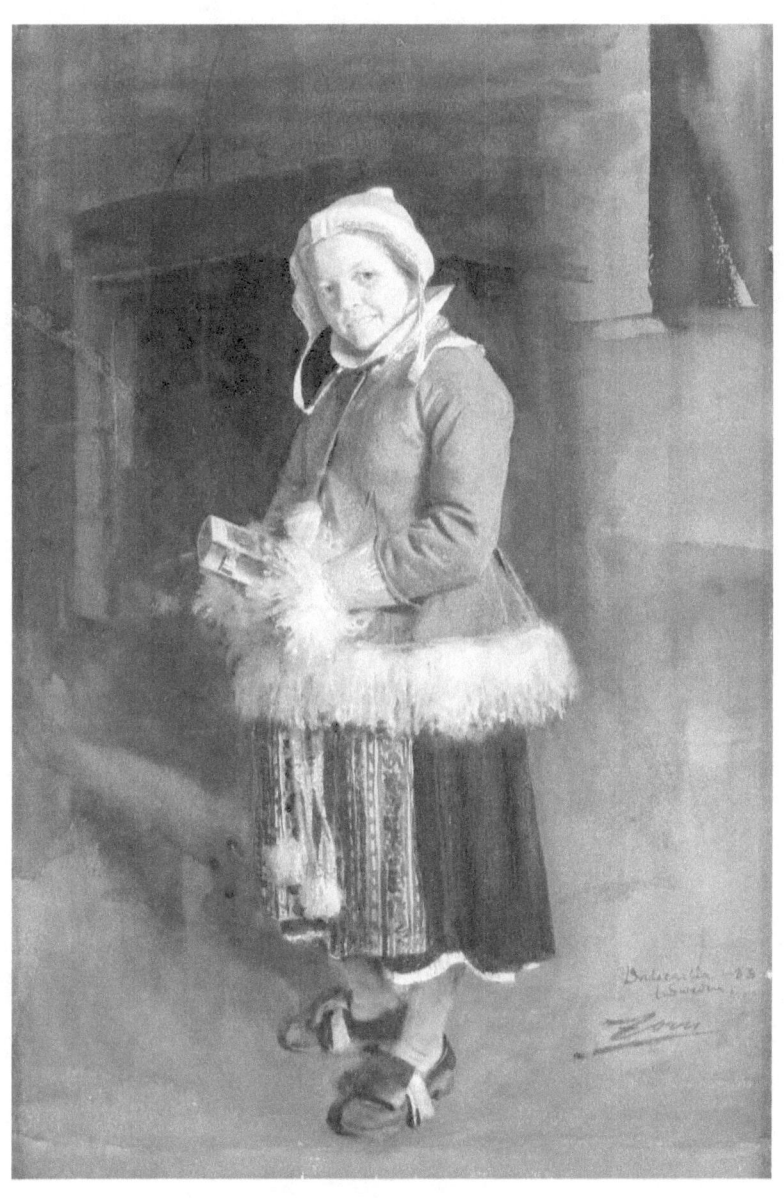

Wedding book, 1883, watercolor on paper

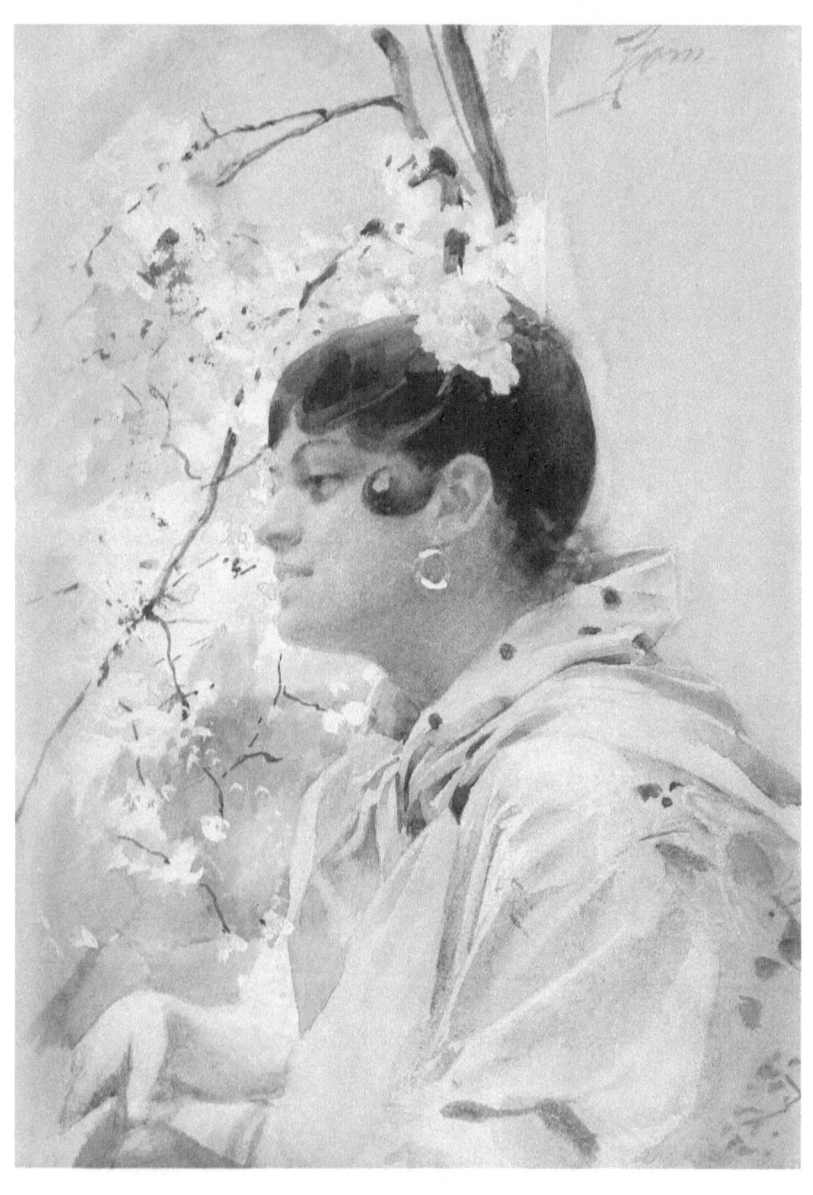

Carmen, 1884, watercolor on paper

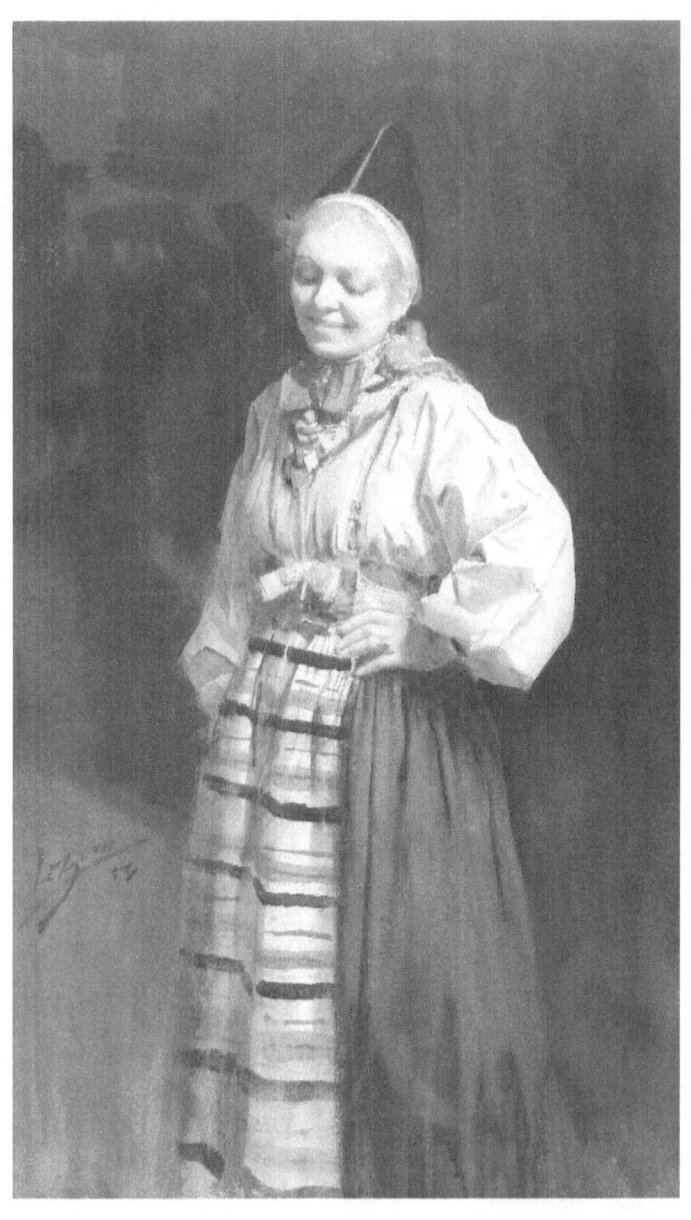

Dalecarlian girl from Rättvik, 1883, watercolor on paper

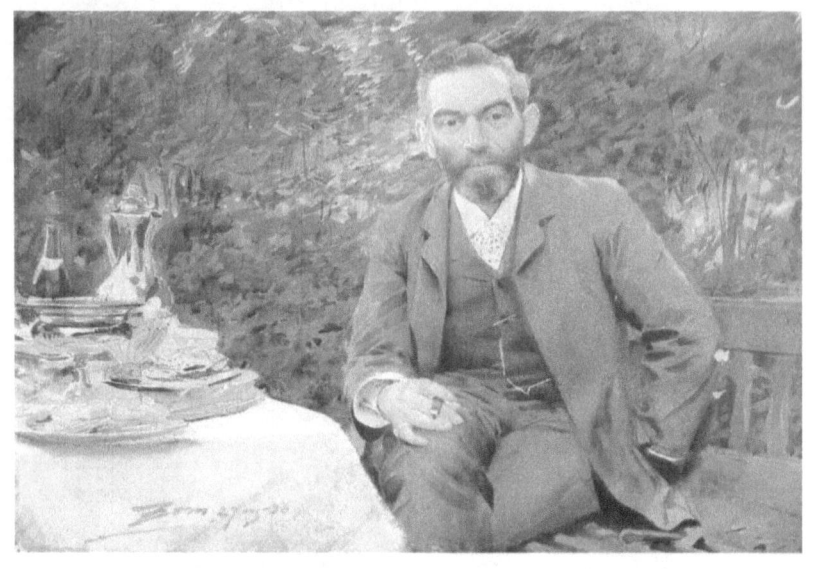

Breakfast in the green, 1920, watercolor

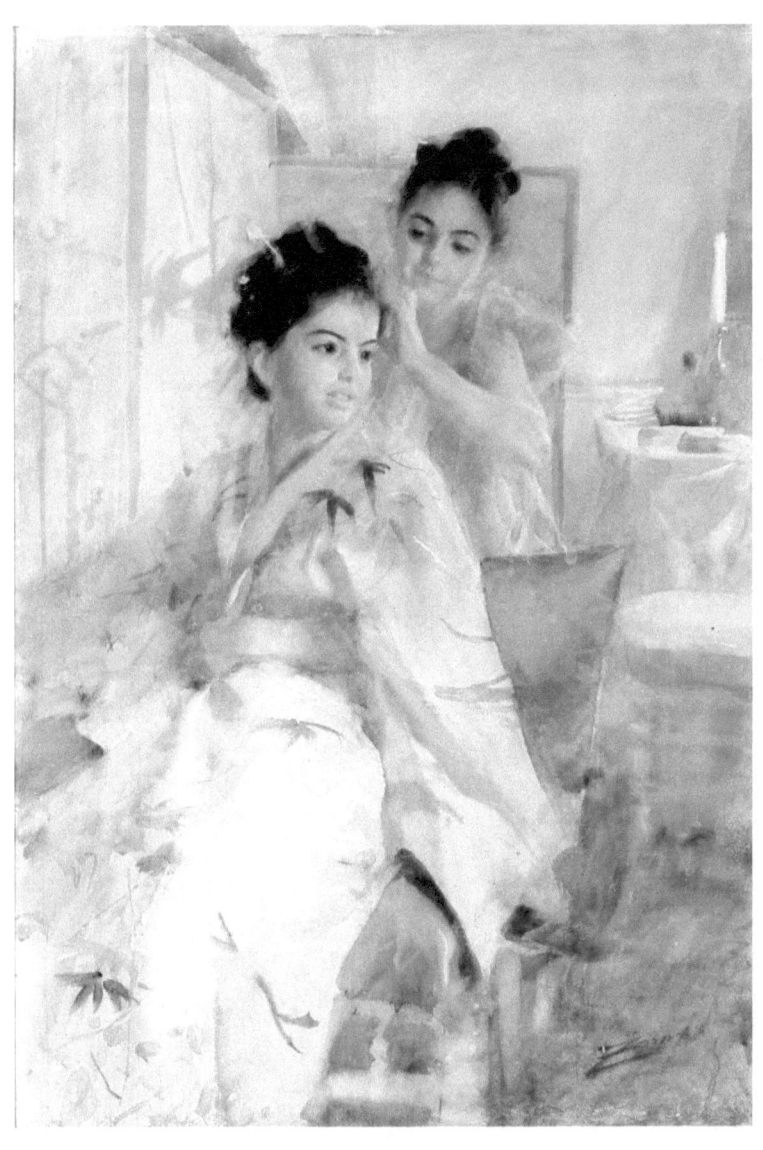

The misses Salomon, 1888, watercolor

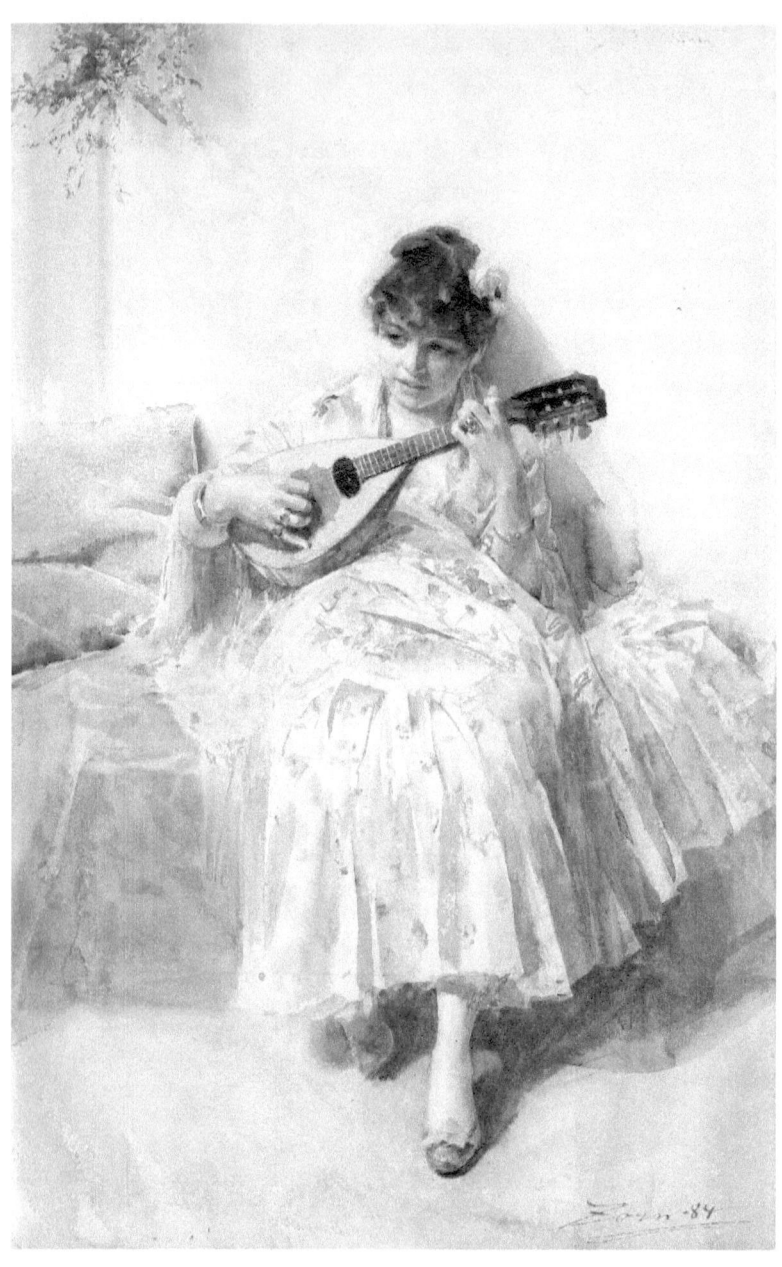

Girl playing mandolin, 1884, watercolor on paper

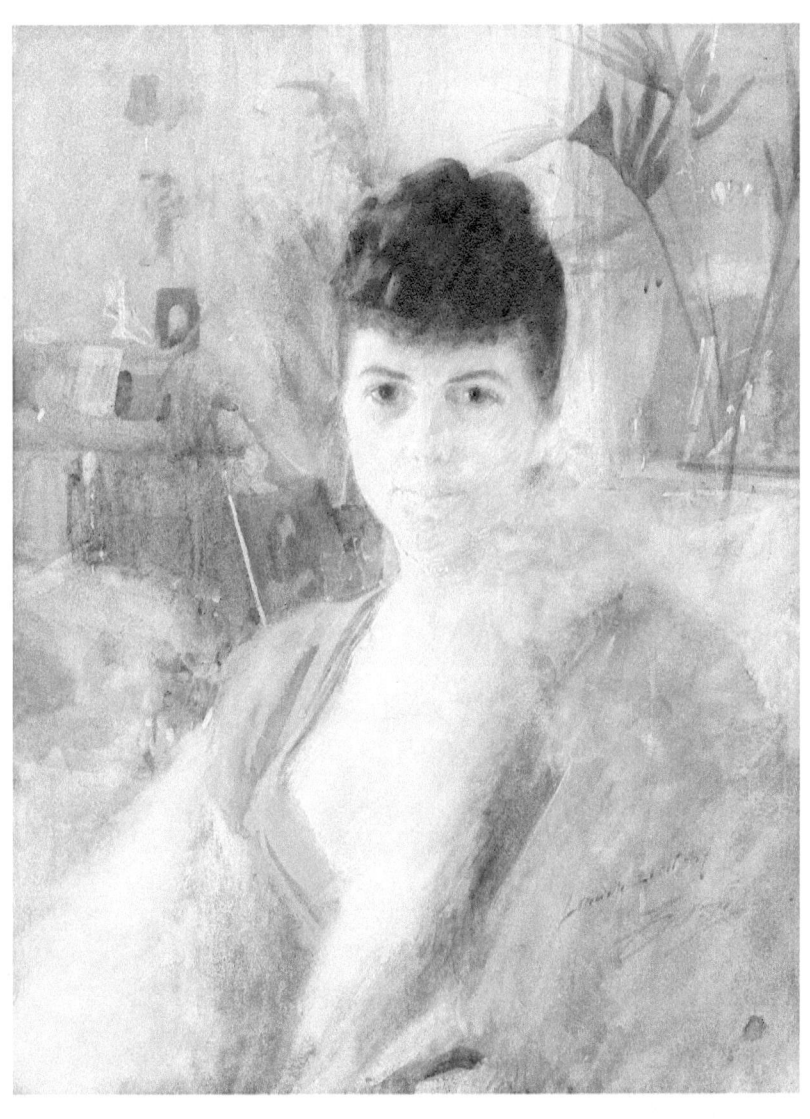

Lady with fur cape, 1887, watercolor on paper

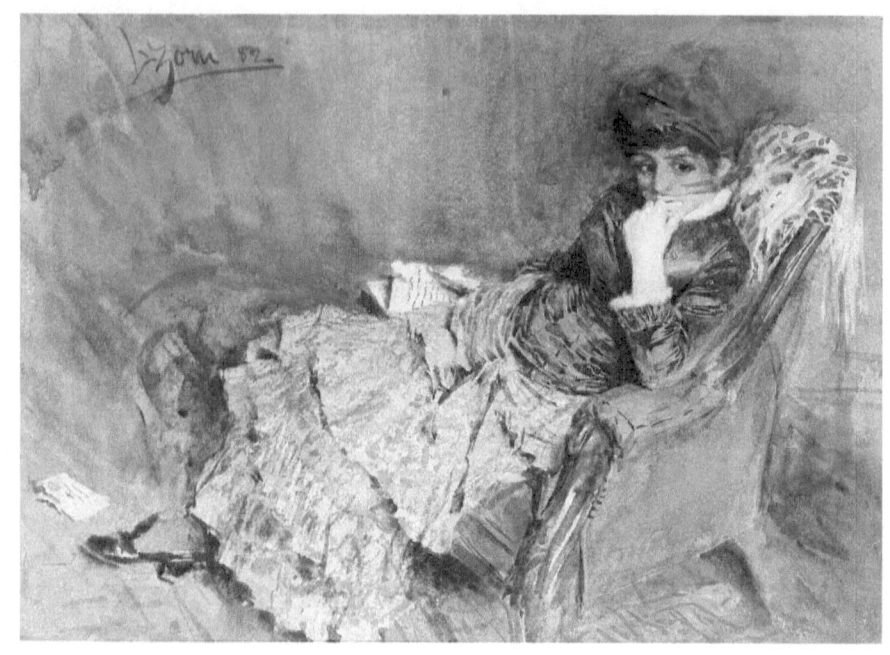

The Letter, 1882, watercolor on paper

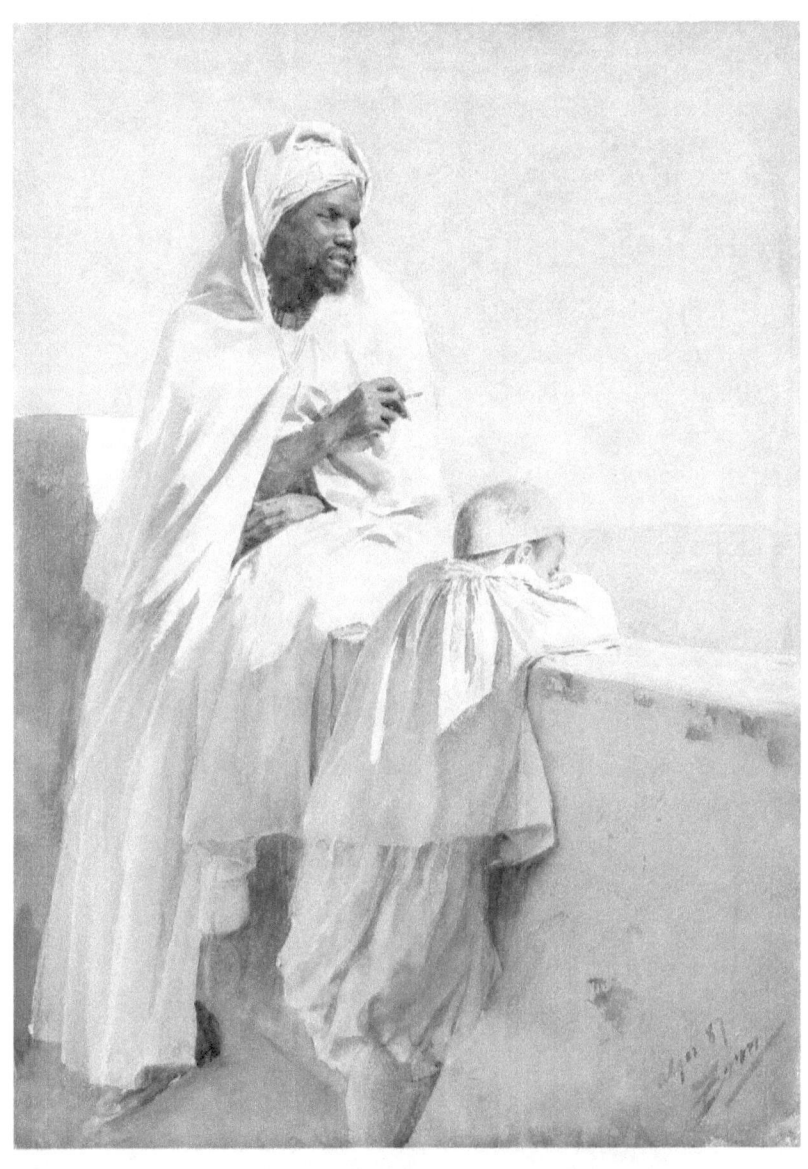

Man and boy in Algiers, 1887, watercolor and gouache
on paper mounted on board

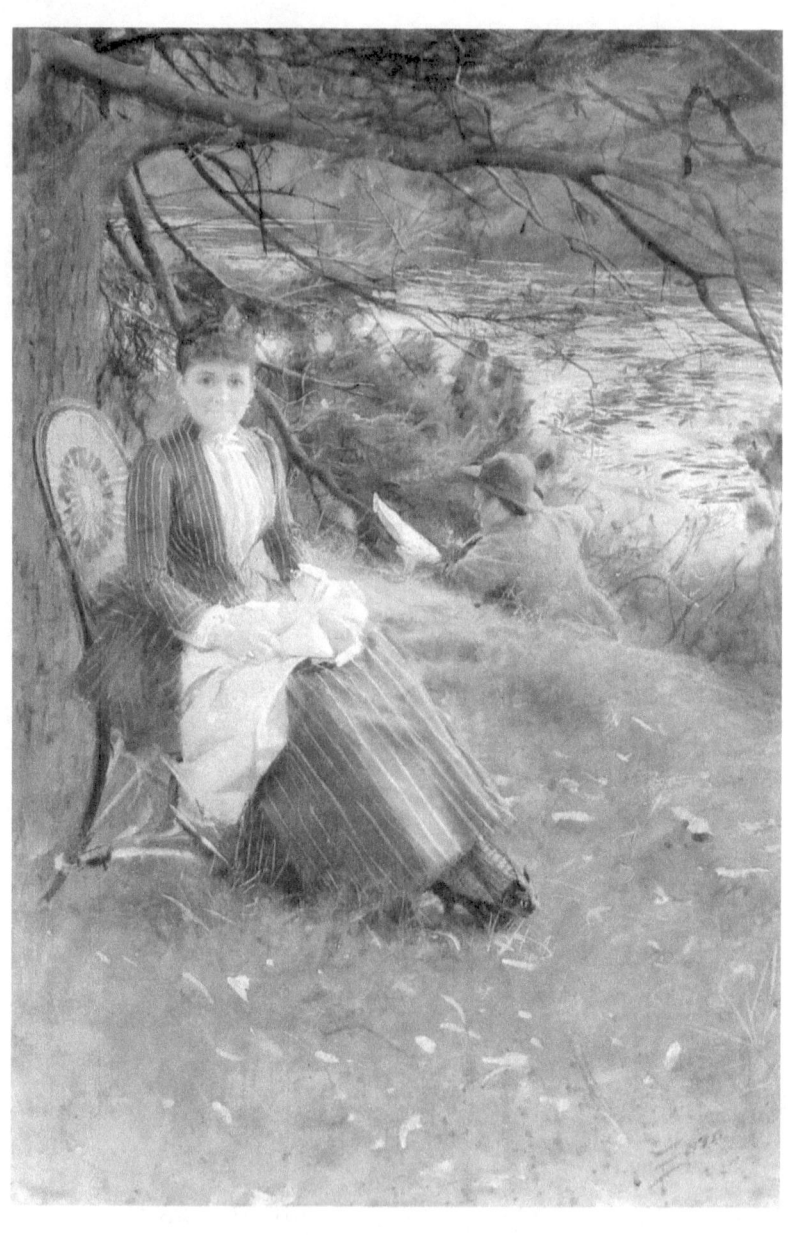

In Scotland (Mrs. Symons), 1887, watercolor

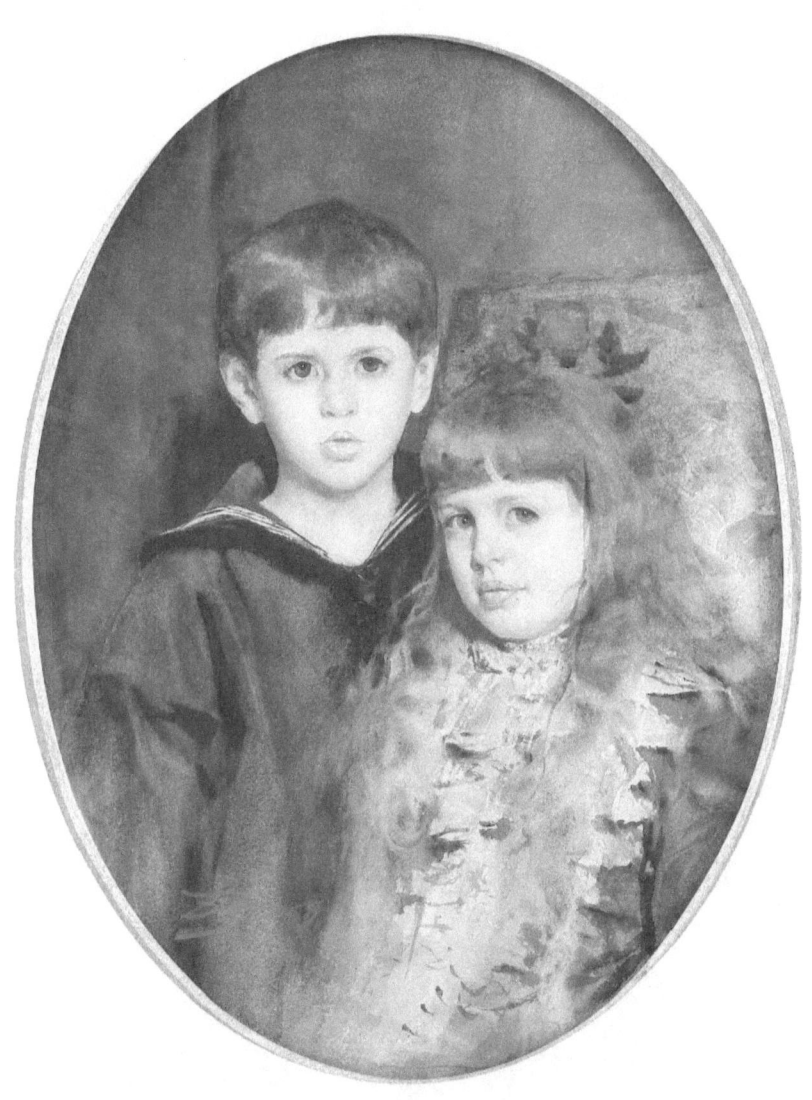

The Children Stuers, 1884, watercolor

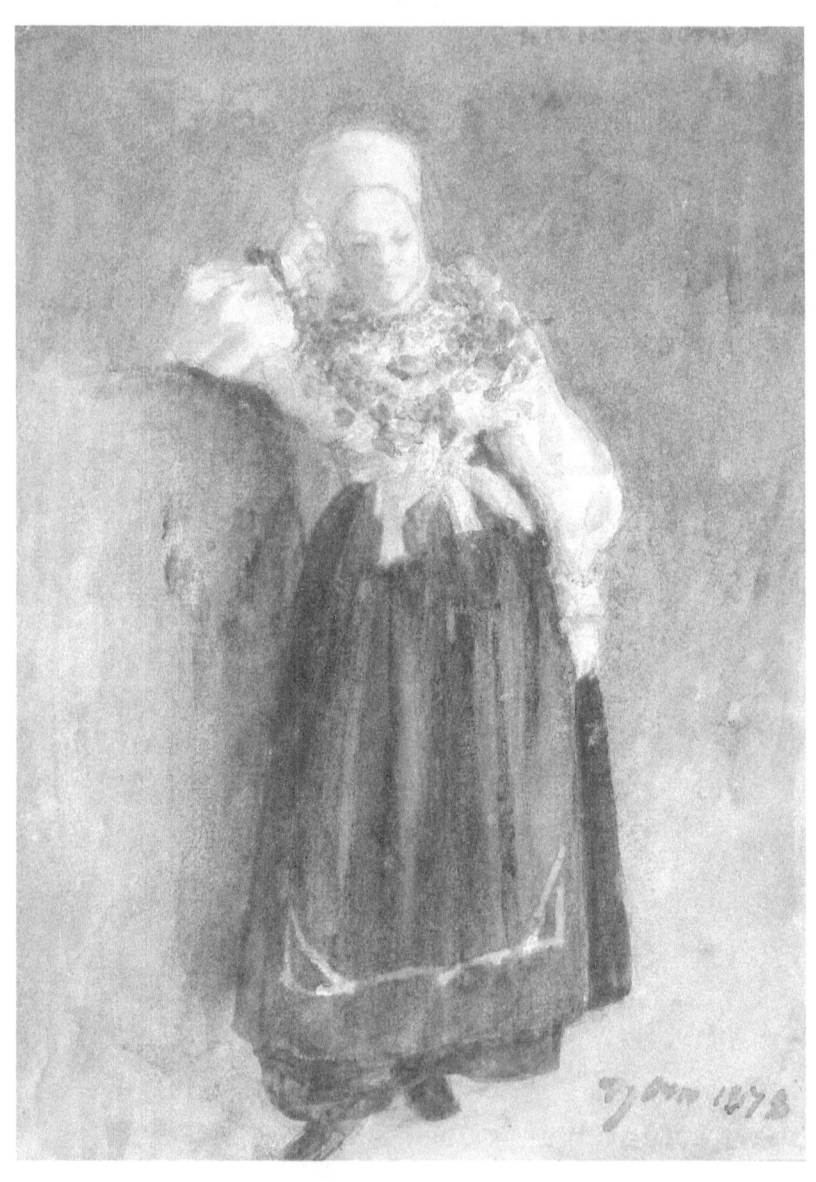

Ball in costume, 1878, watercolor

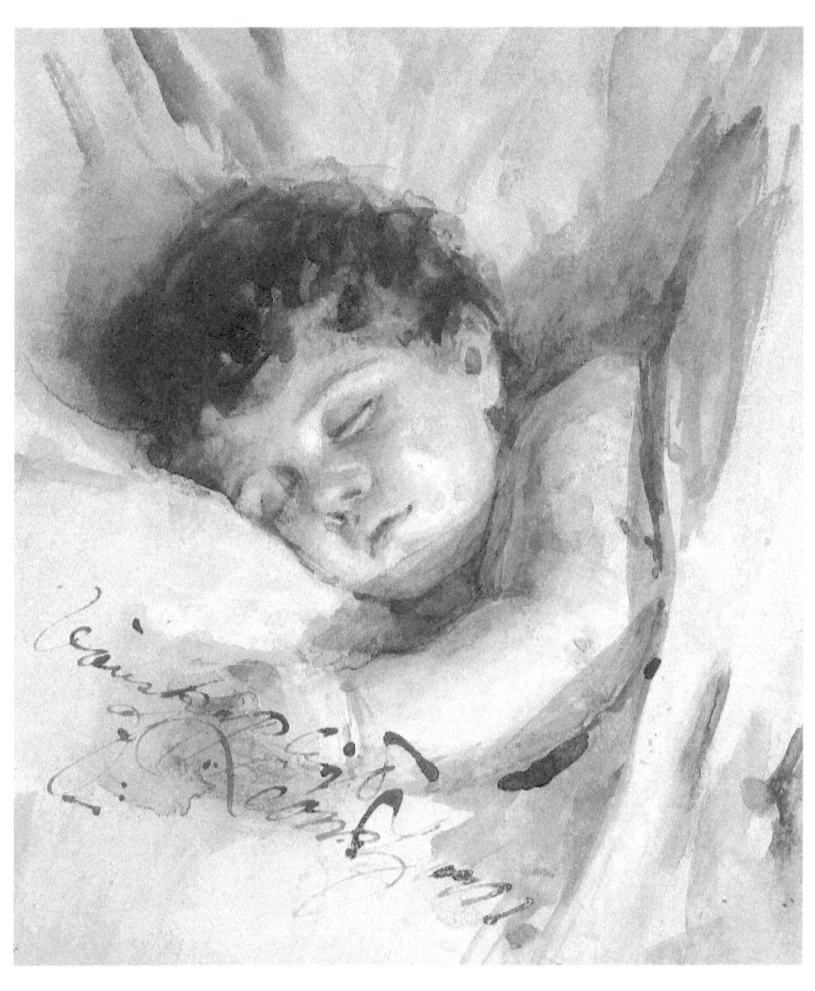

Sleeping Child, watercolor on paper

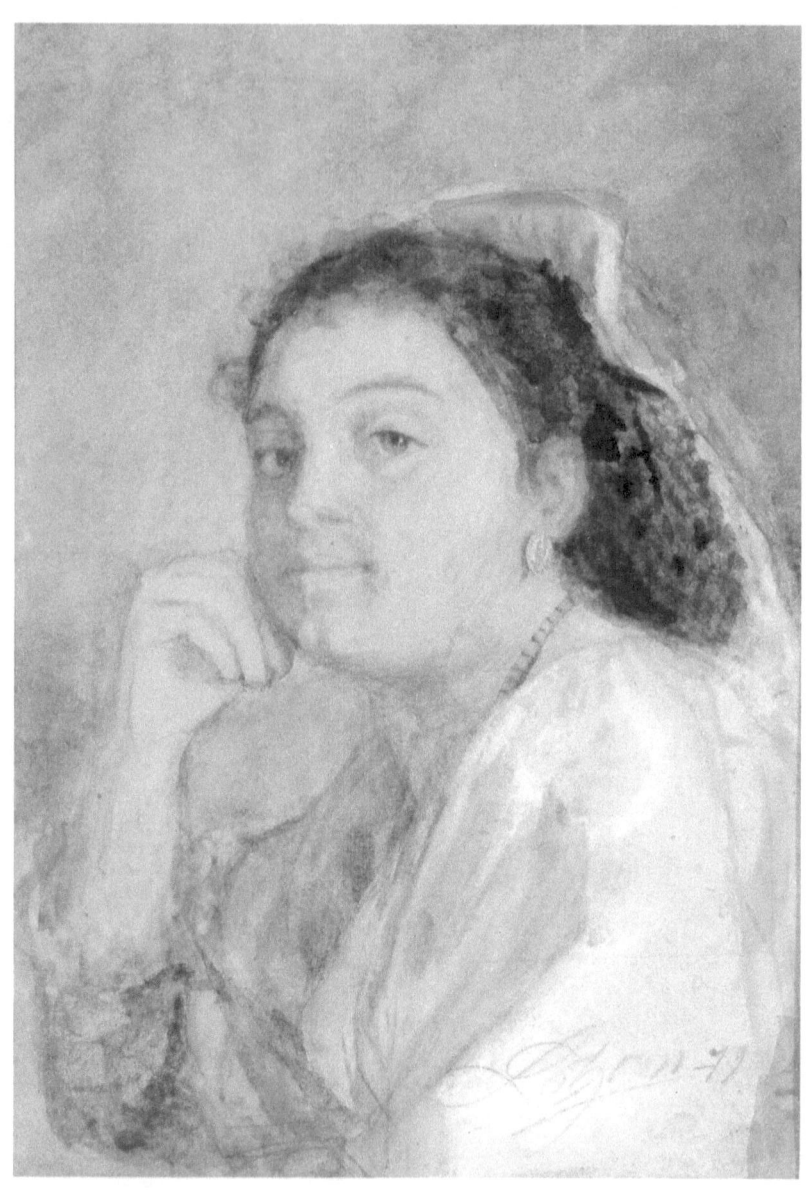

Spanish Woman, 1879, watercolor

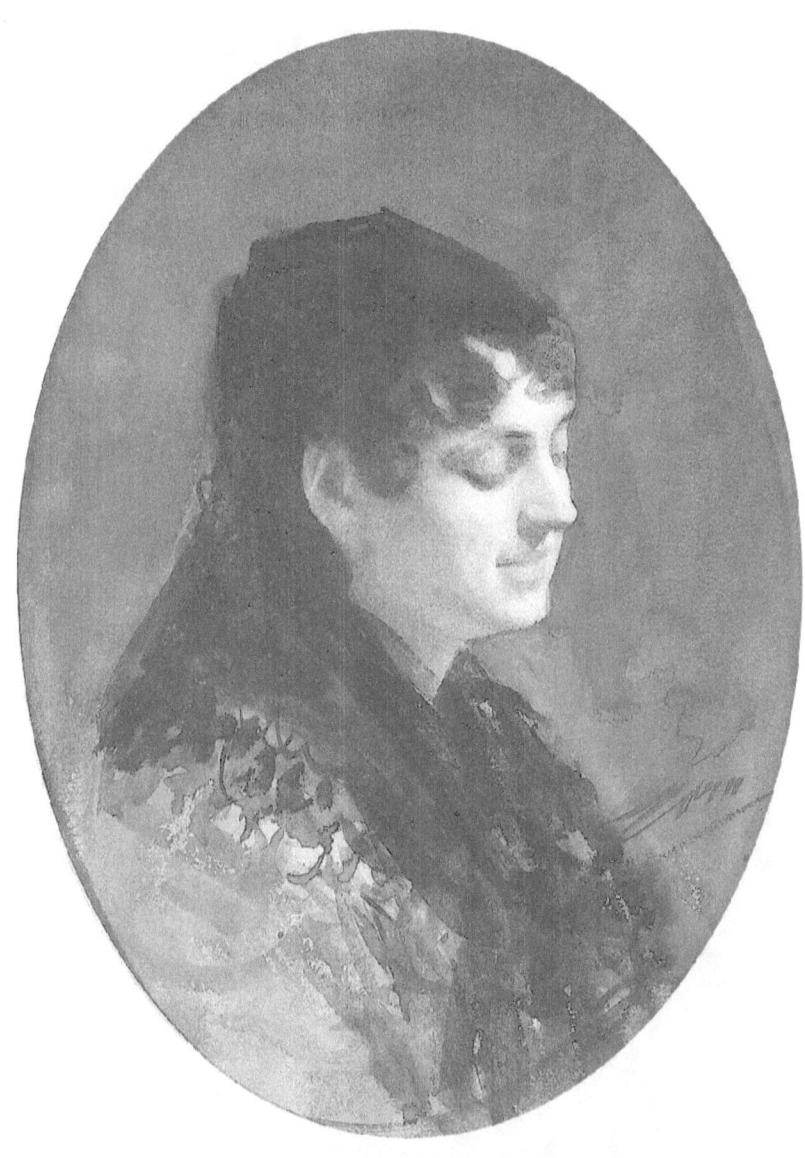

Spanish woman, probably 1884, watercolor on paper

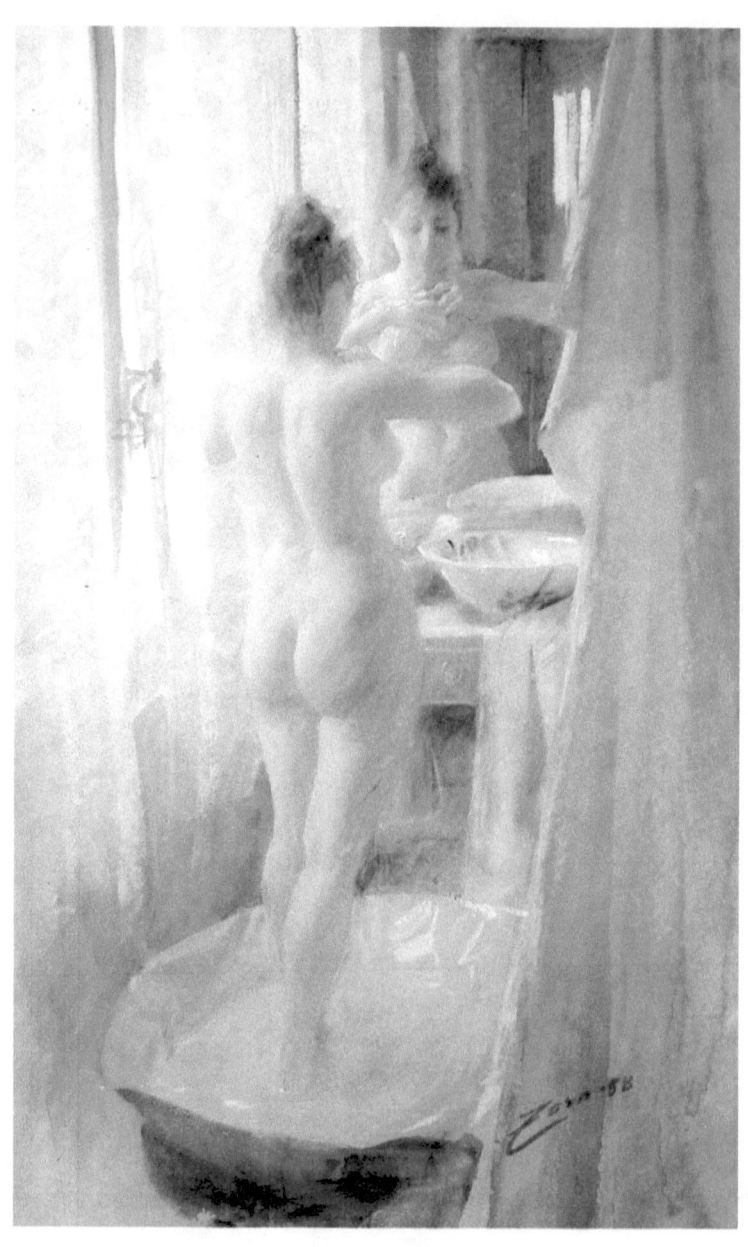

The Tub, 1888, watercolor on paper

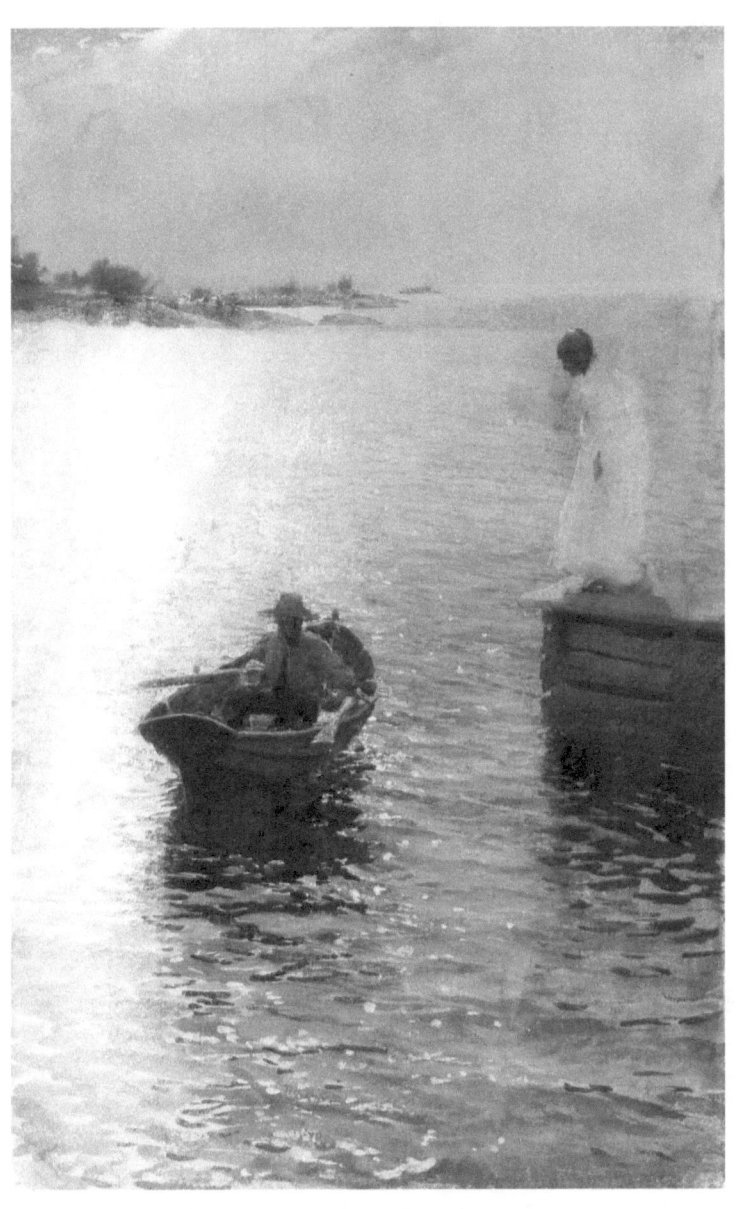

Summer pleasure, 1886, watercolor

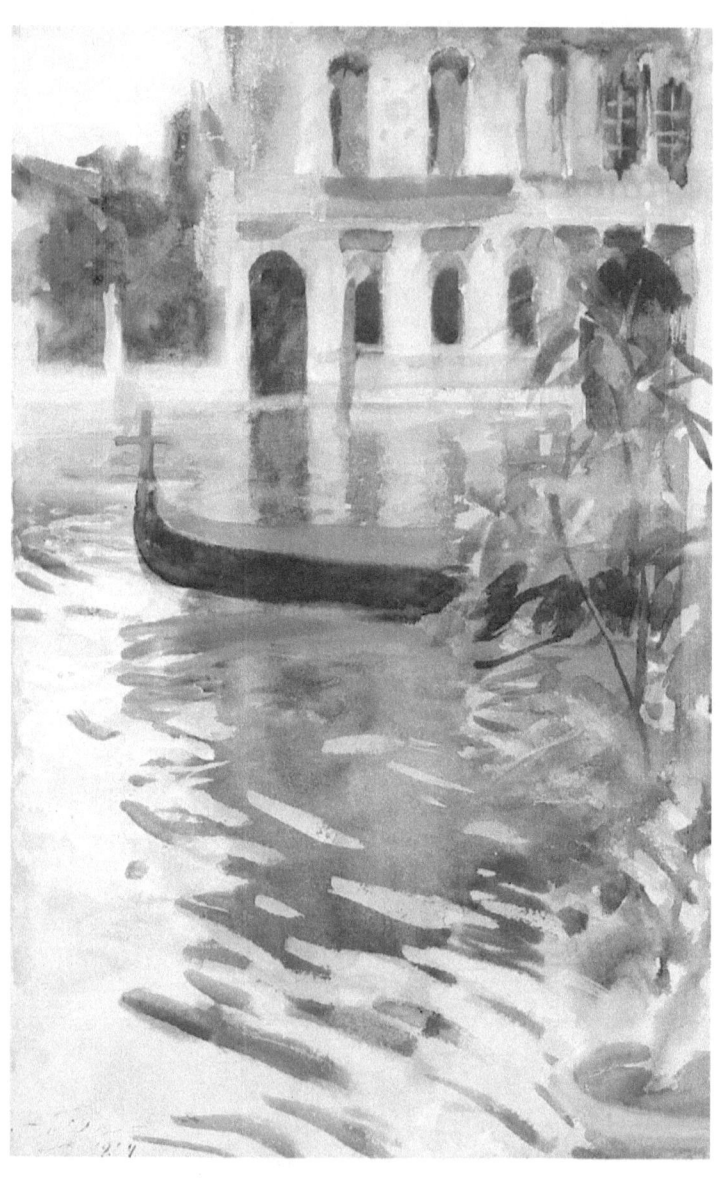

Gondola in Front of the Palazzo Barbaro, 1894,
watercolor on paper

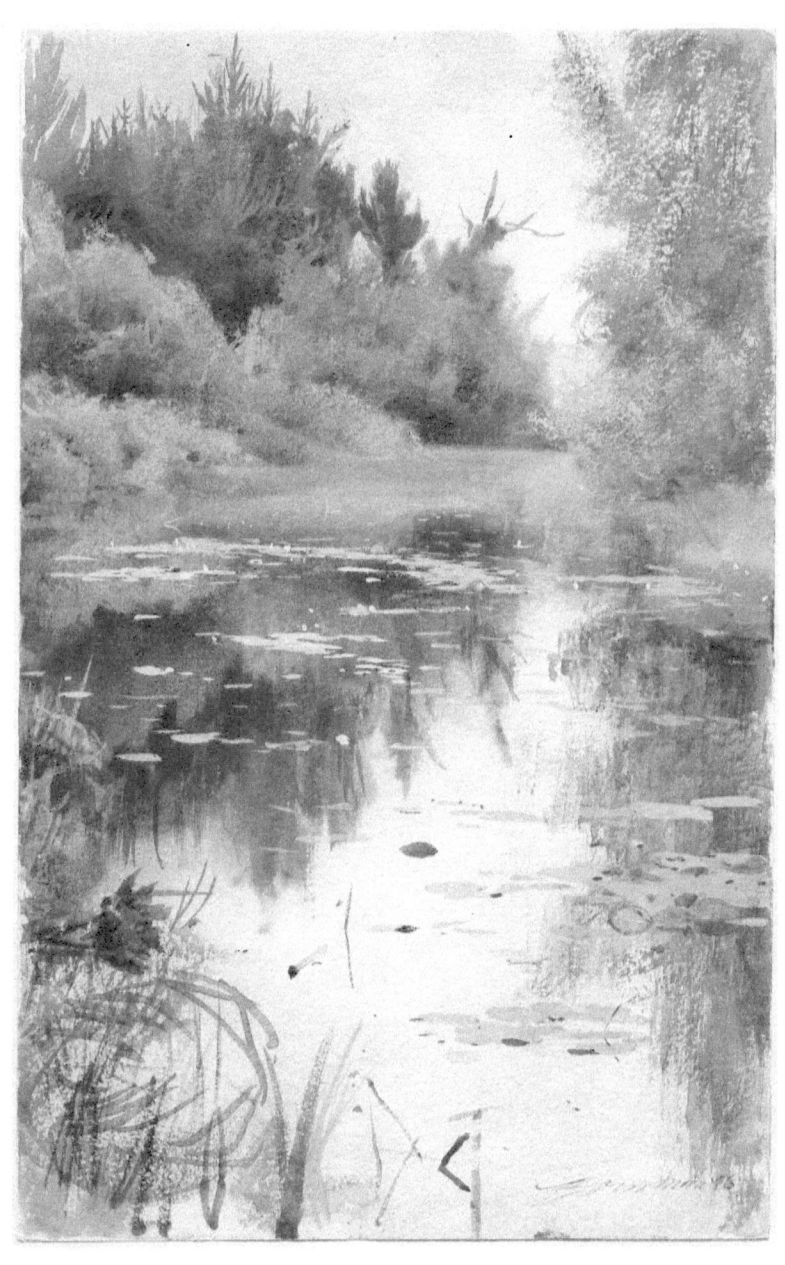

Landscape study of Mora, 1886, watercolor

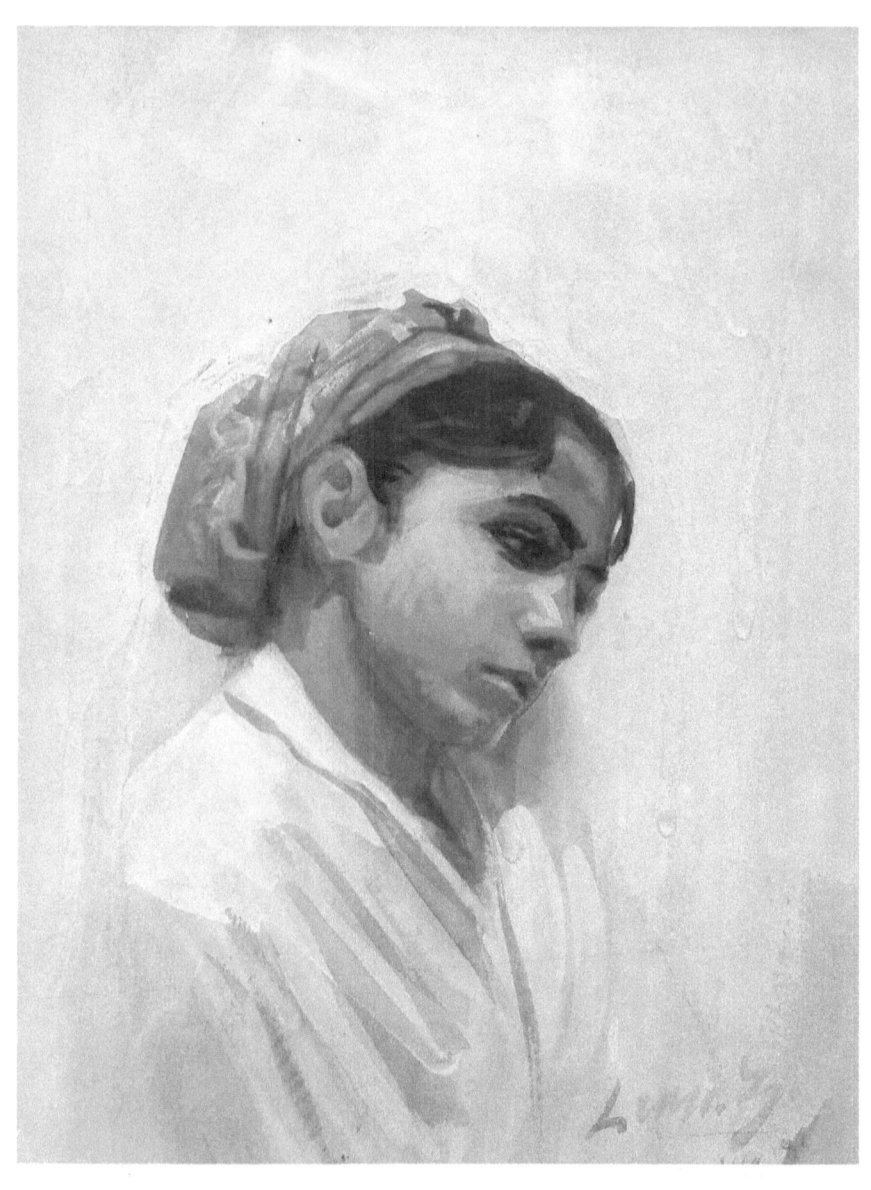

The head of the Spanish girl, Seville, 1881, watercolor

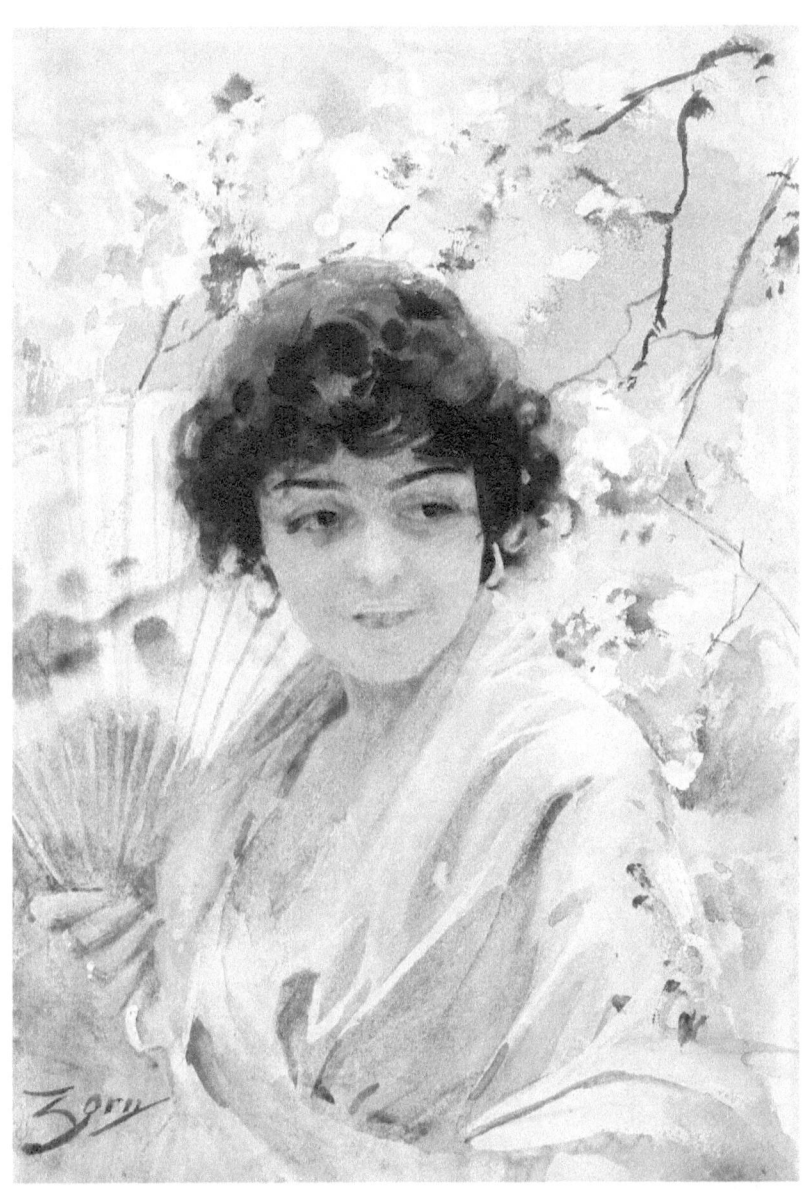

Rosita, 1884-1885, watercolor on paper

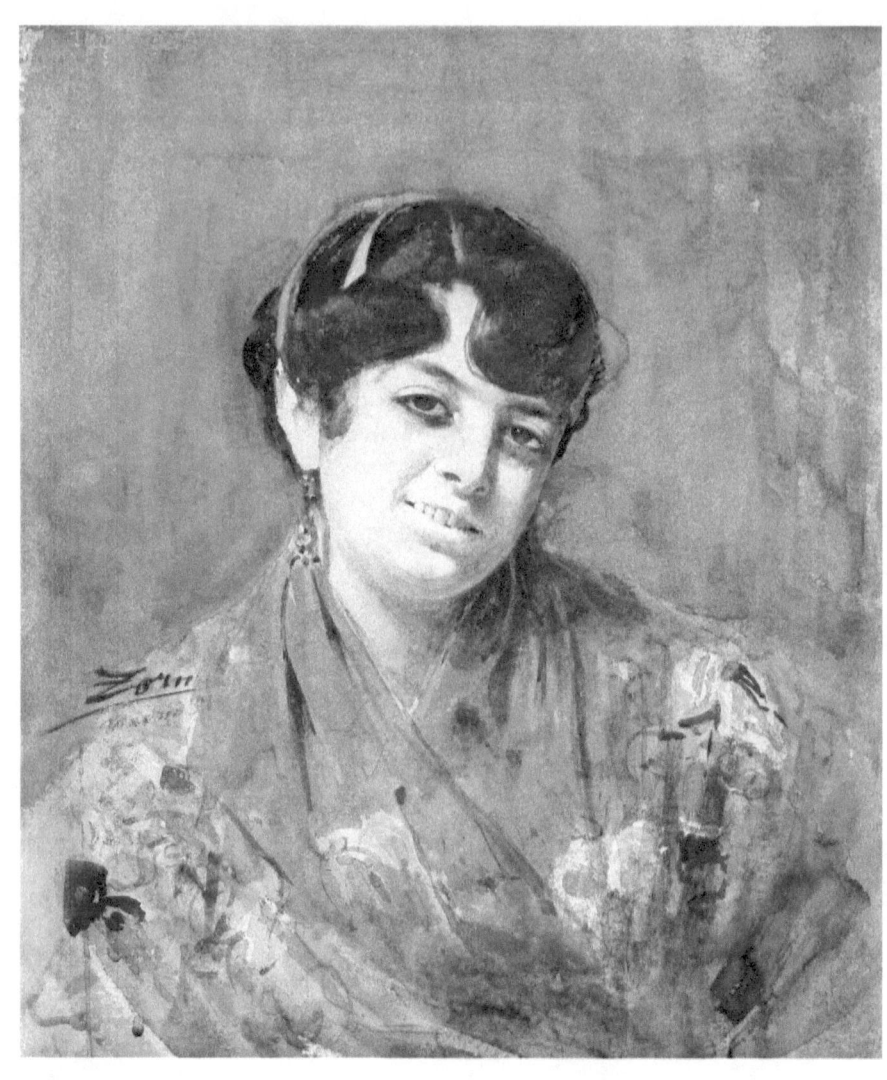

A Spaniard from Madrid II, 1884, watercolor on paper

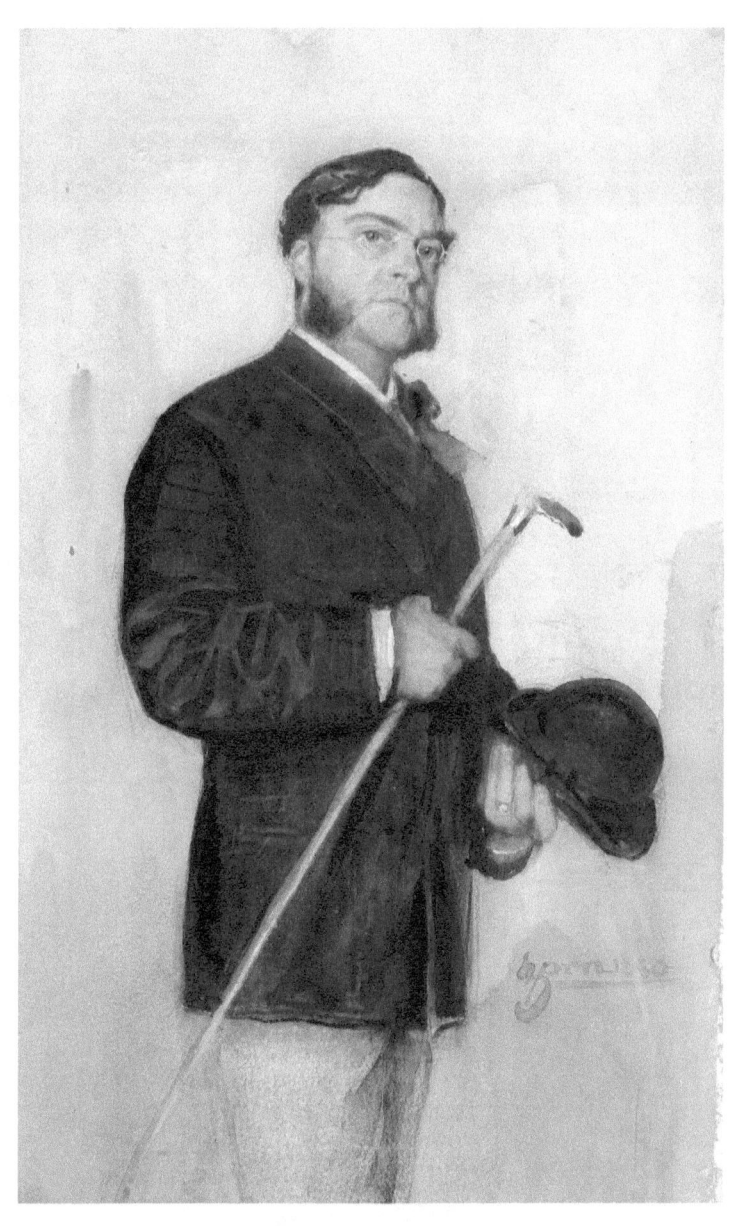

Banker Ludvig Arosenius, 1880, watercolor

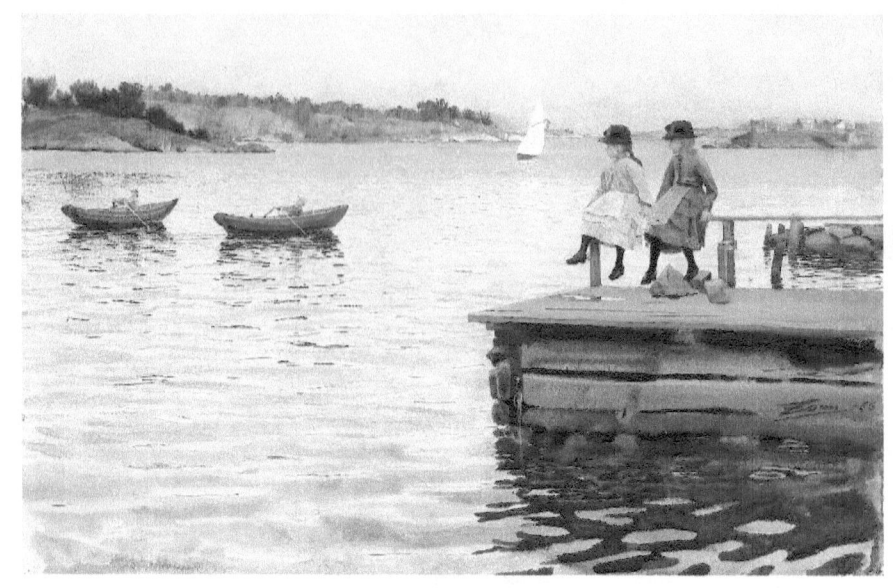

A boat race between two boys at the island of Dalarö, in
the Stockholm archipelago, watercolor

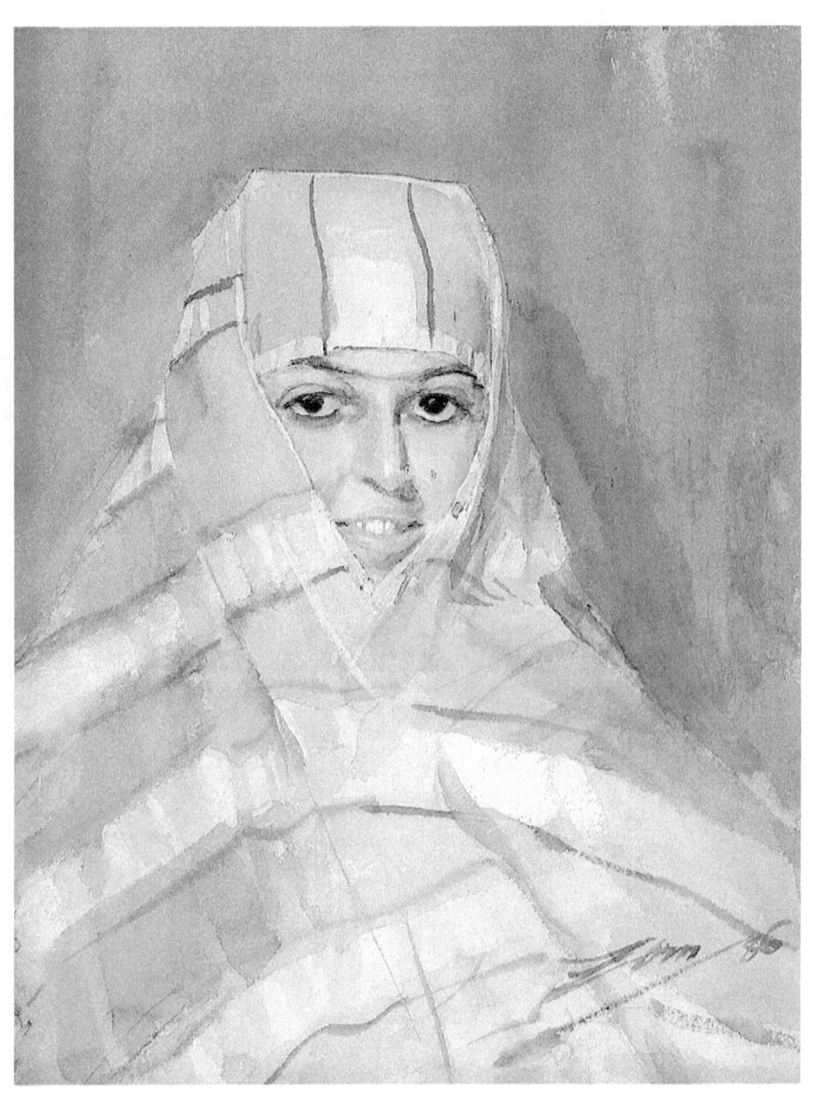

Bedouin girl, 1886, watercolor

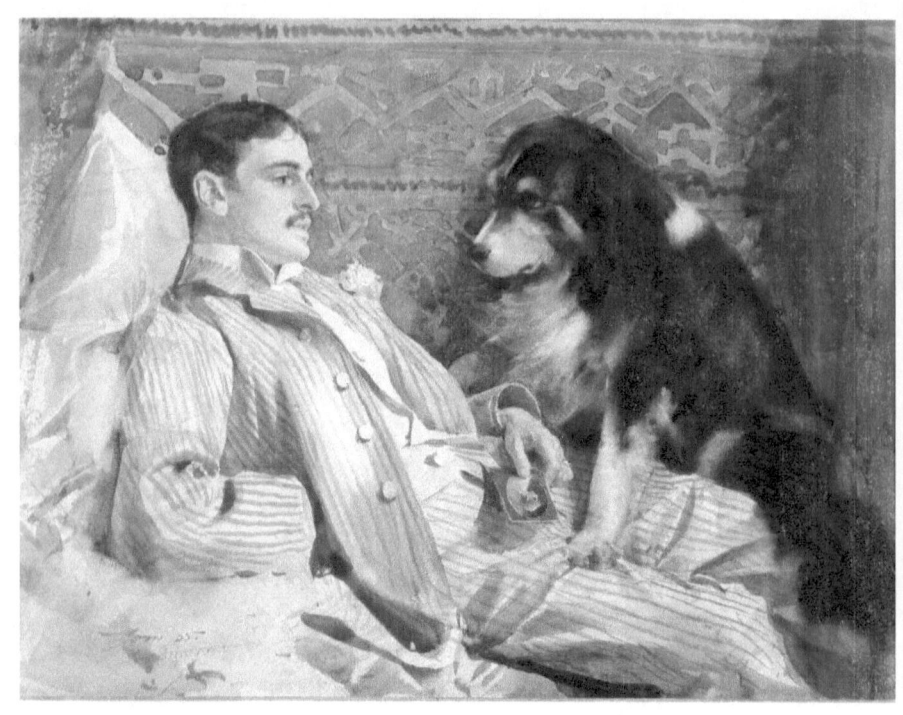

Clarence Barker, 1885, watercolor

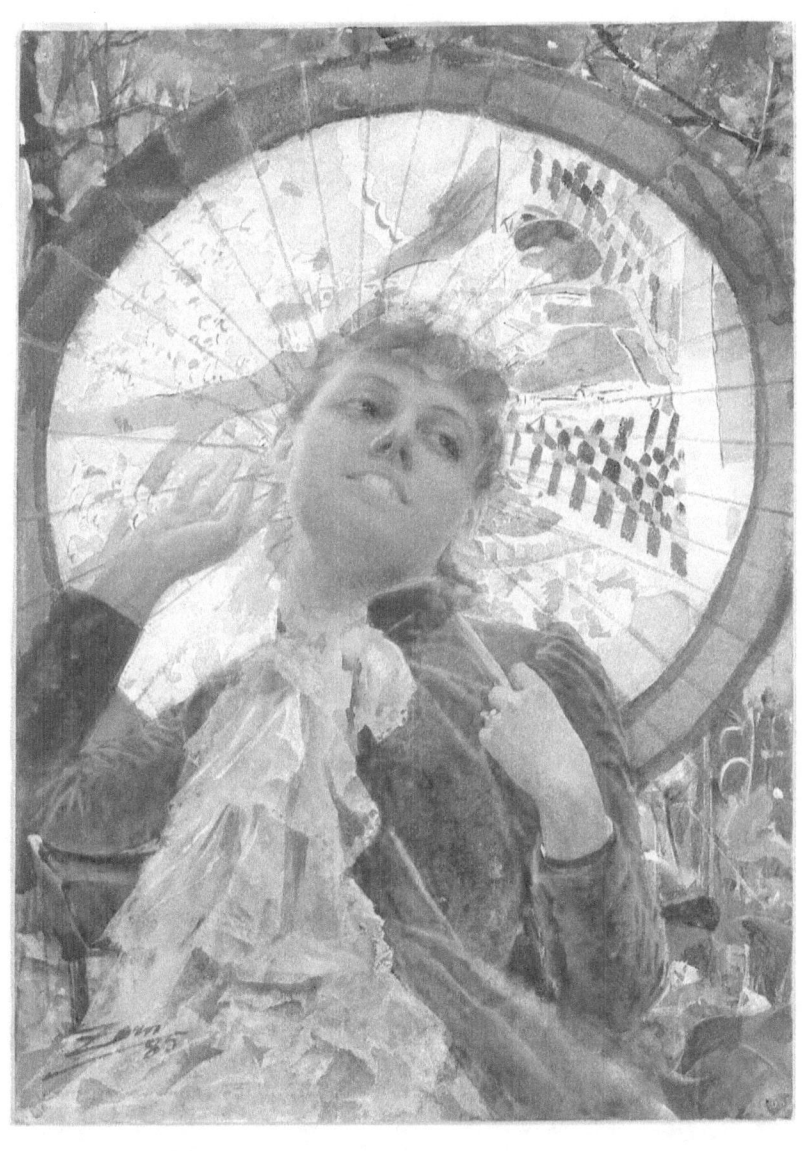

Castles in the Air, 1885, watercolor

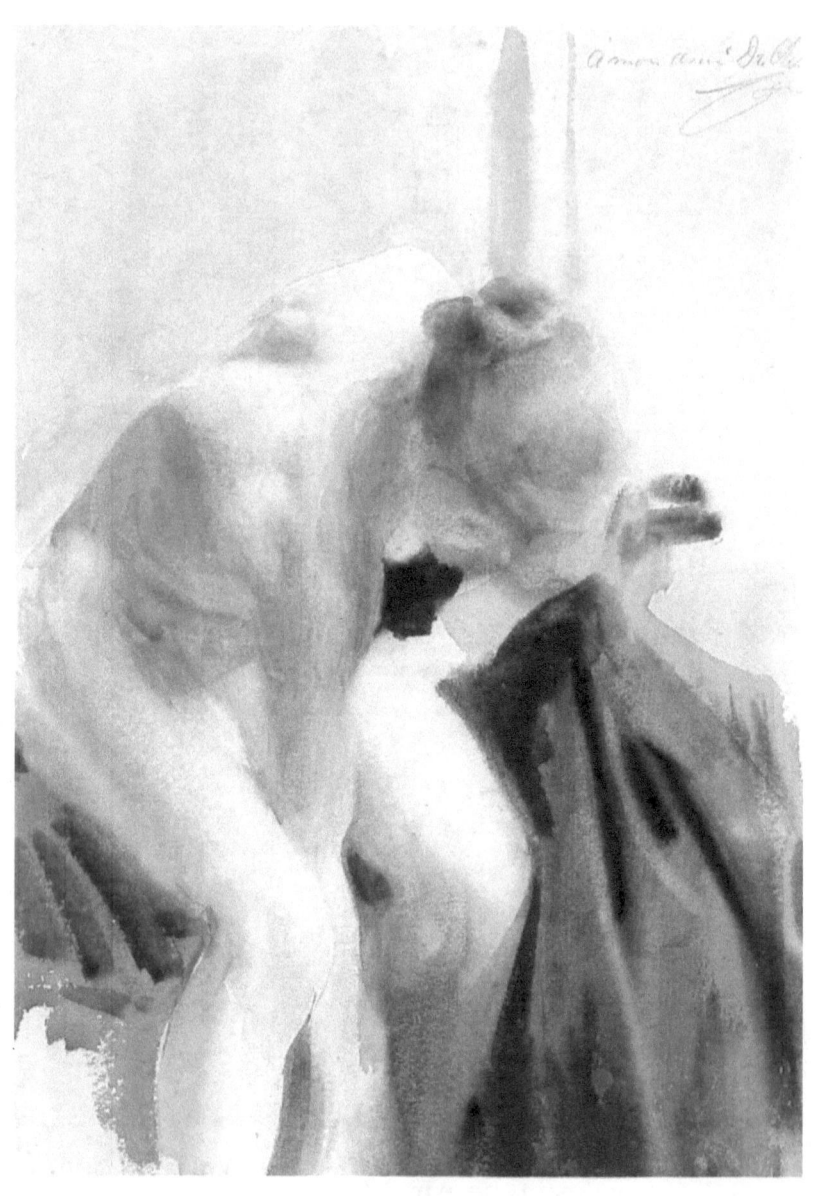

A Female Nude, watercolor

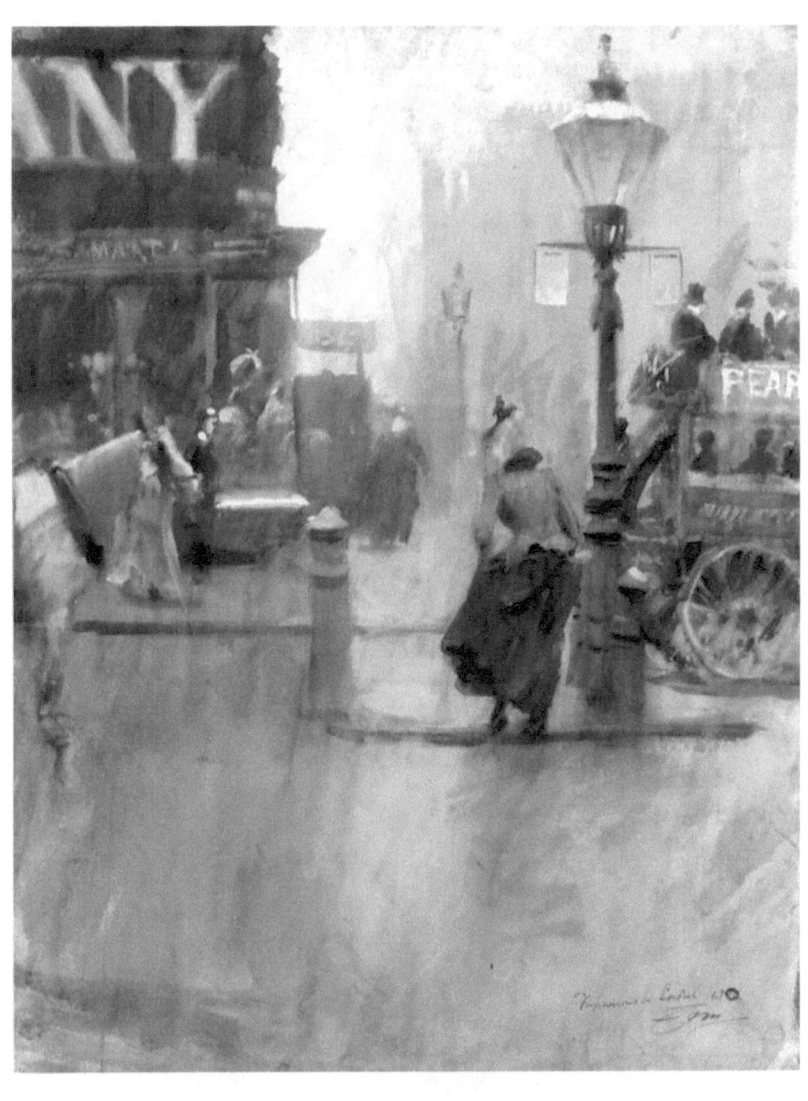

Impressions of London, 1890, watercolor

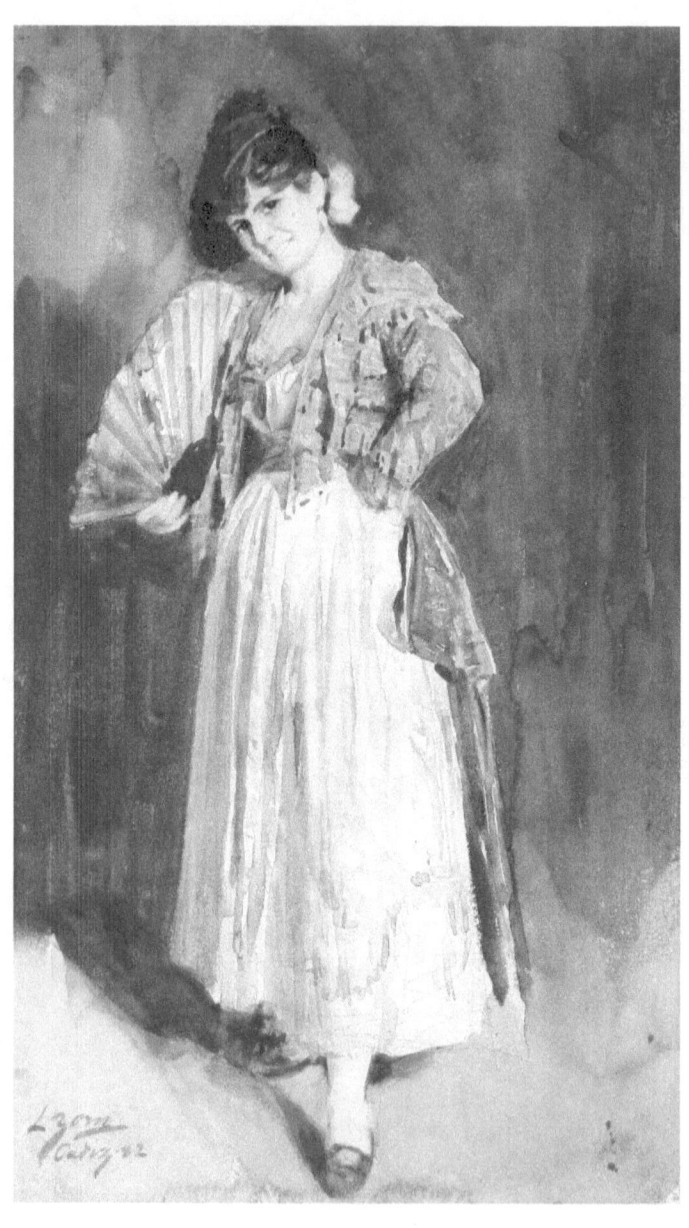

Spanish Lady, 1893, watercolor

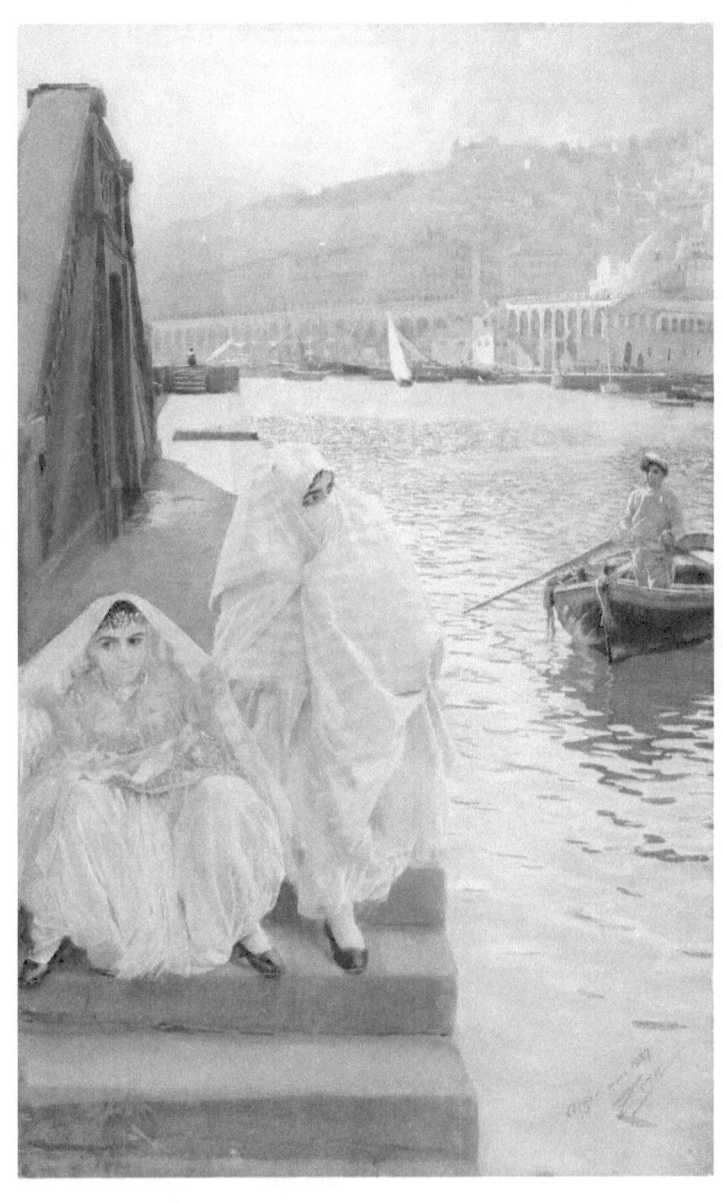

From Algiers Harbor, 1887, Watercolor

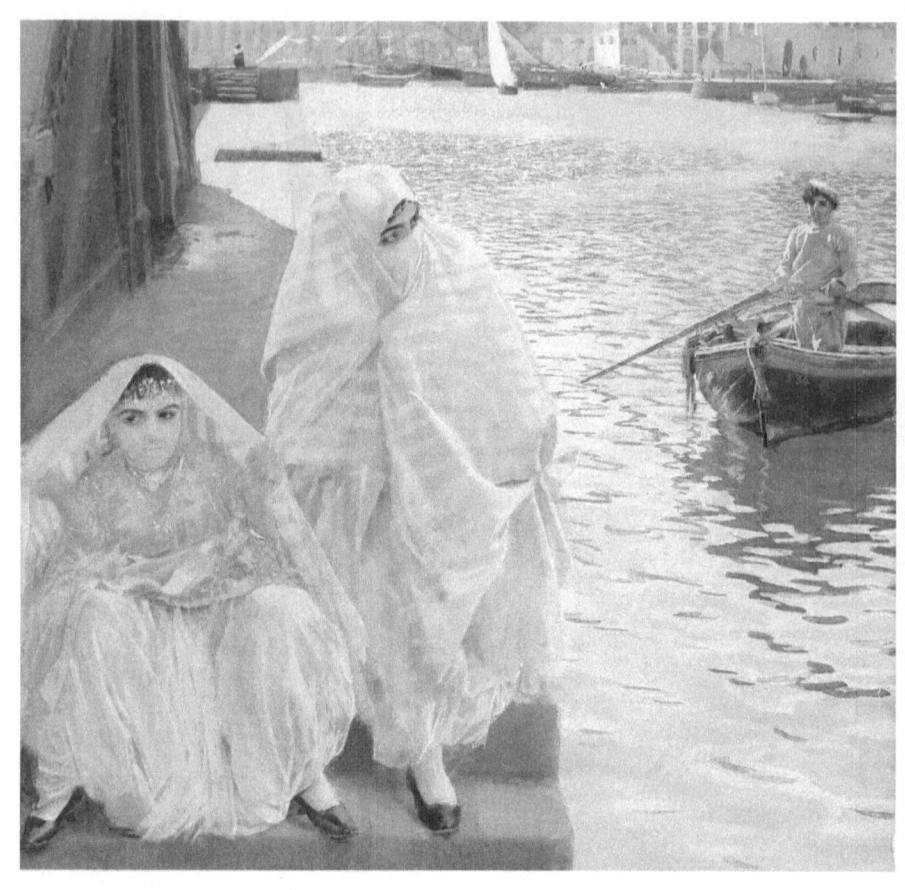

From Algiers Harbor, Detail, 1887, Watercolor

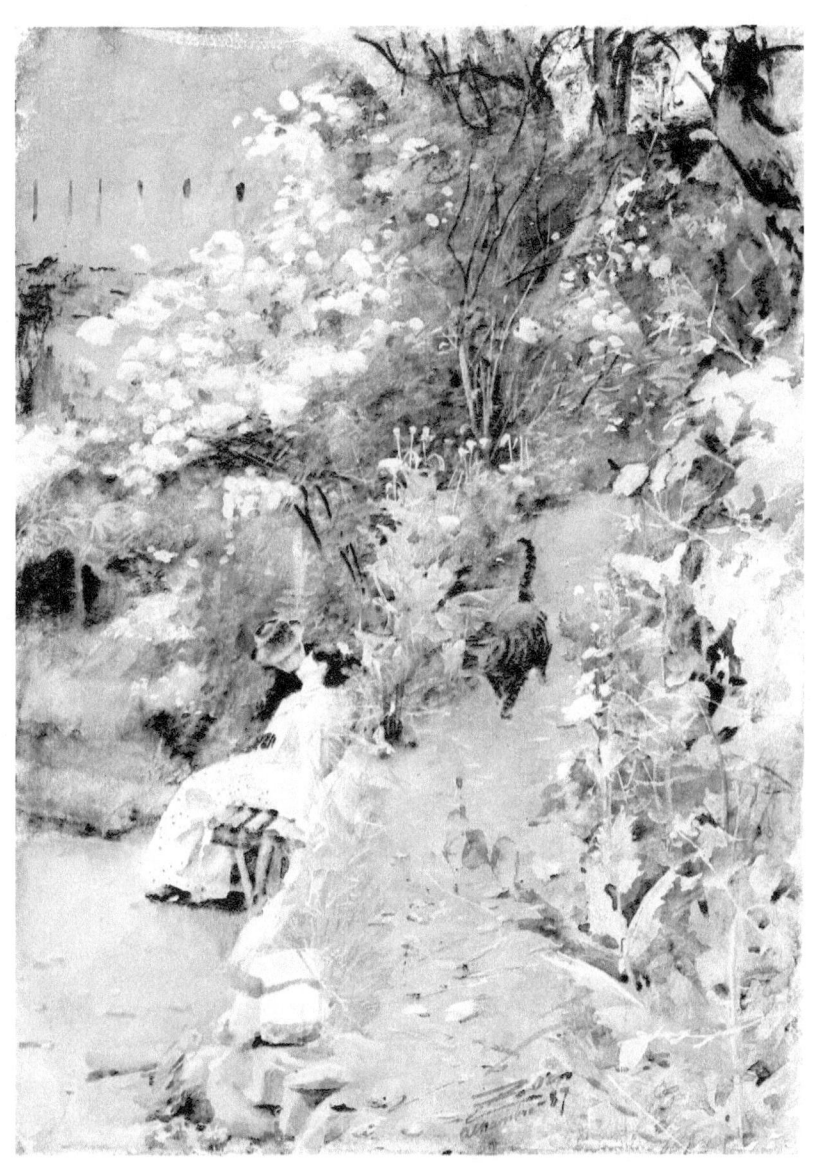

In Alhambra Park, 1887, watercolor

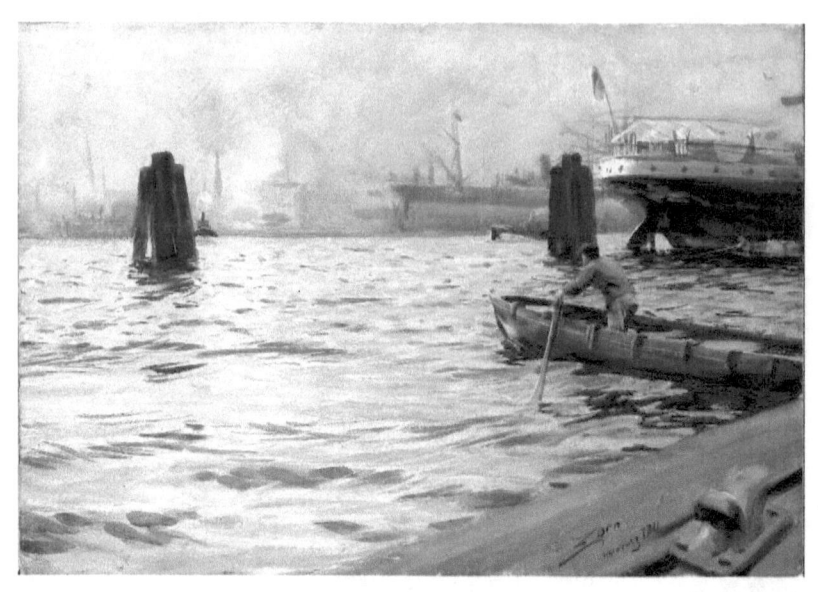

Port of Hamburg, 1891, watercolor

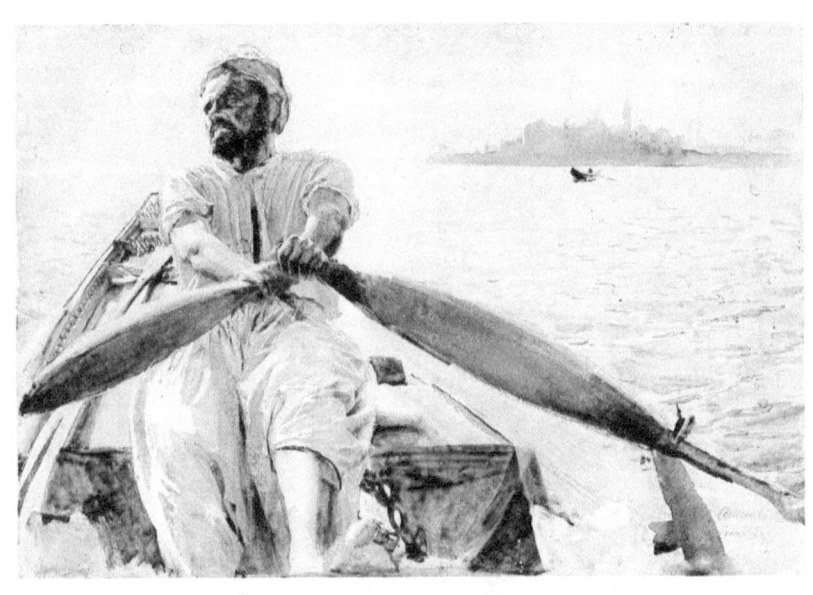

Caique Oarsman, 1886, Watercolor

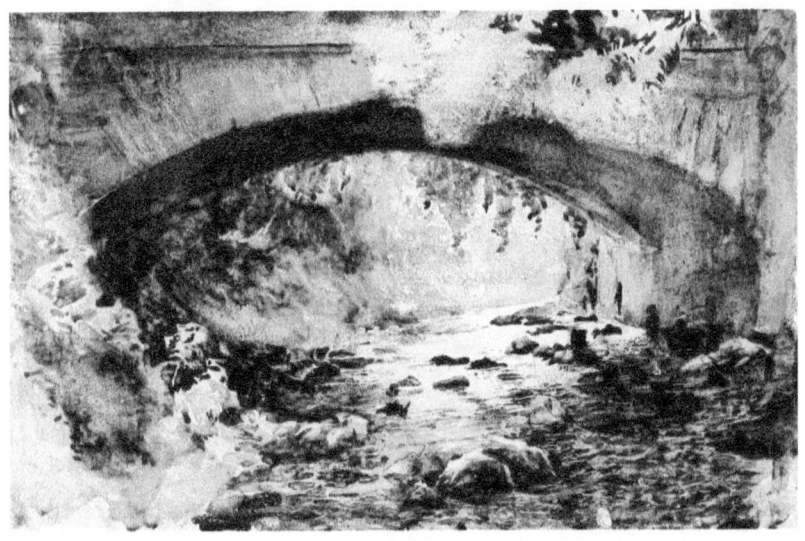

River under Old Stone Bridge, 1884, watercolor

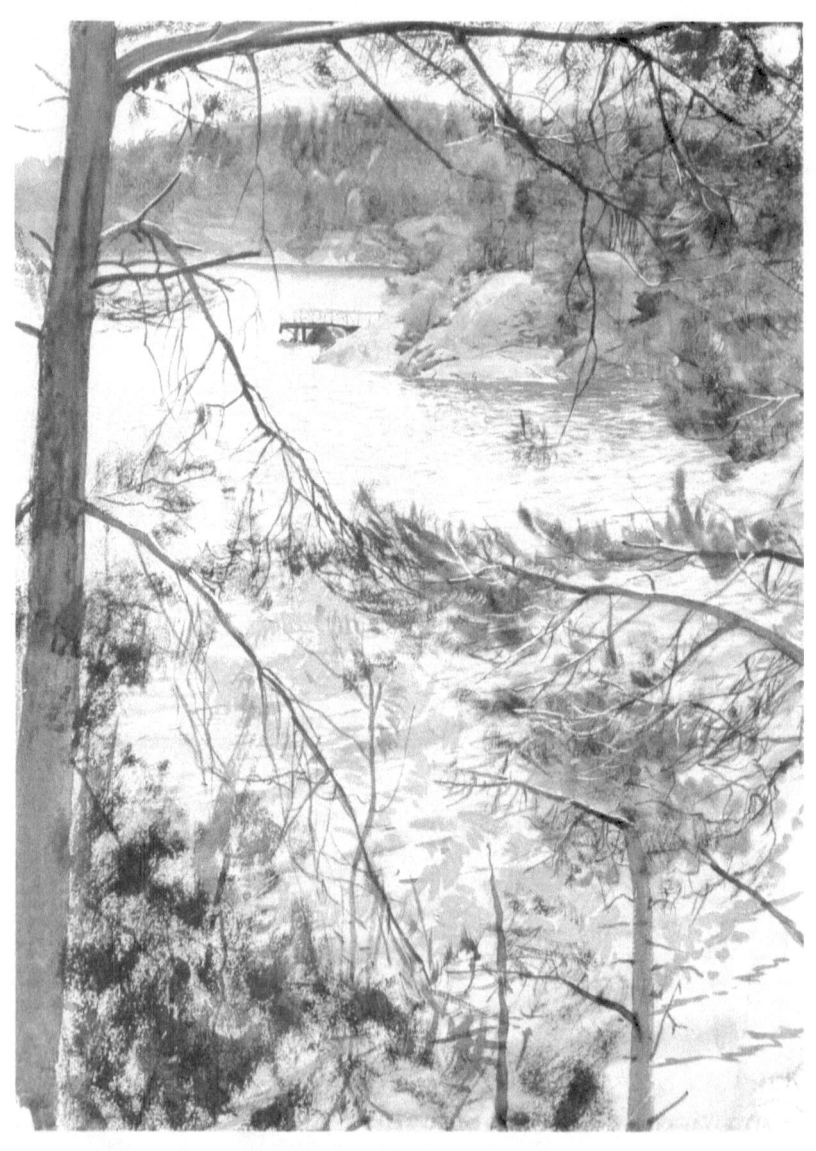

Kyrkviken bei Lidingö, 1883, watercolor and gouache

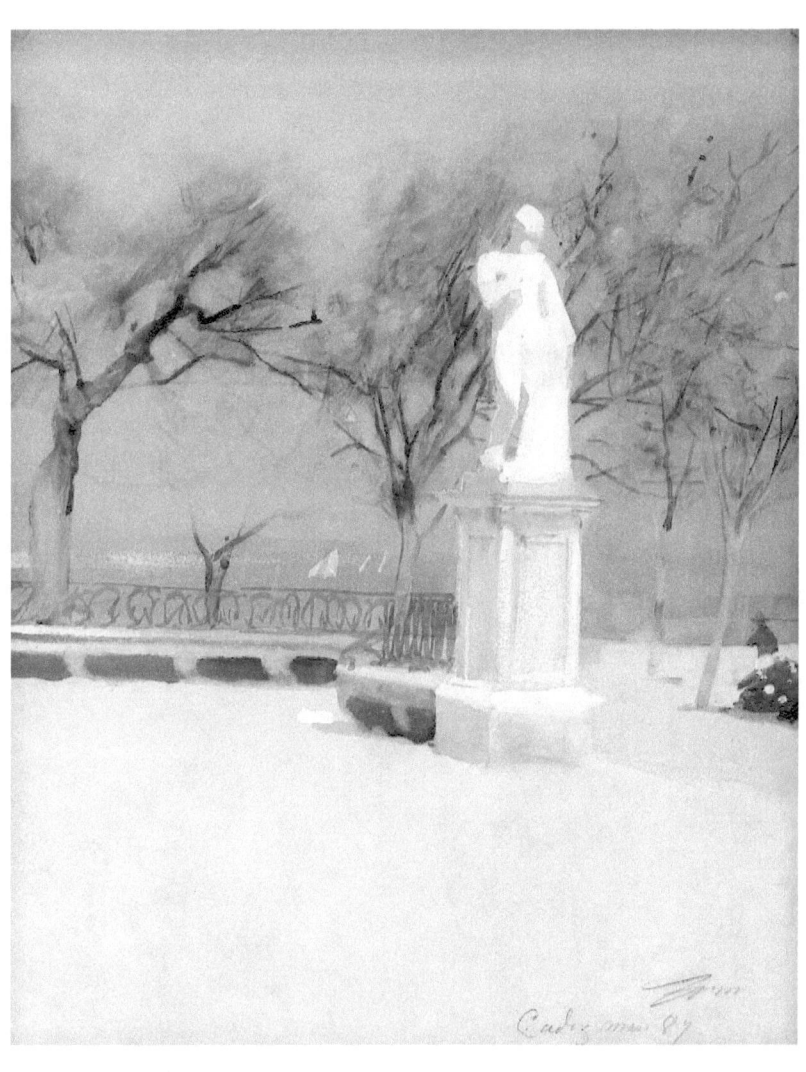

Alameda de Apodaca (Street) in Cádiz, 1887,
watercolor

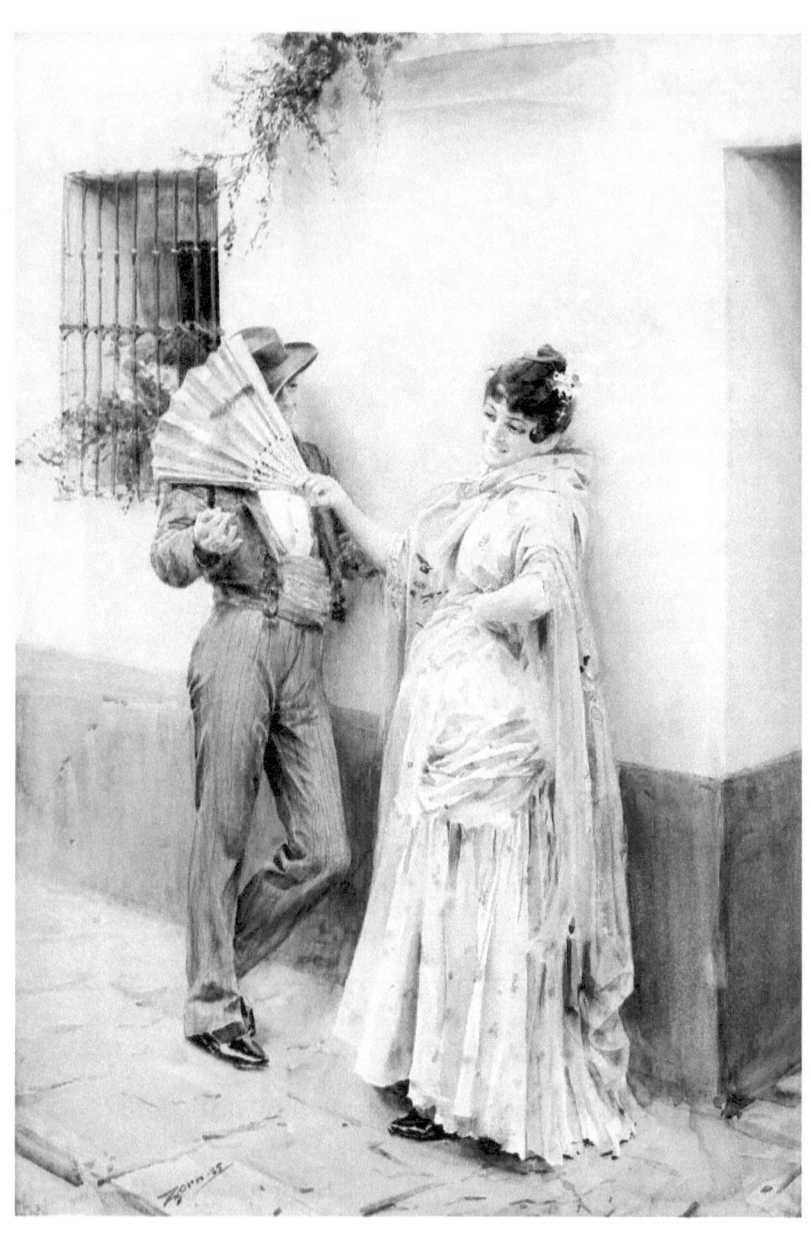

Flirtation, no date, watercolor

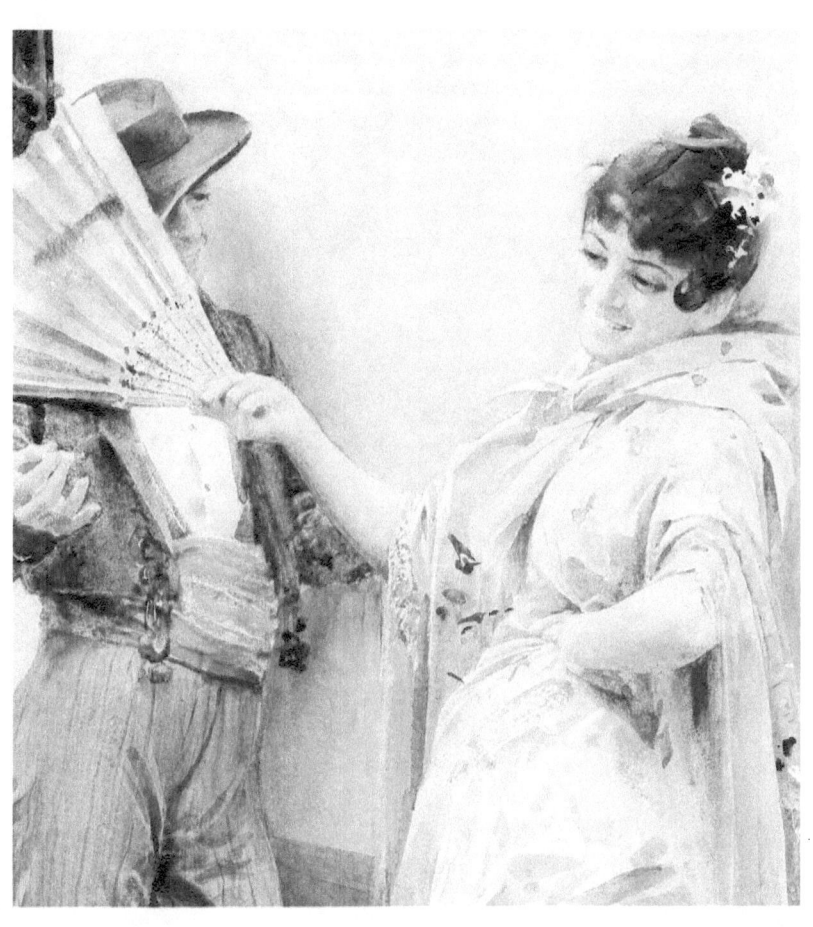

Flirtation, Detail, no date, watercolor

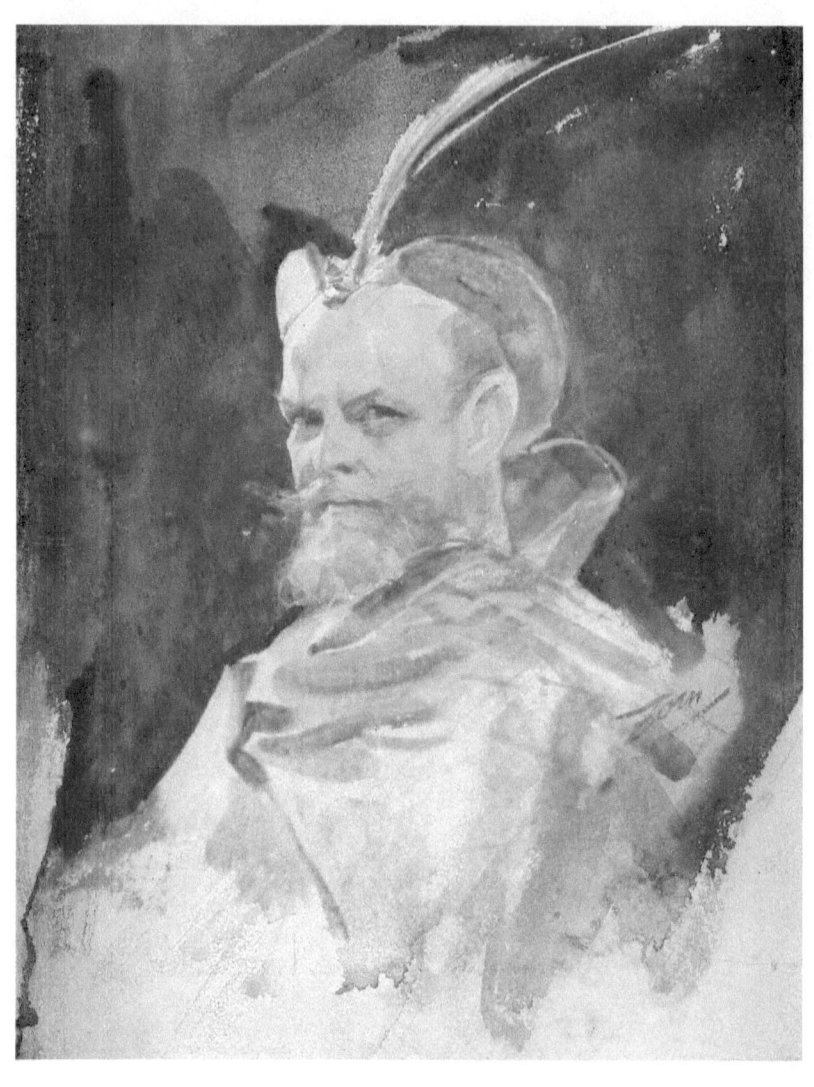

Mefisto (Konsul Dahlander), 1884, watercolor

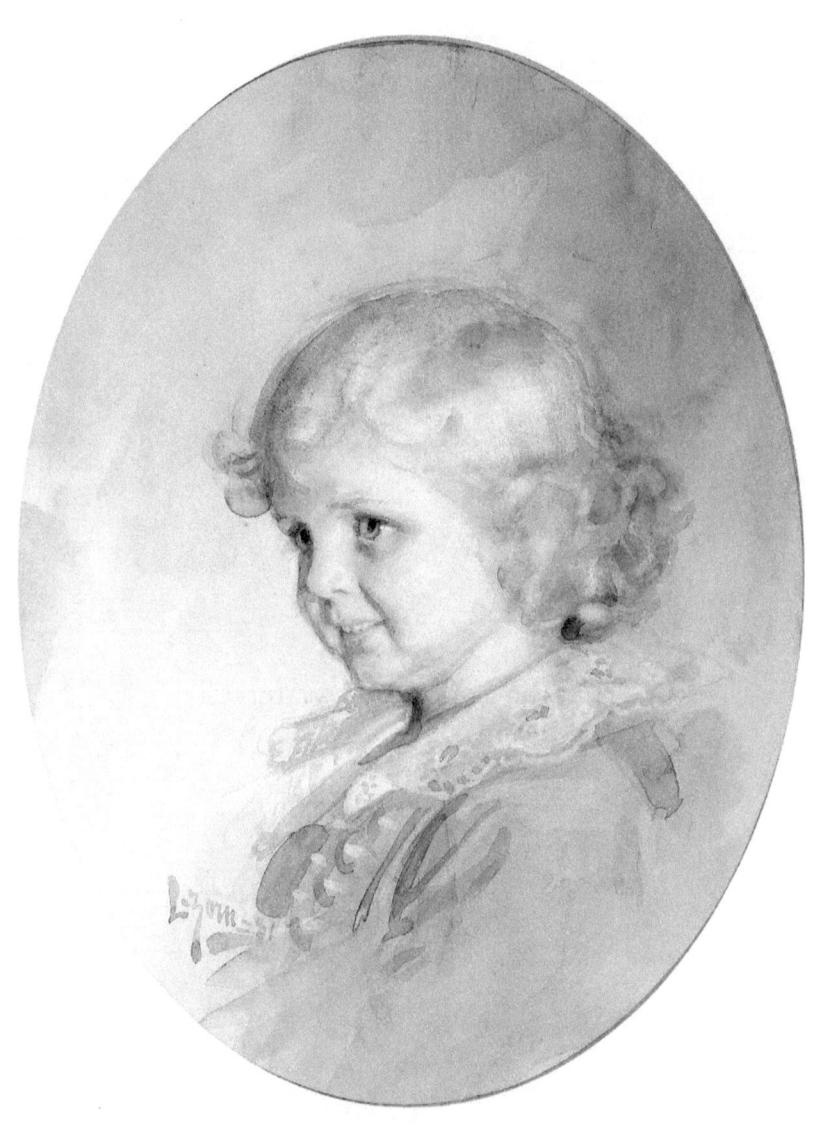

Portrait of a boy, 1881, watercolor

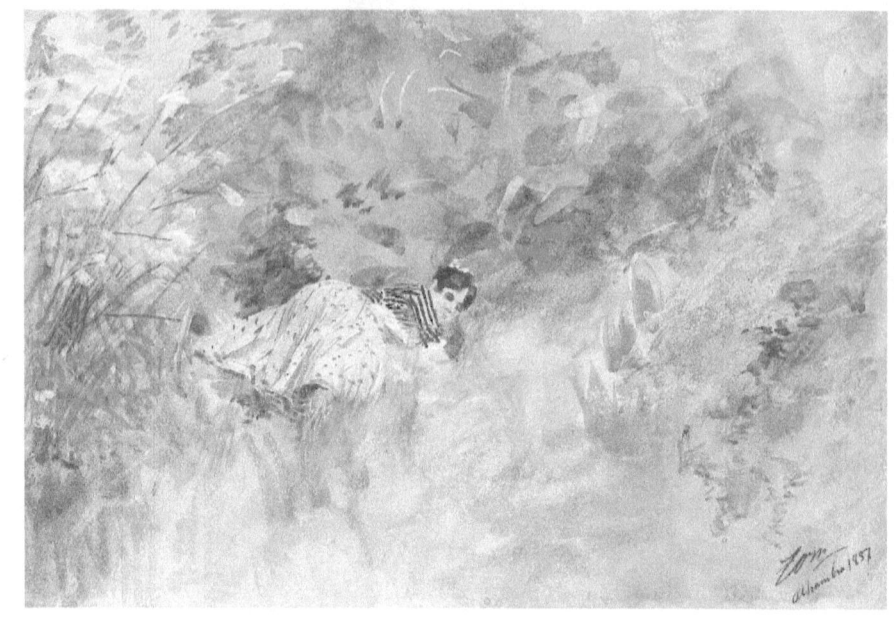

Girl in the grass, 1887, watercolor

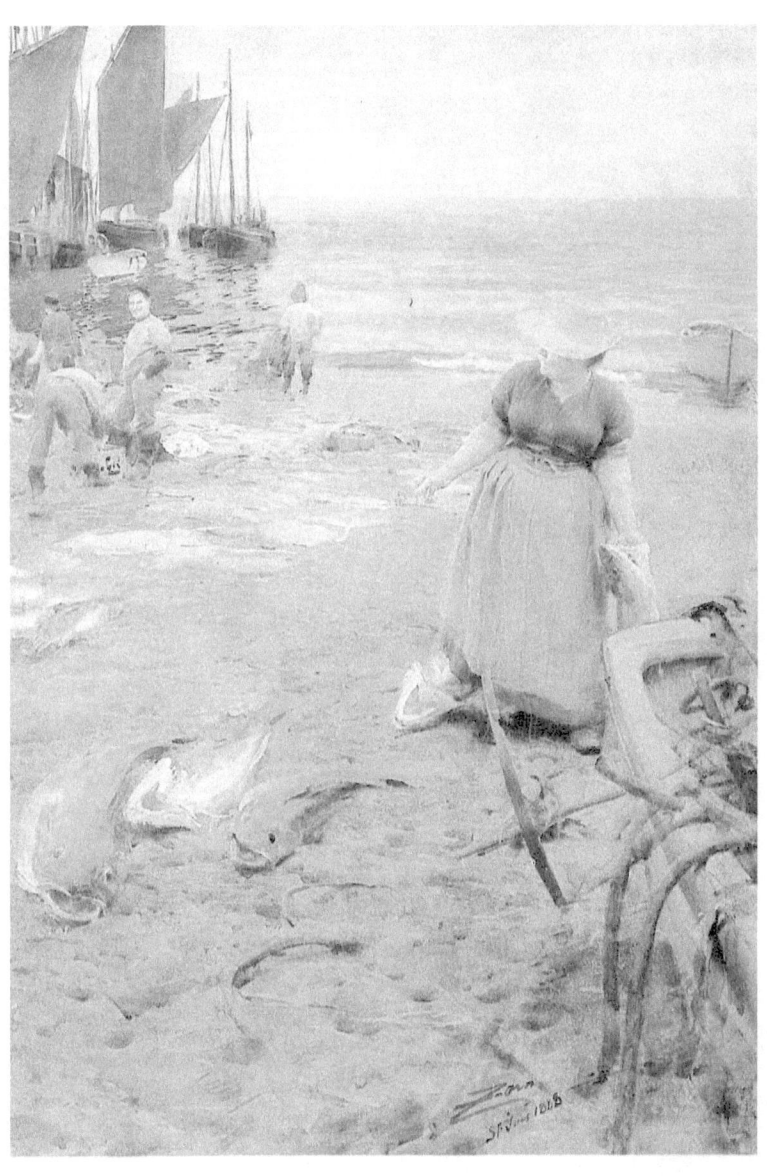

Fish Market in Saint Ives, 1888, watercolor

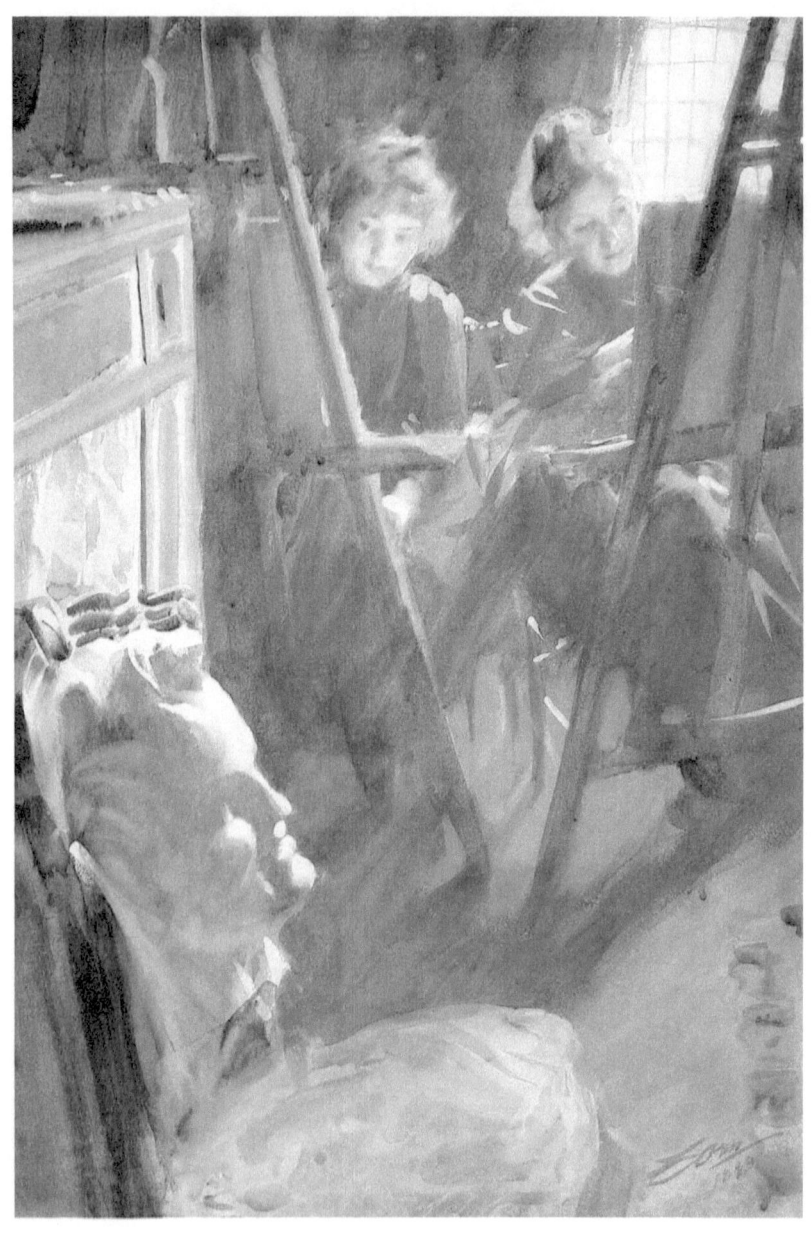

The Schwartz Girls, 1889, gouache over black chalk on cardboard

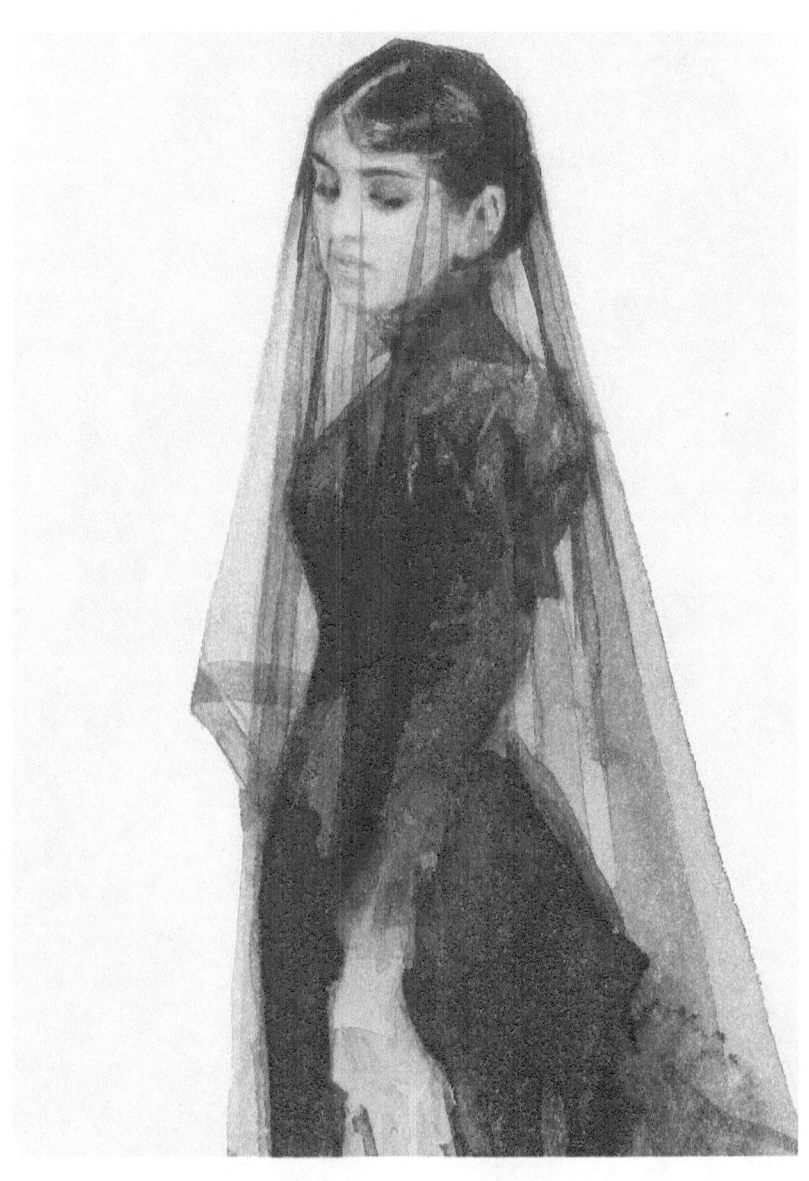

The Widow I, Detail, 1882-85, watercolor

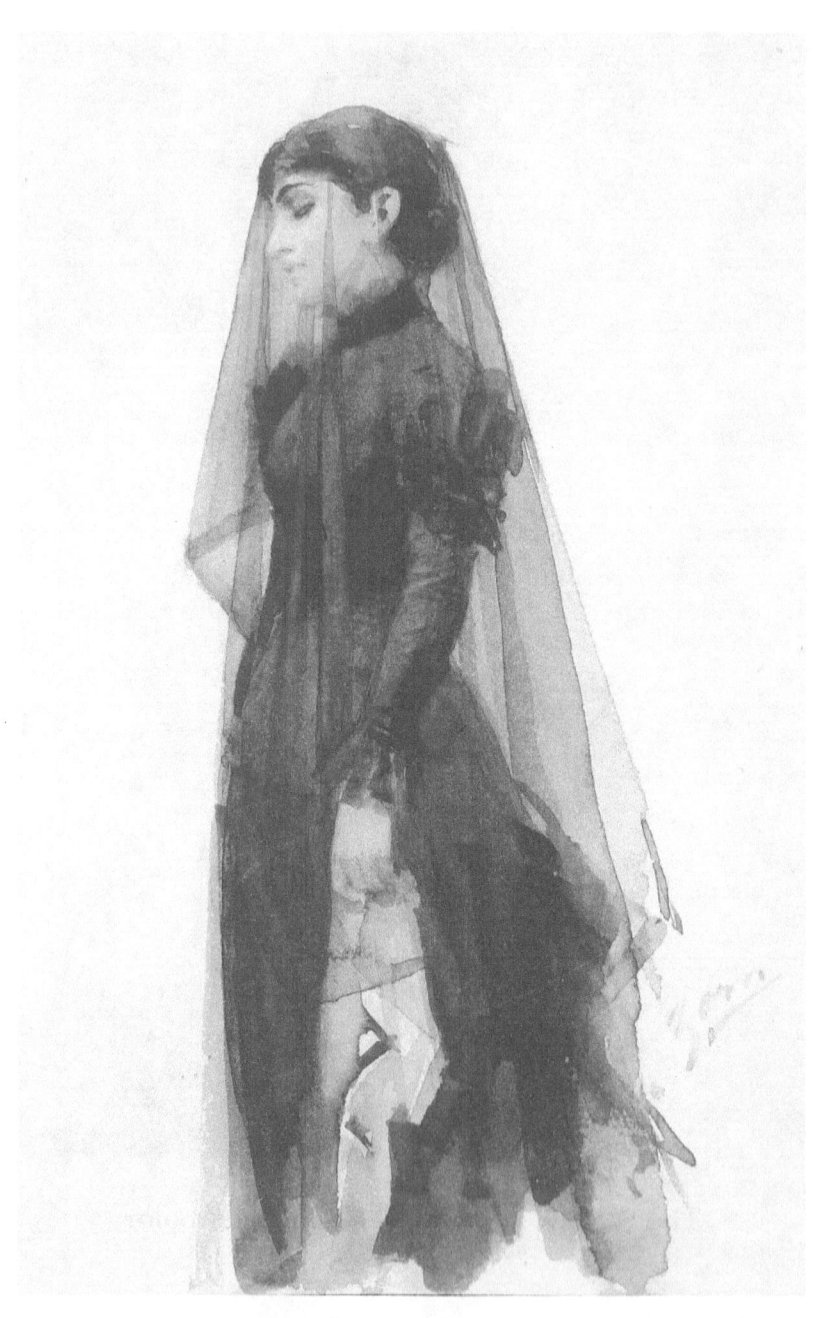

The Widow II, 1882-85, watercolor

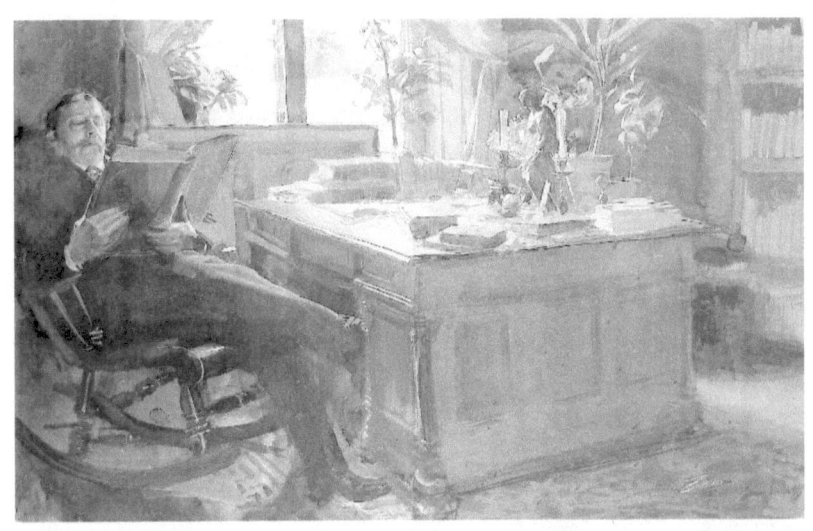

Swedish author Viktor Rydberg reading a book in his
rocking-chair, circa 1890, watercolor

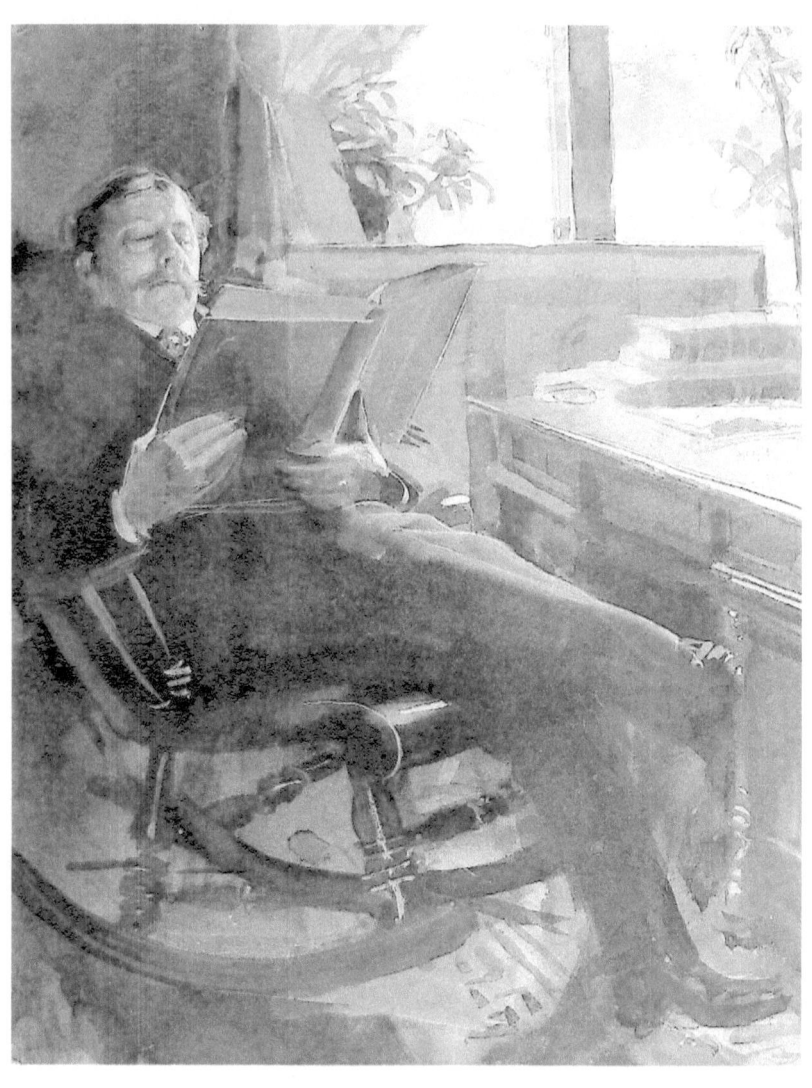

Swedish author Viktor Rydberg reading a book in his rocking-chair, Detail, circa 1890, watercolor